# About AFREPREN

The African Energy Policy Research Network or AFREPREN was created in 1989 with the aim of promoting research relating to the formulation and implementation of appropriate policy in the field of energy in countries of East, Central and Southern Africa. It also seeks to strengthen research capability within the region. Currently, under its sponsorship, over 90 African energy professionals from ten countries are engaged in research on six themes – institutions; management and efficiency; capacity building; financing and markets; local and regional environment; and climate change. The Network is coordinated and administered by a professional secretariat based in Nairobi. AFREPREN is funded by the Swedish International Development Cooperation Agency (SIDA) and the Norwegian Agency for Development (NORAD).

## African Energy Policy Research Series

*African Energy: Issues in Planning and Practice*
AFREPREN (1990)

*Energy Management in Africa*
M. R. Bhagavan and S. Karekezi (eds)
(1992)

*Rural Electrification in Africa*
V. Ranganathan (ed.)
(1992)

*Energy Options for Africa: Environmentally Sustainable Alternatives*
S. Karekezi and G. Mackenzie (eds)
(in association with the UNEP Collaborating Centre
on Energy and Environment)
(1994)

*Biomass Energy and Coal in Africa*
D. O. Hall and Y. S. Mao (eds)
(1994)

*Energy Utilities and Institutions in Africa*
M. R. Bhagavan (ed.)
(1996)

*Transport Energy in Africa*
M. R. Bhagavan (ed.)
(1996)

*Renewable Energy Technologies in Africa*
S. Karekezi and T. Ranja
(1997)

*Biomass Energy Policy in Africa: Selected Case Studies*
D. L. Kgathi, D. O. Hall, A. Hategeka, C. V. Mlotshwa
and  M. B. M. Sekhwela (eds)
(1997)

*Planning and Management in the African Power Sector*
L. Khalema-Redeby, H. Mariam,
A. Mbewe and B. Ramasedi
(1998)

*Petroleum Marketing in Africa*
M. R. Bhagavan (ed.)
(1999)

*Reforming the Power Sector in Africa*
M. R. Bhagavan (ed.)
(1999)

# Capacity Building
# for a Reforming African Power Sector

Edited by

**Mengistu Teferra and Stephen Karekezi**

Contributing authors

J. Baguant
R. Beeharry
J. Kimani
M. Mapako
G. Minas
P. Ngobese
M. Ntsaba
W. Wolde-Ghiorgis

Zed Books Ltd
LONDON & NEW YORK

in association with

African Energy Policy Research Network
(AFREPREN)

*Capacity Building for a Reforming African Power Sector*
was first published in 2002 by
Zed Books Ltd, 7 Cynthia Street, London N1 9JF, UK and
Room 400, 175 Fifth Avenue, New York, NY 10010, USA
www.zedbooks.demon.co.uk

in association with

the African Energy Policy Research Network (AFREPREN),
PO Box 30979, Nairobi, Kenya
www.afrepren.org

Distributed in the USA exclusively by Palgrave, a division of
St Martin's Press, LLC.,
175 Fifth Avenue, New York, NY 10010



Cover design by Sophie Buchet
Typeset by Long House, Cumbria, UK
Printed and bound in the United Kingdom
by Biddles Ltd, Guildford and King's Lynn



A catalogue record for this book
is available from the British Library

ISBN  Hb 1 84277 238 4
      Pb  1 84277 239 2

# Contents

# List of Tables

# List of Boxes

# List of Abbreviations

| | |
|---|---|
| AAU | Addis Ababa University |
| ADB | African Development Bank |
| ADLI | Agricultural Development Led Industrialization |
| AFREPREN | African Energy Policy Research Network |
| BOT | Build, operate and transfer |
| BPC | Botswana Power Corporation |
| BUCSE | Bindura University College of Science Education (Zimbabwe) |
| CAPCO | Central African Power Corporation |
| CBP | Corporate business plan |
| CCS | Central Statistical Services (South Africa) |
| CDG | Carl Duisberg Gesellschaft |
| CEB | Central Electricity Board (Mauritius) |
| CEET | Compagnie d'Énergie Électrique du Togo |
| CFPP | Centre de Formation et de Perfectionnement Professionnel |
| CIDA | Canadian International Development Agency |
| CIE | Compagnie Ivoirienne d'Électricité |
| COBEE | Compañía Boliviana de Energía Eléctrica |
| CSC | Commonwealth Science Council |
| CSO | Central Statistical Office (Mauritius, Zimbabwe) |
| DBSA | Development Bank of South Africa |
| DMEA | Department of Mineral and Energy Affairs (South Africa) |
| DoE | Department of Energy (Zimbabwe) |
| DRC | Democratic Republic of Congo |
| DWAF | Department of Water Affairs and Forestry (South Africa) |
| ECG | Electricity Commission of Ghana |
| ECSA | Engineering Council of South Africa |
| EdD | Électricité de Djibouti |
| EDF | Électricité de France |
| EDM | Énergie du Mali |
| EDM | Electricidade de Moçambique |
| EDRC | Energy for Development Research Centre (South Africa) |
| EEA | (Egypt) Egyptian Electricity Authority |
| EEA | (Eritrea) Eritrea Electricity Authority |
| EECI | Énergie Électrique de Côte d'Ivoire |
| EEI | Electrical and Electronics Institute (proposed, Ethiopia) |
| EELPA | Ethiopian Electric Light and Power Authority |
| EEPCO | Ethiopian Electric Power Company |
| ENA | Ethiopian News Agency |
| ENELGUI | Enterprise Nationale d'Électricité du Guinée (Guinea-Conakry) |
| EOC | Educational Opportunities Council |
| EPE | Ethiopian Petroleum Enterprise |
| EPRDF | Ethiopian People's Revolutionary Democratic Front |
| EPZ | Export Processing Zone |
| ERC | Energy Research Centre (Ethiopia) |

| | |
|---|---|
| ERRP | Economic Reform and Recovery Programme |
| ESAMI | Eastern and Southern Africa Management Institute |
| ESAP | Economic Structural Adjustment Programme |
| ESC | Electricity Supply Commission (Zimbabwe) |
| ESCOM | Electricity Supply Commission of Malawi |
| ESDP | Education Sector Development Programme |
| ESKOM | Electricity Supply Commission of South Africa |
| ESMAP | Energy Sector Management Assistance Programme |
| FRD | Foundation for Research Development (South Africa) |
| FUEL | Flacq United Estate Limited (Mauritius) |
| FWD | Foundation for Woodstove Dissemination |
| GDFI | Gross domestic fixed investment |
| GDP | Gross domestic product |
| GEAR | Growth Employment and Redistribution strategy (South Africa) |
| GJ | Gigajoule (1 million kilojoules) |
| GNP | Gross national product |
| GPA | Grade pont average |
| GWh | Gigawatt hour(s) |
| HEAT | Household Energy Action Training (South Africa) |
| HEPP | Hydroelectric power plant |
| HND | Higher National Diploma (Zimbabwe) |
| HRD | Human resources development |
| HV | High voltage |
| ICS | Interconnected system (Ethiopia) |
| IDA | International Development Aid |
| IDRC | International Development Research Centre |
| IDT | Independent Development Trust (South Africa) |
| IEEC | Interafrican Electrical Engineering College |
| IIED | International Institute for Environment and Development |
| ILO | International Labour Organization |
| IMF | International Monetary Fund |
| IPD | Independent power distributor |
| IPP | Independent power producer |
| IVTB | Industrial and Vocational Training Board (Mauritius) |
| KENGO | Kenya Energy and Environment Organization |
| kgoe | Kilogram of oil equivalent |
| KGRTC | Kafue Gorge Regional Training Centre |
| km | Kilometre |
| KPLC | Kenya Power and Lighting Company |
| KPMG | Klynveld, Peat, Marwick, Goerdeler |
| ktoe | Thousand tonnes of oil equivalent |
| kV | Kilovolt |
| kWh | Kilowatt hour(s) |
| LEC | (Lesotho) Lesotho Electricity Corporation |
| LEC | (Liberia)  Liberia Electricity Corporation |
| LPG | Liquefied petroleum gas |
| MB | Million Birr |
| MEDAC | Ministry of Economic Development and Cooperation (Ethiopia) |
| MHE | Ministry of Higher Education (Zimbabwe) |
| MME | Ministry of Mines and Energy (Ethiopia) |
| MW | Megawatt |
| MWh | Megawatt hour(s) |
| NAMACO | National Manpower Advisory Council (Zimbabwe) |
| NCCRD | National Centre for Curriculum Research and Development (Mauritius) |
| NCHE | National Commission for Higher Education (South Africa) |

| | |
|---|---|
| ND | National Diploma (Zimbabwe) |
| NEC | National Electricity Corporation (Sudan) |
| NELF | National Electrification Forum (South Africa) |
| NEPA | National Electricity Power Authority (Nigeria) |
| NER | National Electricity Regulator (South Africa) |
| NEXCO | National Examinations Council (Zimbabwe) |
| NFC | National Foundation Certificate (Zimbabwe) |
| NIC | Newly industrialized country |
| NIGELEC | Société Nigerienne d'Électricité (Niger) |
| NGO | Non-governmental organization |
| NOCZIM | National Oil Company of Zimbabwe |
| NRTF | National Research and Technology Foresight Programme (South Africa) |
| NSA | National Skills Authority (South Africa) |
| NSF | National Skills Fund (South Africa) |
| NTI | Nangyang Technological Institute |
| NUST | National University of Science and Technology (Zimbabwe) |
| NQF | National Qualifications Forum (South Africa) |
| OECD | Organization for Economic Cooperation and Development |
| ONCCP | Office of the National Committee For Central Planning (Ethiopia) |
| ONE | Office National d l'Électricité (Morocco) |
| PIC | Performance Improvement Centre (ZESA) |
| PIP | Performance improvement programme |
| PMGE | Provisional Military Government of Ethiopia |
| PRISEC | Private Sector Educational Council |
| PTC | Posts and Telecommunications Corporation (Zimbabwe) |
| PV | Photovoltaics |
| PVS | Pre-Vocational Certificate (Zimbabwe) |
| RAU | Rand Afrikaans University |
| RDP | Reconstruction and Development Programme (South Africa) |
| RE | Renewable energy |
| REA | Rural Electrification Agency (Zimbabwe) |
| REDS | Regional electricity distributors |
| REGIDESO | Régie de Production et Distribution d'Eau et d'Électricité |
| Rs | Rupees (Mauritius) |
| RWEPA | Regional Wood Energy Programme for Africa |
| SACHED | South African Council for Higher Education |
| SACOB | South African Chamber of Business |
| SACS | South African Communication Services |
| SADC | Southern African Development Community |
| SAPP | Southern African Power Pool |
| SAQA | South African Qualifications Authority |
| SAREC | Swedish Agency for Research Cooperation with Developing Countries |
| SBEE | Société Béninoise d'Électricité et d'Eau |
| SCS | Self-contained system (Ethiopia) |
| SEEG | Société d'Énergie et d'Eau du Gabon |
| SENELEC | Société Nationale d'Électricité (Senegal) |
| SET | Science, engineering and technology |
| SETAs | Sectoral Education and Training Authorities (South Africa) |
| SGB | Standards Generating Body (South Africa) |
| SIDA | Swedish International Development Cooperation Agency |
| SIRDC | Scientific and Industrial Research and Development Centre (Zimbabwe) |
| SNE | Société Nationale d'Électricité (Congo Brazzaville) |
| SNEL | Société Nationale d'Électricité (Democratic Republic of Congo) |

| | |
|---|---|
| SONABEL | Société Nationale d'Électricité du Burkina Faso |
| SONELEC | Société Nationale d'Eau et d'Électricité (Mauritania) |
| SS | Substation |
| STC | State Trading Corporation (Mauritius) |
| STEE | Société Tchadienne d'Eau et d'Électricité |
| STEG | Société Tunisienne de l'Électricité et du Gaz |
| TANESCO | Tanzania Electricity Supply Company |
| TGE | Transitional Government of Ethiopia |
| TJ | Terajoule (1,000 gigajoules) |
| toe | Tonnes of oil equivalent |
| TRL | Transmission line |
| UCT | University of Cape Town |
| UDI | Unilateral Declaration of Independence (Rhodesia/Zimbabwe) |
| UEB | Uganda Electricity Board |
| UN | United Nations |
| UNCED | United Nations Conference on Environment and Development |
| UNDP | United Nations Development Programme |
| UNEP | United Nations Environmental Programme |
| UNESCO | United Nations Educational, Social and Cultural Organization |
| UPDEA | Union of Producers, Conveyors and Distributors of Electrical Energy in Africa |
| UZ | University of Zimbabwe |
| VRA | Volta River Authority (Ghana) |
| WB | World Bank |
| WCC | Wankie Colliery Company |
| YTL | YTL Corporation Berhad (Malaysia) |
| ZERC | Zimbabwe Electricity Regulatory Commission |
| ZESA | Zimbabwe Electricity Supply Authority |
| ZESCO | Zambia Electricity Supply Corporation |
| ZIE | Zimbabwe Institute of Engineers |
| ZIMDEF | Zimbabwe Manpower Development Fund |
| ZRA | Zimbabwe River Authority |

# Acknowledgements

The publication of this report has been made possible through the kind support of the Swedish International Development Cooperation Agency (SIDA).

The editors wish to thank the contributors to this volume who are AFREPREN principal researchers. Special thanks also go to L. Majoro and W. Kithyoma, who assisted in reviewing the reports, and to J. Kimani, co-author of one of the reports, who not only participated in the reviewing procedure but also provided vital logistical and coordinating support to the editors. In addition, the editors wish to thank the following AFREPREN Secretariat staff and interns who assisted in the formatting and cross-checking of energy data and information, and in providing logistical support to the AFREPREN Capacity Building Theme Group: *A. Mwangi, J. Wangeci, J. Muthui, P. Musyoki, W. Ndoung'u, E. Wamuyu, J. Matogo, I. Mwangi, M. Njoroge, E. Manyara, S. Amenya, O. Kamande, Z. Kinya, K. Mathenge, J. Lwimbuli, R. Mutugi, S. Mbuthia, G. Muthee, B. Mbugua, G. Ababu, C. Awori, I. Oketch, O. Onguru, J. Kabogo, G. Rubiro, F. Ariri and J. Katua.*

# Notes on Contributors

*The views expressed in this volume are the authors' own and should not be attributed to the institutions and organizations in which they are employed.*

**Jawaharlall Baguant**, who died in 1998, was the holder of Bachelor and Masters degrees in Chemical Engineering from Louisiana State University, Baton Rouge, and a PhD in the same field from the University of Tennessee, Knoxville. At the time of his untimely death, Baguant was Pro-Vice Chancellor for curriculum development and distance education at the University of Mauritius, where he had served with distinction since 1974. He had also undertaken several projects for a number of UN agencies, the Commonwealth Science Council (CSC), the International Development Centre (IDRC) and the African Development Bank (ADB). He was a principal researcher and Coordinator of AFREPREN's Capacity Building Theme Group. In addition to sugar engineering, his research work and publications spanned the fields of energy management in the transport and electric power sectors, as well as capacity building with specific reference to engineering and energy services.

**Revin Panray Beeharry** holds an MSc in Chemical Engineering from Illinois Institute of Technology, Chicago and a BTech in Chemical Engineering from the Indian Institute of Technology. He has worked as a consultant for Applied Energy Services in the USA, as a lecturer in Chemical/Sugar Technology at the University of Mauritius, and as a research assistant in Energy Systems. He is currently a senior lecturer in Chemical Engineering at the Department of Chemical and Sugar Engineering, Faculty of Engineering, University of Mauritius. He is the author of several publications on energy, transport and renewables in Mauritius.

**Stephen Karekezi** (BSc and MSc) is Director of the African Energy Policy Research Network (AFREPREN) as well as Executive Secretary of the Foundation for Woodstove Dissemination (FWD) in Nairobi. In 1995, he was appointed to the Scientific and Technical Advisory Panel (STAP) of the Global Environment Facility (GEF) co-managed by the World Bank, UNDP and UNEP. Karekezi is an engineer with postgraduate qualifications in management and economics. He has written, co-authored and edited some 87 publications, journal articles, papers and reports on sustainable energy development. In 1990 he received the Development Association Award in Stockholm in recognition of his work on the development and dissemination of the Kenya Ceramic Jiko, an energy-efficient cooking stove.

**John Kimani** (BA), an energy analyst, is Manager of the Information Programme and Head of the Joint Database Department at the AFREPREN Secretariat. His main responsibilities include developing and managing the AFREPREN energy database and backstopping for the Energy Sector Reform and Special Studies theme groups. He has assisted in the writing of several research papers and publications and co-authored publications and reports on the African power sector and African energy data. He is a graduate (Economics and Sociology) of Egerton University, Kenya.

**Maxwell Mapako** holds a BSc Hons in Environmental Studies and Biochemistry from the University of Wales and a Diploma in Renewable Energy Sources from Urbino, Italy. He has attended various courses in renewable energy technologies and project management. Formerly a senior research officer in the new and renewable energy section of Zimbabwe's Department of Energy, he is currently Director of the African Regional Office of the Biomass Users Network. His numerous publications on biomass energy technologies have been instrumental in shaping Zimbabwean renewable energy policies and programmes.

**Peter Ngobese** holds an MSc in Agriculture Economics from Virginia Polytechnic Institute and State University, and a BSc in Agriculture from the University of Zimbabwe. He has attended courses on programme and environmental management in development; monitoring and evaluation of public sector projects; and agriculture project planning and analysis. His field experience includes project appraisal and evaluation of rural development projects in Zimbabwe, environmental assessment of the proposed Matabeleland water project, and research and publications on local food security and natural resource management in the Southern African Development Community region.

**Mankone Ntsaba** is a Private Researcher in South Africa. She holds BSc Honours and MSc degrees from Rhodes University as well as a BSc from the National University of Lesotho. She is the author of publications on capacity building in the power sector of South Africa and environmental perception management strategy for Engen, a petroleum company. Her professional skills include scoping and public participation methodologies; environmental impact assessments and benchmarking studies; and research and report writing.

**Mengistu Teferra** is a Senior Adviser in Ethiopia's Ministry of Finance and Economic Development. He holds an MSc in Energy Studies from the University of Sussex, a Diploma in Electricity Distribution from the University of Trondheim, Norway and a BSc in Electrical Engineering from the University of Addis Ababa. He was formerly Head of the Department of Mines, Energy and Water Resources, Senior Energy Expert and Energy Team Leader in the Ministry of Economic Development and Cooperation, and Engineer in charge of a hydro station in the Ethiopian Electric Power Corporation. A leading Ethiopian energy analyst, he has authored numerous influential reports and publications on the energy sector of Ethiopia.

# Dedication

This book is dedicated to the late Professor Jawaharlall Baguant, a principal researcher and Theme Group Coordinator of AFREPREN's Capacity Building Theme Group. Professor Baguant (or Jay as he was popularly known) was one of the founding members of the AFREPREN Network and will be dearly remembered by all as a dedicated and influential person who selflessly gave himself both to his work and to others. In addition to preparing high-calibre research work, Jay was a great source of support to the AFREPREN Network and an exemplary model of a brilliant and committed African energy policy researcher and scientist.

# Part I

INTRODUCTION

**Stephen Karekezi**

## Defining capacity building

Sharing the common fate of many development buzzwords, 'capacity building' has been added to the lexicon of popular development catchwords without being defined clearly in the process. In the convoluted style typical of international documents, the citation in UNCED's Agenda 21 (Chapter 37) defines capacity building as follows: 'Specifically, capacity building encompasses the country's human, scientific, technological, organizational, institutional and resource capabilities.' A fundamental goal of capacity building is to enhance the ability to evaluate and address the crucial questions related to policy choices and modes of implementation among development options, based on an understanding of environment potentials and limits and of needs as perceived by the people of the country concerned (United Nations Conference on Environment and Development, 1992). This introduction will confine itself to discussing capacity building with specific reference to the energy sector and the power sector.

The bulk of energy sector involvement in capacity building in Africa takes the form of technical assistance projects that are proving to be expensive and account for a large and increasing share of available financial resources. Typically, a team of between one and three expatriate consultants will be attached to an energy ministry or utility to assist in the development of national energy policy and provide energy training support. This small core team of external energy consultants will then call upon a large pool of short-term external energy experts to undertake specific tasks. The aim of such technical assistance projects is to overcome a perceived near-term shortfall in expertise and skills that will eventually be filled by trained local energy personnel.

So far, actual results of technical assistance projects have been well below expectations (World Bank, 1987). The most dramatic failure has been recorded in sub-Saharan Africa where the need for local capacity building is at its most acute. In spite of significant inflows of technical assistance support, the International Institute for Environment and Development (IIED) has issued a report ('Institutional Development: a Focused View') asserting that Africa provides a worst-case institutional scenario for development (Fowler, 1993).

## Internal barriers to capacity building

The weight of evidence provided by past investigations and studies appears to attribute much of the failure associated with capacity-building programmes to the North and the approach of the bilateral and multilateral development agencies that it controls. In the final analysis, however, capacity building for the energy sector is an important national responsibility, which governments in Africa have to address seriously. The inability or unwillingness of African governments to mobilize the required level of investment in the development of national capacity for the energy sector is, in part, responsible for many of the difficulties faced by past and ongoing capacity-building initiatives.

Too often, the host African government representatives prefer hardware and large-scale infrastructure investments in hydro or thermal plants to technical and training assistance programmes that contribute directly to capacity building. Preference for large-scale energy investments is often a sign of corruption because of the ease with which kickbacks for capital-intensive projects can be arranged.

Poor systems of governance prevalent in the African energy sector, combined with mismanagement, disorganization, entrenched inequity, political instability and repression, compound the problem (Commission on Developing Countries and Global Change, 1992). Writing with reference to the industrial sector in sub-Saharan Africa (although his conclusions apply to other sectors such as energy), Thandika Makadawire explains:

> Disciplined neither by market nor by political forces, the bureaucracy and its cohorts the 'political class' essentially ran amok. They set up projects that had no economic rationale whatsoever. They entered into all kinds of shady deals to set up industries most of which never took off. They realized their mad dreams of grandeur but only through monumental waste. Choices of technology, location of industries, and products were either completely arbitrary or reflected a highly idiosyncratic understanding of how industrialization takes place. Rarely did they reflect anything hinting at national interest (Mkadawire, 1992).

National governments in Africa have also consistently failed to negotiate for a more equitable North–South partnership in technical assistance programmes for the energy sector that will ensure availed resources are utilized in an optimal fashion and not to the detriment of long-term development of local capacity. Negotiating teams representing African countries are often underqualified and poorly prepared for the task (Dag Hammarskjold Foundation, 1990).

This is compounded by the unwillingness of the national governments to call on the substantial energy expertise that exists outside the civil service. Examples include national universities, independent research agencies and non-governmental organizations (NGOs). Unwillingness to use local institutions is often rooted in paranoia-tinged suspicion of organizations that are outside the government's direct budgetary and managerial control and the inability to cope with perspectives that are different from the conventional wisdom prevailing within civil service circles (Commission on Developing Countries and Global Change, 1992).

Hesitation to use local expertise on the part of national African governments is not surprising because technical skills are not always ideologically neutral. Calling on local technical expertise for energy development programmes is linked to strategic decisions by key political actors. Alliances, negotiations and compromises can often lead to the dismissal of politically independent, technically skilled energy personnel in favour of less knowledgeable but loyal experts.

It is, however, important to realize that national recipient agencies are more heterogeneous and complex than is usually assumed. It is not always the case of the 'imperialist North' coming down to assist the 'underdeveloped South'. The South has its own power structures: some élite groups in Africa may look for technical assistance initiatives in order to foster their own interests in local power struggles that are unknown to the donor agencies and their technical teams.

## External barriers to capacity building

External factors in the failure of capacity-building programmes for the energy sector should not be underestimated, however. Far from filling a short-term skill gap, technical assistance initiatives have actually impeded the development of the African energy sector and are, in part, responsible for the problems faced by the continent (Mkadawire, 1992). In sub-Saharan Africa, for example, instead of locals taking over from external energy experts, the number of expatriate energy consultants in the region has continued to increase rapidly: it is now believed that there are more external experts on the scene than there were in pre-independence times (World Bank, 1991). In some sub-Saharan African counties, the cost of external experts is said to be higher than the total civil service wage bill. In Guinea, the cost of a team of experts on a single project was estimated to be equivalent to 80 per cent of the country's total government payroll.

One of the key problems of excessive reliance on external consultants is that they upset the local power structures in a decision-making process often built up painfully over a long period of time and based on subtle and intricate trading between interests and power groups. The advent of powerful external consultants upsets this process and creates a new focus of attention that is usually short-term. On their departure, the reconstruction of the local power structure has to be restarted – until a new external consultant comes in to subvert it again.

Too often, donors define the agenda and priorities of technical assistance development projects, with little consideration given to the cultural, economic, political and social environment in which the assistance is to take place. Technical assistance projects tend to be geared to 'change' and to 'overcoming resistance' rather than to enabling or empowering local agents.

For example, in the African energy sector, external energy experts have prepared tens of thousands of reports, studies and surveys. Few of these reports are read and fewer still are implemented to any significant degree (Pachauri, 1993). A recent review of technical assistance raises alarm over the number of Northern agencies, research institutes and individuals that have become almost wholly reliant on technical assistance projects for employment and continued survival (Bossuyt *et al.*, 1991).

In a trenchant critique of prevailing technical assistance programmes in the energy sector, R. K. Pachauri (1993) provides an illuminating example:

> I fear that the whole question of capacity building might also become a similar example of good programmes being distorted to serve the interests of organizations in the North. This fear is not imaginary. I have recently seen a proposal from a group of professionals in the US to undertake a capacity building activity in Africa for US$4.5 million. Of course, it could be purely incidental that, of this 4.5-million-dollar-budget, roughly two thirds would go to the consultants in the US responsible for the programme, and of the balance amount, the bulk would go towards travel expenses for conducting workshops and seminars on the subject. It is not clear whose capacity will be built through this exercise, but it certainly won't be that of the developing countries identified as the programme's beneficiaries.

A large and growing pool of energy experts has been created through a combination of both blunt and subtle mechanisms. Typical of the blunt approach is donor agencies that insist on the use of expatriate consultants as a condition for the provision of financial assistance to the African energy sector (World Bank, 1991). The subtle tools include the preference for highly sophisticated data-intensive analytical instruments in the development of energy policies. A graphic example is the use of large-scale computerized models for the development of national energy policies. The bulk of these exercises require high levels of skilled expertise and yet few of these initiatives have managed to make a dent on national energy policy formulation and implementation.

Many of these efforts are driven by the argument that sophisticated data collection and analysis tools are required to reach satisfactory policy decisions. The experience in many African countries appears to indicate that the increased technical sophistication of policy analysis has not yet resulted in more coherent energy policy making. The policy analysis and recommendations are largely divorced from policy implementation, which is often erratic and poorly informed. Under such conditions, it is difficult to understand why increasingly higher levels of technical sophistication are being used in policy analysis. A shift towards efforts that lead to a more comprehensive understanding of existing policy formulation and implementation mechanisms needs to be effected. In addition, more robust means and approaches for influencing policy making need to be developed.

A less obvious but highly damaging impact of excessive reliance on external technical assistance in African countries is the stunting of local ability to analyze and develop energy policy and investment options (Commission on Developing Countries and Global Change, 1992). Local energy ministries become reliant on external experts and make little or no recourse to local institutions.

As a result, local skilled energy personnel are marginalized which, in turn, generates frustration and contributes to the brain drain (SAREC, 1993). The chairperson of the 1990 Conference on Capacity Building in Sub-Saharan Africa, held in Maastricht in the Netherlands, argued that 'it was wasteful and unacceptable that technical assistance was taking jobs away from able local people' (Wheeler, 1990).

For example, it is estimated that there are over 10,000 Nigerian professionals working in the US (World Bank, 1989). In total, an estimated 100,000 highly skilled African professionals work in the North (World Bank, 1991). It is interesting to note that this is equivalent to the estimated number of external experts in sub-Saharan African countries (The *East African Standard*, 1995).

The cost of technical assistance is now huge because of a gradual shift (within the donor community) from infrastructure support programmes to projects that are designed to provide short-term expertise. It is estimated that between 1984 and 1987 the cost of technical assistance to sub-Saharan Africa increased by 50 per cent and was estimated to be about US$4 billion a year (World Bank, 1991; Jaycox, 1993). Long-term initiatives for the development of local capacity building would only require a very small fraction of the existing technical assistance development budget.

## The way forward

Some way needs to be found to address the problem of capacity building in the African energy sector. There is no magic bullet approach that will resolve the capacity-building problem. This section briefly discusses a number of national and regional initiatives aimed at building capacity in the African energy sector.

A number of institutions play an important role in capacity building in the energy sector. These key institutions are listed below:

- academic institutions;
- not-for-profit training institutions;
- government;
- private sector and energy utilities.

*Academic institutions*

Many energy analysts argue that development of a comprehensive and sustainable human resource base in energy necessitates the early sensitization of citizens to this central human need. This calls for the inclusion of important energy issues in the existing academic curricula, preferably from the primary level up to the tertiary stages. Ideally, this should focus on local energy resources. At the moment, however, the primary responsibility of initiating and supporting appropriate educational programmes on energy in Africa rests with the institutions of higher learning and other middle-level training venues.

Conventional energy subsectors such as electricity, coal and petroleum fuels more readily find trained staff because training in relevant topics is widely available (Mapako, 1996: 6). However, only a handful of academic institutions offer energy education in their mainstream curricula. Most of them include the subject of energy only as part of other courses such as engineering and agriculture.

For example, the Faculty of Mechanical Engineering at the University of Nairobi provides some energy-related courses, but the bulk of modules concentrate on conventional energy systems such as thermal generation and large-scale power. Walubengo and Kimani (1993) point to the case of Kenya, where there are only two charcoal experts teaching at the four public universities, despite charcoal being used by at least 30 per cent of the population.

The above information reveals that there has been reluctance to develop a programme to cater for education on energy in the region. To overcome the lack of interest in energy at African institutions of higher learning, centres of appropriate technology such as the Appropriate Technology Centre (ATC) at Kenyatta University in Nairobi and the Development Technology Centre (DTC) at the University of Zimbabwe have addressed energy issues (Kimani and Naumann 1993; Karekezi *et al.*, 1994). The ATC undertakes various renewable energy programmes while offering a Bachelor of Science and Master of Science in Appropriate Technology (ATC, 1992; Karekezi *et al.*, 1994). Kenyatta University has also initiated a Bachelor of Environmental Studies degree that has several modules on renewable energy. Similarly, the Kenya Polytechnic has a diploma course on Environmental Science (Kimani and Naumann, 1993). In Tanzania, a research unit at the University of Dar-es-Salaam deals with anaerobic digestion. The Physics Department of the University of Zambia started a renewable energy programme for both undergraduate and postgraduate students in the 1994/5 academic year .

Other postgraduate-level training programmes are sponsored in colleges outside the region to develop the region's capacity in energy. These include the University of Oldenburg in Germany; the University of Twente in the Netherlands; the International Development Technologies Centre in the Faculty of Engineering at the University of Melbourne in Australia; and Loughborough University of Technology in the UK (AIT, 1994).

Table 1.1 summarizes universities and polytechnics providing training with some energy and environment content.

**Table 1.1 Academic institutions and their energy-based programmes in selected countries**

| Country | Academic institution | Programmes with energy and environment content |
| --- | --- | --- |
| Mozambique | Universidade Eduardo Mondlane | Electrotechnical Engineering |
| Mauritius | University of Mauritius | Engineering, Science and Agriculture (degree courses) |
| Kenya | University of Nairobi | Electrical and Mechanical Engineering |
|  | Kenyatta University | Appropriate Technology, Environmental Studies |
|  | Moi University | BSc Technology and Electrical Engineering<br>Environmental Studies (diploma) |
|  | Kenya Polytechnic | Electrical Engineering (diploma) |
| South Africa | University of Cape Town | Energy & Development Studies (Masters)<br>Environmental and Geographical Science |
|  | University of Stellenbosch | Electrical and Electronic Engineering |
| Tanzania | University of Dar-es-Salaam | Anaerobic digestion research<br>Electrical and Mechanical Engineering |
| Uganda | Uganda Polytechnic Kyambogo | Diploma in Environmental Studies |
| Zambia | University of Zambia | Renewable Energy (BSc/MSc) |
| Zimbabwe | University of Zimbabwe | Environmental Studies |
|  | National University of Science and Technology | Electrical Engineering |

Sources: Williams, 1989: 145; Wield, 1991a: 7; Tibicke, 1987: 15; Baguant 1996a: 22; UCT, 1997; Suba, 1991: 18; Sizoomu, 1994: Annex 2.6; University of Stellenbosch brochure, undated

With regard to the power sector, the focus of this volume, it appears that the required training in electrical engineering is still unavailable as demonstrated by Table 1.2, which lists the universities that provide electrical engineering in selected African countries.

**Table 1.2** Number of universities offering engineering and electrical engineering courses (1996)

| Country | Number of universities | Number offering engineering | Number offering electrical engineering |
| --- | --- | --- | --- |
| Nigeria | 29 | 18 | 8 |
| South Africa | 21 | 9 | 3 |
| Egypt | 13 | 12 | – |
| Morocco | 7 | 4 | 4 |
| Madagascar | 6 | 1 | – |
| Kenya | 13 | 4 | 4 |
| Uganda | 3 | 1 | 1 |
| Zimbabwe | 2 | 2 | 2 |
| Ethiopia | 1 | 1 | 1 |
| Gabon | 2 | – | – |
| Côte d'Ivoire | 1 | – | – |
| Burkina Faso | 1 | – | – |
| Rwanda | 1 | – | – |
| Guinea | 1 | – | – |
| Sierra Leone | 1 | 1 | 1 |
| Mozambique | 1 | 1 | 1 |
| Eritrea | 1 | 1 | – |

– = Data not available

Source: Adapted from Europa, 1996

### *Not-for-profit institutions*

One of the approaches adopted to train engineers, technologists, technicians and extension officers in various aspects of energy has been the development of training workshops with the assistance of several international agencies. In the last two decades such efforts have been made by several agencies to alleviate the shortage of skilled energy personnel in the region. The organizations involved include the Canadian International Development Agency (CIDA), the Commonwealth Science Council (CSC), the International Development Research Centre (IDRC), the Swedish Agency for Research Cooperation with Developing Countries (SAREC), the United Nations Educational, Social and Cultural Organization (UNESCO) and several others.

This approach has been used by the Kenya Energy and Environment Organization (KENGO) in its Regional Wood Energy Programme for Africa (RWEPA) which addressed specific energy training needs by organizing annual tailor-made training courses such as its International Biomass Course and Regional Solar Awareness Workshop. A few courses were also organized for participants interested in improved stove production and dissemination.

By the end of 1993, RWEPA had trained a total of 320 renewable energy project managers, entrepreneurs and technicians. These courses were designed to raise or improve the awareness of the participants in energy matters and provide a forum for information exchange among professionals from different countries (Rabar, 1992). However, due to limited financial resources, KENGO/RWEPA is no longer functional. A breakdown of the number of people trained a few years prior to its winding up is shown in Table 1.3.

**Table 1.3  Summary of KENGO/RWEPA's annual training courses**

| Year | No. of persons trained | Countries represented |
|---|---|---|
| 1988 | 8 | Kenya, Madagascar, Uganda, Ethiopia, Burundi, India |
| 1989 | 13 | Sudan, Uganda, Zambia, Tanzania, Kenya |
| 1990 | 11 | Kenya, Sudan, Rwanda, Angola, Tanzania, Zambia |
| 1991 | 11 | Kenya, Uganda, Zaire, Angola, Zimbabwe, Ethiopia, Botswana, Tanzania |
| 1992 | 11 | Kenya, Zambia, Tanzania, Sierra Leone, Malawi, Namibia, Nigeria, Mozambique, Uganda, Ethiopia |
| 1993 | 30 | Ethiopia, Kenya, Tanzania, Uganda, Ghana |
| Total | 84 | |

Source: Karekezi et al., 1994

An emerging regional training institution is the Eastern and Southern Africa Management Institute (ESAMI), which has provided limited energy management training. One of ESAMI's notable achievements has been training contracted by the Southern African Development Community (SADC) for the period between 1994 and 1997. Under this agreement, ESAMI designed and conducted both energy policy analysis seminars and specialist technical courses on rural energy planning and environmental management. A total of 11 training programmes were conducted each year. Two of the programmes were policy-level seminars targeting ministers of energy, permanent secretaries and other senior policy advisers (SADC, undated).

The African Energy Policy Research Network (AFREPREN) is another example of an energy policy research initiative that builds on the significant past achievements of energy policy makers and researchers in East and Southern Africa. AFREPREN assists policy makers and researchers to formulate strategies that would strengthen the short- and long-term performance and sustainability of the region's energy sector. Relying on South–South cooperation programmes has a multiplier effect – it not only builds capacities in the recipient country but also strengthens the skills of the assisting agencies.

In conjunction with the University of Cape Town, AFREPREN runs a Masters degree scholarship programme on energy policy. To date, 15 African energy experts have been awarded scholarships. In addition, AFREPREN also offers orientation training on energy issues to university students. Its Secretariat, based in Nairobi, has provided orientation training to over 300 university students.

### Government

With support from academic institutions, governments throughout Africa (represented by education ministers and later by those responsible for science and technology) are largely responsible for developing educational policies and programmes. High regard for energy subjects within the scientific community and funding of research and development by governments can make this field attractive to young scientists and engineers. Governments in the region have also realized the importance of skilled manpower in the development of energy and have started initiatives to address the existing deficit.

### Private sector and utilities

Naumann (1993) argues that it is not necessary to wait for a new generation of energy experts with all the required qualifications in this field. A popular strategy adopted by industry to overcome the current deficit of trained manpower in the field of energy is in-house or on-the-job training.

A recent development in capacity building is the emerging training companies in the private sector. Although these training companies are not providing specialized training in energy, they provide training in management skills, which is crucial for energy institutions such as the power utilities and petroleum companies. Some of the training companies with the requisite facilities in the region include internationally renowned consulting companies such as PriceWaterhouse Coopers and Deloitte and Touche, among others.

Almost all power and petroleum utilities offer in-house training programmes of some sort for trainee engineers and technicians. These programmes have been instrumental in developing a significant pool of skilled technicians and engineers in many of the region's utility institutions. In addition, utilities provide useful practical training for university and polytechnic students through vocational/attachment programmes. Management training is given less attention and mainly targets senior management staff. The training is undertaken in-house, or by sponsorship to local or overseas universities, polytechnics and technical colleges.

## Capacity building in the power sector

The fact that most power utilities in the sub-Saharan African region are characterized by poor performance is a sufficient indicator of the need for capacity building. Both technical and managerial skills appear inadequate in the power utilities. The majority of power utilities appear to have a high proportion of unskilled/semi-skilled manpower.

Under the aegis of the AFREPREN Capacity Building Theme Group, a regional study and four country studies were undertaken to address the aforementioned capacity-building question in the African power sector. This volume presents the findings of the studies. The regional study provides an extensive background review of capacity building in the African electricity industry. Thereafter, country case studies of Mauritius, Ethiopia, Zimbabwe and South Africa are presented. Both the regional and the national studies systematically analyze the issues of manpower recruitment, training and retention in national power utilities.

In the regional review study, Karekezi and Kimani start by examining the structure and performance of power utilities in the region. They then attempt to link the technical and financial performance of utilities to investment in training and related capacity-building initiatives. Although the data they provide is not fully conclusive, the evidence presented is sufficient to underline the importance of capacity building in improving the performance of the African electricity industry.

Jawaharlall Baguant addresses the capacity-building question in the Mauritius power sector. After reviewing the country's economy and education system, he considers capacity-building efforts at the main institution of higher learning, the University of Mauritius, and the country's main utility, the Central Electricity Board (CEB). Using a methodology that links economic performance to the availability of engineers and technicians, Baguant assesses the projected demand for trained manpower in the country's electricity industry.

He then uses the projection to determine the extent to which the country's output of engineers and technicians will be sufficient to meet the demand for skilled personnel. Baguant ends with a number of recommendations that address the country's capacity-building challenges.

Mengistu Teferra reviews capacity building in Ethiopia's electricity industry. He first reviews the country's electricity sector and provides a succinct summary of the system of higher education.

Using survey statistics, Mengistu then estimates the current and future requirements for qualified personnel in the Ethiopian power sector. He derives a second estimate using the same methodology employed by Baguant in his Mauritius case study. Using both estimates, he demonstrates that the supply of trained manpower is inadequate to meet the current and future needs of the country's electricity industry. Finally he proposes a number of options in addressing the serious capacity-building problems faced by the national utility.

Prepared by Maxwell Mapako, the chapter on Zimbabwe presents a detailed review of the country's education policies from the pre-independence period to the present day. Mapako highlights key weaknesses in Zimbabwe's education system and links these to the difficulties that the power sector faces in recruiting and retaining well-qualified technical personnel.

He then analyzes the capacity-building effort of Zimbabwe's main power utility, the Zimbabwe Electricity Supply Authority (ZESA), demonstrating the significant role it played in reversing the decline that the utility faced in the early 1990s. Mapako stresses, however, that recent socio-economic and political problems that the country is facing may reverse the capacity-building gains realized not only in the power sector but also in the country as whole. As a result of declining economic performance, the departure of skilled and qualified manpower from Zimbabwe is beginning to reach alarming levels.

The final chapter of Mapako's study first suggests a number of options that could be relevant in tackling the capacity-building problems faced by the country's utility. He ends by carefully reviewing the institutional, legal, management and financial barriers that could impede the successful implementation of the identified options, thus arriving at the options that should be given priority.

The final study, by Peter Ngobese and Mankone Ntsaba, brings capacity building in South Africa into focus. They provide convincing evidence of the detrimental impact of the country's past apartheid policy on the development of skills among the previously marginalized black majority. This legacy promotes a significant racial imbalance in the supply of skilled professionals, especially in the technical and engineering disciplines that are crucial for the power sector.

Ngobese and Ntsaba then discuss, at some length, the efforts of ESKOM, the country's main power utility, to address the problem of racial imbalances in skilled personnel. Through a wide array of proactive training programmes, capacity-building initiatives and aggressive headhunting, ESKOM has been able to address the racial imbalance in its professional ranks. In many respects, ESKOM provides a model for capacity building that could be emulated by other utilities in the region.

In conclusion, the four country case studies all endorsed the following recommendations for addressing capacity-building problems in the region's power sector:

- Review of curricula in higher institutions of learning to meet the current and future needs of the power sector.

- Establishment of a national dedicated power sector training fund to finance training of utility employees.

- Enhancement of in-house training programmes and facilities to ensure improved performance of the utility.

- Training in management skills for all utility personnel. Experience shows that management training at all levels of staffing can yield significant benefits to the electricity industry.

- Regional training facilities for power utilities to address some of the region's key capacity-building shortfalls as well as to facilitate the transfer of skills within the region.

- Attractive salary and incentive packages for all utility employees. There is convincing evidence that an attractive incentive package is one of the most important factors in the retention of highly skilled personnel in the region's electricity industry.

## Glossary of terms

| | |
|---|---|
| **Brain drain** | Emigration of qualified personnel |
| **Ideal utility** | Utility chosen as point of reference by authors |
| **Manpower** | Used in non-discriminatory sense to refer to both male and female employees as human units of labour capacity |
| **Non-professionals** | Employees with no formal training (also referred to as unskilled manpower) |
| **Overstaffing** | Exceeding the required number of manpower units |
| **Power sector reforms** | Ownership and structural changes in the power sector |
| **Professionals** | Degree holders |
| **Retention** | Act of minimizing loss of qualified manpower through motivation and incentives |
| **Retrenchment** | Act of reducing employment levels |
| **Semi-professionals** | Non-degree holders with some formal qualifications such as ordinary national diplomas, high national diplomas and high-level certificates (also referred to as semi-skilled manpower) |
| **Staff** | Various levels of employment |

# Part II

---

# OVERVIEW

## CAPACITY BUILDING
## IN SUB-SAHARAN AFRICAN POWER UTILITIES

Stephen Karekezi and John Kimani

# Sub–Saharan Africa

Sub-Saharan Africa (excluding South Africa):
selected indicators
Area (km²): 22,407,000
Population (millions): 600.8 (1999)
Annual population growth rate (%): 2.8 (1999)
Urban population (million): 180.1 (1999)
Urban population growth rate (%): 5.2 (1999)
Rural population (millions): 420.7 (1999)
Government expenditure in real wages and
salaries (Index 1987=100): 130 (1998)
GNP *per capita* (US$): 306 (1999)
Literacy levels (%): 57 (1998)
Male literacy levels (%): 66 (1998)
Female literacy levels (%): 48 (1998)
Adult literacy (%, age 15 and above): 60.5 (1999)
Youth literacy (%, age 15–24): 76.9 (1999)
Female primary age group enrolment (% of primary school age girls): 51.8
Female secondary age group enrolment (% of secondary school age girls): 35.8
Population under age 15 (as % of total): 44.7 (1999)
Population aged 65 and above (as % of total): 3 (1999)
Combined primary, secondary and tertiary gross enrolment ratio (%): 42 (1999)
Average public education spending (US$ per pupil): 252 (1999)
Average public education spending in primary and secondary (US$ per pupil): 190 (1999)
Average public education spending in tertiary institutions (US$ per student): 1,611 (1999)
Average wage and salaried workers (% of total population): 33.5 (1998)
Percentage distribution of the labour force by occupation (1998)
    Professional, technician and related workers (%, male): 4
    Professional, technician and related workers (%, female): 3
    Administrative and managerial workers (%, male): 4
    Administrative and managerial workers (%, female): 0
    Clerical and related workers (%, male): 3
    Clerical and related workers (%, female): 3
    Sales workers (%, male): 6
    Sales workers (%, female): 11
    Service workers (%, male): 5
    Service workers (%, female): 5
    Agricultural and other workers (%, male): 60
    Agricultural and other workers (%, female): 64
    Production and related workers (%, male): 17
    Production and related workers (%, female): 8
Modern energy consumption *per capita* (kgoe): 355 (1997)
Electricity consumption (*per capita* kWh): 126 (1999)
Total electricity generation (GWh): 81,215 (1997)
Installed capacity (MW): 22,745 (1997)
Population with access to electricity (%): 13 (1999)
Rural population with access to electricity (%): 5 (1999)
Urban population with access to electricity (%): 12 (1999)

Sources: World Bank, 2000; World Bank, 2001; AFREPREN/FWD 2001; Zomers, 2001; UNDP 2000; UNDP 2001

# 1

---

## Introduction

In the 1960s and 1970s the bulk of electricity was from hydro generation, mainly because loans for hydropower development were readily available from the World Bank. In recent years, however, power sector development in sub-Saharan Africa has been limited by the heavy debt load, while World Bank loans have become difficult to procure (see brief regional profile opposite, and additional time series data in Part II Appendix 1). Consequently, the region has been experiencing pronounced electricity supply deficits. An interim response to the deficit has been to switch to thermal generation mainly from independent power producers (IPPs), which account for about 80 per cent of the total electricity generation capacity in the continent (*Financial Times*, 1999; IEA, 2000).

Traditionally, power utilities in Africa have enjoyed a monopoly hold on their national electricity industries. The traditional institutional set-up of most African power utilities is similar to the one provided in Figure 1.1, made up of power utilities (publicly and privately owned); the Ministry of Energy; the Ministry of Finance; the Parliament; and the energy/electricity regulatory body.

There has been growing concern that this monopoly power has contributed to the undeniable underperformance in the delivery of electricity services. Power sector institutions are mainly characterized by unreliability of power supply, low capacity utilization and availability factor, deficient maintenance, poor procurement of spare parts, and high transmission and distribution losses – among other problems.

A major consequence is that most of the power utilities in Africa have failed to provide adequate levels of electricity services to the majority of the region's population, especially to rural communities and the urban poor. At national level, with the exception of North African countries, Zimbabwe, Ghana, Côte d'Ivoire, Mauritius, Nigeria and South Africa, the majority of sub-Saharan African countries generally register electrification levels well below 30 per cent. This is a very low figure when compared to other developing countries in Asia and Latin America, where electrification covers over 70 per cent of the population. Figure 1.2 shows the percentage of the total population electrified in selected African countries.

This chapter presents an overview of capacity building in power utilities in the sub-Saharan region. It attempts to address the key aspects

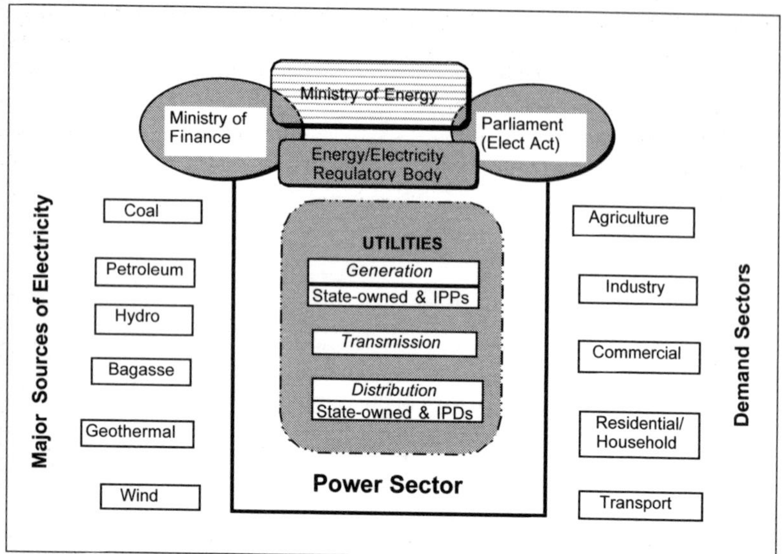


Figure 1.1  Institutional set-up of the power sector

IIPPs = Independent power producers; IPDs =- Independent power distributors
Source: Compiled by authors

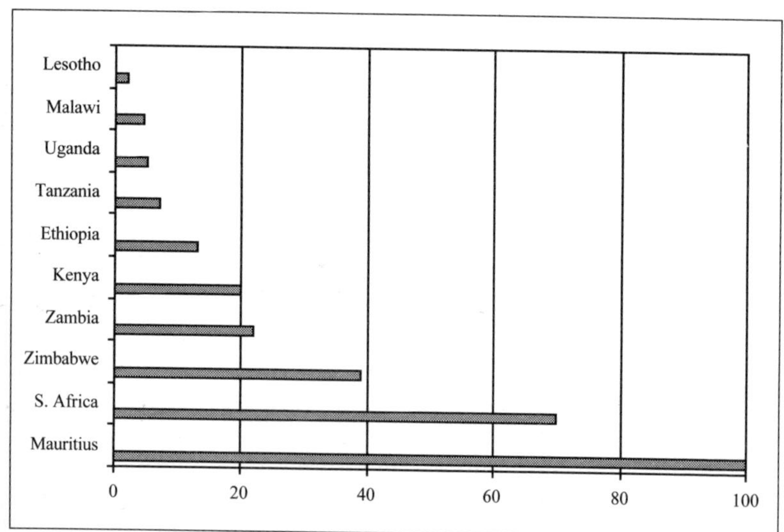


Figure 1.2  Percentage of total population electrified in selected African countries
Source: AFREPREN/FWD, 2001

– manpower recruitment, training and retention – and link them to the performance of the utility, mainly by using case examples of utilities for which data were available. The study proposes policy options that could enhance the performance of power utilities.

It should, however, be noted that the findings of the study could be affected by power sector reform, both ongoing and planned. Where applicable, the implications of power sector reform for capacity building are discussed.

# 2

## Capacity Building
## in the Power Sector in Africa

Power utilities in the African region tend to be small in size, with the majority having installed capacities below 1 GW. The majority of the utilities in the region are state-owned. With a few exceptions, there is little variation in the structure, functions and policy formulation process of power utilities in Africa. However, closer examination uncovers key differences that could have important implications for capacity building.

**Table 2.1 Categorization of utilities by installed capacity (2000/2001)**

| Country/Utility | Installed capacity (MW) |
|---|---|
| *Large (over 4 GW)* | |
| South Africa (ESKOM) | 39186 |
| Egypt (EEA)** | 14600 |
| Nigeria (NEPA) | 6000 |
| Morocco (ONE)* | 4389 |
| *Medium (400 MW – 4 GW)* | |
| Ghana (VRA) | 2600 |
| DRC (SNEL) | 2561 |
| Mozambique (EDM)*** | 2399 |
| Zimbabwe (ZESA) | 1961 |
| Zambia (ZESCO) | 1786 |
| Tunisia (STEG) | 1580 |
| Kenya (KPLC) | 1173 |
| Côte d'Ivoire (CIE & IEEC) | 1100 |
| Tanzania (TANESCO) | 785 |
| Sudan (NEC) | 640 |
| Mauritius (CEB) | 498 |
| Ethiopia (EEPCO) | 422 |
| Senegal (SENELEC) | 422 |
| *Small (below 400 MW)* | |
| Uganda (UEB) | 263 |
| Malawi (ESCOM)*** | 220 |
| Botswana (BPC) | 132 |
| Eritrea (EEA)** | 92 |
| Lesotho (LEC) | 75 |
| Burundi (Regideso)*** | 43 |
| Rwanda (Electrogaz)* | 34 |
| Benin (SBEE)*** | 15 |

* – 1997 data; ** – 1998 data; *** – 1999 data

Sources: BPC, 2000; Chandi, 2001; *Financial Times*, 1999; Ntsaba, 2001; Dube, 2001; *Financial Times*, 2001a; *Financial Times*, 2001b; KPLC, 2001; *Financial Times*, 2002; Hebrard, 2001; Kebede, 2001; Marandu, 2001; Engorait, 2002; ESCOM, 1999; Habtetsion, 2002; Turkson, 2000; UN, 1997

The three categories in Table 2.1, based on the installed capacity, give a quantitative profile of the continent's power utilities.

Figure 2.1 provides electricity generation data for selected African countries. In the case of National Electricity Power Authority (NEPA) (Nigeria) it should be noted that, although the utility has a large installed capacity, its generation is low because of poor maintenance.

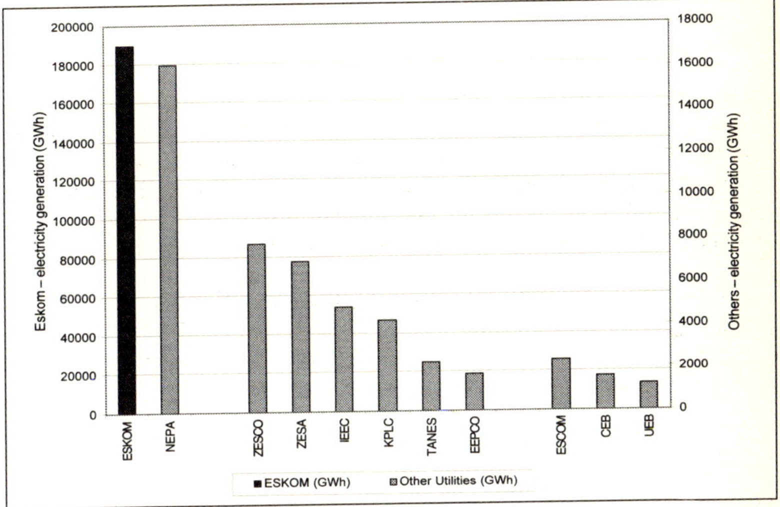


**Figure 2.1  Electricity generation for selected utilities (1999/2000)**

Sources: Ali and Elgizouli, 1996; Chiwaya, 1996; DANIDA, 1991; Dube, 1996; Eshetu and Bogale, 1996; ESKOM, 1994; LEC, 1993; Mugyenzi, 1996; Ntsaba and Ngobese, 1998; Nyoike and Okech, 1996; Sampa, 1996; World Bank, 1993a; World Bank, 1997

## Manpower levels

The World Bank's staff appraisal reports on the power sector highlight insufficient qualified manpower as a problem affecting almost all African utilities. Extreme cases mentioned include utilities in which 60–70 per cent of the total manpower are unskilled or semi-skilled personnel (World Bank, 1993a).

In comparison to power utilities in other developing countries, most African power utilities are overstaffed, with a majority of unskilled and semi-skilled manpower. Indicators of overstaffing include customers per employee and electricity sales per employee. A ratio of 125 customers per employee is considered satisfactory for most developing countries. Most African utilities register ratios below this benchmark (Figure 2.2).

*Estimating manpower requirements in power utilities*
Accurate estimates of the required manpower levels for utilities is an important planning parameter for training institutions. The utilities'

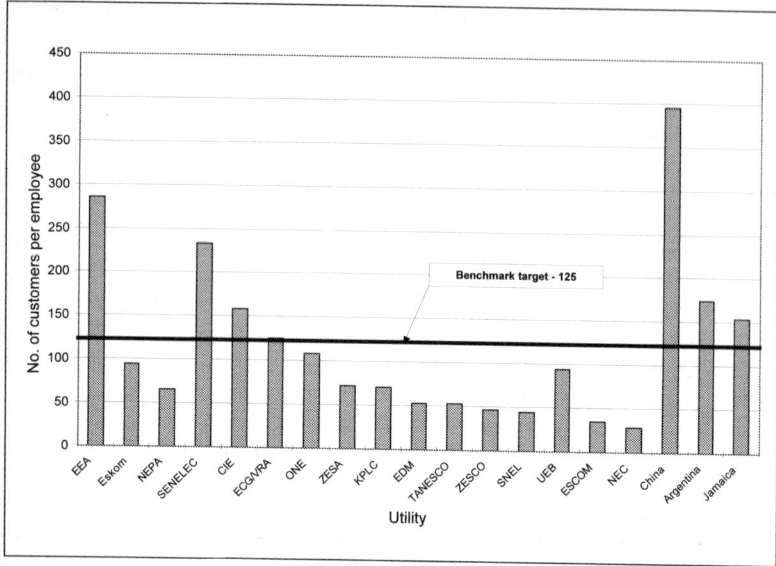



Figure 2.2  Customers per employee by utility (1997)
Sources: AFREPREN/FWD, 2001

estimates of the number of technicians and engineers required on an annual basis would enable the training institutions (mainly universities, technical colleges and polytechnics) to determine whether the prevailing annual output of engineers and technicians can meet the utilities' requirements.

One methodology that can assist in deriving estimates of engineers and technicians required by a national utility was developed by Mordell and Coales (1983). They used it to estimate the future supply of engineers and technicians in developing countries. With some modifications, it is possible to use the methodology to develop ballpark estimates of man-power requirements for the power sector. Mordell and Coales used the methodology to estimate the number of engineers and technicians per thousand of the total population required to attain the desired GDP *per capita*.

The methodology could be adapted to determine the adequacy of the current utility staffing levels as well as to project the future requirement of engineers and technicians. To determine the adequacy of the current levels, the existing national stock of engineers and technicians is used. In a well-functioning economy, a national utility is expected to use about 5 per cent of the total stock of engineers and technicians. This estimated proportion of the current national stock of engineers and technicians is compared to the existing number of engineers and technicians in the utility. If the utility's current staff complement of engineers and technicians is above the estimated proportion, it can be inferred that the utility is overstaffed; when it is less than the estimated proportion, the inference is that the utility is understaffed.

The methodology can also be adapted to estimate future manpower requirements of engineers and technicians for a national utility by using the country's projected number of engineers/technicians per thousand of the total population. To derive the number of engineers and technicians, the population is estimated using the prevailing population growth rate. Using the 5 per cent benchmark, the estimated number of engineers and technicians required by the national utility can then be derived (see chapters 2–5).

Another methodology for estimating the staffing levels required for African utilities is by comparison with the staffing ratios of an 'ideal' African utility. For this study, the ideal African utility selected is the Central Electricity Board (CEB) of Mauritius, which consistently attains the performance indicators that one expects in a developing country utility that functions well. Table 2.2 provides the ideal staffing ratios derived from the CEB as at 1997.

**Table 2.2  Ideal staffing ratios derived from the CEB**

| Ratio | Ideal number |
|---|---|
| Ratio of employees per installed MW capacity | 5 (max) |
| Ratio of employees per GWh (produced) | 2 (max) |
| Ratio of customers per employee | 125 (min) |
| Ratio of technical to administration manpower | 3 : 1 (min) |

Ideal staffing ratios provide a more nuanced assessment of manpower utilization, as shown in Table 2.3, which compares the Ethiopian Electric Power Company (EEPCO) and the Zambia Electricity Supply Corporation (ZESCO). Using the traditional measure of staffing levels – customers per employee ratio – EEPCO would seem to have better staffing levels than ZESCO.

**Table 2.3  Comparison of staffing levels for EEPCO and ZESCO**

| Indicator | 'Ideal utility' ratios (CEB) (1998) | EEPCO (2000) | ZESCO (2000) |
|---|---|---|---|
| Installed capacity (MW) | 400 | 422 | 1786 |
| Customers per employee | 125 (min) | 72 | 47 |
| Manpower per MW installed capacity | 5 (max) | 19 | 2 |
| Manpower per GWh produced | 2 (max) | 5 | 1 |
| System losses (%) | 12 (max) | 17 | 12 |
| National electrification levels (%) | 87 | 13 | 20 |

Sources: Baguant and Beeharry, 1998; Teferra, 2001a; Kalumiana, 2002

## Table 2.4 Comparison of selected utilities in the three categories (1998/9)

| | Installed capacity (MW) | Number of employees | Employees/MW installed capacity |
|---|---|---|---|
| **LARGE** | | | |
| *Ideal utility (CEB)* | *400* | *1934* | *5* |
| ESKOM (South Africa) | 39186[c] | 32832[c] | 0.84[c] |
| NEPA (Nigeria) | 6000[c] | 3,000[c] | 6.3[c] |
| ONE (Morocco) | 4389[c] | 10500[a] | 3.2[a] |
| *Indonesia* | *13630* | *36524* | *2.7* |
| AVERAGE | 16191.7 | 27111 | 3.45 |
| **MEDIUM** | | | |
| *Ideal utility (CEB)* | *400* | *1934* | *5* |
| KPLC (Kenya) | 1132[c] | 6593[c] | 5.8[c] |
| CIE (Côte d'Ivoire) | 1100[b] | 3022[a] | 3.2[a] |
| EEPCO (Ethiopia) | 422[c] | 8200[c] | 19.4[c] |
| TANESCO (Tanzania) | 785[c] | 7107 | 12.5 |
| ZESCO (Zambia) | 1786[c] | 4025 | 2.3 |
| ZESA (Zimbabwe) | 1961[c] | 6968[c] | 3.55[c] |
| ECG & VRA (Ghana) | 1622[c] | 3182[a] | 1.3[a] |
| SNEL (Zaire) | 2561 | 5544[a] | 2.2[a] |
| NEC (Sudan) | 600[c] | 11388[a] | 16.3[b] |
| SENELEC (Senegal) | 422[c] | 1700[c] | 4[c] |
| *COBEE (Bolivia)* | *783* | *1749* | *2.2* |
| AVERAGE | 1239.1 | 5773 | 7.06 |
| **SMALL** | | | |
| *Ideal utility (CEB)* | *400* | *1934* | *57* |
| Jirama (Madagascar) | 220 | 4175[a] | 19.3[a] |
| ESCOM (Malawi) | 220[c] | 2218[c] | 10[c] |
| UEB (Uganda) | 263 | 1903 | 7.24 |
| AVERAGE | 234.3 | 2765.3 | 12.18 |

1  The data provided for the 'ideal utility' refer to 1998 statistics – the base data for utility comparison. See Part III appendices for more recent data

2  The average for the medium utility category excludes Bolivia, while that for the large utility category excludes Indonesia

3  Data provided other than for 1998/9 are for the following years: a: 1994/5; b: 1996/7; c: 2000/1

Sources: ESKOM, 2001; World Bank, 1996c; Kathambana, personal communication, 1998; KPLC, 1997; Girod, 1995; Bhagavan, 1999; AFREPREN/FWD, 2001; Kayo, 2001; Teferra, 2001a

| Employees/<br>GWh<br>generation | Transmission &<br>distribution losses<br>(%) | Customers<br>per<br>employee | Electrification<br>level<br>(%) |
| --- | --- | --- | --- |
| *2* | *11.6* | *125* | *87* |
| 0.17[c] | 5[c] | 95[c] | 70[c] |
| 2.4[c] | 40[c] | 66.4[a] | 39 |
| 1.06[a] | 22 | 108.6[a] | 50 |
| *0.001* | *12.5* | *415.2* | (rural)[c]<br>*38* |
| 1.21 | 22.3 | 90 | 53.15 |
| *2* | *11.6* | *125* | *87* |
| 1.6[c] | 21.3[c] | 71.22[c] | 20[c] |
| 1.7[a] | 13[c] | 159.5[a] | 21[a] |
| 4.8[c] | 17[c] | 72[c] | 13[c] |
| 3.4 | 11.7[c] | 53 | 7[c] |
| 0.5 | 12.1[c] | 46.81 | 20[c] |
| 1.8[c] | 13[c] | 72 | 40[c] |
| 0.4[a] | 26[c] | 125.7[a] | 45[c] |
| 1.01[a] | 12[b] | 45.1[a] | 7[c] |
| n/a | 41[c] | 29[a] | 30[c] |
| 1.3[c] | 17 | 234[c] | 30.4[c] |
| *0.001* | *11.4* | *314.3* | 56 |
| 1.83 | 18.41 | 90.83 | 23.34 |
| *2* | *11.6* | *125* | *87* |
| 8.8[a] | 17[c] | 45[a] | 7 |
| 2.17[c] | 18.5[c] | 35[c] | 5[c] |
| 1.24 | 35 | 94.7 | 5[c] |
| 4.07 | 23.5 | 58.23 | 5.67 |

The ideal ratios, however, seem to indicate that ZESCO performs better than EEPCO. The technical performances of the two utilities appear to corroborate the findings derived from the ideal ratios. Using system losses and electrification levels as indicators of technical performance, ZESCO appears to perform better.

The deductions made in the previous comparison between EEPCO and ZESCO appear to be confirmed by Table 2.4, which compares utilities across the three categories. Utilities within or very close to the ideal staffing ratios (for both installed capacity and generation), register better technical performance (based on electricity losses, customers per employee and electrification levels). For example, utilities such as ESKOM (South Africa), CIE (Côte d'Ivoire), ONE (Morocco), the formerly integrated ECG/VRA (Ghana), SENELEC (Senegal) and ZESCO (Zambia), whose staffing ratios compare relatively well with the ideal, appear to register better performance, especially with regard to national electrification levels.

Conversely, poor performances are registered by utilities with ratios (of both manpower per MW installed capacity and manpower per GWh produced) exceeding the ideal. Utilities such as EEPCO (Ethiopia), TANESCO (Tanzania), Jirama (Madagascar), ESCOM (Malawi) and UEB (Uganda), with staffing ratios below the ideal, all register low electrification levels – less than 10 per cent.

On the whole, it appears that the large and medium-sized power utilities are adequately staffed as compared to the small power utilities. The smaller utilities appear to be largely overstaffed. As shown in Table 2.4, the small utilities have staffing levels that are twice the ideal staffing levels. The fact that the majority of utilities in the region register staffing levels below the ideal staffing ratios would seem to indicate that overstaffing could be a result of inadequate manpower planning skills in the utilities. For example, in the Ethiopia country case study described in Part IV, Teferra indicates that several key utility personnel interviewed at EEPCO were of the impression that the utility had an inadequate number of engineers because many positions remain unoccupied. However, after analysis using the ideal staffing ratios and estimates derived from the Mordell–Coales methodology, Teferra is able to reveal that EEPCO in fact had an excess number of engineers (Teferra, 1998). Figure 2.3 compares the actual and the required number of engineers in 1996 (derived from the ideal staffing levels and the Mordell–Coales methodology).

*Conclusions on manpower levels*

We have thus been able to establish a link between staffing levels and performance, using the ideal utility as the basis for comparison. It is apparent that the overstaffed utilities tend to perform poorly. Utilities with manpower ratios within range or close to the ideal appear to register better technical performance compared to those whose ratios are not within range. Examples of utilities with ratios that are comparable to the

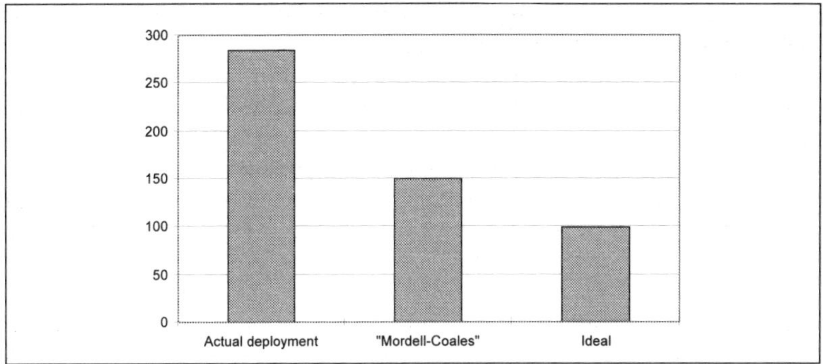

Figure 2.3  Comparison of engineers required in EEPCO (1996)
Source: Adapted from Teferra, 1998

ideal include ESKOM (South Africa), ONE (Morocco), CIE (Côte d'Ivoire), ECG/VRA (Ghana) and SENELEC (Senegal).

The smaller utilities appear to be more overstaffed in comparison to the larger utilities. On average, unlike the large and medium-scale utilities, the smaller utilities appear to register staffing levels twice the ideal. When technical performance indicators are considered, the small-scale utilities turn out to have the highest system losses and the lowest national electrification levels (Table 2.5).

Manpower planning could be hindered by the fact that the number of employees in some utilities has been predetermined through what are referred to as 'established posts'. These posts were established many years ago and may not be relevant to present-day utilities. The case study of Ethiopia and EEPCO by Teferra and his colleagues reveals this weakness quite clearly: the utility considers its staffing levels inadequate on the basis of the unoccupied posts. Conversely, comparative use of the ideal staffing ratios indicates overstaffing in the utility. EEPCO's staffing ratios are 20 employees per MW of installed capacity and five employees per

Table 2.5  Comparison of staffing levels by utility category

| UTILITY CATEGORY | Employees/ MW installed capacity | Employees/ GWh generation | Transmission & distribution losses (%) | Electrification levels (%) |
|---|---|---|---|---|
| Ideal utility (CEB) | 5 | 2 | 12 | 87 |
| Large | 3.5 | 1.2 | 22 | 53 |
| Medium | 7.1 | 1.8 | 18 | 23 |
| Small | 12.2 | 4.1 | 24 | 6 |

Source: Compiled by authors

GWh of generation, compared to the ideal of five and two employees respectively.

With the advent of power sector reform, the majority of the utilities considered overstaffed (UEB of Uganda, for example) are downsizing, mainly in readiness for privatization. Utilities such as KPLC (Kenya) have downsized as a result of the unbundling of the power sector. Power sector reform appears to have reduced the political pressure on utilities to provide employment.

## Status of manpower training

Power utilities generally employ personnel with qualifications from universities, polytechnics and technical colleges. At the utility level, the training provided is more specialized and focused on the utility's operations. The kind of training provided familiarizes the new employees with the equipment that they will use in the course of their work. Specialized training is usually given at the utility training institution and further training, where available, is obtained at local and foreign tertiary institutions (Ali and Elgizouli, 1996; Mugyenzi, 1996; Nyoike and Okech, 1996; Mbewe, 1996).

Most of the power utility training institutions are underdeveloped and lack equipment, adequate training personnel and coordinated training programmes. Examples of poor training facilities include UEB of Uganda and NEC of Sudan, among other utilities (Mugyenzi, 1996; Ali and Elgizouli, 1996).

With the exception of a few, the majority of the utility training facilities have not been expanded to meet growing training needs. The few utilities that have expanded their training institutions have used part of the loans acquired for investment in generation, transmission and distribution. In Mozambique in 1994, part of a $30 million loan was used to renovate and expand the technical training centre run by the Electricidade de Mocambique (EDM) at Songo (ERI, 1994). In Ghana in 1993, part of an International Development Aid (IDA) loan for rehabilitation of the power sector was used to expand the Tema Training Centre (World Bank, 1993a).

Power utilities, generally more technically oriented than other parastatals, tend to provide more training for technical staff (engineers, technicians, artisans) than their non-technical colleagues (Nyoike and Okech, 1996; Ali and Elgizouli, 1996). Non-technical training is mainly provided for management level employees. Although KPLC (Kenya) and ZESCO (Zambia) are not directly involved in the training of non-technical employees, they have policies that encourage employees to develop their skills. These utilities have set aside funds for the reimbursement of fees payable for short courses relevant to an employee's work (Nyoike and Okech, 1996; Mbewe, 1996).

The case studies that follow provide information on the status of training in selected utilities within the sub-Saharan region.

*Training at power utilities*

ESKOM, SOUTH AFRICA

To maintain and improve technical performance, ESKOM's human resource management focuses on creating an adequately skilled and harmonious workforce that keeps abreast of the best worldwide practices (ESKOM, 1992a). To achieve this the utility offers comprehensive training programmes designed to meet individual needs and motivate staff to realize their full potential (*ibid.*).

ESKOM has invested about US$150 million in local training and development-related facilities (Percy, 1996) and each year the utility spends about US$34 million on various educational and training programmes for its employees. Overseas training in technical skills development has been encouraged, and several artisans have been trained as master craftsmen at the Handwerkshammer für Mittelfranken in Germany (ESKOM, 1992a).

Each year, ESKOM trains about 7,000 technical staff members at the Technical Skills Development Centre at ESKOM College (*ibid.*: 39). ESKOM also organizes training for personnel from utilities in neighbouring countries (*ibid.*: 41) as well as from other countries outside Africa. All in all, about 13,000 trainees undergo training in a wide range of technical, managerial and financial skills at ESKOM College annually (*ibid.*). Practical hands-on knowledge of the working of a power station is provided at the Wilge power station in the eastern Transvaal. It is one of the few operational power stations in the world that is run exclusively for training purposes (*ibid.*).

To eradicate illiteracy among some of its employees, in 1996 ESKOM offered adult literacy education opportunities to over 10,000 employees (Percy, 1996). In addition, the utility sponsors the education of its employees' children whom it considers to be future 'Eskomites' (ESKOM, 1992a).

ZIMBABWE ELECTRICITY SUPPLY AUTHORITY (ZESA)

ZESA undertakes most of its staff training at the National Training Centre in Harare. The training centre cost US$830,000 (mid-1998 exchange rate) to construct and is equipped to international standards (ZESA, 1995a). With a maximum capacity of 220 trainees at a time, the training centre meets technical training needs in generation, transmission and distribution up to graduate engineering level (ZESA, undated: 3). In addition, non-technical training in customer care, financial and general management, administration, leadership and supervisory skills is provided to both technical and non-technical staff (ZESA, 1993a; ZESA, 1995a). Additional training, including internships, is provided as part of staff development.

In the mid-1990s a SADC consultant recommended that ZESA's National Training Centre provide training officers to the Kafue Gorge Regional Training Centre in Zambia. The consultant also confirmed the training centre's capacity to host regional training programmes for the SADC region (ZESA, 1995a). ZESA already conducts training of personnel from utilities in parts of the region where training facilities are less developed, such as Tanzania, Mozambique and Botswana.

ZESA provides hands-on training at one of its power plants and through the use of simulators. The simulators enable rapid development of a high level of operational efficiency and are also used for refresher courses. The Hwange power plant is used as a thermal power plant familiarization centre. This particular power station was constructed with training as one of its objectives (ZESA, undated).

To enhance manpower productivity, ZESA targeted 2000 as the year by which it would increase its trained personnel from 10 to 70 per cent and its fully skilled personnel from 30 to 60 per cent (ZESA, 1995a). Training of staff in ZESA can be summarized in the four categories shown in Table 2.6.

**Table 2.6  Categories of training in ZESA**

| Category | Description |
| --- | --- |
| Category I<br>Routine basic training | Apprentice and postgraduate |
| Category II<br>Advancement and reinforcement training | Advanced technical and supervisory skills |
| Category III<br>New technologies | Advanced engineering, total quality management |
| Category IV<br>Targeted training | Live-line working, HIV–Aids awareness, defensive driving, etc. |

Sources: World Bank, 1993b: 20; ZESA, 1995a: 17

KENYA POWER AND LIGHTING COMPANY LIMITED (KPLC)
Most of the training for both junior and senior cadre staff at KPLC is undertaken locally. The junior cadre employees are trained at the company's training school. KPLC also sponsors the junior staff for further training at the local polytechnics. In-house training for professional and semi-professional personnel covers engineering, accountancy and personnel administration (Nyoike and Okech, 1996).

The management-level staff is trained by locally based private management consultancies. This appears to be a cheaper option than sending the employees abroad (*ibid.*: 50–1). It is estimated that between 1989 and 1994 about 3,920 junior cadre employees underwent technical training.

During the same period, about 739 senior cadre employees underwent managment training (*ibid.*: 51). In relative terms, KPLC has spent more on the training of junior cadre than senior cadre staff.

Figure 2.4 shows the level of manpower training at KPLC from 1989 to 1994. The graph demonstrates that the utility provided more technical than non-technical (management) training. In 1994, there appears to be a drastic drop in technical training that corresponds to the drop in the funds allocated for training.

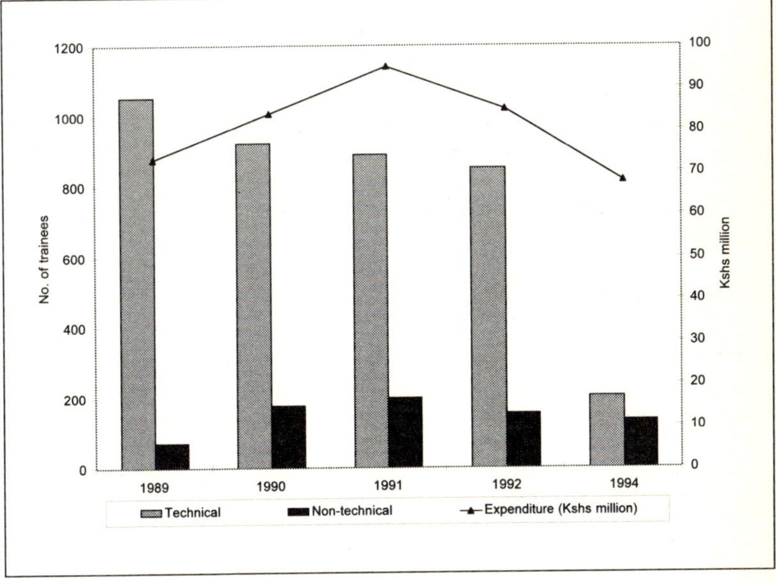


**Figure 2.4 Expenditure and employee training at KPLC (1989–94)**

Data unavailable for 1993
Source: Adapted from Nyoike and Okech, 1996

Brew-Hammond (1995) contrasts KPLC's staff training to that of the Volta River Authority (VRA). KPLC's manpower training appears unsustained and has been on the decline since 1991. VRA's training, on the other hand, has intensified. The increased level of VRA's manpower trained annually, indicated in Figure 2.5, confirms its commitment to long-term manpower training.

NATIONAL ELECTRICITY CORPORATION (NEC), SUDAN
Training in NEC, under the jurisdiction of a Director of Training who reports to the Director of Organization and Training, has been inadequate. In 1989 an Overseas Development Agency (ODA) review mission identified the lack of a training policy at NEC and suggested that the utility

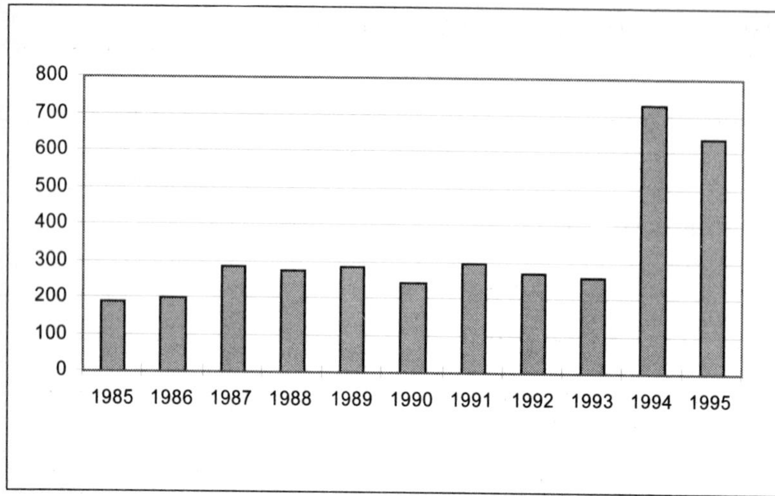


**Figure 2.5  Level of manpower training at the VRA (1985–95)**

Source: Brew-Hammond, 1997

ought to 'quantify training needs at all levels, identify how such needs should be met, and establish priorities' (Ali and Elgizouli, 1996).

No consensus exists within NEC on its level of emphasis on training for technicians and engineers, according to Ali and Elgizouli (1996). Nonetheless, it is clear that there is an urgent training need for craftsmen, semi-skilled and unskilled labourers in the utility. For instance, in the central motor garage there are 96 employees of whom only five, including the manager, are capable of overhauling vehicles. Poorly trained maintenance staff meant that a large proportion of machinery purchased over a decade ago remained unassembled for a long time. Ali and Elgizouli contend that training of craftsmen, semi-skilled and unskilled labourers could significantly reduce the workload on the more qualified staff.

Training at the utility is undertaken in several training centres and on the job (DANIDA, 1990d; Ali and Elgizouli, 1996: 158–9). This training is uncoordinated, however, because the NEC Training Department does not liaise with the training institutes. Table 2.7 lists the key training undertaken locally in 1989.

In 1990 a new training centre was established about 25 km from Khartoum at Um Haruz. The centre was designed to provide training in mechanical and electrical installation, maintenance and operational practices: it targeted engineers, technicians and craftsmen. Instructors for the training centre were drawn from the NEC staff. About 16 instructors went to Ireland in 1988 for instructor training (Ali and Elgizouli, 1996).

There is little motivation for instructors or trainees to participate in training. For instance, although housing is provided for the instructors at

**Table 2.7 Local training given to NEC staff in 1989**

| No. of Employees | Course | Duration | Place of training |
| --- | --- | --- | --- |
| 2 | Personnel management | 1 month | Sudan Academy for Administrative Science |
| 8 | Cable jointing | 2 months | NEC training school |
| 1 | Executive development | 6 months | Sudan Academy |
| 1 | Diploma in administration | 1 year | University of Khartoum |
| 16 | Power station operation and maintenance | 1 year | Khartoum North Power Station |
| 3 | MSc in Planning | 2 years | University of Khartoum |
| 3 | BSc in Electrical Engineering | 3 years | Khartoum Polytechnic |
| 50 | Fitting | 1 month | Burri Power Station |

Source: Ali and Elgizouli, 1996

the Um Haruz training centre, the distance to Khartoum coupled with the lack of transport is a demotivating factor. For trainees, on the other hand, the only inducement to attend training courses is the speculative prospect of promotion (*ibid.*). In addition, although the training centre has a mechanical workshop (NEC, 2001), it is reported to be ill-equipped with regard to the repair and maintenance of diesel engines, one of NEC's most pressing training needs (Ali and Elgizouli, 1996).

To supplement local training, NEC, in conjunction with donor governments and sponsors, offers overseas training to its staff. Table 2.8 lists key overseas training conducted in 1989. Although training abroad has been useful to NEC personnel in terms of exposure to new experience, Ali and Elgizouli identified the following problems:

- *Poor identification of training needs*: The analysis of training needs was conducted in a haphazard and uncoordinated fashion.

- *Delayed approvals*: Slow approval by the National Training Agency, even when there was no government expenditure involved, sometimes led to delays and missed training opportunities.

- *Favouritism*: Overseas training selection showed clear-cut imbalances and favouritism towards certain departments.

**Table 2.8  Overseas training given to NEC staff in 1989**

| No. of employees | Course | Place of training | Sponsor | Duration |
|---|---|---|---|---|
| 1 | Chemical Engineering | UK | Confederation of British Industry | 6 months |
| 1 | Power distribution network | W. Germany | W. German govt | 11 months |
| 1 | PhD in Civil Engineering | USSR | USSR govt | 3 years |
| 1 | PhD in Mechanical Engineering | USSR | USSR govt | 3 years |
| 1 | Development of concrete tower network | Finland | Finnish govt | 2 months |
| 5 | Fuel diesel maintenance | Canada and USA | Japanese govt | 1 month |
| 1 | Power plant design and operation | Philippines | Philippines govt | 2.5 months |
| 1 | Electrical engineering (photovoltaic) | Italy | Italian govt | 1 month |
| 1 | Electrical control systems | W. Germany | W. German govt | 4 months |
| 7 | Operation and maintenance of diesel stations | Netherlands | Dutch govt | 2 months |

Source: Ali and Elgizouli, 1996

There has been little training for non-technical staff in the administrative and financial departments. As at 1996, the last comprehensive management training had taken place in 1984, when 15–20 senior staff went to Ireland. In 1987, the Management Development Centre in Khartoum emphasized that NEC should design training programmes for its staff in senior posts. The Centre recommended 14 topic areas for NEC's consideration. This recommendation, however, was not implemented (Ali and Elgizouli, 1996).

Independent power producer (IPP) developments planned for Sudan are several times larger than the present installed capacity of NEC, which poses a challenge for manpower training in the utility. To meet these projected new needs, additional manpower training and expansion of the training facilities will be necessary. Table 2.9 shows the planned IPP developments in Sudan.

Table 2.9  Planned IPP developments in Sudan

| IPP development | Developer | Installed capacity (MW) |
| --- | --- | --- |
| Merowe | To be solicited | 1000 |
| Kajbar | Unspecified Chinese group | 300 |
| Shirek | To be solicited | 300 |
| Khartoum | Multidiscovery | 100 |
| Port Sudan | Multidiscovery | 100 |
| | TNB | 60 |

Source: *Financial Times*, 2001b

## *Regional training institutions for power utilities*

At the regional level, there are a few training facilities dedicated to training employees from power utilities with less-developed training facilities. Notable examples are the Interafrican Electrical Engineering College and the Kafue Gorge Regional Training Centre.

INTERAFRICAN ELECTRICAL ENGINEERING COLLEGE (IEEC)

The Interafrican Electrical Engineering College (IEEC) is located in Bingerville, Côte d'Ivoire. The IEEC was conceived in 1974 and opened in 1979. It has been run by the Union of Producers, Conveyors and Distributors of Electrical Energy in Africa (UPDEA). The College was established with the aim of providing a quality degree that incorporates practical training in engineering (ESMAP, 1990).

Focused in a single degree course, the objectives of the IEEC include the following (*ibid.*):

- To establish an African institution that provides degrees in electro-mechanical engineering to stem the brain drain that seems to occur when African students attend universities in Europe and North America.

- To provide graduates who are immediately useful to their sponsoring utility. The training provided targets the key engineering problems faced by utilities.

- To foster future interregional cooperation among the continent's power utilities through the establishment of a bilingual (English and French) course.

The quality of training provided in IEEC is said to be almost equivalent to that which in the United Kingdom leads to a Chartered Engineer qualification (*ibid.*). This latter entails a two-year structured industrial training course, known as a graduate industrial traineeship, for persons recruited from national university engineering schools.

By 1990 IEEC had produced 127 engineering graduates who were working in 14 African countries. These graduates may be equivalent to and possibly better suited for service in African power utilities than their counterparts graduating from European or American universities (*ibid.*). Table 2.10 shows IEEC graduates in 1988/9 (*ibid.*: 2). It appears that North and West African utilities send employees to this college rather more freely than do utilities from the rest of Africa.

**Table 2.10  Use of IEEC by power utilities in Africa (1988/9)**

| Utility | Country | Degree graduates | Preparatory course |
| --- | --- | --- | --- |
| EECI | Côte d'Ivoire | 42 | 35 |
| SENELEC | Senegal | 23 | 7 |
| NIGELEC | Niger | 15 | 14 |
| SONABEL | Burkina Faso | 7 | 3 |
| CEET | Togo | 7 | 14 |
| SNEL | DRC | 6 | – |
| SEEG | Gabon | 4 | 6 |
| EDM | Mali | 4 | 4 |
| ENELGUI | Guinea-Conakry | 3 | 2 |
| STEG | Tunisia | 2 | – |
| ENERCA | Central African Rep. | 1 | – |
| EdD | Djibouti | 1 | – |
| SONELEC | Mauritania | 1 | – |
| STEE | Chad | – | 3 |
| SNE | Congo | – | 4 |
| LEC | Liberia | – | 4 |
| Electrogaz | Rwanda | – | 1 |
| TOTAL | | 116 | 97 |

KAFUE GORGE REGIONAL TRAINING CENTRE (KGRTC)

Prior to serving regional interests, the Kafue Gorge Regional Training Centre was dedicated to training the employees of the Zambia Electricity Supply Corporation (ZESCO). In the period 1971–82, approximately 250 of ZESCO's employees underwent training on a wide range of long-term courses in hydroelectric engineering at the training centre (*SADCC Energy Quarterly*, 1990).

Following an assessment carried out by a joint Zambian and Norwegian consultancy team on the training needs of the SADC region, the recommendation was made that the centre should be rehabilitated and reopened as a regional training centre. Its rehabilitation became part of the refurbishment programme for the Kafue Gorge power station (*SADCC Energy Quarterly*, 1990: 33; 1991).

In the early 1990s, the Norwegian and Swedish power consultants (Norpower and Swedpower) jointly managed the centre, providing a manager, the instructor-in-chief and short-term instructors. ZESCO found three instructors and the necessary support staff (*SADCC Energy Quarterly*, 1990: 33–4). ZESA's National Training Centre in Harare collaborated with the regional training centre through the provision of training officers (ZESA, 1995a).

As the regional training centre for the Southern African region, KGRTC offers training designed to meet the curriculum outlined in the SADC's *Five-Year Regional Power Sector Training Programme* (Jordanger, 1992). With the development of the Southern African Power Pool (SAPP), which encompasses the majority of SADC countries, this training institute is likely to continue to be the key training centre for utilities in East and Southern Africa.

*Conclusions on manpower training*

The larger and a number of the medium-scale utilities appear to possess better-equipped training centres than the smaller utilities. The majority of the training centres are equipped with basic machinery but often lack specialized training equipment such as simulators. In addition, most utilities do not have dedicated power plants to provide hands-on training.

Some of the large and medium-scale utilities known to use advanced simulators as part of their training include ZESA (Zimbabwe), ESKOM (South Africa), CEB (Mauritius), ZESCO (Zambia) and ONE (Morocco). Simulators provide the trainees with practical knowledge before deployment to the power plants. The aforementioned utilities seem to indicate better technical performance than those that do not use simulators as part of their training.

Utilities with better-equipped training facilities also tend to face fewer maintenance problems than those without simulators. NEC (Sudan) is an example of a utility that has faced constant maintenance problems that can be traced back to its training technique. According to Ali and Elgizouli (1996), NEC's training centre is ill-equipped and lacks adequate workshop facilities for the repair and maintenance of diesel engines – one of NEC's most pressing training needs. We have also remarked on the non-assembly of NEC's long-purchased equipment and the inability of most staff in its central motor garage to overhaul vehicles.

In addition to simulators to enhance the technical skills of the employees, some utilities such as ZESA and ESKOM have dedicated power plants that are run exclusively for training purposes. These power plants are connected to the national grid. ZESA has used the Hwange power plant as a thermal power plant familiarization centre, while ESKOM uses its Wilge power station for hands-on training.

Complementing the regional training centres are the large and medium-scale utilities with advanced training facilities. They provide valuable training to employees of small utilities with less-developed training facilities, especially those in countries such as Lesotho, Malawi and Botswana. ESKOM and ZESA are once again examples. KGRTC and IEEC both provide training to utilities in their respective regions. Table 2.11 provides examples of utilities with advanced training facilities that have trained employees from utilities with less-developed training facilities. In a few cases, utilities have established bilateral joint training facilities. For example, in 1968 SBEE (Benin) and CEET (Togo) established a

**Table 2.11  Training at regional training centres and in utilities with advanced training facilities**

| Utility/regional training centre | Location | Other utilities trained |
| --- | --- | --- |
| ESKOM | South Africa | Nampower (Namibia), LEC (Lesotho), BPC (Botswana), ZESA (Zimbabwe) |
| ZESA | Zimbabwe | TANESCO (Tanzania), EDM (Mozambique), BPC (Botswana) |
| KGRTC | Zambia | Utilities in the SADC countries |
| IEEC | Côte d'Ivoire | West African utilities in Senegal, Niger, Burkina Faso, Togo, Gabon, Mali, Guinea-Conakry, Chad, Liberia |

Source: Compiled by authors

training facility at Abomey-Calavi, Togo, to provide qualified staff for both utilities during the construction of the transmission line between Benin and Togo (DANIDA, 1991).

Instead of acquiring separate financing for developing their training facilities, some of the small and medium-scale utilities have included a training component in the overall loan for expansion projects. Examples of small and medium-scale utilities that have adopted this financing method include the aforementioned SBEE (Benin) and CEET (Togo), EDM (Mozambique) and ECG/VRA (Ghana). We have seen how Mozambique, in 1994, and Ghana, in 1993, used a part of loans for power sector rehabilitation in this way.

Utilities that have well-defined training programmes appear to perform better than those with poor and uncoordinated programmes. Utilities such as ZESA (Zimbabwe) and ESKOM (South Africa) have carefully devised training targets to meet. Their technical performance indicators also appear to show relatively good performances. By contrast, utilities with poor and uncoordinated training programmes, such as UEB (Uganda) and NEC (Sudan), appear to turn in poor technical performances. Table 2.12 shows how training targets set by ZESA and ESKOM might have contributed to their remarkable technical performances.

A closer examination of the training courses offered at utility level indicates a significant bias towards the technical, with limited training in management and computer use. In-house training programmes seem not to cater for senior employees who mainly require training in financial management, strategic planning and time management. This observation was also highlighted by the Twelfth Congress of the Union of Producers, Conveyors and Distributors of Electric Power in Africa (Khonza, 1997).

Table 2.12  Training targets for ZESA, ESKOM, UEB and NEC

| Utility | Training target | System losses (2000) | Electrification levels (2000) |
|---|---|---|---|
| ZESA | By year 2000, increase level of trained employees from 10% to 70% | 13% | 39% |
| ESKOM | Training of 13,000 employees annually | 5% | 70% |
| UEB | Limited training undertaken | 39% | 5% |
| NEC* | Uncoordinated training programme | 41% | 30% |

* Year 2001 data
Source: Mangwengwende, 2001; Percy, 1996; Kyokutamba, 2001; NEC, 2001

The rationale for introducing management training, especially to senior engineers and technicians in the utility, is that, as they rise up the ranks, they are less involved in the daily routines of technical and operational matters but get more involved in managing and decision-making aspects. At management level, the employees are well versed in technical issues and further technical training may not contribute to meeting the challenges of their management positions. Management training is even more important as the utility grows. As the number of power plants, customers and employees grows, the management of the utility becomes increasingly complex.

The best-performing large and medium-scale utilities in the region are those that provide extensive management training. For example, ESKOM provides management training to its employees and this in part explains the utility's exceptional performance both by regional and international standards. Another example is ZESA, which in the previous decade began to emphasize training in management skills: no doubt as a result, it has demonstrated a significant improvement in performance.

The training of senior cadre employees in management skills should not, however, be to the detriment of training of their junior counterparts. Training statistics from KPLC (Kenya) for the period between 1988 and 1994 reveal an alarming trend whereby the training of junior employees was drastically reduced from about 1,000 trainees in 1988 to about 200 in 1994 (Nyoike and Okech, 1996). During the same period, training of senior employees in management was doubled from about 70 to about 140. This imbalance and neglect of the basics could partially explain recent maintenance problems faced by the utility.

Data available from selected utilities reveal that a modest but effective training programme requires only a small proportion of total expenditure. Figure 2.6 shows as a percentage the expenditure that goes into training for selected utilities. There could be a link between utility technical

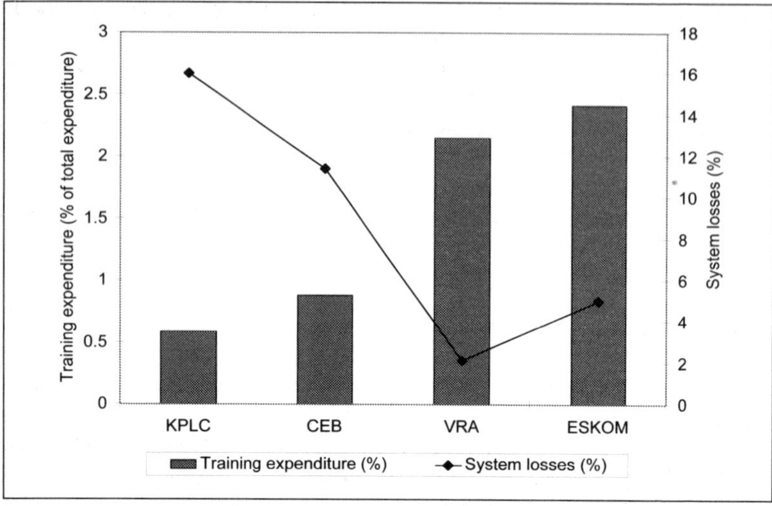



**Figure 2.6  Comparison of training expenditure and system losses in selected countries**

VRA is mainly a generation utility which explains its low system losses
Source: Compiled by authors

performance and the level of expenditure for training. It seems that utilities with low system losses spend a larger proportion of their expenditure on training. This link appears to corroborate earlier findings that utilities with good training facilities and training programmes perform better than those with poor facilities and programmes.

Recent power sector reforms of the electricity industry in the region have resulted in numerous new players joining the power game. Because it may not be possible for every new power company to establish its own training facility, the inevitable question that follows is: who will provide training for the electricity industry? As for more advanced training, the aforementioned regional training centres and national utilities such as ESKOM and ZESA could provide it. For the fundamental and intermediate training courses, however, a local institution would be best placed to provide the training. An option that could be explored is to have a dedicated training facility that would serve all the utilities in the country.

This option would entail handing over the management of the existing training facility under a state-owned utility to a board of trustees with representatives from all key players in the power industry. This arrangement is based on a model from the Kenyan hotel industry where the Utalii College was established to provide training for employees in the country's hotels and restaurants. The College is managed by a fairly autonomous board of trustees that represents the industry and is financed through a 2 per cent levy charged on customers' hotel and restaurant bills. (Until recently, the levy was remitted directly to the board of trustees. This avoided the delay normally associated with levies that go through the Treasury, such as the Rural Electrification Levy.) For this training option to be successful, it is vital that the board of trustees be appointed by the key players in the electricity industry. This will ensure its autonomy and accountability. If necessary, a training levy could be introduced on electricity consumers' bills to help finance the training facility. The power utilities could also contribute a significant proportion of the required finance.

## Manpower retention

Retention in many African utilities is a problem mainly due to poor salary structures and inappropriate incentives. This has been the case for the majority of the small and medium-scale utilities in the region and can be attributed in part to the poor state of their national economies.

In ESCOM (Malawi), for instance, attracting qualified and experienced personnel was difficult until the salary scales were increased to match the salaries provided in the private sector. A meritocratic system of staff rewards was also effected (Chiwaya, *et al.*, 1996). In LEC (Lesotho), following a long-standing problem of retention, a new performance management system started to provide rewards based on measurable achievement (LEC, 1993).

There are, however, other exogenous factors that affect retention in the utilities. One of these factors is political and economic instability, which leads to brain drain: qualified personnel migrate for both job and personal security reasons. This is a serious problem in Sudan's NEC (Ali and Elgizouli, 1996).

Another factor that is increasingly worrying is the impact of HIV–Aids on employees of power utilities. HIV–Aids cases have been on the increase in the region and power sector employees have not been spared. In Zambia, Sampa (1996) contends that ZESCO experiences a higher staff turnover due to the impact of HIV–Aids cases than as a result of resignations and dismissals. Similar sentiments have been voiced with regard to ZESA, with deaths (mainly HIV–Aids related) accounting for about 30 per cent of the total staff turnover (ZESA, 1999).

Apart from good pay packages and attractive training opportunities that serve as incentives, some utilities provide medical services to staff and their families. In addition, the availability of small loan schemes, job security, long-service awards and attractive retirement arrangements have enhanced the level of retention in the utilities. Table 2.13 provides a summary of incentives and rewards provided by various power utilities.

In a significant number of countries, the World Bank-driven economic reform and structural adjustment programmes have led to the ongoing and planned retrenchment of employees in state-owned institutions. To

**Table 2.13  Incentives and awards provided by selected utilities**

| Utility (Country) | Incentives and rewards |
| --- | --- |
| CEB (Mauritius) | Training, medical cover, compensation, attractive, pension, collective bargaining |
| ESCOM (Malawi) | Training, annual salary review, collective bargaining |
| ESKOM (South Africa) | Training, medical cover, subsidies, collective bargaining |
| KPLC (Kenya) | Training, medical cover, car loan, housing, long-service awards |
| LEC (Lesotho) | Training, annual salary review, medical cover |
| NEC (Sudan) | Training, medical cover, loan scheme, collective bargaining |
| ZESA (Zimbabwe) | Training, performance-based rewards, medical cover, annual salary review, collective bargaining, long-service awards, 'Worker of the Year' award |

Source: Compiled by authors

meet retrenchment targets, some utilities have established attractive early retirement schemes dubbed 'golden handshakes'. These retirement schemes target the non-professional and lower-cadre staff. In Kenya, an attempt by KPLC backfired when the scheme unexpectedly attracted the professional technical employees who saw it as an opportunity to launch their own businesses. This defeated the retirement scheme's objective of reducing the proportion of unskilled and semi-skilled manpower.

A significant challenge that is often not highlighted is the retention of the top-level management of the utility. The majority of the state-owned utilities experience a high turnover of top-level management and the board of directors. Frequent changes in the management of the utilities can sometimes help to explain poor performances.

The high turnover is mainly caused by political interference, usually from the Minister of Energy or the relevant Ministry. Prior to the amendment of the Electricity Act in a number of African countries undergoing power sector reform, the former Act gave the Minister wide powers over the management of the utility. The chief executive officer and the board of directors, all appointees of the Minister, had very little power and as a result became implementing agents of the Minister's directives (Mangwengwende, 2001).

For political reasons, ministers have sacked entire boards of directors and top-level management. One such case is in Zimbabwe where, in

1992, the then Minister of Energy sacked the entire board of directors and the chief executive officer of ZESA. In 2001, political interference, again, led to the loss of the entire top-level management team that had turned the utility's record around following the successful implementation of a performance improvement programme (*ibid.*).

*Staff retention initiatives in utilities in the region*
ESKOM has used two main techniques to achieve staff retention. First, it provides a minimum guaranteed wage adjustment for all of its employees annually. Second, ESKOM has reached a flexibility agreement with trade unions on retaining and redeploying surplus staff in order to minimize retrenchment (ESKOM, 1992b).

Staff retention at ZESA, especially of professionals, has been difficult mainly because of the poor remuneration packages offered (ZESA, 1993a; Mapako, 1996). In the early 1990s ZESA was recording an annual staff turnover as high as about 8 per cent for professional employees and about 5 per cent for other employees (ZESA, 1995a). The introduction of a performance improvement programme addressed the issue through job evaluation and review of salary scales (ZESA, 1993a). The ZESA corporate business plan set a target of reducing staff turnover to 5 per cent for the professionals and 2 per cent for the other employees by the year 2000 (ZESA, 1995a). The high staff turnover among professional staff was reported to have been stemmed and this target achieved (Mangwengwende, 2001).

ZESA provides incentives to its employees through long-service awards. In 1995, for instance, a total of 91 employees received 25 years' long service awards (ZESA, 1995a). There is also a 'Worker of the Year' award. Management has further enhanced working relationships with its employees through the formation of a National Employment Council, an impartial body meant to settle cases that the normal procedures at ZESA cannot resolve (*ibid.*).

ZESA provides a model of how the introduction of staff retention measures can have significant impact on a utility's performance. Table 2.14 compares the technical and financial performance of ZESA's selected indicators before and after the introduction of the performance improvement programme (PIP) in 1992/3.

Table 2.14 ZESA's performance before and after its performance improvement programme

| Indicator | 1990 | 1991 | 1992 | 1993 | 1994 | 1995 | 1996 | 1997 | 1998 | 1999 |
|---|---|---|---|---|---|---|---|---|---|---|
| Self-financing ratio | −112.0 | −65.0 | −102.0 | −28.0 | 27.0 | 31.0 | 47.0 | 37.6 | 37.6 | 40.0 |
| Debtor days | 72 | 74 | 85 | 99 | 61 | 50 | 56 | 37 | 32 | 32 |
| Electrification levels (%) | 20.0 | 20.0 | 28.0 | 29.4 | 30.8 | 32.2 | 33.6 | 35.0 | 37.5 | 39.0 |
| Customers per employee | 41 | 40 | 44 | 45 | 44 | 47 | 51 | 55 | 60 | 69 |

Source: ZESA, 1997; Mapako, 1998; Kayo, 2001

In comparison to other government corporations in Sudan, NEC provides better terms of service in terms of remuneration – this, however, since the Ministry of Finance ceased determining remuneration for NEC's employees following Cabinet approval of NEC's autonomy to determine terms of service for its employees (Ali and Elgizouli, 1996).

A medical fund is in operation to back a clinic through which employees receive medical services. Under this medical fund, employees contribute 1 per cent of their salaries and NEC contributes 2 per cent (*ibid.*). Surgery expenses are shared on the basis that the employee foots 25 per cent of the bill while the balance is taken care of by the medical fund.

In spite of these incentives, NEC is reportedly facing difficulties in attracting, retaining and developing a technically competent staff for its power stations (DANIDA, 1990d). Benefits of salary increments are quickly eroded by the country's high rate of inflation (*ibid.*). The haphazard transfer of employees to perform other duties has also been a feature of the working regime at NEC and may have affected motivation. The Director of Organization and Training, for instance, was summarily transferred to perform other duties, leaving his subordinate in charge. In another instance, some employees appointed to instruct on a short-term basis at the Um Haruz Training Centre ended up spending up to four years at the centre (Ali and Elgizouli, 1996: 157). To address the issue, an aid agency proposed that NEC give priority to staff retention by maintaining employees in posts for which they have been trained (*ibid.*).

In Kenya, KPLC provides competitive staff remuneration and benefits comparable to those provided by prominent private sector employers such as banks and multinational corporations. For instance, a KPLC manager's salary is twice that of his civil service counterpart and, in addition, he enjoys fringe benefits such as a generous car loan, a mileage allowance, medical and housing mortgage schemes and attractive training opportunities (Nyoike and Okech, 1996). As well as this incentive package, the utility provides opportunities for career development.


*Conclusions on manpower retention*
In almost all African utilities, especially the smaller ones, manpower retention is undermined by poor salary structures and the inadequacy of other rewards. Even though most utilities provide better salaries than other civil service sectors, the private sector still offers greener pastures. Utilities that provide salaries and rewards equal to or competitive with those provided by the private sector appear to record low and in some cases negative staff turnovers (a negative staff turnover implies that no employee leaves the utility, while new employees join). Examples of such utilities include CEB, KPLC and ZESA. Figure 2.7 provides an illustration of CEB's staff turnover after the introduction of competitive salaries and incentives in 1993/4.

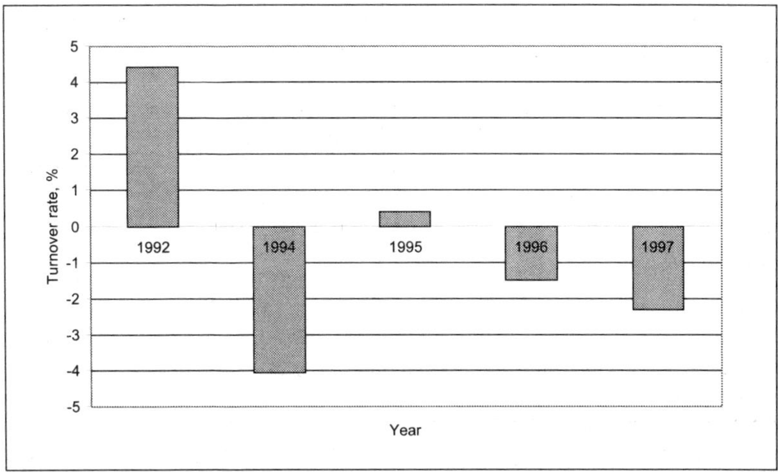


**Figure 2.7  CEB's staff turnover rate (%)**
Source: Baguant and Beeharry, 1998

The experience of ZESA following the introduction of its performance improvement programme clearly demonstrates that good manpower retention policies such as improved salaries and rewards can yield significant improvement in the technical performance of the utility.

Addressing the issue of retention of top-level management and boards of directors is critical to the improved and sustained performance of power utilities. It is, however, a very difficult issue to address. For instance, even though the amendment of the Electricity Act may minimize the powers of the Minister over the utility's management, this may not bring about a significant change in utilities that continue to be state-owned. For as long as the state is the dominant stakeholder ministers will tend to remain powerful *de facto* board members of the utility, and hence likely to influence the appointments and dismissals of the top-level management. This is likely to perpetuate the problem of retention of top management.

Power sector reform may compound the problem. Privatization of the utilities and the awarding of management contracts appear to threaten the retention of local top-level management. This is because, in almost all countries where privatization and management contracts have become the order of the day, management of the utility is handed over to the new foreign owners. Foreigners usually displace the local management teams almost entirely.

# 3

## Policy Options and Analysis

Based on the findings highlighted in the previous section, this section assesses policy options that could enhance the performance of power utilities through improved manpower policies. The findings in the previous section highlighted the fact that overstaffing in the power utilities is linked to poor technical performance. This is particularly the case for the smaller utilities. A significant proportion of the large and medium-scale utilities seem to have the right staffing levels and also appear to perform well.

With regard to manpower levels, the availability of well-equipped training facilities appears crucial. Utilities with advanced training facilities (mainly the large and a few of the medium-scale ones) tend to register better performance. In addition, training in management skills has been highlighted as an important factor in the performance of utilities. The impressive performances of ESKOM and ZESA underscore the importance of management training. On the whole, utilities with well-developed management training programmes appear to perform better. Available data demonstrate that effective training programmes can be organized without accounting for a large portion of the overall expenditure of the utility.

With regard to manpower retention, the key issue of concern is poor salaries and incentives schemes that do not compete with what is offered by the private sector. Good salaries and performance-based incentive schemes seem to be critical in reducing staff turnover and in addition, enhancing the utility's technical performance. Equally important, but often overlooked, is the retention of the top-level management of the utility to ensure sustained performance.

## Policy options

Proposed policy options that would lead to improved manpower effectiveness and improved performance of power utilities are listed below:

- Maintain the number of employees that is commensurate with the size of utility (measured in installed capacity and electricity generation).

- Establish a dedicated fund for training utility employees.

- Utilize advanced training facilities in neighbouring utilities and regional training centres.

- Place greater emphasis on training in management skills.

- Encourage employee motivation through improved salaries and performance-based incentive schemes.

- Pay attention to the retention and autonomy of top-level management.

To assess the viability of the above options, their respective institutional, legal, management and financial implications are discussed in the next few pages.

◆ *Maintain the number of employees that is commensurate with the size of utility (measured in installed capacity and electricity generation)*
As highlighted in the preceding chapters, staffing levels are linked to the performance of the utility. Utilities with adequate staffing levels, in comparison to the ideal utility, seem to perform better than those that are overstaffed. Manpower planning is therefore important to ensure that a workforce commensurate with the size of the utility is maintained. This will not only enhance effectiveness of manpower use but may also lead to improved technical performance.

Manpower planning will involve planning for fresh manpower recruitment to fill vacancies arising from staff turnover and retirements. More important, manpower planning should ensure that the utility moves on from filling in 'established posts' to creating vacancies based on measurable requirements. This implies that there are no permanent posts: if a post becomes defunct, the holder can be deployed to other suitable vacancies. Within the utility, the Human Resource Department is most likely to undertake manpower planning. However, in utilities that have a Corporate Planning Department section, such as ZESA and ESKOM, manpower planning could be part of overall strategic planning.

There are no legal barriers to the adoption of prudent manpower planning techniques. The utility's policy governing its structure can be adjusted to eliminate the rigidity associated with 'established posts' entitlement. For instance, in TANESCO (Tanzania), the post of an area manager entitles him/her to two secretaries, two vehicles (hence two drivers) and one messenger. A similarly inflated entitlement is provided for assistant managers. This allocation of personnel is usually made without taking into account the area's geographical size, customer base and electricity demand. This invariably leads to overstaffing of non-technical employees (Katyega, personal communication).

From a management viewpoint, manpower planning would ensure that the supervisor–subordinate ratios remain within the optimum range of six to seven subordinates reporting to one supervisor. Manpower planning, especially for utilities, may not be a skill widely available. Training in manpower planning would be an important investment for utilities. However, since formal training of this kind is difficult to obtain, utilities could consider 'twinning' with other utilities that have better manpower planning capabilities.

Financially, the foreseeable cost associated with manpower planning is the salary payable to well-trained manpower planning personnel, which is unlikely to significantly affect the financial status of the utility. Where this option is adopted, an additional cost likely to be incurred is the cost of 'twinning arrangements', mainly travel and accommodation costs, which are likely to be modest.

◆ *Establish a dedicated fund for training utility employees*
Developing and expanding existing utility training facilities would involve equipping the facilities with training aids such as simulators and models, which are costly to install. In addition, training programmes need to be elaborate enough to meet the training needs of both technical and non-technical employees.

Dedicated training funds are already in use in different sectors. As we have seen, one exists for the hotel industry in Kenya where the Utalii College was established and, until recently, managed by a board of trustees while being financed by a training levy that hotels and restaurants charge their customers. The training of students at the College is done at a fee. Any hotel or restaurant can arrange with the College to send their employees for refresher courses. An added benefit of this College is that it also runs a hotel on a commercial basis, which serves as a hands-on training facility for the trainees. We have suggested that the parallel for the power sector would be to establish a board of trustees (composed of all key stake holders in the electricity industry) to manage the dedicated training fund for the power sector. In addition, a separate training centre could be established or the board of trustees could take over management of an existing state-owned utility training facility. This would be the ideal arrangement for a liberalized power sector with numerous power companies.

For such a development to occur, legal changes to the status of the training facilities – from the state-owned utility to an independent entity managed by a board of trustees – would be required. A foreseeable problem would be the acquisition of power plants to be used for hands-on training. Another legal requirement would be for Parliament to approve the training levy that would be imposed on the consumer's electricity bill, which we discuss further below.

For the efficient management of the training facility, the board of trustees should be autonomous but accountable. Experiences from similar bodies in the region indicate that delinking the board of trustees from government influence would be a crucial factor for its success.

Examples of similar autonomous bodies that have operated successfully include the National Energy Board of Ghana.

The main financial challenge would be to identify the requisite revenue sources for the fund. One possibility would be to use the proposed hotel industry model, where funds could be raised through a levy imposed on the consumer's electricity bill. The levy could be a small percentage (about 1–2 per cent) of the electricity bill, which is directly remitted to the board of trustees. In countries where the consumers' electricity bills are already laden with other levies, such as the Rural Electrification Fund levy and the Electricity Regulatory Body's levy, an additional levy is likely to meet with stiff resistance from electricity consumers. Another possible way to raise finances is by following the examples of utilities in Zambia, Mozambique, Ghana and Togo/Benin, which used a part of loans advanced for the development of the power sector to expand their training facilities.

A foreseeable problem in managing the fund would be the dependence on the distribution utilities to collect the training levy on the board's behalf. A significant proportion of utilities have poor revenue collection records. Some of the utilities with the worst records include NEPA (Nigeria), with a collection period of 450 days; UEB (Uganda), with 250 days; TANESCO, with 244 days, and ESCOM (Malawi), with 116 days. Interestingly, the utilities with poor revenue collection records also happen to be those in dire need of developing training facilities. By contrast, those utilities with better training facilities also happen to have relatively good revenue collection records: ESKOM, with about 30 days; ZESA, with 32 days; and KPLC, with 81 days (Kayo, 2001; Okech and Nyoike, 2001; World Bank, 1996c: 64).

◆ *Utilize advanced training facilities in neighbouring utilities and regional training centres*

Some of the utilities with advanced training facilities and regional training centres already provide training, mainly to the smaller utilities. Utilities such as ZESA and ESKOM have provided training to their counterparts in neighbouring countries. Regional training centres such as the Kafue Gorge Regional Training Centre (Zambia) and the Interafrican Electrical Engineering College (Côte d'Ivoire) have trained utility staff from the SADC and from North and West African countries, respectively.

There are no legal requirements that could hinder a utility's decision to use training facilities in another country. Utilities would need to decide, however, on what training would be done in-house and what would be undertaken in the advanced training facilities of another country in the region. A difficulty that might hinder use of advanced training facilities would be the variety of languages used in the region: the continent uses English, French, Portuguese and Arabic as well as a host of major and minor indigenous languages. Organizing specialized multilingual training courses is a very difficult undertaking.

In short-to-medium financial terms, utilization of the advanced training facilities in neighbouring utilities or regional training centres is more cost-effective for a utility than developing its own training facility to the standard, for example, of ZESA or ESKOM.

◆ *Place greater emphasis on training in management skills*
At management level, the employee is likely to be well versed in technical issues and further training may not be necessary. Senior cadre utility employees may need to be acquainted, however, with various management tools such as financial management, strategic planning and time management.

Only a limited amount of management training is undertaken at utility training facilities. There are training companies in the private sector, however, that are specifically targeting corporate management training of power utilities. These companies include internationally renowned training and consulting companies such as PriceWaterhouse Coopers, and Deloitte and Touche. An emerging regional training institution is the Eastern and Southern Africa Management Institute (ESAMI), which provides some management training for professionals in the energy sector.

Management courses are generally shorter than technical courses, to suit the tight schedules of the managers. In terms of cost per day, management courses tend to be relatively more expensive than technical courses. Their short duration, however, results in modest expenditure. In addition, the proposed dedicated training fund could be an ideal source of financing management training.

◆ *Encourage employee motivation through improved salaries and*
  *performance-based incentive schemes*
The key objectives of providing employees with good salaries and incentives are to attract qualified employees; to retain competent employees; and to reward all employees for their effort, loyalty, experience and achievement (Cole, 1997: 203).

Even though most utilities have better salaries than other civil service sectors and some form of incentive scheme, they still face high rates of staff turnover, especially among professional staff. Utilities that have succeeded in retaining their most competent employees are those whose salaries and incentive schemes closely match those offered by the private sector.

What seems to be most effective for utilities is the performance-based incentive scheme. Performance-based incentives enhance efficiency and innovation on the part of employees. It is also useful for management since it enables monitoring of employees' performance over time. However, for adequate monitoring of each employee, the supervisor to subordinate ratio has to be low enough: no more than six to seven subordinates per supervisor is said to be an appropriate ratio. Utilities that are overstaffed are, therefore, likely to face difficulties in monitoring employee performance.

The financial implications of improved salaries and performance-based rewarding schemes would generally depend on the magnitude of salaries and rewards in relation to the utility's financial turnover. However, there are some benefits of spending a modest sum of money in staff motivation. Well-motivated employees are invariably more productive. In addition, performance-based incentives could lead to innovative cost reduction initiatives, which would enhance the financial performance of the utility.

Ongoing and planned power sector reform appears to be downsizing the workforce in the state-owned utilities to ensure that it is better paid and motivated. In countries where private power sector entities exist, they appear to pay and motivate better than their state-owned counterparts. Consequently, a large number of professionals from the state utilities are being employed by the new private entities. The state-owned utilities can only curb the loss of professionals through improved salaries and incentives that match those provided by the private power companies.

◆ *Pay attention to the retention and autonomy of top-level management*
The retention of the utility's top-level management is a significant challenge given the heavy influence of the state. As is the case for the majority of the state-owned institutions, government intervention and political interference are rampant. Power utilities have not been spared this interference, and hence top-level management enjoys very little autonomy.

Power sector reform has established some room for autonomy in the management of power utilities. This is as a result of management contracts and the sale of a significant proportion of the utility's stake to private investors. However, the main drawback with these arrangements is that the top-level management of the utility is being handed over to foreigners – displacing the local professionals.

Perhaps the only way of ensuring the retention of the top-level local management, in cases where management contracts and privatization of the utility have taken place, is by awarding the contracts or the licences (in the case of privatization) to the firms that demonstrate willingness to retain a significant proportion of the local professionals in top-level management – at least those with proven track records.

In countries where the utilities are still wholly state-owned, the only option seems to be the drastic reduction of the powers of the Minister to appoint and dismiss the utility's top-level management and the board's members. The appointment and dismissal of the board's members would be more objective if undertaken by Parliament – a fairly autonomous body in countries where multiparty politics is practised. This would give the power utility almost the same status as other autonomous public institutions such as the Central Bank.

Neither of the above options to ensure the retention and autonomy of the utility's top-level management would be easy to implement. They both require alterations of the legal and regulatory framework, mainly through the amendment of the Electricity Act. In the majority of the African countries, Bills of Amendment whose objective is to minimize the political influence of the incumbent government are slow to win the approval of Parliament, or fail to be passed.

## Analysis of the policy options

The policy options discussed in the previous chapter would not be expected to have the same impact on all the utility categories. This section attempts to identify appropriate options for utilities of different size. Table 3.1 presents the policy options compared across the three utility categories. A subjective ranking is undertaken based on the previous discussion of the viability of each policy option based on the following filters: institutional framework, legal requirements, management and financial implications.

In Table 3.1, a tick ($\sqrt{}$) implies that the policy option can be implemented with regard to the specific filter (institutional framework, legal requirements, management and financial). A cross ($\times$) implies that there could be some difficulties, hence the option may not be implemented. Where a tick and a cross appear together ($\sqrt{}\times$), this implies that it is uncertain whether the option would be implemented. The aggregate ranking is obtained by multiplying the values of the ticks and crosses, which effectively implies the ranking difference.

OPTION 1: MAINTAINING THE NUMBER OF EMPLOYEES THAT IS COMMENSURATE WITH THE SIZE OF THE UTILITY (MEASURED IN INSTALLED CAPACITY AND ELECTRICITY GENERATION)
The rankings indicate that the large-scale utilities such as ESKOM would face few problems in implementing this option. It would, however, be very difficult for the smaller utilities.

OPTION 2: ESTABLISH A DEDICATED FUND FOR TRAINING OF UTILITY EMPLOYEES
The rankings indicate that this option would be useful for utilities in all the categories. The smaller utilities, however, are likely to face problems implementing this option, mainly because of tariff constraints. Smaller utilities already register high tariffs and there may be resistance to additional levies.

OPTION 3: UTILIZE ADVANCED TRAINING FACILITIES IN NEIGHBOURING UTILITIES AND REGIONAL TRAINING CENTRES
This option would greatly benefit the small and medium-scale utilities with less developed training facilities. The large-scale utilities such as

## Table 3.1  Policy options ranking

| Legend: | Every √ =10 | x=2 | √x =5 | | |
|---|---|---|---|---|---|

| Policy options | Size of utility | | | |
|---|---|---|---|---|
| | Large | Medium | Small | Total |
| *Adequate no. of employees* | | | | |
| Institutional framework | √ | √x | x | 100 |
| Legal requirements | √ | √x | x | 100 |
| Management | √ | √x | x | 100 |
| Financial | √ | √x | √x | 250 |
| Ranking | 10000 | 1250 | 40 | 550 |
| *Dedicated fund for training* | | | | |
| Institutional framework | √ | √ | √ | 1000 |
| Legal requirements | √ | √ | √ | 1000 |
| Management | √ | √ | √ | 1000 |
| Financial | √ | √x | x | 100 |
| Ranking | 10000 | 5000 | 2000 | 3100 |
| *Use of advanced training facilities* | | | | |
| Institutional framework | √ | √ | √ | 1000 |
| Legal requirements | √ | √ | √ | 1000 |
| Management | √x | √x | √x | 125 |
| Financial | √ | √x | √x | 250 |
| Ranking | 5000 | 2500 | 2500 | 2375 |
| *Emphasis on training in management* | | | | |
| Institutional framework | √ | √ | √ | 1000 |
| Legal requirements | √ | √ | √ | 1000 |
| Management | √ | √ | √ | 1000 |
| Financial | √ | √x | √x | 250 |
| Ranking | 10000 | 5000 | 5000 | 3250 |
| *Improved salaries and rewards* | | | | |
| Institutional framework | √ | √ | √ | 500 |
| Legal requirements | √ | √ | √ | 100 |
| Management | √ | √x | x | 100 |
| Financial | √ | √ | √ | 1000 |
| Ranking | 10000 | 5000 | 2000 | 3100 |
| *Retention and autonomy of top utility management* | | | | |
| Institutional framework | √ | √ | √x | 1000 |
| Legal requirements | √ | √x | x | 1000 |
| Management | √ | √x | x | 100 |
| Financial | √ | √ | √ | 1000 |
| Ranking | 10000 | 2500 | 200 | 1700 |
| Overall ranking | 55000 | 20625 | 11740 | |

ESKOM that have advanced training facilities are likely to be the ones to provide training.

OPTION 4: PLACE GREATER EMPHASIS ON TRAINING IN MANAGEMENT SKILLS
The ranking indicates that all categories of utilities would be able to implement this option.

OPTION 5: ENCOURAGE EMPLOYEE MOTIVATION THROUGH IMPROVED SALARIES AND PERFORMANCE-BASED INCENTIVE SCHEMES
Large-scale utilities such as ESKOM already provide attractive salaries and incentives to their employees. The majority of the utilities in the small and medium-scale categories are often the best-paying public institutions in their respective countries.

For utilities in the small and medium-scale categories, salary increments in utilities with high staffing levels may worsen their already deplorable financial performances.

OPTION 6: PAY ATTENTION TO THE RETENTION AND AUTONOMY OF TOP-LEVEL MANAGEMENT
Some of the larger utilities such as ESKOM are fairly autonomous and have relatively good retention policies for their top-level management. The rankings indicate that the challenge of retention and autonomy of top utility management is greater among utilities in the small and medium-scale categories.

## Conclusions

The overall ranking suggests that large utilities are capable of implementing all six policy options with minimum difficulty. ESKOM, which is in this category, has already implemented most of these options, which perhaps explains its outstanding performance. NEPA (Nigeria), the other utility in this category, is more likely to follow the options and approach of the medium and small-scale utilities owing to the political instability in the country and the utility's past record of poor performance.

For the medium-scale utilities, the most attractive options seem to be: establishing a dedicated fund for training; training in management; and motivation of employees through increased salaries and incentives. The option of retention and autonomy of top-level management appears to be a difficult one to implement for both medium and small-scale utilities. This is due to the difficulty in making the required legal and regulatory changes.

For the small utilities, what seems to be the most attractive option is training in management. This is likely to enhance the performance of the utilities in this category. Another attractive option for the utilities in this category is utilization of advanced training facilities. The least attractive option is maintaining an adequate number of employees. In some utilities, the implementation of this option would imply cutting staffing levels by a half – a move that the trade unions would resist.

Of the six options it appears that, across all three categories, the most attractive one is the emphasis on training in management skills. The other options follow in the order provided below:

- Establish a dedicated fund for training utility employees.

- Encourage employee motivation through improved salaries and performance-based incentive schemes.

- Utilize advanced training facilities in neighbouring utilities and regional training centres.

- Pay attention to the retention and autonomy of the top-level management.

- Maintain the number of employees that is commensurate with the size of the utility (measured in installed capacity and electricity generation).

It would seem to be the case, therefore, that, contrary to the popular belief that overstaffing is the key impediment to capacity building in the power sector, there is a lot more that is needed. Training and retention appear to take higher priority. However, as has been noted, having the correct staffing levels is critical for the utility to be able to provide attractive salaries and incentives as well as ensuring an improved technical and financial performance.

# Part II Appendices

## Part II Appendix 1 Selected time series data, sub-Saharan Africa (excluding South Africa) (table and figures)

Table IIA.1.1. Selected time series data, sub-Saharan Africa

| Year | 1990 | 1991 | 1992 | 1993 | 1994 | 1995 | 1996 | 1997 | 1998 | 1999 |
|---|---|---|---|---|---|---|---|---|---|---|
| Population (millions) | 473.14 | 487.19 | 501.45 | 512.51 | 525.34 | 539.76 | 554.97 | 570.92 | 585.86 | 600.84 |
| GDP (US$ million) | 155200 | 158117 | 157759 | 157859 | 159486 | 167204 | 176123 | 183328 | 189700 | 195452 |
| GDP gowth (%) | 2.40 | 1.90 | -0.20 | 0.10 | 1.00 | 4.80 | 5.30 | 4.10 | 3.50 | 3.00 |
| GNP per capita (US$) | 381 | 369 | 349 | 319 | 286 | 288 | 303 | 319 | 312 | 306 |
| Electricity consumption *per capita* (kWh) | 122.80 | 126.20 | 126.20 | 130.10 | 127.10 | 125.00 | 126.10 | 125.80 | | |
| Government expenditure in real wages and salaries (index 1987=100) | 120 | 129 | 115 | 126 | 136 | 122 | 106 | 106 | 130 | |

Source: World Bank, 2001

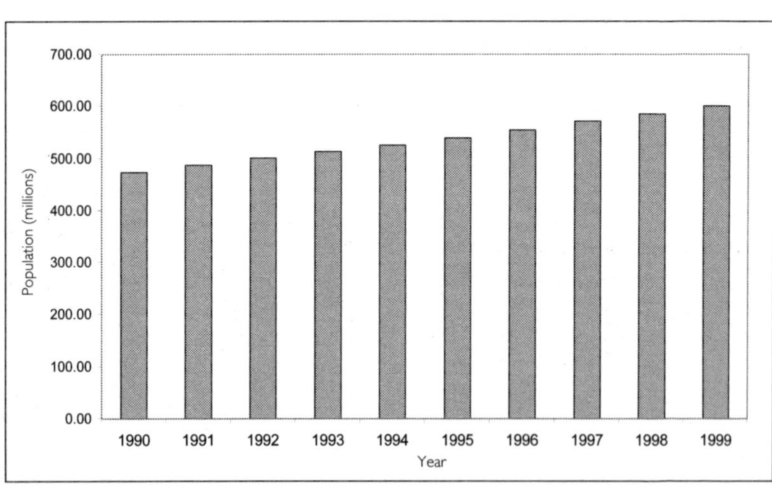

Figure IIA.1.1 Population, 1990–9 (millions)

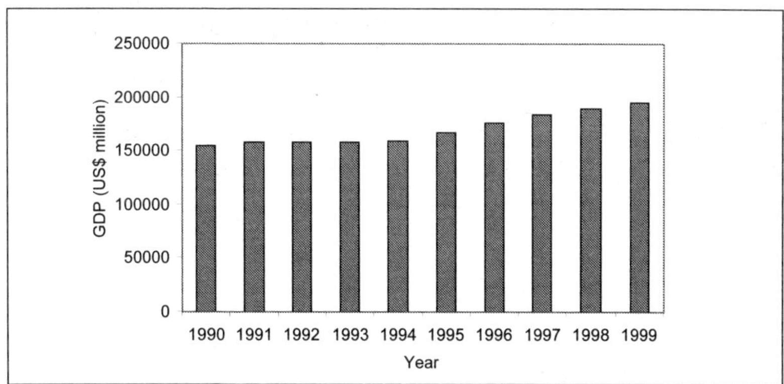

Figure IIA.1.2  GDP, 1990–9 (US$ million)

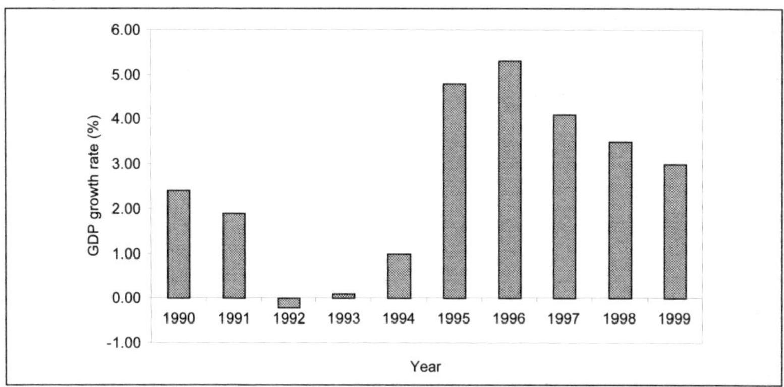

Figure IIA.1.3  GDP growth rate, 1990–9 (%)

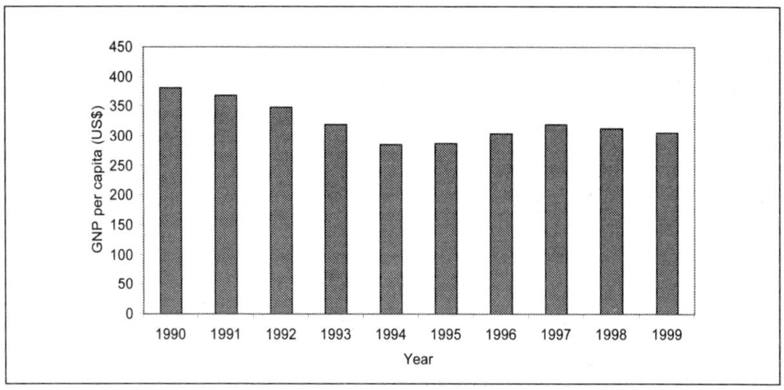

Figure IIA.1.4  GNP *per capita*, 1990–9 (US$)

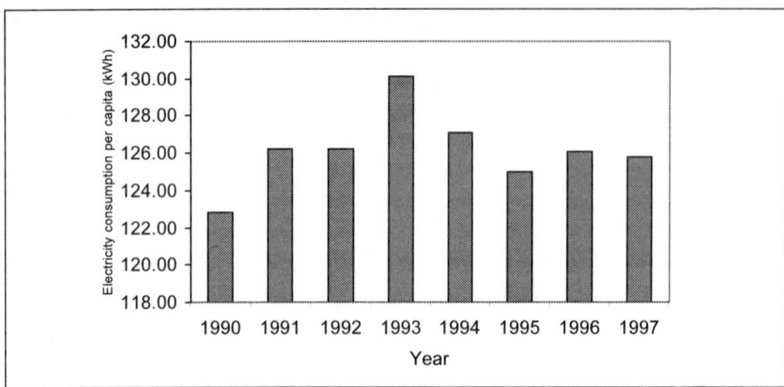

Figure IIA.1.5  Electricity consumption *per capita*, 1990–7 (kWh)

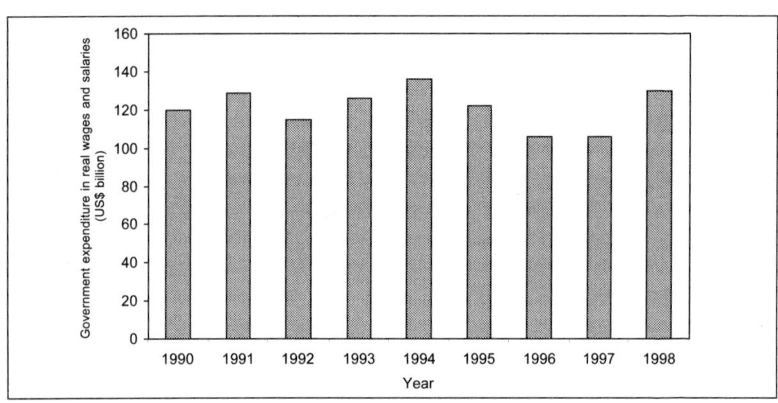

Figure IIA.1.6  Government expenditure in real wages and salaries, 1990–8 (US$ billion)

# Part III

## MAURITIUS

**Jawaharlall Baguant and Revin Panray Beeharry**

# Mauritius

Mauritius: selected indicators

**Area (km²):** 1,865

**Population (millions):** 1.2 (2000)

**Capital city:** Port Louis

**GDP (US$ million):** 4,200 (1999)

**GDP growth rate (%):** 2.7 (1999)

**GNP *per capita* (US$):** 3,600 (2000)

**Literacy levels (%):** (1998)   **Total:** 84

                                    **Male:** 87

                                    **Female:** 80

**Official exchange rate (MRs : US$):** 29 : 5 (December 2001)

**Economic activities:** Agriculture, commerce, financial services, construction, textile manufacture, tourism

**Energy sources:** Hydro, bagasse, solar, imported petroleum, imported coal

**Electrification level (%):** (2001)   **National:** 100

                                    **Urban:** 100

                                    **Rural:** 100

**Name of dominant electricity utility:** Central Electricity Board (CEB)

**Number of customers:** 313,963 (2000)

**Number of employees in dominant utility:** 1,802 (1999)

**Customers per employee ratio:** 169 (1999)

**Installed capacity (MW):** 498 (2001)

**Employees per installed capacity ratio:** 3.61 (2000)

**Electricity consumption *per capita* (kWh):** 2,556 (2001)

**Electricity generation (GWh):** 1,564 (2000)

**Employees per GWh of electricity generation ratio:** 1.26 (2000)

**Electricity generation per employee ratio:** 0.79 (1999)

**System losses (%):** 10.2 (2000)

**Debt collection period (days):** 86.4 (2000)

**Transmission line length (km):** 6,360

Sources: Ministry of Public Utilities, 1999; EIU, 2000b; CEB, 2000; World Bank, 2000b; World Bank, 2001; AFREPREN/FWD 2001

# 4

## Country Background

## Physical and socio-economic characteristics

The State of Mauritius consists of the main island of Mauritius and various tiny specks of land scattered in the south-west Indian Ocean (see brief country profile opposite and additional time series data in Part III Appendix 1). It has a land area of just over 2,000 square kilometres. Under the UN Law of the Sea Convention, the State of Mauritius has jurisdiction over 1.6–1.7 million square kilometres of ocean territory (EIU, 2000b; Deepchand, 2001a).

The population, multilingual and multicultural, is originally from Europe, Africa, the Indian subcontinent and China. The country used to be regarded as a typical monocrop economy based on sugar cane, but over the past 25 years Mauritius has diversified into textiles and tourism. Between independence from the British in 1968 and 1992, Mauritius was governed by a Governor-General appointed by the Queen of England. It then became a republic with a President – nominated by the National Assembly – as head of state.

After the Second World War, Mauritius experienced high population growth rates after a successful campaign to eradicate malaria. The population of 600,000 at the end of the 1950s was expected to reach three million by the year 2000 given then-prevailing fertility rates and declining death rates. Considerable efforts were made to curb population growth and transform Mauritius into a success story for voluntary family planning. The population is currently about 1.3 million and is expected to be between 1.4 and 1.6 million by 2025. The labour force (including those who are unemployed but actively seeking work) was estimated to be 273,000 in 1975, 293,000 in 1983, 513,000 in 1996 and 517,000 in 1999: it is expected to reach between 600,000 and 640,000 by the year 2025. The number of unemployed was estimated at between 20,000 and 30,000 in the mid-1970s and at over 60,000 in the early 1980s. In 1999, the official unemployment figure stood at 33,000, equivalent to 6.4 per cent of the labour force (EIU, 1998a; EIU, 1999b; EIU, 2000b).

Mauritius has no known mineral resources, although its zone of economic sovereignty has renewable resources. Sugar cane is not only the most efficient converter of solar radiation energy into dry matter that is available for commercial exploitation, but is also the crop best adapted to

Mauritius's bio-climatic conditions, which include periodic cyclones. Although Mauritius is no longer the monocrop economy of yesteryear, the sugar industry is still very important. Despite a high population density, Mauritius has a small total population, and therefore a limited internal market. This hampers large-scale activities in commerce and industry. Being relatively far from large markets, Mauritius can be described aptly as a 'sea-locked' economy.

Table 4.1  Sectoral contribution to GDP at factor cost (%)

| Sectors | 1980 | 1985 | 1990 | 1995 | 1997 | 1998 | 1999 | 2000 |
| --- | --- | --- | --- | --- | --- | --- | --- | --- |
| Primary | 12 | 15 | 12 | 10 | 8.3 | 7.5 | 5.7 | 6.8 |
| • Agriculture | | | | | | | | |
| • Forestry | | | | | | | | |
| • Fishing | | | | | | | | |
| Secondary | 26 | 30 | 33 | 34 | 32 | 32.4 | 32.8 | 32.8 |
| • Manufacturing | | | | | 23 | 23.7 | 23.8 | 23.9 |
| • Power production | | | | | 3 | 2.4 | 2.4 | 2.4 |
| • Construction | | | | | 6 | 6.3 | 6.6 | 6.5 |
| Tertiary | 62 | 55 | 55 | 56 | 63 | 56.8 | 58.7 | 57.8 |
| • Trade | | | | | 13 | 13.1 | 13.3 | 13.0 |
| • Tourism | | | | | 5 | 4.5 | 4.6 | 4.6 |
| • Services | | | | | 45 | 39.2 | 40.8 | 40.2 |

Source: EIU, 1998a; EIU, 2000b

Despite such shortcomings, efforts have been made in the promotion of manufacturing industries (especially within the Export Processing Zone), agriculture, tourism, export services and regional economic co-operation. As shown in Table 4.1, the services sector – comprised of tourism, commerce and export services – has remained a key contributor to GDP. The pace of socio-economic development slackened considerably in the second half of the 1970s and the early 1980s, with the downturn in the world economy due to high energy prices and restricted markets for the products of the Export Processing Zone (EPZ). Sugar export prices were either static or declining and input costs in the sugar industry rising. In addition, the high cost of welfare measures and adverse bio-climatic conditions in the second half of the 1970s and the early 1980s compounded the economic malaise.

But by 1984/5 a turnaround in the economy had been realized, unique in Mauritian history because it was not driven solely by the sugar industry. The turnaround was the result of a series of austerity measures taken in conformity with guidelines from the International Monetary Fund (IMF) and the World Bank, such as currency devaluation.

# The energy sector

## Energy supply

Mauritius is not an oil-producing country, nor does it have proven fossil energy reserves. Amongst the locally available energy resources, the most important are hydro, bagasse from the sugar cane industry and woody biomass. Solar energy also has some potential. Table 4.2 shows the evolution of both locally produced and imported fuels, which are petrol, diesel, kerosene, fuel oil, liquefied petroleum gas (LPG) and coal. Figure 4.1 illustrates the flow of energy in the Mauritian economy.

**Table 4.2 Primary energy supply 1972 to 1997 (ktoe)**

| Energy type | Year | | | | | | |
|---|---|---|---|---|---|---|---|
| | 1972 | 1977 | 1982 | 1987 | 1992 | 1997 | 1998 |
| Hydro | 17.28 | 13.53 | 17.57 | 29.22 | 23.38 | 17.27 | N/A |
| Bagasse | 11.04 | 11.52 | 20.65 | 35.52 | 40.80 | 61.00 | N/A |
| Petrol | 24.00 | 43.80 | 31.51 | 41.68 | 65.89 | 83.46 | 95.68 |
| Diesel | 43.73 | 69.03 | 60.48 | 76.70 | 111.08 | 186.77 | 158.13 |
| Kerosene | 16.10 | 25.24 | 17.50 | 22.80 | 43.26 | 79.90 | 61.51 |
| Fuel oil | 21.02 | 56.14 | 57.04 | 67.11 | 124.24 | 217.55 | 208.85 |
| LPG | 0.69 | 1.29 | 2.12 | 8.71 | 30.84 | 44.72 | 43.68 |
| Coal | 0.0 | 0.0 | 0.0 | 24.05 | 44.02 | 18.26 | 42.49 |

Source: Ministry of Public Utilities, 1999

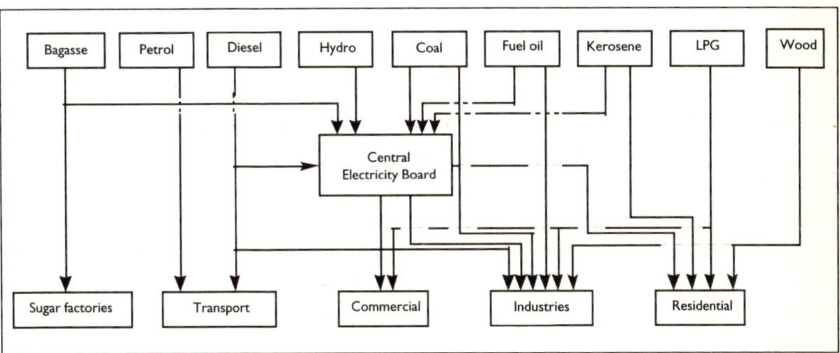


Figure 4.1   Energy flow in the Mauritian economy

Development of hydro sites was initiated well before the 1950s and the most recent major hydropower development of 30 MW capacity was undertaken during the late 1970s and completed in the early 1980s, bringing the total installed capacity of hydropower to around 59 MW. The proportion of hydroelectricity supplied to the national grid, compared to the total electricity requirement, has declined constantly from around 85 per cent in 1955 to around 10 per cent in 1996. Hydroelectricity is fed to the national grid from seven different sites with installed capacities ranging from 1 MW to 30 MW (CEB, 1999).

According to historical data and taking into account climatic conditions, the mean annual generation of hydroelectricity is 110 GWh, representing around 9 per cent of the current total electricity requirement of the island (Ministry of Public Utilities, 1999). Potential for further development of 30 to 50 MW of hydro sites still exists. With proper water management and further hydro site development and adoption of a pump hydro scheme, it is estimated that the total installed capacity could be in the range of 80 to 100 MW, with a mean annual output of around 200 GWh.

Bagasse, a by-product of the sugar industry, is utilized to produce all the energy required (in the form of process steam and electricity) for the manufacture of sugar. Bagasse co-generation power plants have also been developed to produce excess electricity during the sugar cane harvest period, which is then fed to the national grid.

Development of co-generation installations was initiated during the mid-1950s. By 1980, 16 out of the 19 sugar factories were equipped with small turbo alternators, ranging from 0.5 to 3.5 MW, to produce excess electricity for export to the national grid during the harvesting season (June–December). In 1980, the total capacity of the 16 sugar factories was 30 MW. Depending on the availability of bagasse, sugar factories could produce between 20 to 40 GWh annually, representing around 8 per cent of the total electricity demand in 1980.

During the mid-1980s, one of the largest sugar factories on the island – Flacq United Estate Limited (FUEL) – installed a dual-fuel furnace, able to run on bagasse during the harvesting season and on coal during the rest of the year. It was able to produce electricity all year round. The system had an installed capacity of 21.7 MW and was equipped with a high-pressure boiler (42 bars) and a condensing turbine.

Based on the experience of the dual-fuel power generating system at FUEL, the Bagasse Energy Development Programme was formulated and implemented. Currently, the overall capacity for power generation sited at ten sugar factories is about 217 MW. The total annual output of electricity is about 340 GWh, about half of which is produced during the sugar cane crop season using bagasse, and the rest during the inter-crop season using coal. This represents over 23 per cent of the total national electricity requirement (1,424 GWh) in the year 1999.

According to surveys carried out by the Forestry Services of the Ministry of Agriculture, around 56,000 hectares, representing around 25 per cent of the total area of Mauritius, are classified as forest area. This area consists of productive and unproductive woodlands which are partly government-owned and partly privately owned. The wood produced is used as timber, wood poles for scaffolding in the construction industry and directly as firewood or indirectly for making charcoal for cooking. Wood is also used in lime kilns for the production of lime for local consumption. Of all these uses of wood in Mauritius, its use as firewood for cooking in the residential sector is by far the most important.

Since locally available energy resources are limited, imported fossil fuels (petroleum products and coal) remain the major source of energy. The total liquid fuel consumption, currently in the order of 500,000 tonnes of oil equivalent (toe) annually, is just below the figure required to justify the construction of a local oil refinery. As a consequence, the imported fossil fuels are in the final refined form: petrol, diesel, kerosene, fuel oil and LPG. Since 1984, coal has also been imported to supplement the bagasse-fired electricity generation plant, as well as for steam production in the industrial sector.

Currently, the importation of almost all petroleum products (including LPG) and coal is handled by the State Trading Corporation (STC) in collaboration with the oil companies. The distribution is handled entirely by the four major oil companies – Caltex, Esso, Shell and Total – and some smaller auxiliary companies. Kerosene (jet-fuel grade), diesel and other products bunkered in Mauritius for the airline industry and ships are not accounted for in the Mauritian economy.

Since 1984, only premium petrol has been imported to provide the energy requirements of the light transportation industry, which comprises automobiles, motorcycles, mopeds and certain categories of light trucks and vans. Other miscellaneous uses of petrol include motor-boats, lawnmowers and two-stroke engines for operating small water pumps.

A major portion of imported diesel oil is supplied to the heavy transport industry, which consists mostly of buses engaged in the mass transit system and trucks used for the transportation of goods and sugar cane. Diesel is also used in the light transportation of goods, public cars (taxis) and vans, and is supplied to the CEB where it is used for starting up electricity generators and in the industrial sector for purposes such as steam generation.

Kerosene is primarily used to meet the demand for cooking fuel in the residential sector. Since 1988, however, a sizeable proportion of kerosene has also been supplied to the CEB for use in gas turbines for electricity generation. The government has a 'zero tax policy' on kerosene used for cooking purposes to assist low-income households.

The main portion of fuel oil is supplied to the CEB for electricity generation and the rest is supplied to industries such as the beverage industry and the Export Processing Zone where it is used for raising process steam.

LPG, distributed in pressurized gas cylinders (bottled gas), is used mostly for cooking in the residential sector and the commercial sector (in restaurants and hotels). The residential sector is, however, by far the largest user of LPG.

Since 1984, coal has been imported and used primarily by the power plant at FUEL to generate electricity during the inter-crop seasons. The FUEL Sugar Estate furnace is capable of burning coal and bagasse or various mixtures of these two fuels. As from 1989, several manufacturing units in the textile sector have been equipped with coal-fired steam generation plants.

*Energy demand (1970–95)*

Total energy demand increased from around 108,000 toe in 1970 to reach above 550,000 TOE in 1995, representing an average annual increase of 6.5 per cent or a five-fold increase over the 25-year period. Local resources of energy have contributed between 10 and 20 per cent of total supply, the balance being supplied by imported petroleum products and coal (Ministry of Public Utilities, 1999).

Primary energy demand for the transportation sector grew at about 6 per cent annually between 1970 and 1995. Diesel is the predominant road transportation fuel for the heavy transport and bus industry, while petrol is used to power cars, dual-purpose vehicles, motorcycles and mopeds. Both forms of fuel exhibited steady growth until 1978/9 when high oil prices on the world market caused major declines in consumption. Since 1983, consumption of both fuel forms has increased steadily, though fluctuations in the economy caused minor dips between 1989 and 1991.

The residential sector uses a mix of kerosene, LPG, electricity and woody biomass to meet its energy needs. The overall increase in energy consumption in this sector was four-fold from 1970 to 1995, representing an average annual increase of 6 per cent. In the 1970s the residential sector's share of the total energy consumed in Mauritius was about 30 per cent, but this has declined to about 23 per cent owing to the increasing energy demand of the industrial sector. The pattern of energy demand within the household sector has changed significantly over the last 25 years. The average share of kerosene, which was about 76 per cent in the early 1970s, dropped to about 20 per cent, while the share of LPG increased from 3 to 45 per cent. This change in consumption pattern is due to the reduction in tax on LPG, a decision taken in 1986. The share of electricity in 1970 was about 21 per cent, gradually increasing to 35 per cent by 1995 (Ministry of Public Utilities, 1999).

A national survey of household energy consumption carried out in 1988 revealed that woody biomass contributed as much as 50 per cent of the household primary energy requirement, or almost 20 per cent of the total primary consumption of the island. A more recent similar survey carried out in 1995 indicated that the use of firewood has gradually been substituted by kerosene and LPG, and that the share of woody biomass in total primary energy consumption had been reduced to 15 per cent. (Ministry of Public Utilities, 1999).

Electricity is the predominant energy carrier for the commercial sector. End uses include lighting, cooling, cooking and running of office

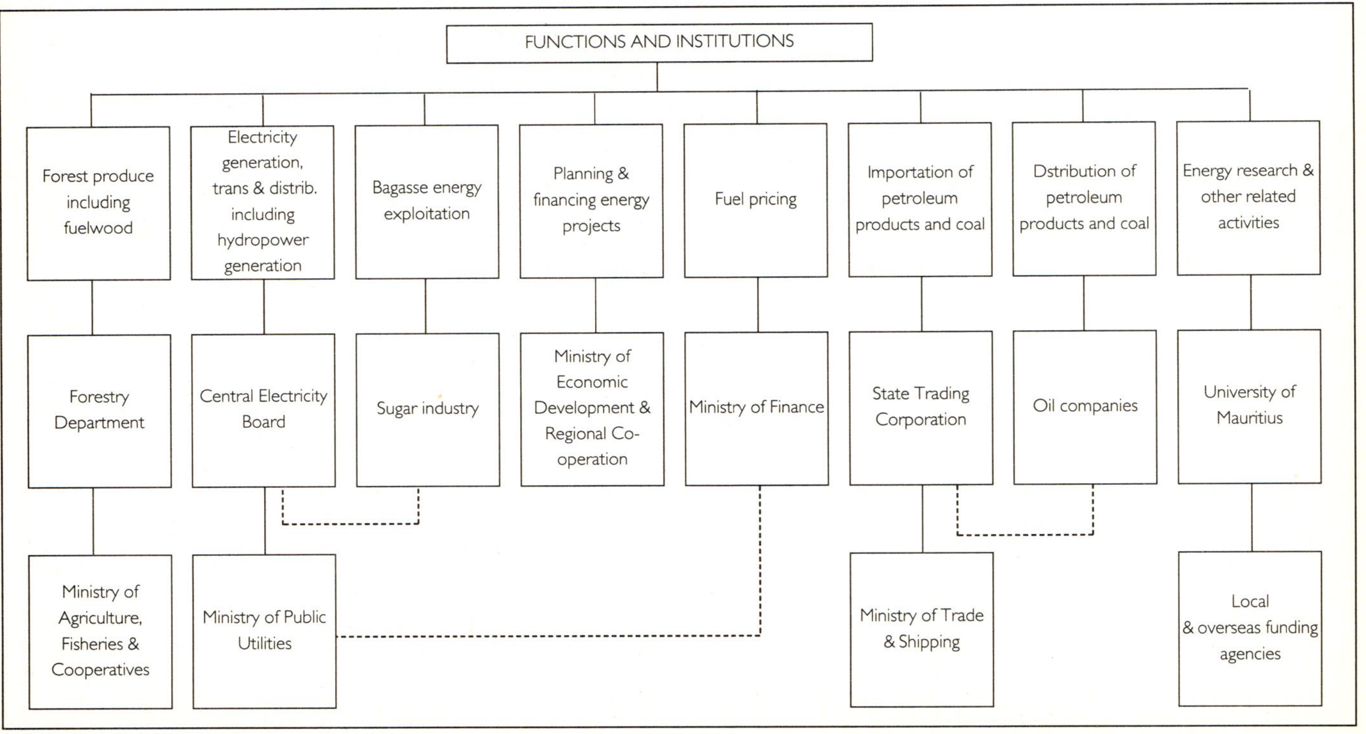


**Figure 4.2  Institutional framework of the energy sector**

equipment. In 1970, the commercial sector was completely dependent on electricity. By 1995, electricity accounted for around 80 per cent of total energy used and LPG supplied the balance (20 per cent). Between 1970 and 1995, total energy use (primary, toe) in the commercial sector increased six-fold, representing an annual growth rate of 7.5 per cent.

Energy consumption in the industrial sector increased from 14,000 toe in 1970 to 155,000 toe in 1995, a more than eleven-fold increase representing an average annual increase of about 10 per cent. The share of the different energy types of this sector in 1995 was 1 per cent for LPG; 14 per cent for diesel, 20 per cent for coal, 23 per cent for electricity and 42 per cent for fuel oil.

*Institutional framework of the energy sector*
Several institutions are responsible for energy production, importation, storage, distribution, energy policy formulation, pricing and energy project planning in Mauritius. The main institutions are the Ministry of Public Utilities, the Central Electricity Board (CEB), the Forestry Services of the Ministry of Agriculture and Natural Resources, and the State Trading Corporation. Figure 4.2 depicts the institutions and their roles in the energy sector.

The Ministry of Economic Development and Regional Cooperation, in conjunction with the Ministry of Public Utilities, is responsible for the planning and financing aspects of energy projects. Fuel pricing and taxation policies primarily fall under the Ministry of Finance. The State Trading Corporation (STC), a parastatal body under the Ministry of Trade and Shipping, manages supply and demand for petroleum products and coal, but distribution of imported fuel is undertaken by privately owned oil companies, namely Total, Esso, Caltex and Shell. These companies are also responsible for the distribution of LPG.

The Forestry Service, a unit of the Ministry of Agriculture and Natural Resources, is responsible for the management of forest products, including woody biomass used as a cooking fuel.

Ever since its creation in 1971, the University of Mauritius has conducted a number of energy-related studies, ranging from the harnessing of solar energy to long-range energy demand forecasting, with funding from both local and international sources.

*National energy policy*
As in most developing countries, energy sector policies in Mauritius are designed to address the problem of allocation of energy resources, as market forces alone are perceived to be inadequate. National energy policies were surveyed and the results are presented by sector in Table 4.3.

Some of the key policies are summarized below:

- Use of locally available bagasse from the sugar industry in combination with imported coal for production of electricity in order to reduce dependence on imported oil.

**Table 4.3 Energy policies review matrix, Mauritius**

| Policies | Energy-consuming sectors | | | |
|---|---|---|---|---|
| | Industrial | Transport | Commercial | Domestic |
| *Legislation* | | | | |
| Energy law | ✓ | None | None | None |
| Law on energy conservation | None | None | None | None |
| Energy efficiency agencies | None | None | None | None |
| *Financial measures* | | | | |
| Investment subsidies | ✓ | None | None | None |
| Reduced import duties and exemptions | ✓ | ✓ | ✓ | ✓ |
| Income tax schemes | ✓ | ✓ | ✓ | ✓ |
| Differential fuel/electricity pricing | ✓ | ✓ | ✓ | ✓ |
| *Loans, soft loans and grants* | ✓ | ✓ | ✓ | ✓ |
| Other (energy tax) | None | None | None | None |
| *Technical measures* | | | | |
| Standards on insulation | None | NA | None | NA |
| Standards on boilers | ✓ | NA | NA | NA |

✓ – Policies exist
NA – Not applicable

- Use of solar water heaters for domestic purposes in order to reduce use of electricity in the residential sector.

- Use of the mass transit system, which runs on diesel, in order to reduce reliance on individual cars, thus reducing petrol consumption.

- Development of wind energy projects through a BOT (build, operate and transfer) scheme in order to reduce dependence on imported fuel for electricity production.

- Provision of adequate electric power and other sources of energy at acceptable prices to ensure economic growth through industrialization and tourist sector development.

- Provision of affordable high-quality energy such as electricity, LPG and kerosene for the residential sector in order to control deforestation and improve the quality of life.

The next section will assess the country's education and human resource development policy, setting the stage for examination of the key capacity-building issues in the power sector.

## Review of education and human resource development policy

The Republic of Mauritius attaches great importance to education at all levels from pre-primary to tertiary, as well as to pre-vocational and vocational training. Various Acts have been passed in Parliament for the creation of educational and training institutions. Funding for education and training is sourced from the government budget, from donor agencies and through bilateral and multilateral agreements. Government's recurrent expenditure on education for the financial year 1998/9 was Rs2,556 million, representing 13 per cent of the total budget. Out of this sum 1.3 per cent went to pre-primary education; 34.5 per cent to primary education; 40.3 per cent to secondary education; 12.8 per cent to post-secondary education; and 11.8 per cent to technical and vocational training (including the Industrial and Vocational Training Board, IVTB).

**Table 4.4** Student population at the University of Mauritius

| Year | Faculties | | | | | Student population |
| --- | --- | --- | --- | --- | --- | --- |
| | Agriculture | Engineering | Management & Social Studies** | | Science* | |
| 1980–81 | 63 | 198 | 209 | | – | 470 |
| 1981–82 | 51 | 161 | 176 | | – | 388 |
| 1982–83 | 75 | 179 | 236 | | – | 490 |
| 1983–84 | 88 | 102 | 240 | | – | 430 |
| 1984–85 | 58 | 122 | 278 | | – | 458 |
| 1985–86 | 107 | 172 | 276 | | – | 555 |
| 1986–87 | 86 | 236 | 321 | | – | 643 |
| 1987–88 | 133 | 318 | 427 | | – | 878 |
| 1988–89 | 114 | 355 | 796 | | 60 | 1325 |
| 1989–90 | 103 | 365 | 869 | | 150 | 1487 |
| 1990–91 | 132 | 403 | 978 | | 137 | 1650 |
| | | | HSS | L&M | | |
| 1991–92 | 126 | 469 | – | 963 | 241 | 1799 |
| 1992–93 | 99 | 471 | 333 | 599 | 250 | 1858 |
| 1993–94 | 130 | 595 | 464 | 742 | 230 | 2161 |
| 1994–95 | 135 | 537 | 546 | 719 | 249 | 2186 |
| 1995–96 | 144 | 578 | 608 | 742 | 272 | 2344 |
| 1996–97 | 157 | 682 | 657 | 659 | 341 | 2496 |
| 1997–98 | 231 | 909 | 753 | 777 | 465 | 3135 |

* Created in 1988/9
** Split into two faculties since 1990/1: Faculty of Humanities and Social Studies (HSS); Faculty of Law and Management (L&M)
Source: *Digest of Educational Statistics* (Central Statistics Office), 1997

---

**Box 4.1  Relevant education policies**

1   Education at all levels is practically free – state-funded.
2   Primary education is compulsory for children aged 5–11.
3   Places are available at secondary schools for all candidates (ages 12–20) who successfully complete primary school. Not compulsory.
4   Secondary school has two parts: I: 5 years leading to 'O' levels; II: 2–3 years leading to 'A' levels.
5   Vocational institutions/polytechnics cater for students not keen to follow the academic stream. Areas of focus: engineering (mechanical, electrical, etc.); accountancy; information technology.
6   The University of Mauritius caters for students with 'A' levels. Places are available for two out of every three qualified applicants. Diplomas and degrees are in the following areas: agriculture, including food and biotechnology; engineering, including textile and information technology; physical and social sciences; humanities; management; accountancy; economics; law.

---

Mauritius is one of those few countries in the region where education at *all levels* is essentially free. For example, tuition fees are not charged. Public expenditure on education, however, declined from 4.1 per cent of GNP in 1980 to 3.5 per cent at present. In addition, 14 per cent of the total public expenditure on education – the current Mauritian level – falls short of the average of 15–20 per cent expended by other newly industrialized countries (NICs).

The education sector is modelled on the British education system and the current structure is divided into four major subsections: pre-primary/primary, secondary, vocational and tertiary. This structure, generally considered to be effective, has remained practically unchanged for decades

With the exception of the Central Electricity Board (CEB), which has its own training centre, no institution in Mauritius provides training in energy-related subjects. There is no specific policy related to training in energy. Institutions involved in energy production and distribution rely mainly on technicians and graduates from the University of Mauritius and overseas universities to run their relevant institutions. As shown in Table 4.4, the University's enrolment in engineering has fluctuated between 20 and 30 per cent.

A review of the current curriculum used at primary, secondary and tertiary institutions revealed that energy-related concepts are taught at the various levels. The outcome of the curriculum review is summarized below.

- Simple energy concepts are introduced through courses in environmental studies that form part of the primary school curriculum.

- Some energy concepts are included in subjects – such as economics, geography, physics, chemistry, biology, and design and technology – which form part of the secondary school curriculum.

- Energy-related concepts are also included in several modules taught at diploma and degree levels. The Faculty of Engineering has also introduced modules covering energy resources and energy technologies, which are options, offered to engineering students.

The Faculty of Engineering also runs special workshops in energy engineering/technology for practising engineers, managers and economists. The Faculty plans to offer a joint Engineering Degree in energy technology/engineering.

Key education policies as well as relevant information on the education system in Mauritius are presented in Box 4.1.

# 5

---

## Capacity Building in the Mauritian Power Sector

## Structure of the power sector

The power sector in Mauritius is made up of the Central Electricity Board and independent power producers (IPPs) based on the sugar industry. Electricity generation, transmission and distribution, as well as hydro-power generation, are carried out by the Central Electricity Board, a parastatal body under the Ministry of Public Utilities. Bagasse-based electricity produced by the sugar industry, is sold to the Central Electricity Board for distribution.

*The Central Electricity Board (CEB)*
The CEB, the sole distributor of electricity in Mauritius, was established in December 1952 with the objective of developing, controlling and co-ordinating electricity supply services throughout the island. During its first three years of operation, the CEB purchased the assets of the various small private holdings which were then producing electricity, and consequently became the sole institution responsible for electricity generation and distribution on the island. By the end of 1955, the total electricity generating capacity of the CEB was 11 MW, of which 7.6 MW was hydro-based and the balance diesel-based. With around 607 km of overhead line, the utility had about 30,000 customers.

To supplement the Board's own generation resources, an agreement was reached with the St Antoine Sugar Estate in 1956 to supply power during the sugar cane harvest season (June to December), using excess high-pressure steam produced from bagasse. In 1957, the St Antoine Sugar Estate exported electricity to the national grid for the first time. Gradually more electricity supply agreements were signed with other sugar factories.

From the early 1960s, several other development programmes were undertaken, namely:

- rural electrification;

- hydropower development;

- installation of additional bagasse-based power plants; and

- installation of oil-based power plants.

Table 5.1 Electricity demand by major user categories (GWh)

| Users | Year | | | | | | |
|---|---|---|---|---|---|---|---|
| | 1988 | 1990 | 1992 | 1994 | 1996 | 1998 | 1999 |
| Domestic | 167 | 199 | 249 | 296 | 358 | 422.7 | 440.3 |
| Commercial | 102 | 126 | 168 | 207 | 254 | 318.6 | 333.5 |
| Industrial | 163 | 212 | 244 | 277 | 337 | 392.5 | 413.1 |
| Irrigation | 11 | 14 | 16 | 19 | 21 | 25.3 | 22.5 |
| Others | 7 | 8 | 10 | 12 | 15 | 17.3 | 19.9 |
| Total | 450 | 559 | 687 | 811 | 985 | 1175.9 | 1229.3 |

Source: CEB, 1995 and CEB, 1999

Table 5.2 Key socio-economic and power sector indicators 1955–99

| | 1955 | 1975 | 1995 | 1999 |
|---|---|---|---|---|
| *Socio-economic parameters* | | | | |
| Population ($10^3$) | 563 | 860 | 1129 | 1300 |
| GDP *per capita* (1980 US$) | 300 | 1040 | 2500 | 3610 |
| *Electricity consumption* | | | | |
| KWh *per capita* per year | 66 | 260 | 927 | 1187 |
| Total (GWh/year) | 37 | 224 | 1047 | 1424 |
| No. of customers | 33500 | 122482 | 253066 | 304029 |
| Peak power demand (MW) | 15 | 54 | 201 | 265.8 |
| *Electricity supply* | | | | |
| Total installed capacity – MW | 11 | 91 | 365 | 522 |
| Local sources (bagasse & hydro) | | | | |
| [GWh] | 32 | 73 | 218 | 214 |
| (%) | (86) | (33) | (21) | |
| Imported sources (fossil) | | | | |
| [GWh] | 5 | 151 | 829 | |
| (%) | (14) | (67) | (79) | |
| Network (km) | 607 | 3279 | 5515 | 6360 |
| *Manpower* | | | | |
| Total employees | NA | 1507 | 1985 | 1845 |
| Customer served/employee | NA | 78.6 | 130 | 165 |
| Production/employee | | | | |
| [manpower/GWh] | NA | 7 | 2 | 1.3 |

Source: EIU, 2000b; Deepchand, 2001b; CEB, 1995; CEB, 1999; Ministry of Public Utilities, 1999

Power sector development during the 1960s progressed steadily and by 1970 the island had a complete distribution network. The data presented in Table 5.1 depict the trend in electricity demand by major user categories. Rising costs of fuel oil and diesel in the late 1970s and early 1980s, coupled with heavy dependence on imported energy sources, led to the development of projects to harness locally available energy resources for power generation.

Table 5.2 shows data on key socio-economic and power sector indicators in Mauritius from 1955 to 1999. Over this period the population almost doubled, while the GDP *per capita* increased almost seven-fold. Consequently, electricity requirements increased as illustrated by the increase in the number of customer connections, which rose from 33,500 to over 304,000, a nine-fold increase. *Per capita* electricity consumption increased almost fourteen-fold from 66 to 938 kWh *per capita*, and total electricity production increased from 37 GWh to 1,424 GWh, a thirty-eight-fold increase. The CEB had to increase its installed capacity from 11 MW to 522 MW and its network from about 600 km to approximately 6,360 km.

The development of local energy resources for power production did not keep pace with the demand driven by economic development. As illustrated in Table 5.2, the contribution of local energy resources decreased from 86 per cent (bagasse and hydro) in 1955 to 21 per cent in 1995.

*Independent power producers (IPPs) – bagasse-based electricity generation*
As mentioned earlier, since the late 1950s sugar factories in Mauritius have produced electricity for the national grid based on co-generation using bagasse. From the early 1980s, coal was introduced to generate electricity in dual-fuel furnaces during the inter-crop season. By 1999, the sugar factories were producing 184 GWh, representing 13 per cent of the total annual electricity production (Table 5.3).

All of the power generation plants in the sugar factories are run by sugar engineers, technologists and technicians who have been trained primarily to produce steam and electricity for sugar manufacturing purposes. Currently, it is estimated that about 45 to 50 such personnel are involved, on a part-time basis, in producing power at the sugar factories for export to the national grid.

## Estimating the power sector's trained manpower requirement

For the purpose of this study, two methods have been used to estimate the current and future trained manpower (engineers, technologists and supporting technicians) requirement for Mauritius.

**Table 5.3 Electricity generation by source**

| Year | Hydro | | Co-generation | | Coal | Fuel oil/Diesel | | Kerosene | | Total | | Bagasse % | |
|---|---|---|---|---|---|---|---|---|---|---|---|---|---|
| | IC | GWh | IC | GWh | GWh | IC | GWh | IC | GWh | IC | GWh | IC | GWh |
| 1989 | 57 | 148 | 42 | 56 | 68 | 149 | 310 | 23 | 7 | 270 | 589 | 15.6 | 9.5 |
| 1990 | 57 | 85 | 42 | 53 | 45 | 149 | 449 | 23 | 36 | 270 | 668 | 15.6 | 7.9 |
| 1991 | 57 | 76 | 42 | 70 | 54 | 148 | 494 | 47 | 44 | 294 | 738 | 14.3 | 9.5 |
| 1992 | 53 | 113 | 42 | 85 | 43 | 142 | 498 | 47 | 69 | 284 | 808 | 14.8 | 10.5 |
| 1993 | 54 | 104 | 43 | 71 | 40 | 163 | 615 | 47 | 40 | 308 | 870 | 14.0 | 8.2 |
| 1994 | 54 | 75 | 43 | 77 | 46 | 163 | 699 | 48 | 48 | 308 | 945 | 14.0 | 8.1 |
| 1995 | 54 | 134 | 43 | 84 | 41 | 154 | 682 | 80 | 106 | 332 | 1047 | 13.0 | 8.0 |
| 1996 | 54 | 104 | 43 | 119 | 98 | 155 | 699 | 80 | 219 | 332 | 1151 | 13.0 | 10.3 |
| 1997 | 54 | 92 | 53 | 125 | 23 | 182 | 857 | 80 | 154 | 370 | 1252 | 14.3 | 10.0 |
| 1998 | 54 | 104 | 90 | 194 | 62 | 176 | 842 | 76 | 162 | 397 | 1365 | 22.7 | 14.2 |
| 1999* | 54 | 30 | 90 | 184 | 155 | 205 | 912 | 76 | 137 | 425 | 1424 | 21.2 | 12.9 |

IC = Installed Capacity (effective), MW

Year 1999 was a severe drought year when only 373,000 tonnes of sugar were produced compared to the normal of about 630,000 tonnes

Source: Deepchand, 2001b

*Method I:* This method is based on the Commonwealth Board of Engineering Education and Training's *Proposal for the Developing Commonwealth: the Need for Engineers and Technicians and How to Meet It Effectively and Efficiently* (Mordell and Coales, 1983). In this method, the total number of trained engineers, technologists and technicians required by the Mauritian economy is estimated first. Then the number of trained personnel for the energy sector is derived from the results, based on historical ratios of types of trained manpower.

*Method II:* This method is based on ratios agreed on as being representative of an ideal utility in the region.


*Method I*
To estimate the number of engineers and technologists (including technicians) required by the Mauritian economy, the following studies and concepts were considered.

- Analyses carried out by the Vice-Chancellor, University of Mauritius and the publication *Varsity at Réduit: The Outcome of a Calculated Risk, 1965-90*, which depicted the relationship between economic development and trained manpower requirement.

- Outcome of an ongoing investigation in the Faculty of Engineering on student enrolment, output of the Faculty and job prospects.

- Discussion amongst academic staff in the Faculty of Engineering.

- Discussion held at several course advisory committees of the Faculty of Engineering.

- Recommendations made by external examiners and visitors (under link programmes) from the UK and to a limited extent from the US and elsewhere.

- The development trend of the Faculty of Engineering for the period 1988/9–1993/4, when the enrolment increased from 369 to about 600.

- The economic development envisaged by our policy makers and the current population growth.

- Indicators available for estimating numbers of engineers/technicians required for economic development through industrialization and the modernization of the agricultural sector.

- The accuracy of the methodology for projecting the human resource requirement on the basis of GDP growth and on the growth of population is at best ± 30 per cent.

- The number of engineers and technologists (including qualified technicians) per 1,000 population is expected to reach a range of 2.0–2.5 by the year 2010.

It is estimated that the total number of engineers and technologists (including technicians) required in Mauritius is currently about 2,000, and that this will increase to between 2,800 and 3,500 by 2010. Taking into account that the stock of such trained personnel was about 900 in 1998, and that the age of retirement is between 60 and 65, about 1,500 additional engineers and technologists will be required in the near future and about 2,000 more by the year 2010.

As far as energy engineers and technologists are concerned, experience indicates that 20 per cent of the total number of engineers and technologists need to have an in-depth knowledge of energy engineering/technology/management. Thus at the turn of the century some 300 engineers and technologists, out of the additional pool of 1,500, needed to be trained to handle energy issues. By the year 2010, an additional 400 of these specialists need to be trained out of the total of 2,000 engineers and technologists that wil be required in addition to the existing manpower pool.

Box 5.1 below presents some relevant data on the proportion of engineers and technicians produced locally and overseas, as well as some economic indicators relating to the availability of engineers in Mauritius.

---

**Box 5.1  Manpower data and economic indicators**

- Stock of practising engineers as at 1992 is estimated at 450 – about a third trained in the Faculty of Engineering, University of Mauritius, and about two thirds overseas.

- By 1998, the stock of technicians holding diplomas was estimated at 600 – almost alll trained in the Faculty of Engineering; for our calculation, two diploma holders are equated to one engineer.

- By 1998, 0.7 engineers per 1,000 population or 0.25 per US$$10^6$ (1992) GDP. Targeted to increase two- to three-fold and reaching 2.0–2.5 per 1,000 population or 0.5 per US$$10^6$ (1992) GDP towards the year 2010.

- GDP *per capita* increasing annually at 5 per cent in real terms and population increasing at the current rate.

---

*Method II*

Using the ratios of human resource requirement of an ideal utility in the region, as agreed upon by the AFREPREN members (Table 5.4), and the projected electricity demand of Mauritius, this method estimates the total manpower required by the Central Electricity Board (CEB).

Based on energy analysis carried out at the University of Mauritius, the total annual electricity demand is around 1,047 GWh. By the year 2010, the annual electricity demand is expected to increase further to reach 2,100–3,000 GWh, with 2,500 GWh/year as the mean projected demand. Again using the load factor of 0.3, the total installed capacity required would be 992 MW. Using the above projection together with the ratios

**Table 5.4  Ratios of an ideal utility in the region**

| Ratio | Ideal number |
| --- | --- |
| Ratio of manpower per GWh (produced) | 2 |
| Ratio of customers per employee | 125 |
| Ratio of technical to administrative manpower | 3:1 |
| Ratio of semi-professional to professional manpower | 6:1 |
| Ratio of non-professional to professional manpower | 43:1 |
| Ratio of manpower per installed capacity (MW) | 5 |

**Table 5.5  Projected manpower requirements – CEB**

| | Professional | Semi-professional | Non-professional | Total |
| --- | --- | --- | --- | --- |
| *1995/6 (Ideal)* | | | | |
| Technical | 30 | 180 | 1290 | 1500 |
| Administrative | 10 | 60 | 430 | 500 |
| Total | 40 | 240 | 1720 | 2000 |
| *2010* | | | | |
| Technical | 75 | 450 | 3225 | 3750 |
| Administrative | 25 | 150 | 1075 | 1250 |
| Total | 100 | 600 | 4300 | 5000 |

indicated in Table 5.4, the number of personnel as well as type of personnel for both technical and managerial sectors of the CEB have been computed: the results are summarized in Table 5.5 (Ministry of Public Utilities, 1999).

From the results, by the year 2010 the total staff needs to increase to 5,000, of which around 700 would have to be semi-professionals and professionals. The CEB would require about another 250 of such staff by the year 2010.

The following assumptions were made in the above analysis:

1   Professionals and semi-professionals are those who possess (or are obtaining) a university degree.

2   Non-professional staff are those who will get on-the-job training provided by the CEB.

3   In 1998, 280 semi-professional and professional staff were adequate to ensure the smooth operation of the CEB.

4   It is assumed that part of the staff will move to the sugar factories (the new IPPs) which will be generating around 50 per cent of the power requirement of the island by the turn of the century.

*Comparing the results – Methods I and II*
Comparing the results of the two methods (Table 5.6), it can be concluded that the difference of about 13–25 per cent is well within the limit of accuracy ($\pm$ 30 per cent) of the methods.

**Table 5.6  Comparing results of Methods I and II**

| | Method I | | Method II | Difference |
|---|---|---|---|---|
| | Total | CEB* | Semi-professional and professional (CEB only) | (%) |
| Year 2010 | 400 | 200 | 250 | 25% |

* Assuming 50 per cent are required by the power sector, which caters for around 50 per cent of the total energy supply and demand of the island

# Supply of manpower

*University graduates*
Towards the end of the colonial era, most countries in our region had established universities as centres of higher-level learning and research. In general, these universities are replicas of European universities (mostly in the UK and France). These universities and other tertiary institutions were established with the purpose of developing a critical mass of scientists and technologists. The need for knowledge, skills, innovation and productive capacities that could absorb and adapt imported technology, including energy technology, was recognized implicitly. Other goals were local technology development for the identification, exploration and exploitation of natural resources, including energy, and conversion of raw materials into semi-finished and finished goods and products.

In Mauritius, the above aspirations led to the establishment of a College of Agriculture at Reduit in 1923. The Mauritian College of Agriculture became an internationally respected agricultural training institute that played an important role not only in Mauritius but also in the agricultural sector of the African region.

Beyond any doubt, the University of Mauritius has made a significant contribution to the development of Mauritius through the provision of skilled technologists, administrators, economists and accountants who replaced the departing European expatriates after independence. Its role in national development, however, is now no longer seen as particularly valuable by politicians in view of the resources it utilizes. It is further argued that for more than a quarter of a century funds have been invested in human resource development at the University and other tertiary institutions with little to show for it in terms of more rapid economic development. There are also complaints that, whereas the curricula in

European universities have evolved considerably in the last two decades to meet the changing needs of society in Europe, the curricula at the University of Mauritius have remained practically unchanged. This rigidity has limited the role the University has been able to play in the development of the country.

To illustrate this issue, Box 5.2 provides a typical honours-level curriculum for a Bachelor of Technology (Mechanical Engineering) Degree at the University of Mauritius. This curriculum, operating on a sandwich basis, does provide a programme of training that will produce a traditional mechanical engineer of the sort Mauritius needed after independence. But it fails to train a mechanical engineer who can adapt to the current changing needs of Mauritius.

---

**Box 5.2**  **Typical mechanical engineering programme at the University of Mauritius**

| Year One | Mathematics |
| | Computer Programming |
| | Engineering Drawing |
| | Engineering Management |
| | Applied Mechanics & Strength of Materials |
| | Thermodynamics & Fluid Mechanics |
| | Electrical Engineering |
| | Electronics |
| | Instrumentation & Signal Analysis |
| **Year Two** | Mathematics & Statistics |
| | Computation & Application of Numerical Methods |
| | Engineering Management |
| | Instrumentation & Microprocessors |
| | Electrical Machines |
| | Textile Machinery |
| | Applied Thermodynamics & Fluid Mechanics |
| | Structural Mechanics & Dynamics |
| | Engineering Design, Materials & Production Technology |
| **Year Three** | Numerical Analysis & Computation |
| | Engineering Management |
| | *Four out of Six* |
| | Control Systems |
| | Machine Element Stress Analysis & Design Practice |
| | Dynamics of Systems, Condition Monitoring & Robotics |
| | Heat Transfer in Thermal Systems |
| | Energy Production & Utilization |
| | Refrigeration & Air Conditioning |
| | Computer-aided Design & Manufacture |
| | *Plus* |
| | Project – Design/Research-Oriented |

When an engineering curriculum such as the one in Box 5.2 is analyzed, it can be seen to fall into two parts. The first part is what is known as the foundation, which includes the necessary science subjects such as mathematics, physics, chemistry and the basic engineering sciences: mechanics and dynamics of solids and fluids, thermodynamics, electricity and electronics, and the strength of materials. Generally, this foundation accounts for up to 60 per cent of the curriculum, and goes up to the end of the second year of the three-year programme. Although this section is (or should be) the same for any engineering curriculum – mechanical, chemical, civil or electrical/electronic – it is generally taught separately by the various departments of the engineering faculty, which is a waste of resources.

The second part consists of specialization in one of the various disciplines – civil, mechanical and the rest – and this represents the other 40 per cent of the curriculum. Because of limited human and financial resources, the options offered during the specialization year are restricted. In many cases, the rigidity of this second part of the curriculum does not allow the introduction of such modules as 'Co-generation and IPP studies' or any other module that diverges from the regular engineering subjects. Consequently, this curriculum produces engineers trained within a relatively narrow field of specialization, who are often criticized for being too theoretical and not flexible enough in the workplace. Similar criticisms of accountancy, management, economics and agriculture curricula have been raised.

The various points discussed above lead to several questions:

- Who decides on the priorities and needs as far as the training of engineers, technologists and managers is concerned?

- What methodology should be adopted to plan the future human resource requirements of each nation and of the region?

- What methodology should be adopted to estimate the number of technologists and engineers?

- To what extent must the curriculum be modified in order to produce technologists and engineers knowledgeable in energy matters?

- To what extent should the University move nearer to marketplace realities, where the short term is at a premium, when its central worth to society is linked to the medium and long term?

To answer the above questions one may turn to the above-mentioned *Proposal for the Developing Commonwealth* formulated by D.L. Modell and J.F. Coales for the Commonwealth Board of Engineering Education and Training and widely circulated among Commonwealth governments and universities. The methodology developed in the study has been used to estimate the requirement of engineers and technologists in Mauritius in general and for the power sector in particular (see below).

*Training at the Central Electricity Board (CEB)*
The CEB established an Education and Training Committee in September 1961 to define the general aspects of education and training required within the CEB and to coordinate training programmes. Unfortunately, this Committee did not complete its mandate. Then, in 1964, the Students' Engineering Training Scheme was set up to ensure the provision of courses in electricity for the benefit of switchboard attendants and foremen.

Scholarships from the UK and France were granted to members of staff in fields such as engineering (both electrical and mechanical) while sponsorships were also provided for Accountancy, Concrete Technology and Business Management courses at the University of Mauritius.

By 1970 the Board had already established links with overseas authorities such as Electricité de France (EDF), Bell Engineering Works, Compagnie Vaudois d'Electricité in Switzerland, the Electricity Commissions of Victoria and New South Wales and the Eastern Electricity Board at Southgate in London. Such links were fruitful in the sense that the personnel of the CEB had the possibility to visit these places, even during their holidays, and hence gain exposure to new techniques. In addition, the Board operates a loan scheme for employees interested in further training.

One of the main achievements of the Central Electricity Board in the training field was the establishment of the Centre de Formation et de Perfectionnement Professionnel (CFPP) in 1975. Its aim is to train young apprentices and to provide refresher courses for both manual and staff employees. The CFPP provides all the training of linemen, wiremen and apprentices. The complete set of training modules run by the CFPP is presented in Box 5.3. Foreign aid in terms of equipment and expertise was received from the French government for the creation of this training centre.

As far as the supply of engineers, managers, accountants and economists is concerned, the CEB relies heavily on graduates of the University of Mauritius. Collaboration between the two institutions exists in the following forms:

- CEB members are invited to participate in the advisory committees of the University which are responsible for curriculum development.

- University graduates in areas such as engineering (electrical and electronic, mechanical and civil), management and accountancy often secure employment at the CEB.

- The CEB provides facilities to University students for industrial training and attachment.

- Fresh graduates in engineering are given the opportunity to undertake their mandatory two-year training prior to professional registration at the CEB.

### Box 5.3  Courses at the CFPP

| Courses | Objective | Duration |
| --- | --- | --- |
| Basic Technical Course for Apprentices | Prerequisite for the basic course in electro-mechanics | 1 year |
| Apprenticeship Course in Electro-mechanics | Training to integrate groups involved in production | 2 years |
| Apprenticeship Course in Networks | Training to integrate groups involved in distribution | 2 years |
| Professional Course for Labourers in the Transport and Distribution Division | Provide essential technical training | 10 days |
| Professional Course for Linemen/Wiremen Mates (1st Stage) | Provide theoretical, technological and practical training of HT/BT networks | 15 days |
| Professional Course for Linemen/Wiremen Mates (2nd Stage) | Continuation of the 1st Stage | 20 days |
| Course for Linemen/ Wiremen Working with Low Voltage | Training in techniques of intervention under low voltage, methods of contact with networks and connection of overhead cables | 20 days |
| Course for Inspectors/ Supervisors Working with Low Voltage | Training in techniques of intervention under low voltage, methods of contact with networks and connection of overhead cables | 15 days |
| Course for Updating Staff Working with Low Voltage | Updating staff supervising the above tasks | 2 days |
| Course for Training of Linemen/Wiremen and Inspectors/Supervisors Working with Low Voltage | Further training for carrying out the above tasks | 5 days |
| Training Course on Lighting Public Places | Training in setting up and repair of the lighting network | 3 days |
| Professional Course For Linemen/Wiremen | Provide essential technical training | 10 days |
| Continuation of the Above Professional Course | Completion and enlargement of general professional knowledge | 10 days |

| | | |
|---|---|---|
| Initiation Course for Linemen/Wiremen in Transport and Distribution Techniques | Technical knowledge in the Transport and Distribution field | 5 days |
| Sensitization of Charge-hands in their Role in Transport and Distribution | Sensitization of participants in their respective roles and responsibilities in Transport and Distribution | 5 days |
| Professional Course for Chargehands in Commercial Service | Provide theoretical, technological and practical training in customer-related activities | 10 days |
| Initiation Course for Commercial Chargehands in Transport and Distribution Techniques | Provide technical training in the HT/BT network, needed for understanding the district-level functions and requirements | 20 days |
| Professional Course for Chargehands in Transport and Distribution | Provide theoretical, technological and practical training in transport and distribution of electricity | 10 days |
| Initiation Course for Charge-hands in the Transport and Distribution Division in Commercial Techniques | Give trainees necessary information on materials and techniques in the Commercial Division | 5 days |
| Professional Course for adaptation of Chargehands in the Transport/Distribution and Commercial Services | Help participants to fully exploit HT /BT network and Commercial Services | 10 days |
| Further Professional Training for Junior/Senior Inspectors in the Commercial Service | Update on techniques and sensitization of staff working in the Commercial Department | 5 days |
| Further Professional Train-ing for Assistant Supervisors/Supervisors in Transport and Distribution | Update on techniques and sensitization of staff working in the Transport and Distribution Department in their respective roles | 5 days |
| Professional Training for Junior Inspectors in the Commercial Service | Provide theoretical, technological and practical training in customer-related activities | 15 days |
| Initiation Course for Junior and Senior Inspectors in Transport and Distribution Techniques | Provide technical training necessary for better understanding of the way the Transport and Distribution sectors work | 20 days |

| | | |
|---|---|---|
| Initiation Course for Assistant Supervisors/ Supervisors in Commercial Techniques | Provide technical training necessary for the better understanding of the way the Commercial Service functions | 15 days |
| Professional Course for Adaptation of Inspectors of the Commercial Service and District Supervisors | Increase communication between Inspectors and Supervisors of the Commercial and Transport/ Distribution Services<br>Further on-the-job technical training | 5 days |
| Professional Training for Electricians of the Central and Transformation Work-shop (1st Stage) | Professional and basic technical training to help in the construction, maintenance and repairs of central and substation connections | 15 days |
| Professional Training for Electricians of the Transformation Workshop | Further theoretical, technological and practical training | 15 days |
| Training of Electricians of the Meter Laboratory | Training in the tuning and maintenance of meters | 5 days |
| Initiation Course for Cadet Engineers/Assistant Supervisors in Transport and Distribution Techniques | Practical and technological training of new recruits<br>Facilitate their adaptation to the job | 10 days |
| Professional Training for Cleaners and Greasers | Provide to new recruits training important for working in the diesel generating station | 18 days |
| Professional Training for Fitters (Thermal) | Further professional training in the maintenance and exploitation of diesel engines | 12 days |
| Professional Training for Fitters/Cleaner and Greasers | Provide technical training indispensable for the job | 18 days |
| Professional Training for Foremen/Assistant Foremen | Introduction to their role and responsibilities in the exploitation of groups | 6 days |
| Professional Training for Fitters (Hydro) | Further professional training in the maintenance of hydraulic turbines | 12 days |
| Professional Training for Electricians Working in an Electricity Generating Station (2nd Stage) | Further theoretical, technological and practical training | 15 days |
| Initiation Course in Welding | Introduction to the principles and disadvantages of welding, nature and importance of possible risks, collective and individual protection | 15 days |

## Efficiency of manpower utilization

There are two commonly used ratios for assessing the efficiency with which manpower is used by utilities or the power sector as a whole, namely:

- ratio of customers served per employee in any one year;

- ratio of total employees to total electricity generated in any one year.

Both ratios are used for power sector analysis but need to be interpreted with caution. Analysis of time series data of these ratios very often reveals inflections and ruptures in past trends. Also, inter-country comparisons of these ratios should recognize that differences in performance of power sectors may stem from structural or geographical factors. Countries with large and sparsely populated electrified territories will tend to employ more personnel for transmission and distribution compared to densely populated countries. Because of the scale of economies, large centralized power plants (>150 MW) will tend to employ fewer personnel and deliver larger amounts of power per employee than the smaller power stations.

As shown in Table 5.2 and Figure 5.1 the number of customers served per employee at the CEB gradually increased from around 79 in 1975 to about 130 in 1995, to come within the generally accepted range for developing countries (125 to 150). Available data from selected African countries shows that the ratio ranges from 10 to 90 customers per employee, while East Asian countries such as the Philippines and Malaysia have ratios comparable to that of Mauritius. Indonesia, Singapore and the Republic of Korea are able to service between 200 to 330 customers per employee.

Unit manpower utilization per GWh of electricity should normally show a decreasing trend as the amount of electricity generated increases. In the case of Mauritius (Figure 5.2), a similar trend was observed for the period 1970–94. The efficiency with which manpower was utilized for power production [manpower/GWh] on an annual basis declined from about 9 in 1970 to around 2 in 1995.

The observed trend in Mauritius can be explained using the so-called 'learning curve' approach. If manpower utilization [manpower/GWh] is plotted against accumulated production (Figure 5.2), two distinct departures from the proposed model are noticeable. After the year 1977 unit manpower utilization increased, while after 1988 the performance was below the learning curve prediction. This is partially explained by the slackening of Mauritian economic growth, due to adverse climatic conditions during the late 1970s and the downturn in the world economy with high energy prices during the same period.

Using the outcome of the above analysis, results from similar studies in the region and comparative data from developed countries, the AFREPREN Capacity Building study group agreed to use the ratios of

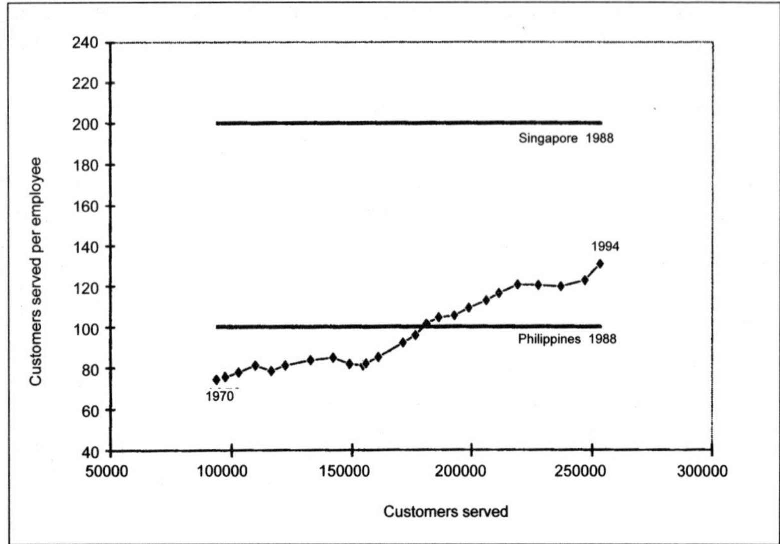


Figure 5.1  Efficiency in customer service (1970–94)

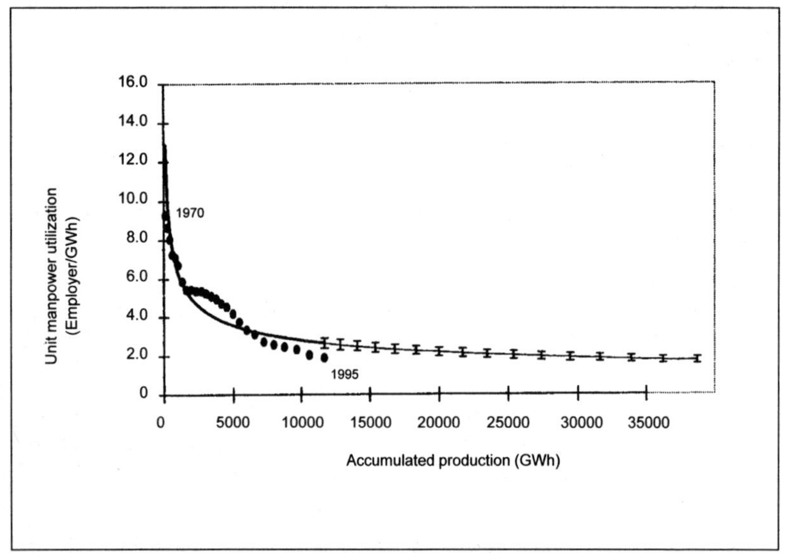


Figure 5.2  Manpower utilization efficiency (1970–95)

manpower utilization at an ideal power utility in the region as a benchmark for comparison.

## Manpower retention at the CEB

More than 50 per cent of the employees of the CEB (Table 5.6) are non-professional staff whose training is carried out by the CFPP. Staff retention incentives for the non-professionals consist of:

1  Prospects for further education and upgrading of skills through 'City and Guilds' type courses.

2  Possibility of appointment as cadet tradesmen.

3  Soft housing loans payable over 20 years.

4  Generous medical scheme whereby medical vouchers issued by the CEB enable employees to seek medical treatment in hospitals of their choice.

Retention incentives for the administrative and technical staff range from soft housing loans to company cars and a medical provident scheme that covers expenditure on dental treatment for sums up to Rs1,500. As shown in Figure 5.3, the measures in place at the CEB were effective. Statistics for later years indicate that the staff turnover problem has been overcome, and in part this can be attributed to the CEB's retention incentive schemes.

The wage bill as a percentage of operating cost has been fairly constant at 11–13 per cent but the expenditure on training as a percentage of operating cost has declined considerably from around 18 per cent in the period 1990–5 to around 13 per cent in 1997.

## Summary of main findings

The outcome of the analyses together with key policy challenges are summarized below.

- The outcome of Method II suggests that by the year 2010 the CEB could require a total staff of 5,000, of whom around 700 would have to be semi-professional and professional. The CEB would require a further 250 such staff by the year 2010.

- Manpower utilization efficiency at the CEB, as measured by 'customers served per employee' as well as by 'unit manpower utilization (employee/ GWh)', has shown signs of improvement over the last two decades.

- Energy concepts are taught at all levels of the national educational curricula but the contents of the courses need to be continuously

### Table 5.7  Staffing and training at the CEB

| Year | 1990 | 1992 | 1994 | 1995 | 1996 | 1997 |
|---|---|---|---|---|---|---|
| Total no. of employees | 1816 | 1975 | 1934 | 1945 | 1917 | 1880 |
| Administrative & technical staff | 718 | 763 | 759 | 771 | 769 | 764 |
| Semi-professional | 26 | 54 | 49 | 75 | 38 | 42 |
| Non-professional | 1072 | 1158 | 1126 | 1099 | 1110 | 1074 |
| No. of customers | 219067 | 236802 | 253066 | 266767 | 276178 | 284576 |
| No. of training facilities – CFPP | 1 | 1 | 1 | 1 | 1 | 1 |
| No. of instructors | 4 | 4 | 4 | 4 | 4 | 4 |
| No. of employees trained/year | | | | | | |
| Own facilities | 78 | 352 | 215 | 290 | 340 | 366 |
| Locally | 10 | 13 | 17 | 76 | 200 | 100 |
| Abroad | 15 | 4 | 5 | 16 | 23 | 16 |
| Wage bill % operating cost | 13 | 12 | 13 | 11 | 12 | N/A |
| Training % operating cost | 16 | 15 | 19 | 21 | 12 | 13 |
| Expenditure on training per employee (Rs) | 18035 | 6369 | 9267 | 10861 | 4613 | 6612 |
| Staff turnover rate (%) | N/A | 4.43 | –4.07 | 0.42 | –1.5 | –2.3 |

Source: CEB, 1995 and CEB, 1999

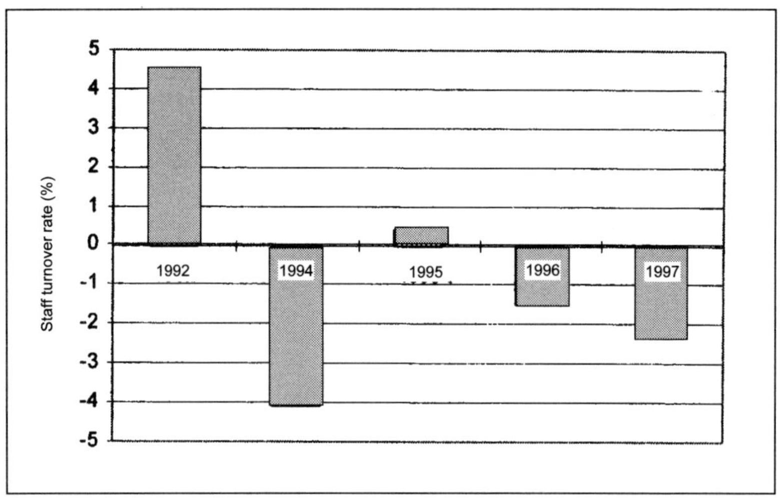


**Figure 5.3  CEB staff turnover rate**

updated to reflect the changes taking place around energy and environmental issues and technologies.

- Professional staff for the power sector are either trained locally at the University of Mauritius or in overseas universities. Technical training for semi-professional and manual workers of the CEB is carried out in-house by the CEB's own training centre (CFPP).

- The investment in training at the CEB is considerable and is currently around 13 per cent of the CEB's operating cost. Given their relatively smaller scale of operations, it is not certain how IPPs would be able to cope with the provision of in-house training for their power sector personnel.

- At the CEB, incentives are in place for staff retention which have largely overcome staff turnover problems

- It is projected that in the near future (6–8 years), that up to 50 per cent of Mauritian power could be generated by some six to eight IPPs based on the sugar industry. An exodus of qualified CEB professionals and semi-professionals is to be expected.

- The emergence of IPPs as major players in the electricity market will give rise to the need for new skills development. Effective negotiations, skills and the drawing-up of long-term power sales contracts between the utility and IPPs, while taking customer needs into consideration, are crucial elements for efficient development of the power industry.

- The CEB is considering a major overhaul of its human resource deployment. The utility may resort to the option of contracting out its non-core activities such as the running of its transport department, the extension and maintenance of power lines, and the processing of bills. This strategy of restructuring would again alter the ratios of employee per MW installed, employee per GWh produced and number of customers served per employee.

# 6

## Policy Recommendations

Broad national policies are in place to enhance capacity building in sectors of importance to the Mauritian economy as a whole. Although the essential elements of training in the power sector are provided, distinct policies need to be developed that address the specificity of the electricity industry. The following recommendations take into account the nature of the country, existing resources and facilities, and the roles of government, other state institutions and power sector operators. The main policy areas are:

- curriculum reform and development;
- dedicated power sector training fund;
- incentives for capacity and skills retention;
- effective negotiation skills and long-term power sales agreements;
- regional capacity building.

## Curriculum reform and development

The national educational curriculum needs to be continuously updated to reflect the technological changes that are taking place with respect to energy issues and energy technologies. Government through its national policy on education and training can pass a bill to include curriculum reform and development with regard to the power sector. This option would entrust the National Centre for Curriculum Research and Development (NCCRD) with the coordination of the various academic bodies to ensure that issues related to the power sector are addressed at all levels of education and training.

The NCCRD was created in 1993 to make the curriculum a continuous process of development in education and training reforms. Whereas curriculum reform and development is within the purview of the NCCRD, management of the curriculum can be undertaken by the Industrial and Vocational Training Board (IVTB). The necessary collaboration between these two institutions already exists.

The NCCRD already draws funds from the national budget for curriculum reform and development. If and when additional funds are required they may come from the national budget or be levied on power sector revenue.

## Dedicated Power Sector Training Fund

The Central Electricity Board has its own centre for in-house training. Independent power producers do not enjoy the same advantage and they presently rely on private or public institutions for the training of their staff and workers. Capacity building issues related to the gradual change from centralized power generation at the CEB to IPPs claiming a half-share of total power production could be addressed by the establishment of a Dedicated Power Sector Training Fund to finance training up to the semi-professional level.

At present there is no legal framework for funds to be dedicated to the power sector. This option, therefore, requires Parliament to pass a Bill establishing a training levy on power sales. In Mauritius, a law to collect a levy for training from employers already exists for vocational training (in the case of the Industrial Vocational Training Board) and this could serve as a model. The IVTB is the institution responsible for:

1   Advising the responsible Minister on matters related to training.

2   Monitoring needs for training in consultation with the relevant authorities.

3   Administering, controlling and operating training schemes.

4   Providing for, promoting, assisting in and regulating the training or apprenticeship of persons who are or will be employed in commercial, technical and vocational fields.

Alternatively, the IVTB could set up a Power Sector Advisory Committee comprising of professionals from the public and private sector to identify training needs, design courses and examine certification matters related to the electricity industry.

For Mauritius, the obvious choice of a training centre is the CEB's existing CFPP. The CEB could still own the centre, with its management falling under the IVTB. The proposed Power Sector Training Advisory Committee, consisting (among others) of professionals from the CEB and IPPs, could define training courses adapted to the specific requirements of the changing power sector.

## Incentives for capacity and skill retention

Capacity and skill retention is particularly important in the light of changes likely to take place with regard to competitive power generation in Mauritius. Internal organizational regulations should guarantee rewards such as salary hikes and promotions, organization-sponsored scholarships for further studies and sponsorship to attend international seminars.

While each organization, private or public, should have its own sources to finance internal seminars, scholarships and monetary rewards, the industry may well opt, drawing on the model of the Southern African Power Pool (SAPP), to institute and manage a common fund for the retention of capacity and skills. This would provide a strategic framework within which each organization would continue to address capacity and skill retention as an in-house responsibility.

## Effective negotiation skills and long-term power sales agreements

Effective negotiation skills, planning and long-term power sales agreements will be crucial instruments for the efficient development of the power sector. The training of professionals in these areas will become important as IPPs capture an increasing share of the electricity market.

Such training is best carried out in the form of seminars and workshops targeting personnel from government, utilities and IPPs. A regional network like SAPP or AFREPREN could become the focal point for such an initiative. Funding for specialized training programmes in negotiation and long-term power sales agreements could come from the proposed Dedicated Power Sector Fund.

## Regional capacity building

Several reports indicate that capacity building in most of the African countries in the power sector is weak. As a result, there has been a significant shortage of skilled manpower for the African electricity industry. Each country has its own training programme, conducted either by major operators in the power sector or by universities and other training organizations. Little attempt has been made so far to make use of specific competence in specific member states for the benefit of the region in general. The proposed pooling of resources, therefore, could yield significant economies of scale.

The most logical option for promoting regional capacity building in East and Southern African countries is SAPP: the question is whether its aims and objectives may be reviewed to include a capacity-building component. This existing organization might then provide the umbrella under which a secretariat responsible for the monitoring and control of capacity-building initiatives could be established.

# Part III Appendices

Part III Appendix 1 Selected time series data, Mauritius (table and figures)

Table IIIA.1.1 Selected time series data, Mauritius

| | 1992 | 1993 | 1994 | 1995 | 1996 | 1997 | 1998 | 1999 | 2000 |
|---|---|---|---|---|---|---|---|---|---|
| Population (millions) | 1 | 1 | 1.1 | 1.12 | 1.13 | 1.15 | 1.16 | 1.17 | 1.2 |
| GDP (US$ million) | 2724 | 2724 | 3037 | 3919 | 3770 | 4393 | 4628 | 4200 | |
| GDP growth rate (%) | 6.1 | 5.4 | 4 | 4.7 | 5.8 | 5.5 | 5.6 | 2.7 | |
| GNP *per capita* (US$) | 2700 | 3080 | 3200 | 3410 | 3710 | 3800 | 3700 | 3610 | 3600 |
| Installed capacity (MW) | 280 | 305 | 305 | 330 | 332 | 370 | 397 | 425 | 474 |
| Electricity generation (GWh) | 808.6 | 869 | 945 | 1047 | 1151 | 1251 | 1365 | 1422 | 1564 |
| Exchange rate M rupees : US$ | 15.6 | 17.6 | 18 | 17.4 | 17.9 | 21.1 | 24 | 25.2 | 29.5 |
| System losses (%) | | | | 12.1 | 12.1 | 11.5 | 11.2 | 10.8 | 10.2 |
| No. of employees | 1940 | 1967 | 1890 | 1898 | 1870 | 1828 | 1816 | 1802 | 1710 |
| No. of customers | 236802 | 246815 | 253066 | 266767 | 276178 | 284576 | 293887 | 304029 | 313693 |
| No. of customers per employee | 122 | 125 | 134 | 141 | 148 | 156 | 162 | 169 | 184 |
| No. of employees per installed capacity | 6.92 | 6.45 | 6.19 | 5.75 | 5.63 | 4.94 | 4.57 | 4.24 | 3.61 |
| No. of employees per GWh of generation | 2.4 | 2.26 | 2 | 1.81 | 1.62 | 1.46 | 1.33 | 1.27 | 1 |
| Electricity generation per employee | 0.42 | 0.44 | 0.5 | 0.55 | 0.62 | 0.68 | 0.75 | 0.79 | 0.91 |

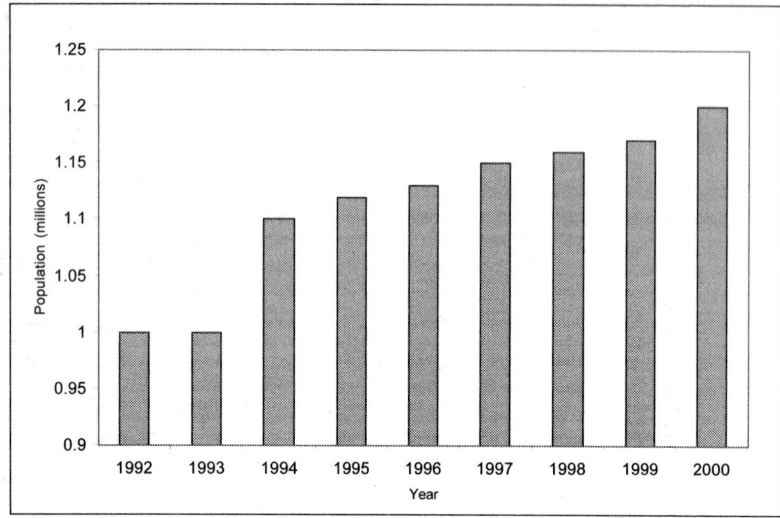

Figure IIIA.1.1  Population, 1992–2000 (millions)

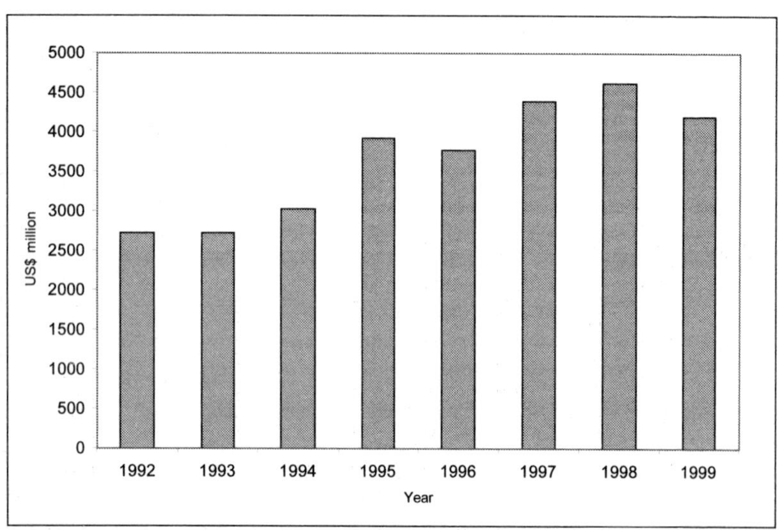

Figure IIIA.1. 2  GDP, 1992–9 (US$ million)

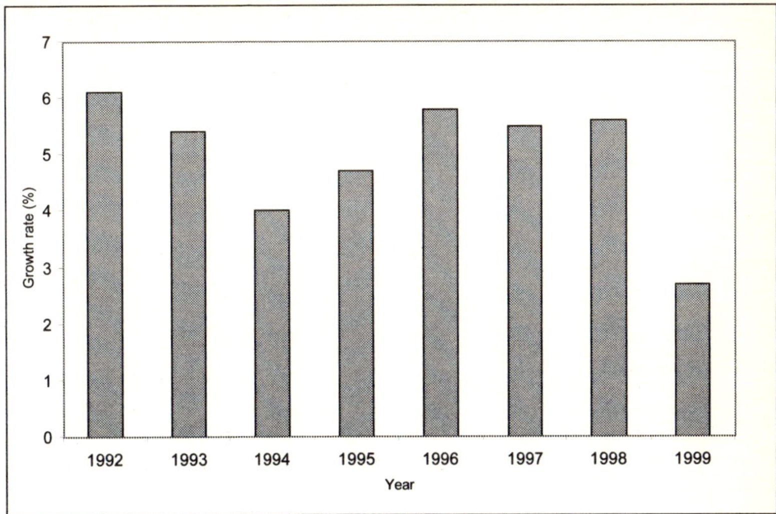


Figure IIIA.1.3  GDP growth rate, 1992–9 (%)

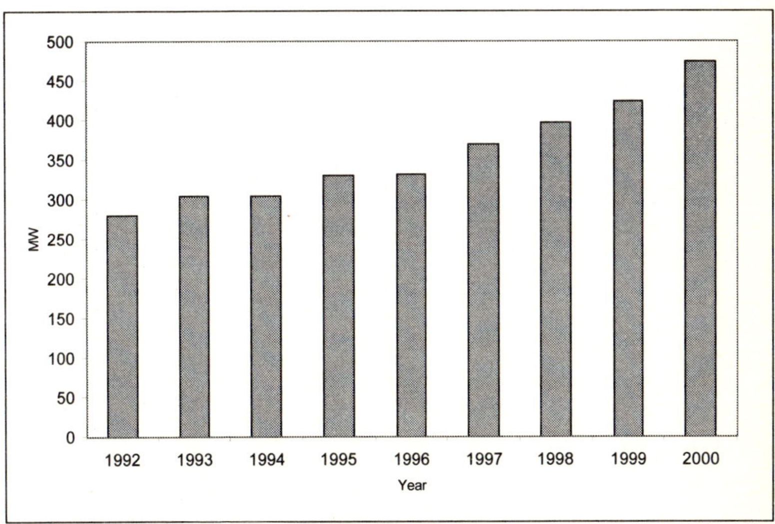


Figure IIIA.1.4  Installed capacity, 1992–2000 (MW)

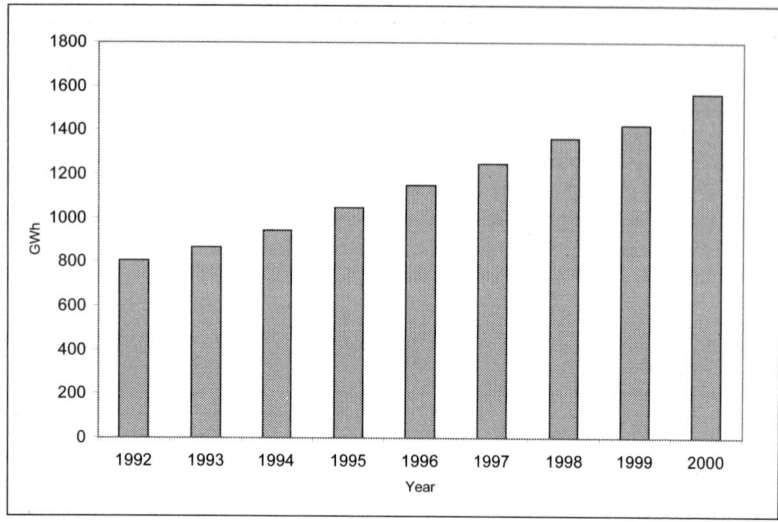

Figure IIIA.1.5  Electricity generation, 1992–2000 (GWh)

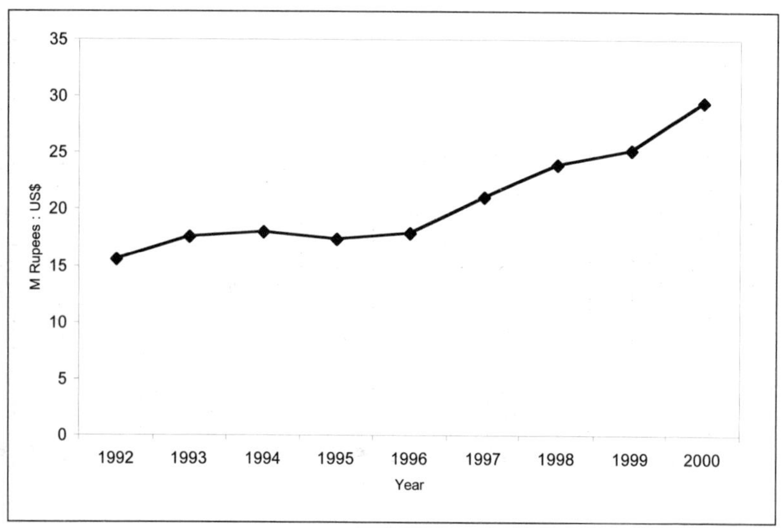

Figure IIIA.1. 6  Exchange rate, 1992–2000 (M Rupees : US$)

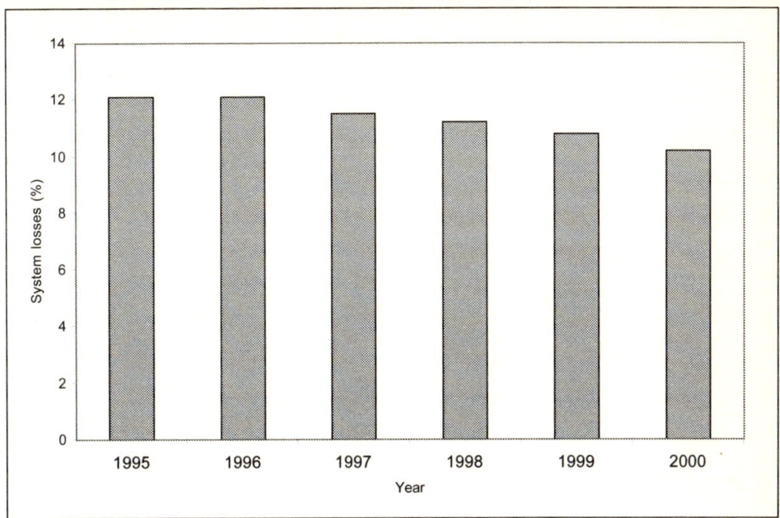

Figure IIIA.1.7  System losses, 1995–2000 (%)

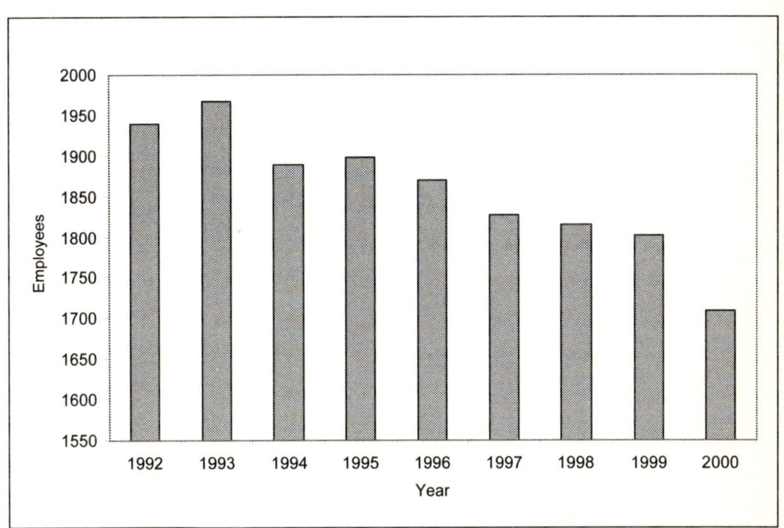

Figure IIIA.1.8  Number of employees, 1992–2000

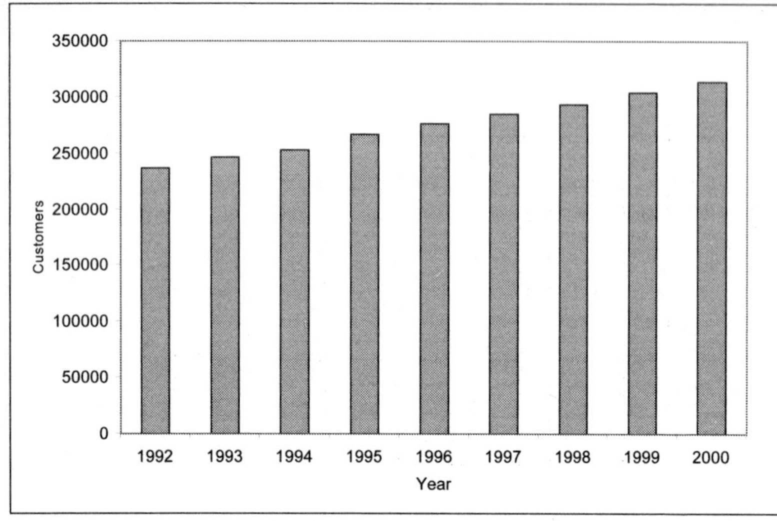

Figure III.A.1.9  Number of customers, 1992–2000

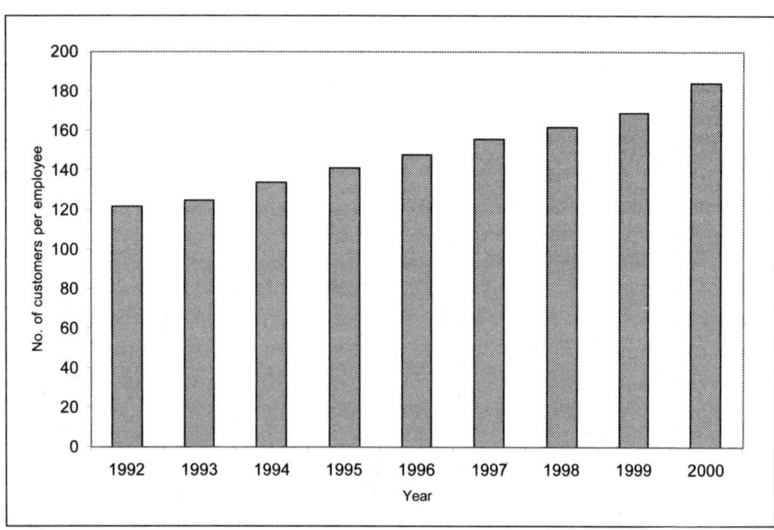

Figure IIIA.1.10  Number of customers per employee, 1992–2000

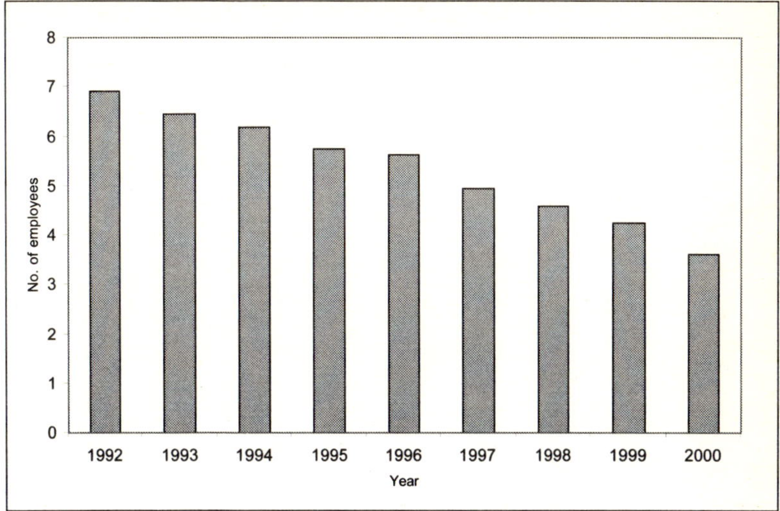

Figure IIIA.1.11  Number of employees per MW installed capacity, 1992–2000

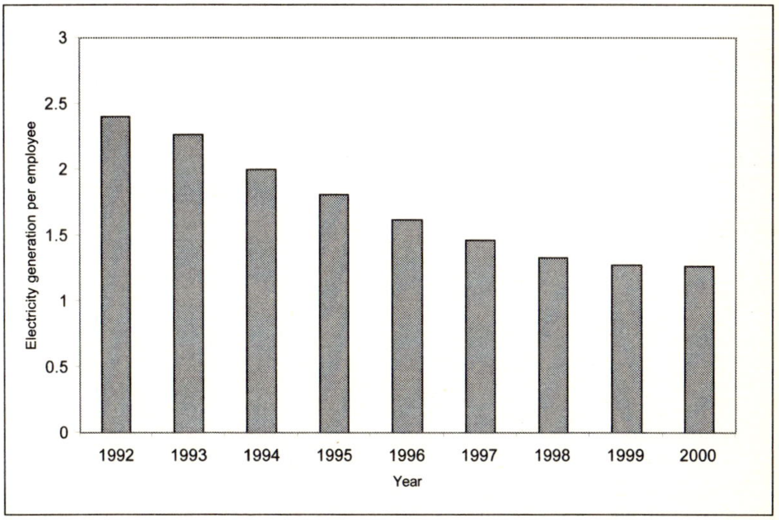

Figure IIIA.1.12  Number of employees per GWh generated, 1999–2000

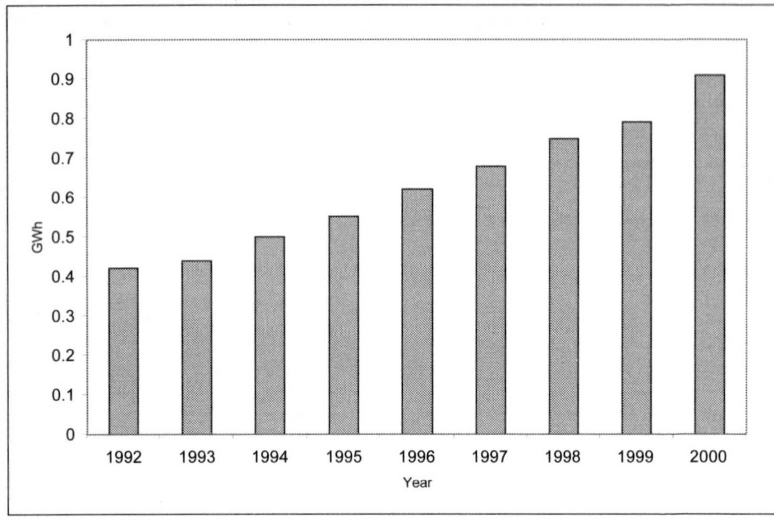

Figure IIIA.1.13  Electricity generation per employee (GWh)

# Part IV

## ETHIOPIA

**Mengistu Teferra**
**with Getachew Minas and W. Wolde-Ghiorgis**

# Ethiopia

Ethiopia: selected indicators

**Area (km²):** 1,097,000

**Population (millions):** 63.5 (2000)

**Capital city:** Addis Ababa

**GDP growth rate (%):** 3.8 (2000)

**GNP** *per capita* **(US$):** 115 (1998)

**Literacy levels (%):** (1998)   **Total:** 36

                        **Male:** 42

                        **Female:** 30

**Official exchange rate:** Birr 8.25 = US$1 (February 2001)

**Economic activities:** Agriculture, forestry, fishing, mining, manufacturing

**Energy sources:** Biomass, natural gas, hydropower, imported oil, dung

**Main electricity utility:** Ethiopian Electric Power Corporation (EEPCO) formally Ethiopian Electric Light and Power Authority (EELPA)

**Electrification levels (%):** (2000)   **National:** 13.00

                        **Urban:** 12.83

                        **Rural:** 0.7

**Installed capacity (MW):** 420 (2000)

**Electricity generation (GWh):** 1,670 (2000)

**System losses (%):** 17 (2000)

**Length of transmission line (km):** 12,755 (1995)

**Electricity consumption** *per capita* **(kWh):** 23 (2000)

**Number of customers in utility:** 594,400 (2000)

**Number of employees in utility:** 8,200 (2000)

**Number of customers/employee:** 72 (2000)

**Debt collection period (days):** 45 (2000)

**Electricity tariffs (US cents/kWh):** 5.1 (2000)

**Profit/loss (US$):** 19.42 million (2000)

**Number of employees/installed capacity:** 20 (2000)

**Number of employees/generated capacity:** 4.91 (2000)

**Modern energy consumption levels (000 metric toe):** 1,082 (2000)

**Modern energy consumption** *per capita* **(kgoe):** 17 (2000)


Sources: *Business in Africa*, 2001; AFREPREN/FWD Database, 2001; EIU, 2000c; World Bank, 2001; Energy Balances for Non-OECD Countries, 2000; *World Development Report*, 2001

# 7

## Country Background

Situated in the Horn of Africa, Ethiopia has a land area of 1.10 million square kilometres and a population of 63.5 million (World Bank, 2001a; EIU, 2000c). It is estimated that about 86 per cent of the population live in the rural areas (see brief country profile opposite and additional time series data in Part IV Appendix 1). Addis Ababa, the capital city, is located in the central highlands, and has a population approaching 3 million. Gold deposits constitute a major mineral endowment. Agriculture is the mainstay of the economy. Its share of GDP is roughly 45 per cent and it generates about 90 per cent of export earnings. Coffee, the main export, accounts for about 65 per cent of merchandise export earnings (EIU, 2000c). The livestock population is one of the highest in the continent. Agricultural production was negatively affected, however, by civil war, drought and the policies of the Derg (military) regime (1974–91). An overall stagnation of the economy was also experienced under this regime.

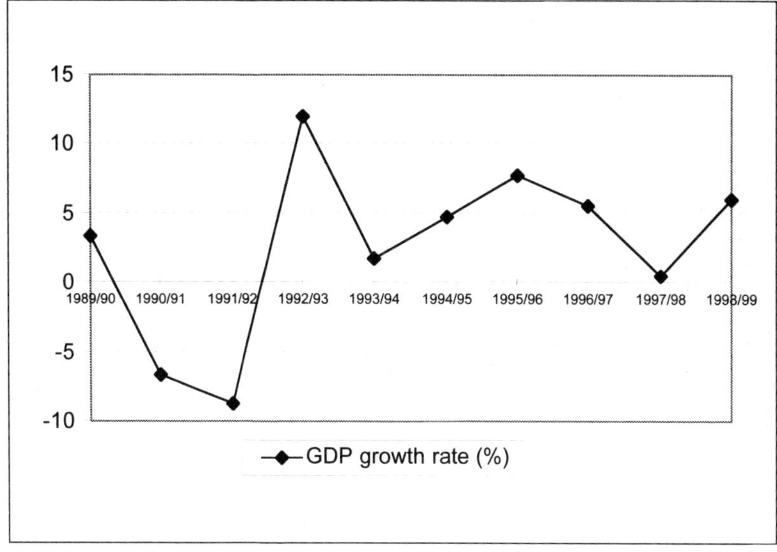


**Figure 7.1  GDP growth rates for Ethiopia**
Source: EIU, 1995; EIU, 1997; EIU, 1999a

Consequently, Ethiopia remains one of the poorest countries in the world, with a GNP *per capita* of around US$120 (World Bank, 2001a). Economic growth is hampered by weak infrastructure (notably roads), low productivity in agriculture, heavy dependence on one export commodity (coffee), a small industrial base and the shortage of skilled manpower. As shown in Figure 7.1, GDP growth rates were negative between 1990 and 1992 (the period immediately after the Derg regime). Growth rates improved from 1992, however, and have been positive. This is mainly attributable to the change in political orientation, new economic policies and economic recovery programmes instituted by the new government.

The economic policy instituted by the new government in 1991 aimed at transforming the Ethiopian economy from a centrally planned economy to a market-based economy. It featured the following notable aspects:

- Limiting the role of the state in most economic sectors and encouraging private investment, which was stifled under the previous regime.

- Increasing the role of regional governments in economic development and public investment in the various regions of the country.

- Reforming previous policies, laws and regulations regarding labour, money supply, credit, interest, taxes and investment.

- Reforming public enterprises to enhance management autonomy and promote higher efficiency and productivity.

- Strengthening the link between agriculture and industry, with significant support being given to peasant agriculture, which constitutes the backbone of the economy.

An Economic Reform and Recovery Programme (ERRP) was proposed as the first phase of the implementation of the new economic policy. The programme has rehabilitated the facilities and infrastructure that were neglected during the civil strife that preceded the fall of the Derg.

With respect to the decentralization of activities, regional governments have taken over water supply and road infrastructure development, the building of schools and health facilities, and the management of agricultural enterprises. The development of the energy and communications infrastructure is still centralized.

The Agricultural Development Led Industrialization (ADLI) strategy was endorsed as the basic framework for national economic development. The focus of the strategy is the rural sector, where most people live. Key objectives include improvement in agricultural productivity through the provision of agricultural inputs and extension services; introduction of small-scale irrigation; establishment of agro-based industries; and, improvement of infrastructure in rural areas. The next section reviews key characteristics of Ethiopia's energy sector.

# The energy sector

Ethiopia is endowed with vast energy resources, which include biomass, hydro, coal, geothermal, natural gas and solar energy. The gross hydro-energy potential of the country is estimated at 650 TWh per year (CESEN–Ansaldo, 1986), 25 per cent of which can be exploited for power. Between 30 and 50 billion cubic metres of natural gas, more than 1,000 MW of geo-thermal power and several hundred million tons of coal and oil shale exist.

About 95 per cent of the total energy consumed in Ethiopia is derived from traditional energy resources such as fuelwood, dung, crop residues and human as well as animal power. Electricity and oil products supply the balance. Electricity is wholly supplied by local generating stations, with hydroelectricity accounting for over 90 per cent of supply (Khalema-Redeby *et al.*, 1997). Oil is imported in the form of crude petroleum and refined products.

Annual energy consumption stands at about 25 kWh *per capita* for electricity, 16 kgoe *per capita* for petroleum and 276 kgoe *per capita* for other sources, mainly biomass. The *per capita* electricity consumption is among the lowest in the world, while petroleum consumption is signi-ficantly lower than the world average of about 600 kgoe *per capita* per annum. The major consumer of the energy is the household sector, which accounts for 90 per cent of the total energy supplied. The transport sector utilizes more than 70 per cent of imported oil, while agriculture uses only 3 per cent (Teferra, 2001b; Ghiorgis, 2000).

The importation of petroleum places a heavy burden on scarce export earnings. For instance, net importation of petroleum fuels was equivalent to 54 per cent of export earnings for the period 1992/3. The corresponding figures for 1995 and 1996 were 22 and 34 per cent, respectively (Teferra, 2001b; EIU, 2000c), the decline being largely due to improvements in revenue accrued from coffee exports.

Only an estimated 12 per cent of the population has access to electricity at national level. The figure is 0.2 and 12.3 per cent for rural and urban areas respectively. It was estimated in 1992 that 9 per cent of the population had access to hydro-based electricity, while only 1 per cent had access to diesel-based electricity (Teferra, 2001b). The assessment also indicated that 13 towns with a population greater than 10,000, and another group of 80 towns with populations between 5,000 and 10,000, were awaiting electrification. To date, this state of affairs has not changed significantly.

The grid electricity network is confined within an approximate radius of 500 km of Addis Ababa. In addition, substations are located far apart which constrains the distribution of power to intermediate villages. Attempts are, however, being made to extend the interconnected system (ICS) grid to various demand centres at transmission voltages of 230 kV, 132 kV, 66 kV, 33 kV and 15 kV (CSA, 1998).

Electricity supply is currently capacity-constrained, with the installed hydro-generation capacity often failing to meet peak power demand (AEG, 1997). Consistent low levels of rainfall exacerbate the situation. Reservoir siltation in older plants has also reduced the storage capacity, thereby accentuating spillage requirements during floods, and aggravating water shortage in dry years.

Hydropower development is increasingly faced with important sustainability issues, namely environmental, technological and political. Lending institutions have stringent appraisal criteria for the performance of client institutions and the viability of proposed hydropower projects. Even local governments are invoking criteria such as capacity building, science and technology transfer considerations, and maximization of local inputs. All the aforementioned considerations indicate the need for capacity building in all aspects of electricity supply.

Provisions of a recent Investment Law restrict foreign investors in the electricity sector to hydropower generation only, while local investors are allowed to invest in hydro generation (unlimited capacity) and thermal generation (up to 25 MW) (Teferra, 2001b). Local investors can also engage in the distribution of electricity. This provision has important implications for raising trained manpower for the power sector.

## Institutional structure of the Ethiopian energy sector

The role of upstream and downstream government institutions involved in the planning and policy formulation, implementation, supervision and coordination of activities in the energy sector in Ethiopia are summarized in Table 7.1.

Various departments have been established under the Ministry of Mines and Energy to monitor and coordinate the implementation of energy projects at a national level. Regional energy bureaux were established with the advent of regional governments (autonomous administrative regions) to address regional energy issues.

As shown in Table 7.2, as at 1995 an estimated 422 professions were employed in public institutions that deal with energy.

## Energy policy

The first officially acknowledged National Energy Policy was finalized and endorsed by the government in May 1994. The priorities of the policy are:

- hydroelectricity development;
- traditional energy development through reforestation programmes;
- oil and gas resources development;

**Table 7.1  Roles of the Ethiopian energy institutions**

| Institution | Role |
| --- | --- |
| Prime Minister's Office | Overall supervision and control; approval of plans and budget |
| Ministry of Economic Development & Cooperation | Overall monitoring & coordination; plan and budget assessment |
| Ministry of Mines and Energy | Monitoring & control of oil and gas development; regulatory role in the electricity supply sector; monitoring and control of activities in new and renewable energy subsectors |
| Supervising Authority for Public Enterprises | Monitoring and control of activities of the Ethiopian Petroleum Enterprise |
| Ministry of Agriculture | Assisting reforestation programmes & public forest management |
| Regional administrations | Monitoring & control of energy sector activities, except for supply of large-scale electricity, oil & gas in their respective regions |
| Petroleum Operations Department | Monitoring & control of oil and gas development by investors |
| Ethiopian Electric Power Corporation (EEPCO) | Electricity generation and distribution |
| Ethiopian Petroleum Enterprise (EPE) | Petroleum products import and bulk sales to distribution companies |
| Energy Research Centre (ERC) | Research, development & dissemination of new and renewable energy technologies |
| Forest and Wildlife Authority | Assisting reforestation, conservation and development programmes; management of public forests |
| Regional energy bureaux | Monitoring and control of woody biomass trade; development of small-scale electricity generation systems |

- energy use efficiency improvement and environmental protection;
- energy sector manpower development.

In line with the priorities of the policy, hydropower development is accorded priority, with the main focus on:

- rehabilitation of old hydropower plants;
- study of new hydropower schemes;
- construction of new hydropower plants.

**Table 7.2  Ethiopia – deployment of energy professionals in public institutions (1995)**

| Ministry and place of organization | Number of professionals | Span of activities |
| --- | --- | --- |
| 1  The Prime Minister's Office | 2 | Planning and policy formulation |
| 2  Ministry of Mines and Energy, Head Office | 22 | Planning and policy implementation |
| 3  Ministry of Economic Development and Cooperation | 4 | Planning, policy formulation and implementation |
| 4  Energy Research Centre | 22 | Research |
| 5  Ministry of Education | 20 | Permanent teaching staff at the Faculty of Technology, University of Addis Ababa |
| 6  Ministry of Agriculture, Forestry Authority | 12 | Firewood and charcoal supply administration: forestry management |
| 7  Regional bureaux of energy | 14 | Heads of energy departments |
| 8  Ethiopian Petroleum Enterprise | 26 | Petroleum supply and distribution |
| 9  EEPCO | 320 | Electricity generation, transmission and distribution |
| TOTAL | 442 | |

A notable change in policy is the shift from traditional large hydro schemes to medium-scale hydro schemes. Medium-scale hydro schemes (35–100 MW) were introduced to counter the weaknesses of small and large hydro: small hydro is too small to meet annual demand growth, while large hydro is very expensive. Three medium-scale hydro schemes are under construction, and three others are in the study and design phase. The split of responsibility for medium-scale hydro development is between the Ministry of Water Resources, responsible for study and design; and EEPCO, responsible for construction.

The next section reviews important elements of Ethiopia's human resource development from primary school level to tertiary institutions. Essentially, this is the base on which capacity building for the sector has to be initiated.

## Education and human resources development policy

*Student enrolment, educational financing and employment*
The number of students in primary education rose from 859,800 in 1973/4 to 2,884,033 in 1988/9 and then declined to 1,855,894 in 1992/3. Between 1973 and 1993, the number of teachers rose from 18,640 to 69,743, registering an annual growth rate of 7.2 per cent. The number of primary schools also increased from 2,754 to 8,120 (Ministry of Education, 1993–5).

Enrolment in junior secondary education rose from 101,800 in 1973/4 to 348,803 in 1992/3, reflecting an average growth rate of 6.7 per cent per year during the period. The number of students in senior secondary education also increased from 81,300 to 363,686 in the same period, equivalent to an average annual growth rate of 8.1 per cent for the period. In the same period, the total number of students in both junior and senior secondary schools was 1.3 per cent of the total population in 1993.

At the tertiary level of education, the enrolment levels have remained constant, despite the growth in enrolment at primary and secondary school level. Students who pass the school-leaving examination are often unable to join universities and colleges owing to space limitations.

Statistics for 1995 indicate that total enrolment in the primary, secondary and tertiary education levels stood at 5.7, 1.4 and 0.029 per cent, respectively, of the total Ethiopian population (Ministry of Education, 1997). The corresponding figures for Singapore in 1990 stood at 10, 8.5 and 2.2 per cent (Selvaratnam, 1994). The largest difference in the two countries is in the enrolment levels at the tertiary level.

The number of students in technical and vocational schools is only 0.1 per cent of the total number of students in general education. This indicates the slow progress of the prevailing education strategy which aims to shift high school students towards vocational training. Moreover, the graduates from vocational and technical schools find it hard to secure jobs in their field of training.

The annual public expenditure on education increased from Birr 376.3 million in 1982/3 to Birr 1,106.7 million in 1992–4. Though it tripled in these 12 years, its share in the total government budget (13.1 per cent) remained fairly constant. The recurrent budget was 71.4 per cent of the total education budget for 1992–4 (UNDP, 1994). Out of the total recurrent budget for the education sector, the share of the institutions of higher education stood at about 10 per cent.

The new economic policy of the government encourages private sector involvement in all sectors of the economy. In the education sector, however, there has been very limited new private investment.

The budget allocation for education has been decentralized in accordance with the new economic policy. Of the total budget of Birr 1,106.7 million (1993/4), for example, the share of the central government was only 19.5 per cent, while the balance was allocated to the regional governments. One of the largest regional governments accounts for 24.2 per cent of the total national education budget (EIU, 1998c).

During the military regime, all university graduates were centrally placed by the then Office of the National Committee For Central Planning (ONCCP). Ministries, authorities and public sector corporations and enterprises submitted their requirements for graduates with their annual plans to the ONCCP. The ONCCP assessed these requirements in relation to the supply of graduates, and assigned the requisite number of graduates to institutions, with the necessary budget allocation for salaries. The productive sectors were given priority in the allocation of manpower.

However, after the change of government in May 1991, the Transitional Government of Ethiopia (TGE) launched a new economic policy that removed the centrally controlled system and placed greater reliance on market forces in determining supply and demand. The government relinquished its dominant role in economic management. As a result, university graduates are no longer centrally placed in the various sectors of the economy and the government does not guarantee them jobs, as was the case before 1992.

*Education sector policy and strategy*
Three main policy documents and strategies define the government's policies on the education sector. The salient features of the education sector policy are spelled out in the five-year programme of the Ethiopian People's Revolutionary Democratic Front (EPRDF). The programme aims at improving the quality, relevance and equity aspects of education in the country. To bring about the required improvement, government support focuses on:

- reorganization of the primary, secondary and tertiary levels of education, along with changes in curricula at the three levels;

- revision of the incentive and remuneration systems for teachers;

- reorientation of training at various levels to ensure that it reflects the skills demanded by the various sectors of the economy;

- limiting free education to the primary and secondary levels only;

- encouraging private sector investment in the education sector.

Admittedly, the policy direction is radically different from the past in areas such as:

- emphasis on vocational training;

- provision of free education;

- use of ethnic languages in formal education;

- private sector participation in the education sector.

The education sector strategy recognizes the problems facing the educational system in Ethiopia, and proposes the following strategies to remedy the situation:

- revision of the existing educational infrastructure;

- review of curricula, with special emphasis placed on science and mathematics;

- upgrading and expanding vocational and technical education and training;

- encouraging community and private sector participation in education.

To translate the government's policy and strategy into concrete programmes of implementation, an Education Sector Development Programme (ESDP) for the next 20 years has been developed. The objectives of the ESDP are to improve the overall educational level of the population and achieve greater social equity by expanding access to education, with the emphasis placed on primary education in rural areas. Expansion of the tertiary sector, according to the ESDP, is limited to meeting the immediate needs of the country for educators, engineers, health workers and public administrators. The estimated budget for tertiary education, which is partly financed by the World Bank and the African Development Bank, is in the order of US$122.2 million.

Before discussing the issue of human resource development and capacity building in the power sector, the next chapter first describes the key characteristics of Ethiopia's electricity industry.

# 8

## The Power Sector in Ethiopia:
## an Overview

## Structure of electricity supply

The Ethiopian Electric Power Company (EEPCO) is the national agency responsible for public electricity generation and supply in Ethiopia. It was established in 1997, following recommendations of a Task Force set up to assess the performance of the then-existing power utility, the Ethiopian Electric Light and Power Authority (EELPA). EEPCO, the new corporation, is essentially a restructured EELPA. The key drivers behind the formation of EEPCO were capacity building; improvement of efficiency; reduction in time taken to make decisions; and a better division of labour.

EEPCO is different from EELPA in the following significant ways:

- EEPCO is a public enterprise that reports to a management board, which makes all the key decisions, and is no longer under a sector ministry, which eliminates lengthy loops in the process of decision making;

- EEPCO is governed by commercial principles and is expected to be financially self-sustaining, with no subsidies from the state Treasury;

- EEPCO is subject to competition, as it is one of the many electricity supply institutions that may be established according to the Electricity Proclamation No. 86/1997. EEPCO, therefore, lost the near-monopoly status that EELPA enjoyed in the past (FDRE, 1997a).

In addition to EEPCO, there are a few private generating units, mostly with small capacities, operating outside the EEPCO system. However, these account for less than 5 per cent of the total supply.

EEPCO operates two systems: the interconnected system (ICS) and the self-contained system (SCS). The ICS has an installed capacity of 453 MW, with seven hydropower stations providing 444 MW and diesel stations contributing 9 MW. The total energy output capability of the ICS is about 2060 GWh/ year (Teferra, 2001b; Kebede, 2001). The ICS supplies demand centres within a radius of 500 kilometres around Addis Ababa. Isolated service areas out of reach of the ICS are supplied by the SCS, with an aggregate capacity of 38 MW, 84 per cent of which is from diesel-powered stations.

Transmission voltages in the EEPCO system are 230 kV, 132 kV, 66 kV and 45 kV. The 45 kV transmission lines are being replaced by 60 kV lines,

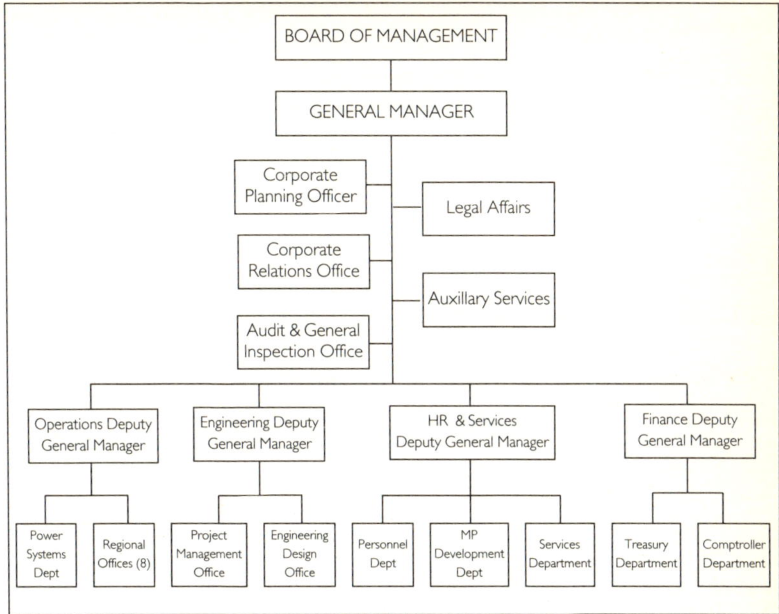


Figure 8.1  Organizational structure of EEPCO, 1997

and there are plans to introduce 33 kV transmission lines. The distribution system voltage is 15 kV and 0.4 kV (CESEN, 1986).

## Organizational structure of EEPCO

Since its formation in 1997, EEPCO has undergone a number of changes in its organizational structure. These include:

1 Replacement of the Ministry of Mines and Energy as the decision making body with a board of management, which has executive powers over the management of EEPCO (see Figure 8.1).

2 Reorganization of departments, divisions and sections within the former EELPA to improve the flow of activities.

3 Strengthening of EEPCO's regional offices by giving them decision-making powers.

The restructuring however, did not go as far as subdividing the former EELPA into separate agencies for electricity generation, transmission and distribution, which was one of the key recommendations of the study of Ethiopia's energy sector carried out by the Energy Sector Management Assistance Programme (ESMAP) (UNDP/World Bank, 1996). The current organizational structure of EEPCO is presented in Figure 8.1.

## Growth of the supply system

EEPCO's supply system has undergone quantitative and qualitative changes since the 1950s. The most important feature is the progressive expansion of the hydroelectric system (ICS) and the diminishing significance of the thermal system (SCS).

As shown in Table 8.1, annual *per capita* production of electricity in Ethiopia is one of the lowest globally and by regional standards (Uganda, Sudan and Kenya generate 40, 50 and 150 kWh *per capita*, respectively). Future expansion of the supply system would entail the extension of the hydroelectric grid and installation of additional diesel units.

Table 8.1  EEPCO supply system growth indicators

| Indicators | 1956 | 1974 | 1984 | 1996 | 2000 |
| --- | --- | --- | --- | --- | --- |
| Installed capacity (MW) | | | | | |
| ICS | 9.7 | 213.7 | 213.7 | 371 | 453 |
| SCS | – | 35.6 | 35.6 | 38 | 38 |
| Actual generation (GWh) | | 383.5 | 753 | 1548 | 2060 |
| ICS | – | 322 | 670 | 1495 | – |
| SCS | 33 | 61.5 | 83 | 53 | – |
| Length of HV lines for ICS (45 kV and above) (km) | – | 684 | 1383 | 5085 | – |
| *Per capita* generation for ICS & SCS (kWh) | 1.6 | 11.6 | 17.7 | 26.3 | 26.3 |

Source: EEPCO, 1996; Teferra, 2001b

## Electricity demand futures

Electricity demand is bound to increase in Ethiopia, given that it is a developing country. Factors that are likely to contribute to increased electricity demand in the foreseeable future include:

1  Increased private sector investment.

2  Increased public sector services.

3  The growing shift to modern fuels in household energy consumption, as a result of better access to the supply infrastructure, improved purchasing power and diminishing supply of biomass fuels.

4  The emphasis on Agricultural Development Led Industrialization (ADLI) and its implications for rural electrification.

A proxy analysis of the effects of these developmental factors on electricity demand was attempted in 1996. The analysis was based on demand growth forecasts for various categories of electricity consumers. The study revealed that electricity demand would increase by 9.6 per cent annually for the period 1997–2015 (Table 8.2). This meant that additional electricity generation capacity of about 1,600 MW would be required in the same period. Likewise, annual electricity generation would be expected to reach about 9,600 GWh in total and 90 kWh *per capita* by the year 2015.

Table 8.2  EEPCO electricity generation: past records and future forecast for indicative years (generation in GWh)

| Year | Interconnected system (ICS) | Self-contained system (SCS) | Total |
| --- | --- | --- | --- |
| 1972 | 289 | 55 | 344 |
| 1982 | 541 | 84 | 625 |
| 1983 | 575 | 79 | 654 |
| 1990 | 1054 | 76 | 1130 |
| 1995 | 1400 | 50 | 1450 |
| 1996 | 1495 | 53 | 1548 |
| 1997 | 1755 | 29 | 1784 |
| 1998 | 2301 | 18 | 2319 |
| 1999 | 1931 | 32 | 1963 |
| 2000 | 2000 | 27 | 2027 |
| 2001 | 2520 | 20 | 2540 |
| 2002 | 2745 | 23 | 2768 |
| 2003 | 3017 | 26 | 3043 |
| 2004 | 3320 | 30 | 3350 |
| 2005 | 3654 | 34 | 3688 |
| 2006 | 4025 | 39 | 4064 |
| 2007 | 4434 | 44 | 4478 |
| 2008 | 4882 | 50 | 4932 |
| 2009 | 5372 | 56 | 5428 |
| 2010 | 5908 | 61 | 5969 |
| 2013 | 7867 | 82 | 7949 |
| 2015 | 9531 | 100 | 9631 |

Source: EEPCO, 1996

## Quality of service

Annual growth rates in electricity demand for household, industrial and commercial sectors average 8.1, 7.1 and 7.4 per cent, respectively. Both the generation capacity and the distribution infrastructure face constraints in meeting this rate of demand growth. The generation reserve margin in the ICS is below 20 per cent. The distribution system is characterized by overloaded transformers and voltage drops exceeding 30 per cent of nominal values in certain areas. Wait-listed customers numbered about 120,000 in 1997 (EEPCO, 1996). In some cases, dry winters have forced the institution of electricity rationing (in October–December 1997, for example). Indicators of EEPCO's performance as an electricity supply enterprise are presented in Table 8.3.

**Table 8.3  EEPCO: enterprise performance indicators, 1996/7**

| Performance indicator | EEPCO current performance | Comparative figures* |
|---|---|---|
| 1  *Customer service* | | |
| i  Average reaction time for faults | 110 minutes | 71 minutes (2) |
| ii  Time lapse between application & new connection | 4–5years | 109 days (1) |
| iii  No. of wait-listed customers | 120000 | – |
| iv  Average tariff (US cents/kWh) | 4.8 | 3.5 (2); 3.06 (3) |
| v  Line loss (transmission + distribution) | 18% | 14% (1); 14% (2); 7.1% (5); 8.4% (6) |
| vi  Voltage regulation under-voltage problems | Common | – |
| vii  Load factor (%) – ICS | 60.3 | 66 (1); 75 (3) |
| viii Plant factor (%) – ICS | 46.5 | 46.8 (3); 56 (4)** |
| 2  *Finance* | | |
| i  Return on assets | 2% | – |
| ii  Operating expenses as % of revenue | 79% | 64% (1) |
| iii  Billing lag | 60 days | 90 (1) |
| iv  Payroll as % of total operating expenses | 21% | 12% (1) |
| v  Training as % of total operating expenses | 0.2% | 3% (1) |
| vi  Transport cost as % of total expenses | 1.1% | 8.5% (1) |
| 3  *Labour and productivity* | | |
| i  Professional staff as % of total | 4% | 8% (2) |
| ii  Customers/employee | 63 | 6 (3); 21 (1); 41 (2) |
| iii  MWh sales/employee | 170 | 345 (1); 300 (3) |
| iv  Power line km/employee (all voltages) | 2.3 | 5.0 (3); 3.3 (1) |

* Numbers in brackets indicate utilities compared:
(1) ESCOM – Malawi (ESCOM, 1995); (2) ZESA – Zimbabwe (ZESA, 1995a); (3) ESKOM – South Africa (ESKOM, 1991); (4) KPLC – Kenya (Brew-Hammond, 1995); (5) Privatized utilities, USA (Bacon, 1995); (6) Privatized utilities, UK (Bacon, 1995)
** Highest performance for Africa (Brew-Hammond, 1995)

## Problems and challenges

EEPCO is currently overburdened with power plant construction projects (four power plants are set to go into the construction phase), transmission line extension, reinforcement projects and a backlog of distribution works. Although consultants and constructors undertake construction of power plant and transmission line, the administration of such contracts requires competent staff. There is a shortage of qualified individuals in the public sector since the private sector is more attractive to upcoming professionals.

Some of the fundamental problems and challenges facing EEPCO in relation to human resource capacity building are:

- Achieving adequate capacity for study, design, construction, performance monitoring, operation and maintenance of the power supply infrastructure.

- Keeping abreast of state-of-the-art power supply technology and management.

# 9

# Capacity Building in Ethiopia's Power Sector

## Human resource assessment at EEPCO

Table 9.1 presents the distribution of EEPCO's manpower as of June 1997.

**Table 9.1  Manpower distribution in EEPCO (June 1997)**

|  | Technical | Administration | Total | Percentage |
|---|---|---|---|---|
| Professional | 210 | 120 | 330 | 4 |
| Semi-professional | 932 | 2613 | 3545 | 42.4 |
| Non-professional | 2727 | 1751 | 4478 | 53.6 |
| Total | 3869 | 4484 | 8353 | 100 |

Source: Based on data provided by EEPCO (1996)

The number of second degree (MA, MSc) and third degree (PhD) holders stood at 134 and 3, respectively, for 1996 (EELPA Task Force, 1996). Most of the second and third degree holders were from East European universities.

An assessment of manpower in EEPCO was undertaken in June 1996. The aim of this assessment was to obtain basic data required for this research study. The data collected were used to:

- derive relevant indices for staffing levels in various departments in order to forecast trained manpower demand for the medium-to-long term;

- assess training needs in the power sector;

- assess appropriateness of energy education curricula at higher institutions and universities;

- assess budgetary implications and foreign assistance requirements for supplying the required manpower to the power sector in the medium-to-long term.

# Manpower demand forecasts by various methodologies

*Survey data*

Each department in EEPCO was requested to fill in a questionnaire on the extent of lack of expertise, personnel mobility, training and staffing levels in the department. All the 13 departments responded to the questionnaires. From the responses, it was possible to derive a few indices for projecting manpower requirement for any future power sector development scenario. The indices were also used to forecast professional manpower demand and the demand for technicians for indicative years in the period 1996–2015.

A reconstruction of the manpower requirements for EEPCO for the years 1972 and 1983 was also done to validate the forecast methodology through retroactive application. The backward projection results testified strongly to the appropriateness of the methodology used. The derivation and use of indices were based on the following set of assumptions:

ASSUMPTIONS IN THE DERIVATION OF INDICES FOR 1996

1   EEPCO staff constructs transmission lines of up to 132 kV.

2   All operational activities in the generation, transmission and distribution system are carried out by EEPCO's staff.

3   The study, design, supervision and construction of major hydropower plants and transmission lines over 132 kV are undertaken by external contractors and consultants.

4   The requirements for counterpart Ethiopian professionals and contract administration in electricity generation and construction will grow in pace with electricity production levels.

5   Transmission line (66 kV and 132 kV) lengths added per year are equal to 200 km.

6   Growth in electricity sales will require commensurate growth in distribution infrastructure construction. However, some portion of sales growth is attributable to existing consumers. To simplify the analysis, this detail is ignored.

7   EEPCO's electricity production for 1996 was 1,548 GWh, while the electricity sales figure for 1996 was 1,238 GWh.

ASSUMPTIONS IN THE USE OF INDICES

1   Assumptions 1–3 above are valid for the period 1996–2015. They are also applicable for the period 1970–96 without substantially affecting the results of the projection.

**Table 9.2  EEPCO: ideal deployment level of professionals as at June 1996**

| Area of deployment | Engineers | | | | Accountants | Economists | Other professionals | Total professionals |
| --- | --- | --- | --- | --- | --- | --- | --- | --- |
| | Electrical | Civil | Mechanical | Total | | | | |
| 1 Generation | 24 | 9 | 11 | 44 | – | – | – | 44 |
| Construction | 6 | 8 | 1 | 15 | – | – | – | 15 |
| Operation | 18 | 1 | 10 | 29 | – | – | – | 29 |
| 2 Transmission & substations | 39 | 25 | – | 64 | – | – | – | 64 |
| Construction | 15 | 25 | – | 40 | – | – | – | 40 |
| Operation | 24 | – | – | 24 | – | – | – | 24 |
| 3 Distribution, construction & operation | 77 | – | – | 77 | 4 | – | 9 | 90 |
| 4 Engineering | 22 | 16 | 4 | 42 | – | – | – | 42 |
| 5 Planning & programming | 15 | 6 | 3 | 24 | – | 5 | 5 | 34 |
| 6 Supply services | – | – | – | – | 2 | 5 | 8 | 15 |
| 7 Technical services | 2 | – | 6 | 8 | – | – | – | 8 |
| 8 Finance & human resource dev. | 1 | – | 1 | 2 | 43 | – | 30 | 75 |
| 9 Other services, including customer services | 23 | – | – | 23 | 1 | 6 | 24 | 54 |
| Total | 203 | 56 | 25 | 284 | 50 | 16 | 76 | 426 |

* Ideal deployment level = actual deployment + 'deployment gap'
Source: Questionnaire responses

2   Energy production by EEPCO will follow the 'reference' scenario in the electricity generation forecast adopted by EEPCO in 1996 (see Table 9.2). The assumptions made in the electricity generation forecast were retained for the manpower demand forecast. In particular, the envisaged expansion of private investment in the economy and the assumed overall growth of the economy at 7.5 per cent per year (average) were used. The assumption that EEPCO will remain the single major supplier of electricity in Ethiopia in the coming two decades was implicit in the exercise. If ownership of electricity supply infrastructure changes, the manpower requirement per unit of electricity supply expansion would have to be adjusted.

3   There is a linear relationship between the production/sales GWh of electricity and the professional (degree-holder) manpower requirement of EEPCO. Reliable data for professional manpower were not available for EEPCO on a time series basis. There were at least two occasions, however, when fairly accurate records were made: in 1983, when the 'ten-year perspective plan' was prepared; and in 1996, when manpower assessment was done for this study. The professional manpower size and the electricity production figures for the two periods are as follows:

| Period | Number of professionals | Production (GWh) |
| --- | --- | --- |
| 1983 | 102 | 654 |
| 1996 | 269 | 1548 |

From the above figures it can be noted that:
- growth of professional manpower = 164 per cent;
- growth of electricity production = 137 per cent.

4   The relationship between the number of professionals and the total number of employees, however, is non-linear. The total numbers of employees for 1983 and 1996 were 5,708 and 8,247, respectively:
- growth of professional manpower (1983–96) = 164 per cent;
- growth of total number of employees (1983–96) = 44 per cent;
- thus ratio of these growth rates (professionals/total number of employees) = 3.7.

This key ratio is used to predict the total number of employees in the forecast period 1997–2015.

5   A serious shortage of professionals existed in 1983 and 1996. As will be demonstrated later, manpower demand estimates based on regional ideal utility indices negate this particular assumption. However, for parallel scenario development the assumption is retained.

*Survey data results analysis*
From the answered questionnaires, it was possible to derive the 'ideal deployment (manning) level' for each department (Table 9.2). The ideal

deployment level is in effect the sum of existing manpower and additional manpower required for smooth execution of jobs in each department. The indices used for the manpower forecast are based on these ideal manpower figures for 1996.

**Table 9.3 EEPCO: indices for ideal deployment level, based on 1996 data (for projection of aggregate requirement for professional manpower)**

| No. | Index | No. of professionals | | |
| --- | --- | --- | --- | --- |
| | | Engineers | Other professionals | Total |
| 1 | Generation construction and operations professionals per 1000 GWh/year electricity production | 28.4 | – | 28.4 |
| 2 | Transmission line and substation operations professionals per 1000 GWh/year electricity transmission | 15.5 | – | 15.5 |
| 3 | Transmission line construction professionals per 1000 km/year construction | 200 | – | 200 |
| 4 | Distribution line construction and operations professionals per 1000 GWh/year electricity sales | 62 | 10.5 | 72.5 |
| 5 | Professionals engaged in all other support activities per 1000 GWh/year electricity sales | 80 | 104 | 184 |

The indices for the ideal deployment level are shown in Table 9.3. For simplicity, the indices are shown for engineers, other professionals and total number of professionals. These indices could, of course, be further disaggregated by type of engineers, accountants and economists. Based on these indices, an initial estimate of the requirement for engineers and technicians in the forecast period was derived (Table 9.4).

The following ratios are derived from Table 9.4:

- The ratio of engineers to technicians in 1996 = 0.25.

- The ratio of engineers to technicians in 2015 = 0.82.

- The ratio of non-professional, non-technical staff to the total number of employees in 1996 = 0.81.

- The ratio of non-professional, non-technical staff to the total number of employees in 2015 = 0.68.

**Table 9.4 EEPCO: initial estimate of requirements for engineers and technicians***

| Year | 1996 | | 2000 | | 2005 | | 2010 | | 2015 |
|---|---|---|---|---|---|---|---|---|---|
| 1 Total number of engineers | 284 | | 405 | | 647 | | 1022 | | 1666 |
| 2 Total additions between years | | 121 | | 242 | | 375 | | 644 | |
| 3 Annual additions (average) | | 30 | | 48 | | 75 | | 129 | |
| 4 Total number of employees | 8247 | | 9253 | | 10826 | | 12558 | | 14730 |
| 5 Total number of technicians* | 1139 | | 1277 | | 1494 | | 1733 | | 2033 |
| 6 Total additions between years | | 138 | | 217 | | 239 | | 300 | |
| 7 Annual additions (average) | | 34 | | 44 | | 48 | | 60 | |
| 8 All professionals | 426 | | 618 | | 1006 | | 1603 | | 2636 |
| 9 Non-professionals | 7821 | | 8635 | | 9820 | | 10955 | | 12094 |
| 10 Non-professional, non-technical staff | 6682 | | 7358 | | 8326 | | 9232 | | 10061 |

* Estimate based on the ratio of technicians to total number of employees remaining constant at 0.138 for period 1996–2015

It is possible to optimize the various ratios by adjusting the percentage annual growth rate for technicians. However, care should be taken to keep the ratio of engineers to technicians above 0.5 for the year 2015 and beyond. This will ensure that certain operational and maintenance jobs now left for technicians will be carried out by engineers, thereby raising the quality and reliability standard of the work done. On the other hand, raising the ratio over unity would be unduly expensive for the utility.

It is also possible to optimize the various ratios by a proactive control of growth rates for the non-professional, non-technical employees. However, this measure would have negative social impacts. In addition, this is an issue that should be considered in the context of the financial viability and profitability of EEPCO, rather than as a factor of capacity building. From the latter viewpoint, the issue of upgrading the skills of the non-professional and non-technical employees through an active training scheme is more important. Ratio optimization, therefore, is not investigated in this study.

The annual additions for engineers and technicians indicated in Table 9.4 do not take into account attrition due to:

* retirement due to old age;

- voluntary resignations;

- involuntary resignations before pension.

The above considerations are difficult to estimate because of their inherent unpredictability. In theory, it is possible to estimate how many of the existing engineers or technicians would retire due to old age in a particular year in the period 1996–2015. However, it is difficult to generate reliable estimates for new engineers and technicians joining EEPCO in the future. It is also difficult to estimate the number of voluntary or involuntary resignations.

One way of estimating the size of annual attrition would be to assume a 'total replacement period' of 30 years for both engineers and technicians. For the respective population to be replaced in 30 years, the current population can be 'depreciated' (depleted) by a factor of 1/30 per year (Table 9.5).

**Table 9.5** Forecast of average annual attrition levels for engineers and technicians

| Period | Average annual attrition | |
| | Engineers | Technicians |
| --- | --- | --- |
| 1996–2000 | 10 | 38 |
| 2000–5 | 14 | 43 |
| 2005–10 | 22 | 50 |
| 2010–15 | 34 | 58 |

Adding the average annual attrition (Table 9.5) to the first estimate of additional requirements (Table 9.4) gives the annual incremental demand for engineers and technicians (Table 9.6).

**Table 9.6** Forecast of annual incremental demand for engineers and technicians in EEPCO

| Period | Average annual demand | |
| | Engineers | Technicians |
| --- | --- | --- |
| 1996–2000 | 40 | 73 |
| 2000–5 | 62 | 86 |
| 2005–10 | 97 | 98 |
| 2010–15 | 163 | 118 |

As will be demonstrated later, the supply of engineers from local universities barely matches the average annual demand, for EEPCO alone, for the years 1996–2000. For technicians, the issue may be one of shortage of skills rather than shortage of supply.

The present attrition rates for professionals in EEPCO are alarmingly high. According to the survey responses from the various departments of

EEPCO, 52 professionals left the corporation in the two years between June 1994 and June 1996. Most of these professionals are engineers lured by better pay in the private sector

Table 9.7 lists the current shortage of skills in EEPCO as identified from the survey responses. These skills are not entirely absent in EEPCO. Rather, threshold-level skills currently available should be strengthened in a process of formal education or formal on-the-job training. The shortage depicted in Table 9.7 does not have serious implications if EEPCO was to continue dominating electricity supply in Ethiopia. However, in a scenario where there was strong competition from independent power producers, the shortage *would* have serious implications.

**Table 9.7  EEPCO: missing skills and training needs at various levels of education (1996)***

| No. | Missing skills/Training needs | University | Technical school |
|---|---|:---:|:---:|
| 1 | Power systems engineering (including study & design) | × | |
| 2 | Power projects' techno-economic analysis | × | |
| 3 | Hydropower engineering (including study & design) | × | |
| 4 | Power line communications | × | |
| 5 | Power systems' protection and control instruments engineering | × | |
| 6 | Computer science: application to the power sector | × | |
| 7 | Computer-aided network analysis for distribution systems | × | |
| 8 | Geothermal power engineering | × | |
| 9 | Diesel- and gas-turbine technology | × | |
| 10 | Information science | × | |
| 11 | Labour law | × | |
| 12 | Laws of contract | × | |
| 13 | Human resources management | × | |
| 14 | Manpower planning and training | × | |
| 15 | Organizational analysis | × | |
| 16 | Transmission line construction | × | × |
| 17 | Electro-mechanical equipment installation | × | × |
| 18 | Electrical installations' practice and standards (customer services) | × | × |
| 19 | Energy auditing and management | × | × |
| 20 | Procurement of materials & service | × | × |
| 21 | Wood pole treatment & concrete pole production | × | × |
| 22 | Financial systems and management | × | × |
| 23 | Automotive vehicles turbocharger maintenance | | × |

* Identified from survey responses

## Estimates of manpower requirement based on indices of more efficient utilities in the region

Basic data for the ideal utility are as follows:

| | |
|---|---|
| Installed capacity | 400 MW |
| Number of customers | 250,000 |
| Electrical production | 1,000 GWh/year |

The indices for the ideal utility are as shown in Table 9.8.

**Table 9.8   Ratios for the ideal utility in the region**

| Indicator | Ideal ratios |
|---|---|
| Manpower per installed capacity (MW) | 5 |
| Manpower per GWh produced | 2 |
| Customers (direct) per employee | 125 |
| Technical to administrative manpower | 3 : 1 |
| Semi-professional to professional manpower | 6 : 1 |
| Non-professional to professional manpower | 43 : 1 |

Data for EEPCO in June 1996 were as follows:

| | |
|---|---|
| Installed capacity | 409 MW |
| Number of direct customers | 519,000 |
| Electricity produced | 1,545 GWh |

Thus, based on the ideal utility figures, the reference manning level and staff distribution for EEPCO, 1996, using the indices shown in Table 9.8 are as follows in Table 9.9.

**Table 9.9  Reference manning level for EEPCO in 1996 per ideal utility indices for the region**

| | Technical | Administration | Total | Percentage |
|---|---|---|---|---|
| Professional | 99 | 33 | 132 | 2 |
| Semi-professional | 594 | 198 | 792 | 12 |
| Non-professional | 4257 | 1419 | 5676 | 86 |
| Total | 4950 | 1650 | 6600 | 100 |

For the reference manning level shown in Table 9.9, the required number of engineers for 1996 is only 99. The actual number of engineers in EEPCO in 1996 was 185. Thus EEPCO can afford to deplete its existing stock of engineers through natural attrition (1/30 of existing stock per year) for a number of years into the future, before the ideal manning level (which is assumed to grow in proportion to the annual electricity demand) is achieved.

Such a scenario is illustrated in Figure 9.1. According to this scenario, EEPCO would not need to recruit additional engineers until the year 2001. However, it would need to recruit about 30 engineers per year in the period 2001–10 and beyond to compensate for natural attrition and to meet the increasing manpower demand for expanding and running the electricity supply system. The scenario does not take into account manpower losses occurring due to individuals resigning from the utility for better employment terms in the private sector.

According to the reference manning forecast, EEPCO would have to recruit additional non-engineering professionals as well after the year 2000. With regard to the overall number of employees, various indices such as electricity production per employee, transmission and distribution line length per employee – indicated earlier in Table 8.3 (page 118) – consistently attest to the overmanned nature of EEPCO. Thus the need to prune the number of non-professional staff is apparent.

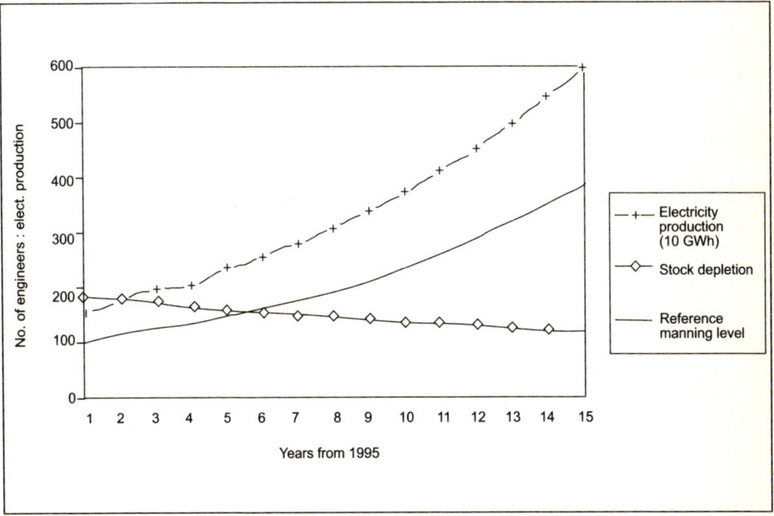


**Figure 9.1** Human resource depletion vs. reference manning levels for engineers in EEPCO

## National-level demand projection for engineers and technicians

Application of a methodology used in a 1983 study for Commonwealth countries (Mordell and Coales, 1983) yields a rough estimate of the requirement for engineers and technicians for the period 1995–2005. The study uses indices of manpower requirement per thousand of the population for countries at various levels of GNP *per capita*. In the Ethiopian case, the results can only be taken as indicative, since the base data for the present stock of engineers and technicians are at best crude estimates, calculated from annual graduate records (PMGE, 1984). The assumptions with regard to key variables are as follows:

| | |
|---|---|
| Annual GNP growth rate | = 5% |
| Total number of engineers and technicians per 1000 population at a GNP *per capita* of US$150–175 | = 0.75 |
| Annual population growth rate | = 3% |
| Percentage of engineers out of total number of engineers and technicians | = 15% |
| Annual attrition level for engineers and technicians | = 3.3% |

Under these assumptions the profiles for years 1995, 2005 and 2010 are summarized in Table 9.10.

**Table 9.10  Ethiopia: national-level demand for engineers and technicians by year 2010**

| Key variable | 1995 | 2005 | 2010 |
|---|---|---|---|
| Estimated population (millions) | 57 | 77 | 89 |
| GNP *per capita*, US$ | 125 | 150 | 165 |
| Total number of engineers and technicians per 1000 population | 0.47 | 0.75 | 0.75 |
| Estimated stock of engineers | 3000 | 8700 | 10000 |
| Estimated stock of technicians | 24000 | 49000 | 56700 |

Assuming an annual attrition rate of 3.3 per cent for the 1995 stock of engineers and technicians, the annual incremental supply requirement at the national level works out to about 550 and 2,800, for engineers and technicians respectively, for the period 1995–2010. It is important to note that this supply level is about three times the present supply capacity of local institutions in both cases.

EEPCO's share of the national stock of engineers is estimated at 5 per cent, on the basis of the total number of engineers in EEPCO in 1996 (which stood at 185) and the national stock of engineers (which stood at about 3,000 – see Table 9.10). On this basis, EEPCO's share of the national stock of engineers would be about 435 and 500 for years 2005 and 2010, respectively.

It is worth noting that only 15 per cent of the engineers in EEPCO are involved in electricity generation (construction and operation of power plants). The advent of IPPs will therefore lower EEPCO's demand for engineers at the generation end (as provided for in Proclamation No. 86/1997) to a maximum of 15 per cent on all forecasts.

## Comparison of results from various forecast methodologies for the requirement of engineers in EEPCO

Figure 9.2 illustrates the number of engineers required in EEPCO for the years 1996, 2005 and 2010, based on the three methods of estimation. The ideal manning forecast (based on the ideal utility requirements) appears to represent the lowest demand scenario. It should be noted that the indices on which the ideal forecast is based do not encompass the effect of the size of electricity transmission and distribution infrastructure on manpower requirements. EEPCO's manpower requirements would be overestimated if the ideal utility were located in a small, densely populated country. In contrast, load centres and power plants in Ethiopia are thinly spread over a large territorial area. This, to some extent, could explain the high forecast in the reference deployment scenario. On the other hand, the division of labour among the present stock of engineers

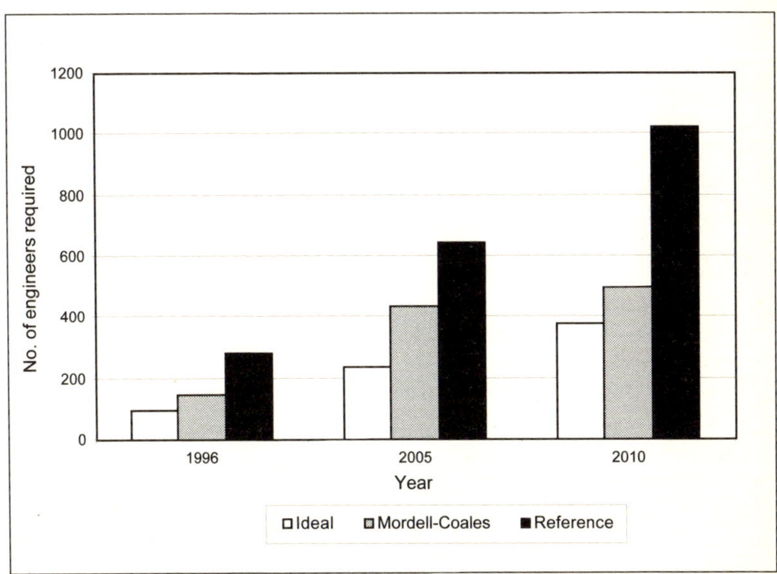


Figure 9.2  Comparison of demand forecasts for engineers in EEPCO

and other professionals in EEPCO is probably not optimized. In actual fact, a few engineers carry the bulk of the workload in the utility. It is likely that fewer engineers could manage if the workload was distributed more evenly.

As shown earlier using the ideal forecast, the annual incremental demand for engineers from the year 2001 onwards would be about 30. This translates into a national-level demand of 600 engineers per year, if it is assumed that EEPCO's present share of about 5 per cent of the national total will continue to apply in the future. This level of national demand for engineers tallies closely with the annual incremental demand of 545 engineers for the period 1995–2010 estimated previously using the method adopted by Mordell and Coales. Meeting this level of demand, as we shall see below, would imply a tripling of the current level of annual graduates in engineering.

## Supply of graduates

The number of graduates from the Faculty of Business and Economics and the Faculty of Technology of the Addis Ababa University (AAU) is shown in Table 9.11 (page 134). For engineers, in particular, the present level of output of about 150 engineers from the local universities cannot match the forecast annual national demand of about 600 engineers. The national-level demand for accountants and economists is also high and the supply from these institutions is not expected to meet the demand. As for foreign universities, in the fields of technology and social sciences there were only six and thirteen graduates, respectively, from this source in the academic year 1995/6 (Ministry of Education, 1997).

The alternative of increasing the supply of graduates from the various faculties and departments at AAU faces the following constraints:

*Faculty of Technology*
The critical bottlenecks in increasing the number of engineering graduates can be identified as follows:

1  Limited number of pre-engineering students at the second-year level; this consists of about 240 regular students and 30 continuing education (or evening) students.

2  Lack of laboratory facilities that restrict electrical engineering students to about 50, and civil and mechanical engineering students to about 100 and 70 respectively. The laboratory facilities were designed to handle a maximum number of 20 to 25 students per laboratory session, and aging equipment and measurement systems have only partially been replaced (or strengthened).

3  Lack of teaching staff, due to the fact that many PhD graduates in electrical engineering have not returned to their posts after acquiring their degrees abroad. Presently the staff consists of seven PhD, five MSc and three BSc graduates, barely adequate to sustain the courses offered.

4  Lack of library facilities, especially new books and technical journals, due to the inability of the AAU to keep abreast of the latest publications because of budgetary limitations in hard currency, a problem that has remained severe since the 1980s.

*Faculty of Business and Economics*
The problems of shortage of teaching staff and other constraints on increasing enrolment size are prominent in both the Department of Accounting and the Department of Economics.

DEPARTMENT OF ACCOUNTING
As at 1997, the Department of Accounting had a weak staff profile with a total of 14 lecturers, including two foreigners. Seven held MA and five BA degrees. There were no PhD graduates among the Ethiopian teaching staff. The Department faced a serious problem of staff shortage as it could not attract and retain qualified accountants.

Part-time lecturers were engaged in courses that otherwise would have been undertaken by permanent staff. Part-time lecturers, however, are not as effective since they are engaged in their own regular work. Retired professionals are not interested because of the low level of remuneration.

In the 1980s students were admitted to the Department of Accounting through a central quota system. The intake to the second-year class was centrally imposed and the number of students at that level was 120. The available number of teaching staff could not meet the lecturing load this imposed.

In 1995, the intake was reduced by 50 per cent. In 1995/6 the Department accepted 70 students and it was envisaged that by 1996/7 there would be two sections with 40 students in each, bringing the total number of students to 80. Adjustment in enrolment size is needed in order to match the capacity of the Department with the available teaching staff and facilities.

DEPARTMENT OF ECONOMICS
This Department also faces shortages in teaching staff, mainly because most of the staff do not return once they go abroad for training. Most of the staff who take sabbatical or research leave also fail to return. The Department cannot retain its staff owing to delayed promotions, lack of staff development programmes, low remuneration, lack of fringe benefits, inadequate health services and housing problems. All these missing incentives are provided by institutions in other sectors of the economy.

**Table 9.11** Tertiary-level enrolment and graduation for selected faculties in Addis Ababa University (academic years 1993/4 and 1995/6)

| Faculty/Department | Enrolment* | | | Graduation | | |
|---|---|---|---|---|---|---|
| | 1 | 2 | 3 | 1 | 2 | 3 |
| *Faculty of Technology* | | | | | | |
| Civil Engineering | – | 3 | 5 | 6 | – | 1 |
| Electrical Engineering | – | | 3 | 33 | 18 | 2 |
| Mechanical Engineering | – | | – | 32 | 5 | – |
| Chemical Engineering | – | – | – | 18 | – | – |
| Total for 1995/6 | 211 | 757 | 6 | 149 | 23 | 3 |
| Corresponding total for 1993/4 | 210 | 690 | 9 | 123 | 28 | 1 |
| *Faculty of Business and Economics* | | | | | | |
| Accounting | 68 | 652 | – | 76 | 63 | – |
| Economics | 63 | 530 | – | 32 | 33 | – |
| Management and Administration | 89 | 590 | – | 47 | 40 | – |
| Economic Policy & Planning & HRE** | – | – | 22 | – | – | 16 |
| Total for 1995/6 | 220 | 1772 | 22 | 155 | 136 | 16 |
| Corresponding total for 1993/94 | 258 | 815 | 16 | 286 | 141 | 13 |

1   Undergraduate, regular degree programme for day students
2   Undergraduate extension programme
3   Postgraduate programme
* Enrolment at first or second year, as appropriate, except for extension programme where the enrolment figures are for all classes (which range from first to eighth years)
** Human Resources Economics
Source: Ministry of Education, 1995; Ministry of Education, 1997

In the 1980s, enrolment in the second-year Economics class was 80–100, but this has reduced to about 50. As mentioned earlier, student placement was centrally decided and imposed irrespective of the intake capacity of the Department. With students being given freedom to choose their field of study, there is a noted shift in enrolment from economics to other fields.

This section has concentrated on examining the adequacy of the current supply of graduates from Addis Ababa University. The next section will review the effectiveness of EEPCO's internal training programme in meeting the utility's need for trained technicians and engineers.

## EEPCO training school's capacity to meet internal training needs

EEPCO has been running a training school since 1961. The school is part of the Human Resources Development Department in EEPCO. The Department is responsible for manpower planning and training. Most of the training at the EEPCO training school is local, with overseas training being offered to candidates who are selected by a training committee. The school has the following major programmes:

- Full-time training for prospective technicians.

- On-the-job training for employees.

*Full-time training for prospective technicians*
Entrants to the full-time programme are graduates of vocational/technical or secondary schools. For vocational/technical school graduates, the training lasts only 3–6 months. For secondary school leavers, the training takes 1–2 years. The duration of training has largely been dictated by the urgent demand for technicians. The training given to all candidates is identical in content, but the shorter the duration the more condensed the course. Graduates of the two-year programme are awarded diplomas whereas the 3–6 month programmes receive certificate accreditation. The six-month training programme has an average annual intake of 100 trainees.

The technical training programme covers major fields such as electrical generation, transmission, distribution, vehicle maintenance, electrical and mechanical workshop technology, civil construction and computer operation and maintenance. Full-time trainees also receive on-the-job training intermittently in management and supervisory skills. Skills improvement training is also offered, intermittently, for personnel employed in administrative, financial, supply and secretarial services.

The school's teaching facilities include the following:

- Classrooms for basic electromechanical theory and mechanical drawing.

- Laboratories for training in electrical instruments, electrical machines and power system protection.

- Workshops for electrical wiring, overhead distribution lines, underground cabling, welding, transformer testing, machine parts production, sheet metal technology and diesel engine maintenance.

- Simulation rooms for power station and substation operations.

There are 14 instructors with work experience ranging from 3–30 years, who teach on a permanent basis. Other instructors, currently working in various departments within EEPCO, can also be called upon as required.

*On-the-job training for employees*
Data provided by EEPCO on training activities for 1996/7 indicate that 91 professionals, 206 semi-professionals and 20 non-professionals went through the various on-the-job training programmes at EEPCO's training school (Table 9.12).

It should be noted that the training provided at the EEPCO training

**Table 9.12 On-the-job training activities in EEPCO, 1996/7**

| Areas of training | Total duration of training | No. of trainees by area of service | | No. of trainees by qualification | |
|---|---|---|---|---|---|
| | | Technical | Admin. and support services | Pro-fessionals | Semi-professionals |
| Management for branch managers | 1 month | – | 25 | 1 | 24 |
| Basic management concepts and function | 5 days | – | 34 | 12 | 22 |
| Computer operation and maintenance | 2 months | – | 136 | 47 | 89 |
| Electrical inspection | NA | 47 | – | 4 | 43 |
| Meter reading | NA | – | 17 | – | 17 |
| Budget control | NA | – | 33 | 22 | 11 |
| Internal auditing | NA | – | 1 | 1 | – |
| Purchasing | NA | – | 1 | 1 | – |
| Financial management | NA | – | 3 | 3 | – |
| Total | | 47 | 250 | 91 | 206 |

NA – Information not available
Source: EEPCO, 1996

school for professionals does not address the skill gaps indicated earlier in Table 9.7, especially with respect to engineering tasks. Such skill gaps are partly filled by overseas training. Data for 1995/6, provided by EEPCO, indicates that about 16 engineers pursued overseas training courses lasting between one month and two years. The courses included:

- hydropower development;
- energy and environment;
- electrical distribution;
- power systems operations;
- geothermal energy technology.

COUNTERPARTING/ 'TWINNING' SCHEMES
Apart from classroom lectures in EEPCO's training centre, attachment of counterpart staff to project consultants or contractors can assist skills

development. EEPCO has an ongoing training programme with Danube Hydro, Austria. The training covers managerial skills development as well as skills for hydro plant maintenance. The courses are offered for on-the-job trainees, partly in Ethiopia and partly in Austria.

In the past, there was a well-established practice in EEPCO of sending engineers, technicians and managerial staff abroad for attachment to companies that manufacture and assemble generation equipment. This practice is no longer common. If counterparting were incorporated in the definition and preparation of new technical or managerial projects, technology and skills transfer would be guaranteed. This is especially important for fresh graduates who would have the opportunity to do their in-service training on actual projects. Areas where counterparting would be important are applications of electrical and civil engineering in planning feasibility studies and designs, construction works involving the latest technologies and machinery, the operation of advanced computer and engineering systems, and basic and advanced management skills.

*Upgrading the EEPCO training school*
In the 1980s there was a major initiative to upgrade the EEPCO training school to an 'Electrical and Electronics Institute' catering for the needs of EEPCO, the Telecommunications Authority and other similar government institutions that largely depend on electrical equipment and machinery for the execution of their primary duties. The initiative secured government support, although it was feared that the efforts of the new Institution would overlap with the mandate of the Addis Ababa University. A large complex, consisting of classrooms, a library, dormitories and a dining hall was built for the upgrading. As a result of higher-level decisions, however, the complex now houses a Civil Services College, which is unrelated to the EEPCO training school.

Although the Faculty of Technology at Addis Ababa University is, in theory, expected to be equipped with facilities that offer practical courses to its students, this is not the case. The University and the 'Electrical and Electronics Institute' could complement each other: the University's strength resting on the theoretical aspects and the Institute's strength lying in practical, hands-on experience. The Institute could be open to the public as well, with short-term practical training offered to those with the necessary level of technical education. It is also possible that university graduates would make use of such training because of its practical emphasis.

Singapore's Nangyang Technological Institute (NTI) was established in 1981, in spite of the presence of the Faculty of Engineering at the National University of Singapore. The rationale for its establishment was the need to produce practice-oriented engineers (Selvaratnam, 1994). The NTI has since developed into a fully-fledged university.

The next section will discuss the retention of skills. As previously noted, EEPCO faces difficulties in retaining its skilled professionals.

## Retention and capacity mobilization

The effective use of manpower requires the retention of trained manpower. It also requires the proper utilization of individual as well as group capacity in carrying out utility tasks. Sourced from the questionnaire responses obtained from 13 departments in EELPA in June 1996, the number of professional staff who resigned from the utility between June 1994 and June 1996 is shown in Table 9.13.

**Table 9.13  Professional staff mobility in EELPA (1994–6)**

| Department | Number of professional staff resigned from departments* | Number of professional staff who resigned from the utility |
| --- | --- | --- |
| Addis Ababa Region | 11 | 1 |
| Construction | 29 | 13 |
| Engineering | 26 | 15 |
| Finance | 15 | 9 |
| Operations | 20 | 8 |
| Special Services | 6 | 6 |
| Others | None | None |
| Total | 107 | 52 |

* Out of the total number, some quit the departments to transfer to other departments within the utility; others left the utility altogether
Source: EELPA, 1996

Thus, the average number of professionals leaving the utility annually is about 26. This translates to a professional staff turnover ratio of 7.9 per cent, on the basis of the total number of 330 professionals in 1997. On the departmental level, the ratio is about 16 per cent. The staff turnover ratio for the utility as a whole (for professionals, semi-professionals and non-professionals) is shown in Table 9.14.

**Table 9.14  Staff turnover ratio for EELPA/EEPCO**

| Year | Number of staff who resigned from the utility | Total number of employees | Staff turnover ratio, % |
| --- | --- | --- | --- |
| 1994 | 405 | 8377 | 4.8 |
| 1995 | 326 | 8414 | 3.9 |
| 1996 | 471 | 8247 | 5.7 |

Source: EELPA, 1996

The number of professionals freshly recruited in the last two years (1996/7) was 18, all from Addis Ababa University. This is lower than the lower attrition rate of 26 professionals per year. Thus, the utility is probably losing the best of its workforce with an overall degradation in the quality of its manpower. Appropriate retention mechanisms are needed to arrest the exodus of professional staff.

In contrast, the number of engineers in EELPA/EEPCO in 1996 stood at double the figure predicted by an ideal manning level for a utility. Although there may be genuine country-specific reasons for this disparity, it is an overall indication of problems in the proper utilization of the professional and technical staff in the utility. Either all the engineers are underutilized, or some are overburdened. Our observations support the latter case.

# 10

## Policy Recommendations

From the previous discussion, it is clear that capacity building in Ethiopia's power sector is faced with the following major challenges:

- A major gap between the supply and demand for professionals in the foreseeable future.

- A need to upgrade the skills of current staff in the electricity industry.

- An urgent need for management and structural reforms that will ensure the retention of skilled professionals.

To address the above challenges, this study proposes the following recommendations:

1 Resolve enrolment capacity constraints for engineering students at the Faculty of Technology, Addis Ababa University.

2 Review the curricula for energy (especially electrical energy) training at the tertiary level of education to ensure relevance to market demand.

3 Revitalize and strengthen EEPCO's training centre for technicians.

4 Improve EEPCO's pay level and incentives system to attract and retain professionals.

5 Institute national-level manpower planning in Ethiopia.

## Resolve enrolment capacity constraints for engineering students in the Faculty of Technology, Addis Ababa University

When it was established nearly 30 years ago, the Faculty of Technology appeared to possess excessive capacity. First, the classrooms, drawing rooms, laboratories and workshops were considered to be sufficient to meet growing enrolment for many years. Due to a relatively low enrolment that rarely exceeded 400 students, the facilities were rarely fully utilized. Second, prospective students were encouraged to join the Faculty with less stringent entrance requirements, provided they had the interest and aptitude to go through a relatively rigorous academic programme. In addition, graduates of technical institutes were enrolled after completing the necessary courses in mathematics, physics and technical drawing.

Gradually, the facilities were also made available to evening students for pre-engineering and diploma courses. However, within a period of ten years after its establishment, acute constraints in capacity began to appear. It therefore became necessary to set a ceiling on the intake capacity for the Faculty at a maximum enrolment of about 1,100 students.

The annual intake into the Faculty for BSc studies currently stands at around 240–245 students, with the following approximate distribution:

| | |
|---|---|
| Civil Engineering | 90 |
| Electrical Engineering | 55 |
| Mechanical Engineering | 40 |
| Chemical Engineering | 30 |
| Architect & Town Planning | 30 |

This enrolment level has to be increased to meet demand for engineers in the country at large, and in the power sector in particular. Various estimates in the preceding sections point to the need to triple this level of intake (and corresponding output level of graduates). One way of achieving a higher output of graduates is by increasing enrolment at the Faculty of Technology in the AAU.

An increase in enrolment in the Faculty of Technology would imply increasing the number of classrooms, laboratories and other facilities. For example, a 50 per cent increase over the present enrolment of 1,100 students would require about 16 more classrooms, four additional laboratories for Civil, Electrical, Mechanical and Chemical Engineering, a new library and one more workshop to be built. In addition, except for a modest computer centre with old processors, the Faculty lacks proper and up-to-date computer facilities.

The total floor area requirement for such infrastructure would be about 1,600 square metres. Building such infrastructure would cost an estimated Birr 2.4 million. Furnishing classrooms and equipping laboratories and workshops would cost a further Birr 2.5 million, giving a total capital outlay of Birr 4.9 million. Preliminary calculations also indicate that the increase in recurrent budget allocation resulting from a 50 per cent increase in enrolment at the Faculty of Technology could amount to as much as Birr 2 million per year.

There are plans to set up four new universities in various regional locations. These universities will have Colleges of Engineering catering for engineering/technology subjects (ENA, 1998; personal communications). Assuming that these colleges will contain departments of Electrical, Civil and Mechanical Engineering, the number of engineering graduates from each college could be as many as 60 per year. This would be a 140 per cent increase over the current number of engineering graduates. This is, therefore, an attractive alternative to increasing the enrolment level at the Faculty of Technology in the AAU.

## Review the curricula for energy (especially electrical energy) training at the tertiary level of education to ensure relevance to market demand

The only dependable source of trained manpower for the power sector is the continued enrolment of engineering students in technical institutions of higher learning. In Ethiopia, there are currently nine establishments engaged in the teaching of engineering courses, covering agricultural engineering, mining engineering, industrial engineering, urban planning and architecture, as well as the standard programmes in civil, electrical, mechanical and chemical engineering. The Faculty of Technology, AAU, is the oldest technical institution, currently offering the following six standard programmes:

- Electrical Engineering (Senior Diploma, BSc and MSc);
- Civil Engineering (Senior Diploma, BSc and MSc);
- Mechanical Engineering (Senior Diploma and BSc);
- Chemical Engineering (BSc);
- Architecture and Town Planning (BSc);
- Building Technology (Senior Diploma).

The programmes, which were introduced in 1969, have to date undergone no change except for the introduction of computer courses. The viability or usefulness of the programmes have been challenged in many instances. Successful graduates are adequately prepared theoretically to join any employing organization interested in recruiting all-round electrical engineers. There is a missing link, however, between theoretical lessons offered at the University and practical experience. The University must create a firm link with major employers and familiarize its students with actual practical expertise in the employing industries.

EEPCO could suggest changes and improvements in the existing curricula. While an academic programme of study is not intended to produce skilled civil, electrical or mechanical engineers, there should be openings for the improvement of courses that were last revised in the early 1980s. Such changes would benefit both the Faculty of Technology and EEPCO. It is also likely that EEPCO's engineers could enrol in the revised MSc programmes (on a part-time basis) in the departments of Civil and Electrical Engineering.

# Revitalize and strengthen EEPCO's training centre for technicians

The *raison d'être* for EEPCO's training centre is established on the following set of premises:

1 It is essential that technical/vocational school graduates with a general knowledge of electrical theory and practice undergo orientation on electricity generation, transmission and distribution.

2 It is not possible to meet EEPCO's demand for technicians by recruiting technical/vocational school graduates alone. EEPCO needs to recruit additional secondary school graduates who undergo a longer duration of training.

3 On-the-job training has to be given to employees at all levels for upgrading of skills.

It is unlikely that the role of EEPCO's training centre will change in the foreseeable future, even with the restructuring of EEPCO. Thus the training centre needs to be equipped adequately in terms of teaching facilities and instructors.

The issue of upgrading the training centre to an Electrical and Electronics Institute (EEI), however, requires deeper reassessment. A UNDP evaluation mission treated this issue at considerable depth in 1993 (UNDP, 1993). The mission's objective was to assess the achievements of the preparatory phase of the project and make recommendations with respect to the actual start-up of operations of the EEI. At the time of the mission's visit, about 80 per cent of the infrastructure for the Institute was already in place. A UNDP grant of about US$700,000 was already approved and expended by the end of 1992.

The Institute's training scope would be centred on training high-level technicians in the fields of electric power and electronics. Trainees would have exposure to basic components of electrical systems and electronic equipment. They would develop the capacity to operate, assemble, modify and adapt such equipment. To this end, the Institute would have to be equipped with up-to-date training facilities. A twinning arrangement could be made with reputable technical institutions abroad, in order to sustain the quality of training. The scheme would benefit EEPCO, the telecommunications industry and the aviation industry. Trainees with appropriate pre-qualifications could be drawn from public and private sector entities.

The mission raised the important question of whether or not to place the Institute under EEPCO or within the Ministry of Education. It appears that the mission was ultimately convinced that although the Ministry of Education seemed the appropriate location for the Institute, it would not be possible to run the Institute without the financial support of EEPCO.

An alternative option was that EEPCO could run the EEI on commercial principles by charging a training fee to cover all costs. However, this would not strictly be within the mandate of EEPCO, which is primarily established to supply electricity. Under the circumstances, the best alternative was to place the EEI under the Ministry of Education. Under such a scenario, EEPCO would still have the option to run its low-level technical training courses in its present training centre. The budgetary implications of running the Institute would be substantial for the Ministry of Education, but they can be eased through assistance from donors and by charging trainees a nominal fee.

It is expected that the classrooms, laboratory, library, office, dormitory and building infrastructure that are already in place, but currently house the Civil Service College, would be returned to the EEI if and when the policy decision is taken to revitalize the Institute. Similarly, the bulk of the teaching equipment, worth about US$0.5 million and purchased prior to 1993, is expected to be available to the EEI. The Institute's curriculum has already been worked out. Major budgetary requirements would be in the areas of training instructors (numbering about 50), the purchase of additional equipment and the actual running of the Institute. Indications are that an additional amount of about US$5 million would be required for training instructors and additional equipment.

## Improve EEPCO's pay level and incentives system to attract and retain professionals

Prior to 1991, there were at least three factors that contributed to high retention rates for professionals in government institutions:

- Very few private sector ventures employed professionals.

- Stringent control with regard to releasing employees.

- Individual workers were not laid off on grounds of inefficiency or restructuring of government institutions.

In the context of the new economic policy built on market principles, these factors are no longer valid. Professionals are often offered better opportunities in the private sector. Obtaining release from government institutions has become a simple formality. At the same time, government institutions are no longer a haven for idleness, with a little effort just to keep routine tasks going. The present threat of lay-offs is likely to continue as a wave of restructuring sweeps across government institutions.

These new realities are pushing experienced professionals to the private sector. Government institutions are thus faced with the challenge of competing with the private sector in terms of pay and other incentives in order to retain their professional staff.

EEPCO's salary level for professionals is not particularly low in comparison to other government institutions in the country. Its board of management approves salary increases from time to time, based on the financial performance of the utility. Pay increases are not automatic, however, in any given year.

In comparison, the Ethiopian Petroleum Enterprise (EPE) has a board of directors that approves salary increases rather more predictably, although they are subject to the enterprise making profit in the previous year. The EPE is also composed of professional staff who previously worked at the Assab refinery, where they were paid higher salaries to compensate for the harsher working environment (the Assab refinery was located in a remote part of what is now Eritrea). EPE salary levels are, therefore, relatively higher than those of EEPCO. In a typical government ministry such as the Ministry of Economic Development and Cooperation (MEDAC), the Civil Service Commission controls the salary scale. The salary levels are low but more predictable. Figure 10.1 compares the salary levels at EEPCO, MEDAC and EPE.

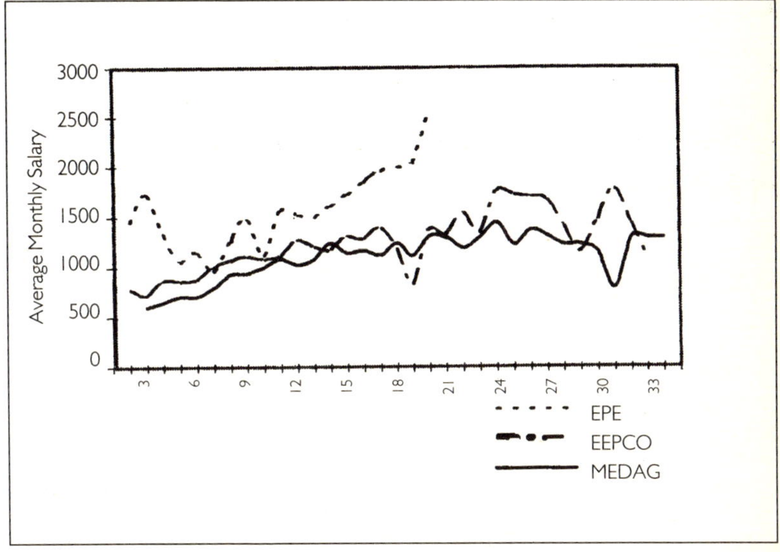


Figure 10.1  Average monthly salary for professionals

Migration of EEPCO staff would mainly be to EPE or to the private sector, where typically the pay level would be double that of EEPCO. Attempts have to be made to narrow the salary gap between EEPCO and the private sector. The financial impact of such measures is not expected to be very significant for EEPCO, because the wage bill for the professional workers is only about 7 per cent of the wage bill for EEPCO employees as a whole. For public enterprises like EEPCO and EPE, which operate under a state-controlled price regime, it is not appropriate to link salary increases to profit levels. Rather, the use of pre-set salary scales that can be revised from time to time is more applicable. Performance requirements can then be imposed on the employees as prerequisites for moving up the salary scale.

## Institute national-level manpower planning in Ethiopia

Manpower planning alleviates the problem of discrepancy between the demand and supply of manpower at various levels. It helps to identify gaps and to develop training schemes. It generates information on the utilization of trained manpower at regional and sectoral levels.

In Ethiopia's new economic policy, the private sector has been given a major economic role to play and greater decision-making powers have been given to regional governments. It is assumed that the private sector will become a major employer. In this setting, the institution of national manpower planning becomes a complex matter.

Central ministries are responsible for setting standards and for providing technical assistance to regional governments, which have their sectoral bureaux for planning and implementing development activities, including manpower planning. Although the regional planning bureau is responsible for planning activities within a region, its assumption of manpower planning tasks presupposes the existence of capacity for such duties. Therefore, the availability of skilled and qualified personnel to undertake manpower planning and labour market information tasks should be given priority. The government should entrust manpower and labour questions to national agencies until regions develop the required capacity. In the long-run, however, regions should assume the task of manpower planning both at regional and sectoral levels.

Manpower planning should be recognized as part of the medium- and long-term development plan of the country. The responsibility of guiding, streamlining, prioritizing and integrating the development plans of various sectors lies with the Ministry of Economic Development and Cooperation (MEDAC). However, MEDAC is neither expected nor adequately equipped to carry out planning on its own for any sector. It only reprocesses initial plans presented to it by line ministries.

Drawing the parallel with other sectors of the economy, a Department of Manpower Planning at the Ministry of Labour and Social Affairs, coupled with a similar department at MEDAC, should be established to ensure proper planning of manpower. The inputs of the Ministry of Education, representing the supply side, and the Federal Civil Service Commission and Employers Federation, representing the demand side for manpower planning, are vital. At the national level, The Ministry of Economic Development and Cooperation should continue to assume the task of overall manpower planning even after regions have gained manpower planning capacity in their local contexts.

Staff training for national manpower planners can be undertaken through seminars, workshops and other relevant technical meetings, and through international fellowships. The skills needed for national manpower planning personnel relate largely to the ability to analyze different sets of data. The training should be in the relevant disciplines such as labour economics, labour statistics, manpower planning, computer science and other macro-economic aspects, such as employment and wages.

It is proposed that national manpower planning be undertaken within the existing institutions, with MEDAC as a coordinating organ responsible for overall planning activities. This will save resources that would otherwise have to be used for the creation of new institutions and placement of staff. The existing staff could have their skills upgraded through the staff development programmes mentioned earlier. The recurrent budget to be allocated for staff salaries, transportation, fuel, allowances, per diem, stationery, telephone and sundry costs will depend on the level of expansion of the manpower planning and coordinating organs.

# Part IV Appendices

Part IV Appendix 1 Selected time series data, Ethiopia (table and figures)

Table IVA.1.1 Selected time series data, Ethiopia

| Ethiopia | 1991 | 1992 | 1993 | 1994 | 1995 | 1996 | 1997 | 1998 | 1999 | 2000 |
|---|---|---|---|---|---|---|---|---|---|---|
| Population (millions) | 48.8 | 50.2 | 51.6 | 53.1 | 54.6 | 56.4 | 58.1 | 59.9 | 61.7 | 63.5 |
| GDP (US$ million) | 5360 | 5197 | 5920 | 4545 | 5026 | 5543 | 5875 | 6028 | 6003 | 6230 |
| GDP growth rate (%) | −4.4 | −3.5 | 12.4 | 2.0 | 6.0 | 10.0 | 6.0 | 2.6 | 0.0 | 3.8 |
| GNP *per capita* (US$) | | 110 | 120 | 100 | 100 | 100 | 110.7 | 115 | 115 | |
| Electrification levels (%) | | | | | | | | | | |
| National | 10.26 | 10.54 | 10.82 | 11.10 | 11.60 | 11.94 | 12.24 | 12.52 | 12.87 | 13.00 |
| Urban | 10.13 | 10.41 | 10.68 | 10.94 | 11.41 | 11.76 | 12.08 | 12.36 | 12.70 | 12.83 |
| Rural | 0.13 | 0.13 | 0.14 | 0.16 | 0.19 | 0.18 | 0.16 | 0.16 | 0.17 | 0.17 |
| Installed capacity (MW) | 407 | 407 | 409 | 417 | 417 | 417 | 417 | 420 | 420 | 420 |
| Electricity generation (GWh) | 1129 | 1147 | 1278 | 1389 | 1470 | 1554 | 1604 | 1610 | 1650 | 1670 |
| System losses (%) | 16 | 15 | 19 | 19 | 19 | 18 | 18 | 16 | 19 | 17 |
| Number of customers | 400785 | 428841 | 450634 | 472912 | 499552 | 519105 | 535606 | 551790 | 574400 | 594400 |
| Number of employees | 7861 | 8269 | 8207 | 8377 | 8414 | 8247 | 8353 | 8361 | 8205 | 8200 |
| Number of customers/ employee | 51 | 52 | 55 | 56 | 59 | 63 | 64 | 66 | 70 | 72 |
| Debt collection period (days) | 90 | 90 | 90 | 90 | 90 | 90 | 50 | 45 | 45 | 45 |
| Average electricity tariffs (US cents/kWh) | 9.8 | 7 | 4.1 | 4 | 3.9 | 4.1 | 4.6 | 4.4 | 5.6 | 5.1 |
| Profit/loss (million US$) | 7.73 | −8.00 | 17.00 | 11.40 | 2.67 | 7.59 | 11.42 | 33.76 | 54.61 | 19.42 |
| No. of employees/installed capacity | 19 | 20 | 20 | 20 | 20 | 20 | 20 | 20 | 20 | 20 |
| Electricity generated per employee (GWh) | 0.14 | 0.14 | 0.16 | 0.17 | 0.17 | 0.19 | 0.19 | 0.19 | 0.20 | 0.20 |

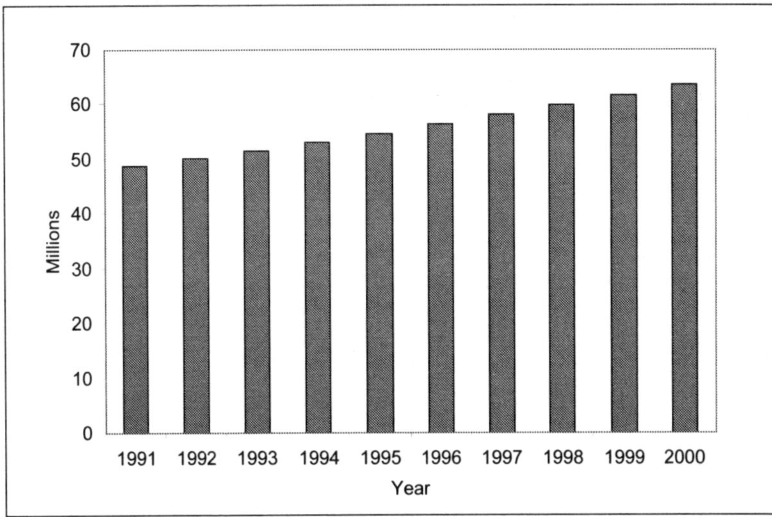

Figure IVA.1.1  Ethiopia: Population, 1991–2000 (millions)

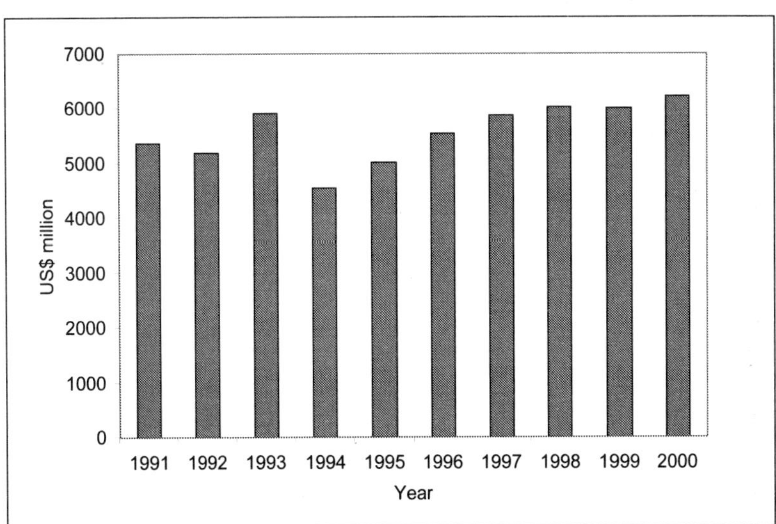

Figure IVA.1.2  Gross domestic product, 1991–2000 (US$ million)

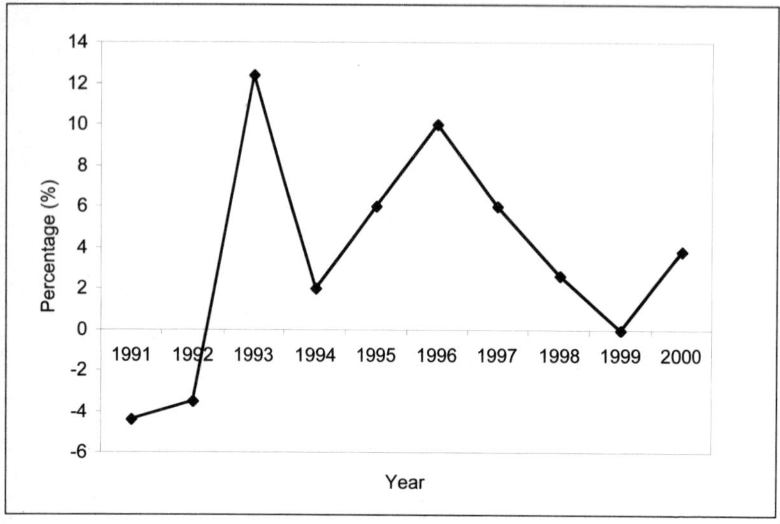

Figure IVA.1.3  GDP growth rate, 1991–2000 (%)

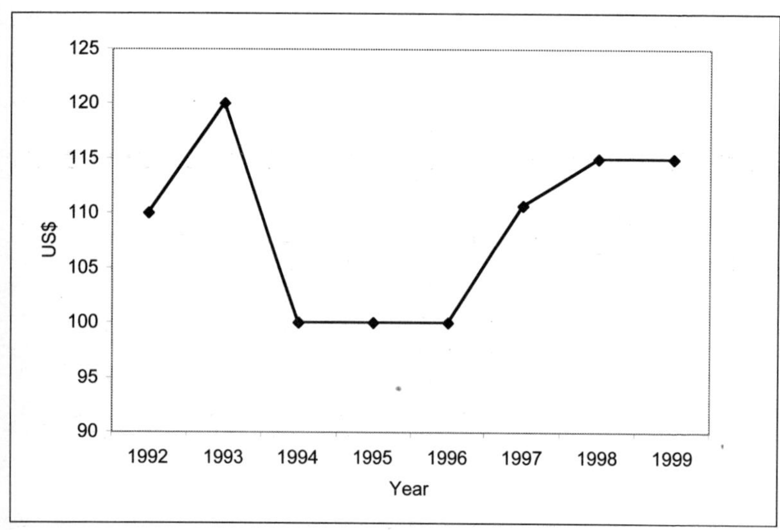

Figure IVA.1.4  GNP *per capita*, 1992–9 (US$)

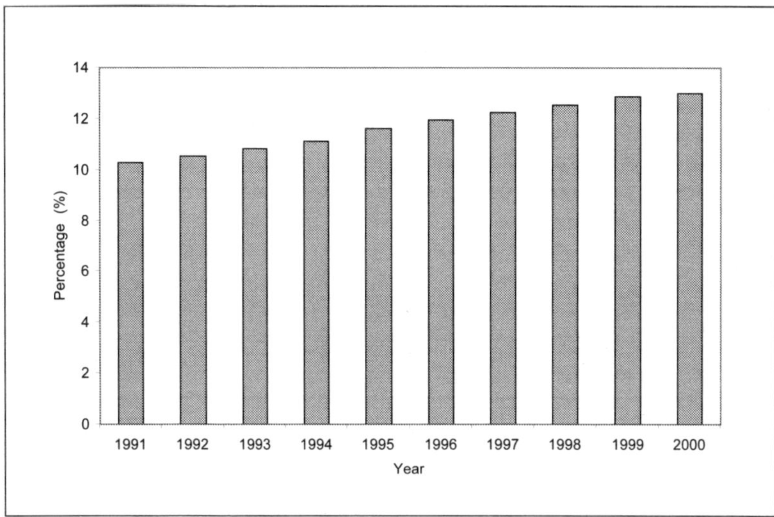

Figure IVA.1.5  National electrification levels, 1991–2000 (%)

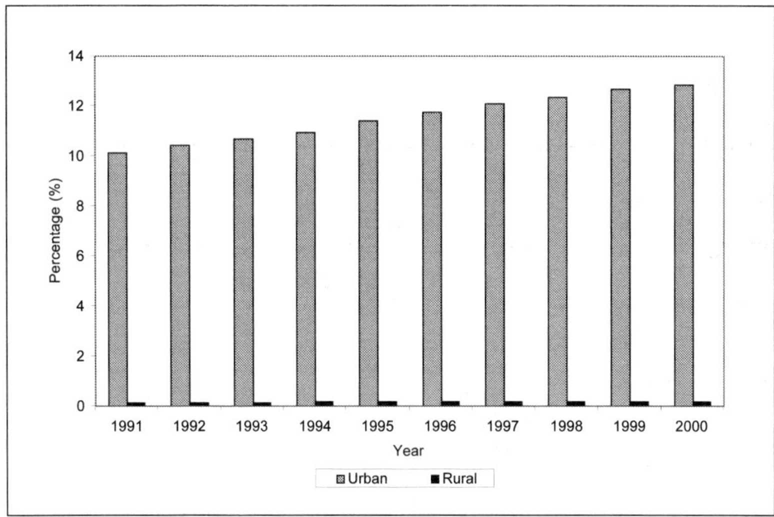



Figure IVA.1.6  Urban and rural electrification levels, 1991–2000 (%)

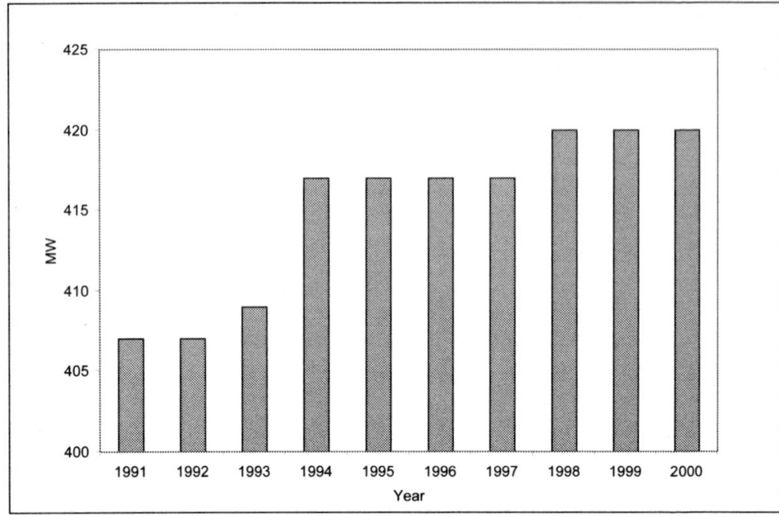

Figure IVA.1.7  Installed capacity, 1991–2000 (MW)

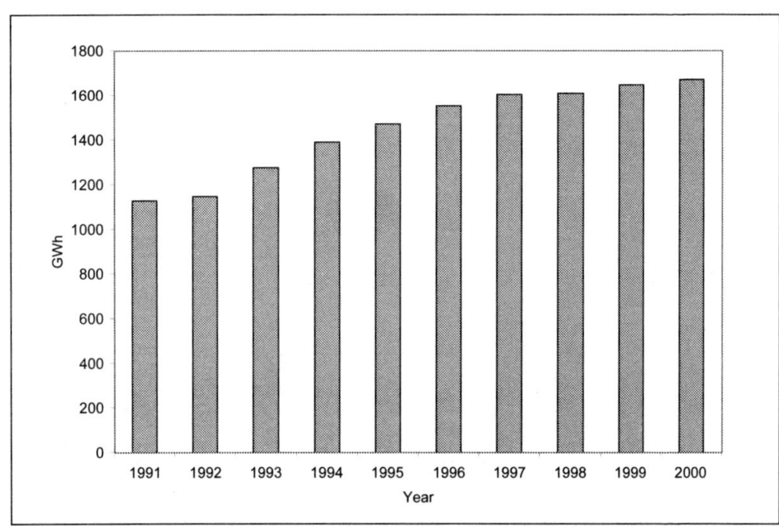

Figure IVA.1.8  Electricity generation, 1991–2000 (GWh)

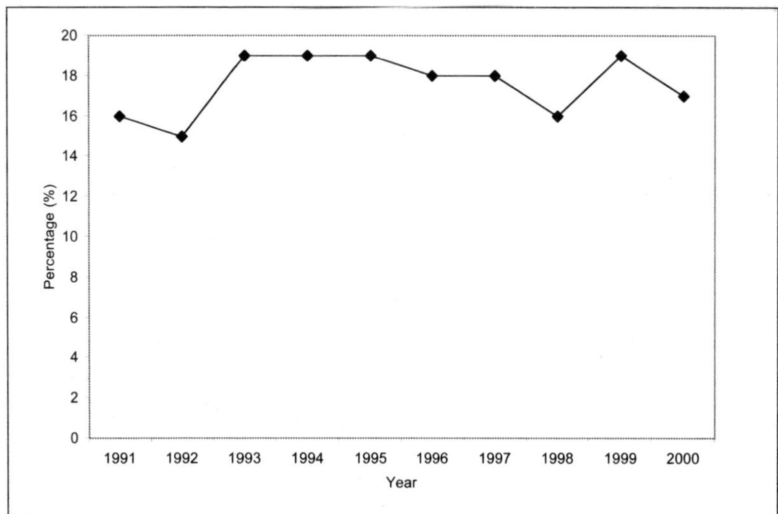

Figure IVA.1.9  System losses, 1991–2000 (%)

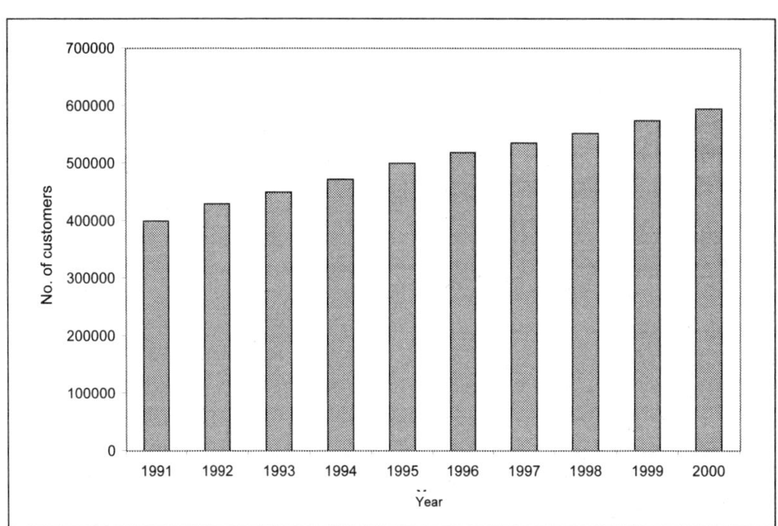

Figure IVA.1.10  Number of customers, 1991–2000

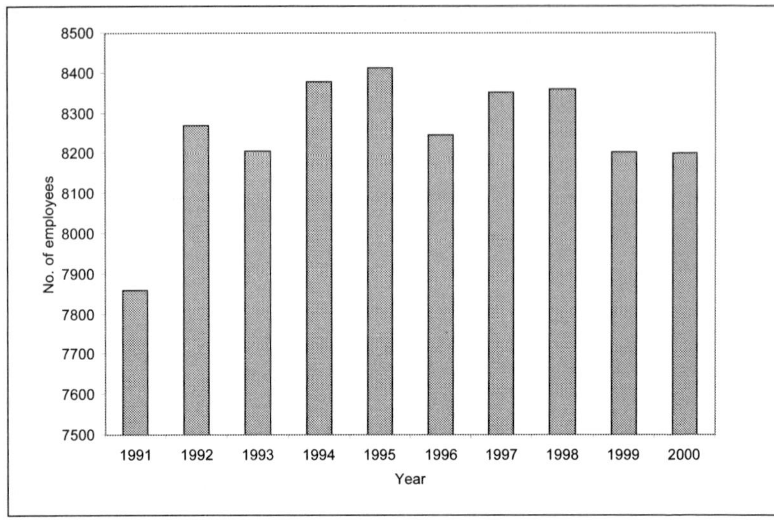

Figure IVA.1.11  Number of employees, 1991–2000

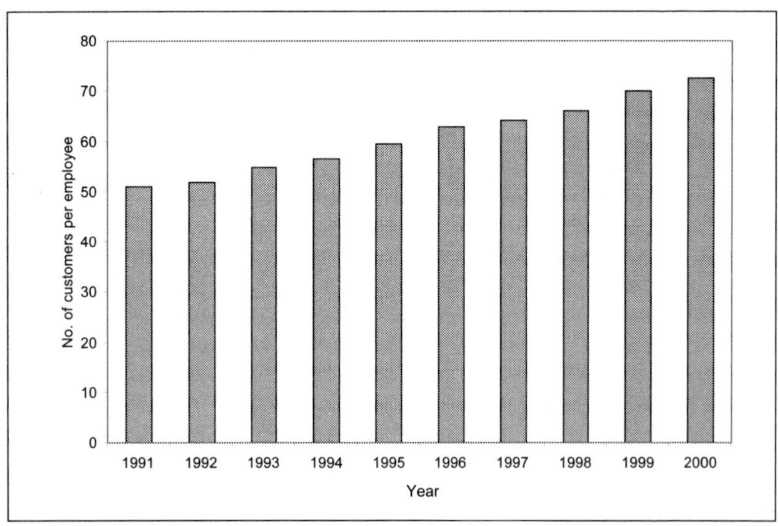

Figure IVA.1.12  Number of customers per employee, 1991–2000

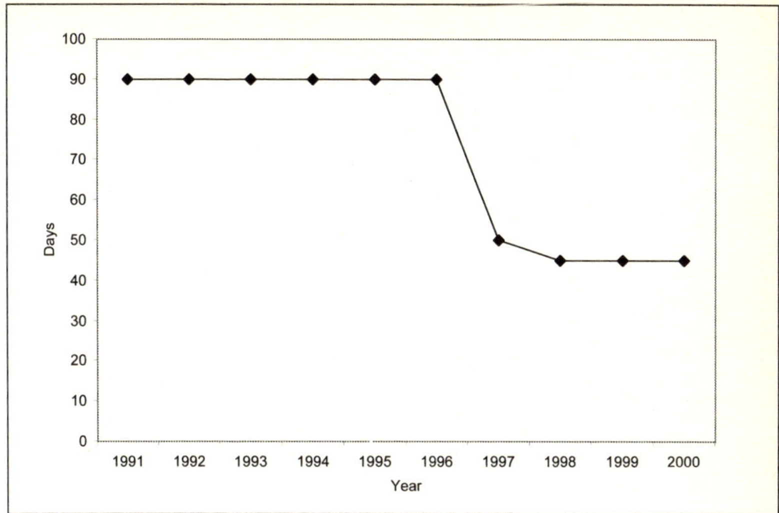

Figure IVA.1.13   Debt collection period, 1991–2000 (days)

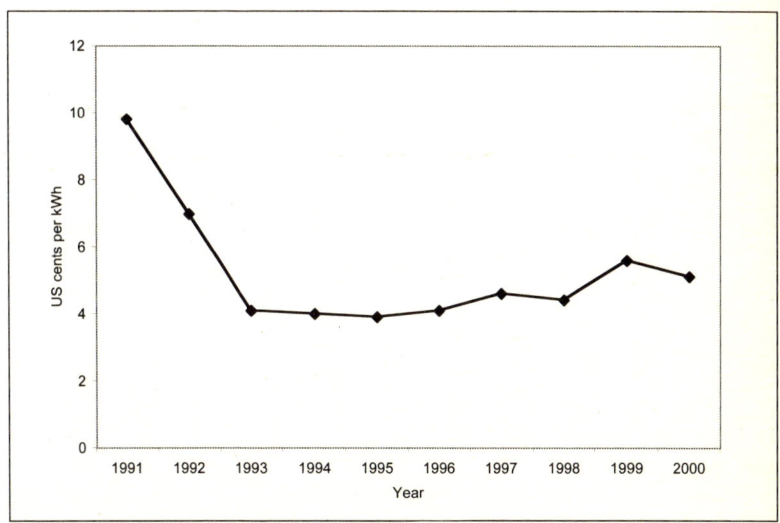

Figure IVA.1.14  Average electricity tariffs, 1991–2000 (US cents per kWh)

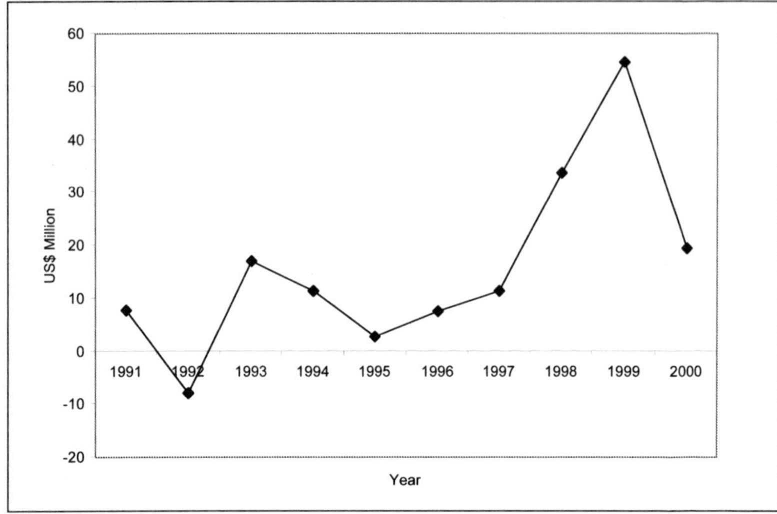

Figure IVA.1.15  Profits/losses, 1991–2000 (US$ million)

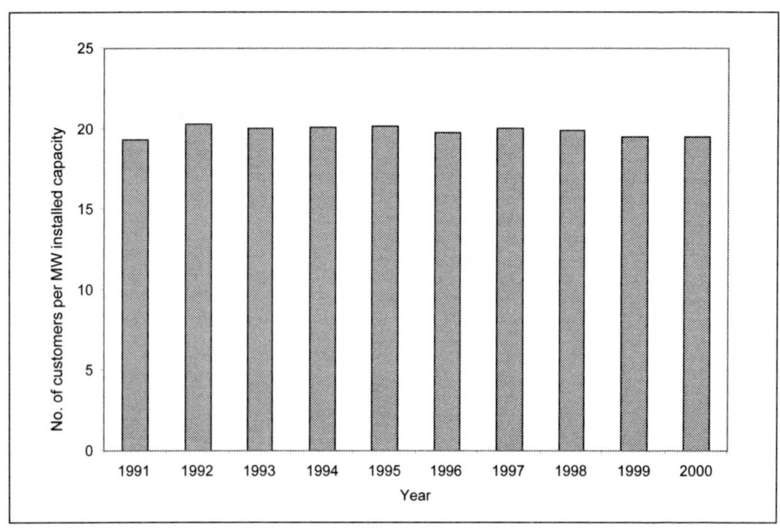

Figure IVA.1.16  Number of employees per MW installed capacity, 1991–2000

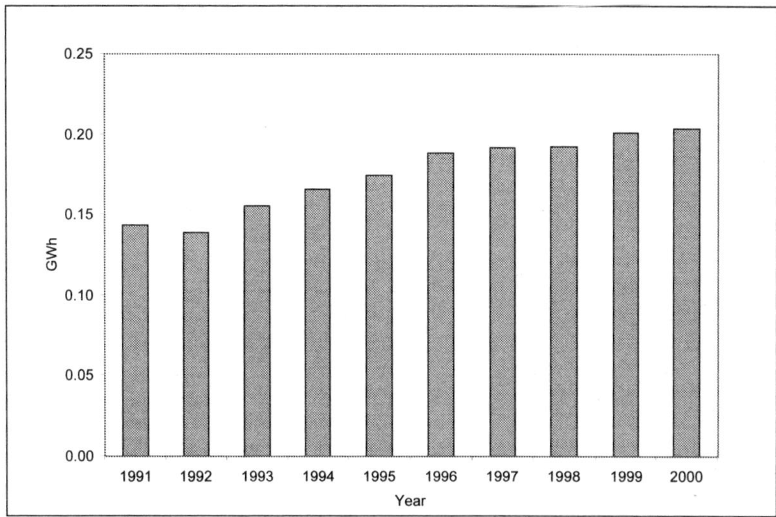

Figure IVA.1.17 Electricity generated per employee, 1991–2000 (GWh)

## Part IV Appendix 2 EEPCO: professional manpower deployment (ideal deployment level) by major categories

Year = 1996
Production (GWh)= 1548
Sales (GWh) = 1238
TRL/year (km)=200

| No. Professionals | Engineers | Other professionals | Total |
|---|---|---|---|
| | | No. of professionals | |
| 1  Generation construction & operations professionals | 44 | | 44 |
| 2  Transmission line operations professionals | 24 | | 24 |
| 3  Transmission line construction professionals | 40 | | 40 |
| 4  Distribution line construction and operations professionals | 77 | 13 | 90 |
| 5  Professionals engaged in all other support activities | 99 | 129 | 228 |
| Total | 284 | 142 | 426 |

Total no. of professionals = 426

Total no. of employees = 8247

## Part IV Appendix 3 EEPCO: projection of professional manpower requirement (based on indices for ideal deployment level)

Year = 2000
Production (GWh) = 2319
Sales (GWh) = 1855
TRL/year (km) = 200

| | | No. of professionals | | |
| | | | Other | |
| No. Professionals | | Engineers | professionals | Total |
| --- | --- | --- | --- | --- |
| 1 | Generation construction & operations professionals | 66 | | 66 |
| 2 | Transmission line operations professionals | 36 | | 36 |
| 3 | Transmission line construction professionals | 40 | | 40 |
| 4 | Distribution line construction and operations professionals | 115 | 19 | 135 |
| 5 | Professionals engaged in all other support activities | 148 | 193 | 341 |
| | Total | 405 | 212 | 618 |

Total no. of professionals = 618

% change in no. of professionals from 1996 = 45%

Therefore, % change in no. of employees from 1996 = 12.2%

Therefore, total no. of employees = 9253

## Part IV Appendix 4 EEPCO: projection of professional manpower requirement (based on indices for ideal deployment level)

Year = 2005
Production (GWh) = 3688
Sales (GWh) 3135
TRL/year (km) = 200

| | | No. of professionals | | |
| | | | Other | |
| No. Professionals | | Engineers | professionals | Total |
| --- | --- | --- | --- | --- |
| 1 | Generation construction & operations professionals | 105 | | 105 |
| 2 | Transmission line operations professionals | 57 | | 57 |
| 3 | Transmission line construction professionals | 40 | | 40 |
| 4 | Distribution line construction and operations professionals | 194 | 33 | 227 |
| 5 | Professionals engaged in all other support activities | 251 | 326 | 577 |
| | Total | 647 | 359 | 1006 |

Total no. of professionals = 1006

% change in no. of professionals from 2000 = 62.8%

Therefore, % change in no. of employees from 2000 = 17%

Therefore, total no. of employees = 10826

# Part IV Appendix 5  EEPCO: projection of professional manpower requirement  (based on indices for ideal deployment level)

Year = 2010
Production (GWh) = 5969
Sales (GWh) 5074
TRL/year (km) = 200

| | | No. of professionals | | |
| No. Professionals | | Engineers | Other professionals | Total |
| --- | --- | --- | --- | --- |
| 1 | Generation construction & operations professionals | 170 | | 170 |
| 2 | Transmission line operations professionals | 93 | | 93 |
| 3 | Transmission line construction professionals | 40 | | 40 |
| 4 | Distribution line construction and operations professionals | 315 | 53 | 368 |
| 5 | Professionals engaged in all other support activities | 406 | 528 | 934 |
| | Total | 1022 | 581 | 1603 |

Total no. of professionals = 1603
% change in no. of professionals from 2005 = 59.3%
Therefore, % change in no. of employees from 2005 = 16%
Therefore, total no. of employees = 12558

# Part IV Appendix 6  EEPCO: projection of professional manpower requirement  (based on indices for ideal deployment level)

Year = 2015
Production (GWh) = 9630
Sales (GWh) = 8470
TRL/year (km) = 200

| | | No. of professionals | | |
| No. Professionals | | Engineers | Other professionals | Total |
| --- | --- | --- | --- | --- |
| 1 | Generation construction & operations professionals | 273 | | 273 |
| 2 | Transmission line operations professionals | 149 | | 149 |
| 3 | Transmission line construction professionals | 40 | | 40 |
| 4 | Distribution line construction and operations professionals | 525 | 89 | 614 |
| 5 | Professionals engaged in all other support activities | 678 | 881 | 1559 |
| | Total | 1666 | 970 | 2636 |

Total no. of professionals = 2636
% change in no. of professionals from 2010 = 64%
Therefore, % change in no. of employees from 2010 = 17.3%
Therefore, total no. of employees = 14730

## Part IV Appendix 7  EEPCO: backward projection of professional manpower requirement (based on indices for actual deployment level for 1996)

Year = 1983
Production (GWh) = 654
Sales (GWh) = 523
TRL/year (km) = 100

| | | No. of professionals | | |
| --- | --- | --- | --- | --- |
| No. Professionals | | Engineers | Other professionals | Total |
| 1 | Generation construction & operations professionals | 12 | | 12 |
| 2 | Transmission line operations professionals | 10 | | 10 |
| 3 | Transmission line construction professionals | 12 | | 12 |
| 4 | Distribution line construction and operations professionals | 20 | 3 | 23 |
| 5 | Professionals engaged in all other support activities | 26 | 33 | 58 |
| | Total | 80 | 36 | 115 |

Total no. of professionals = 115
% change in no. of professionals from 1996 = 134%
Therefore, % change in no. of employees from 1996 = 36%
Therefore, total no. of employees = 6064 (cf. actual = 5708)

## Part IV Appendix 8 EEPCO: backward projection of professional manpower requirement (based on indices for actual deployment level for 1996)

Year = 1972
Production (GWh) = 344

| | | No. of professionals | | |
| --- | --- | --- | --- | --- |
| No. Professionals | | Engineers | Other professionals | Total |
| 1 | Generation construction & operations professionals | 6 | | 6 |
| 2 | Transmission line operations professionals | 5 | | 5 |
| 3 | Transmission line construction professionals | 6 | | 6 |
| 4 | Distribution line construction and operations professionals | 11 | 2 | 12 |
| 5 | Professionals engaged in all other support activities | 14 | 17 | 31 |
| | Total | 42 | 19 | 60 |

Total no. of professionals = 60
% change in no of professionals from 1983 = 70%
Therefore, % change in no of employees from 1983 = 19%
Therefore, total no. of employees = 4797, on the basis of 5708 employees for 1983
(The actual no. of employees for 1972 was 4682)

# Part V

---

## ZIMBABWE

**Maxwell Mapako**

# Zimbabwe

**Zimbabwe: selected indicators**
**Area (km²):** 391,000
**Population (millions):** 12.1 (2000)
**Capital city:** Harare
**GDP growth rate (%):** −6.1 (2000)
**GNP** *per capita* **(US$):** 688 (2000)
**Literacy levels (%):** (1998)   **Total:** 87
                                  **Male:** 92
                                  **Female:** 83
**Official exchange rate:**  Z$ 55.5 = 1 US$ (February 2002)
**Parallel market exchange rate:** Z$300 = 1 US$ (February 2002)
**Economic activities:**  Agriculture, mining, manufacturing, commerce, forestry
**Energy sources:**  Coal, imported petroleum, solar, biomass, hydro
**Dominant electricity utility:** Zimbabwe Electricity Supply Authority (ZESA)
**Electrification levels (%):** (2000)   **National:** 40
                                         **Urban:** 84
                                         **Rural:** 18
**Installed capacity (MW):** 1,961 (2001)
**Electricity generation (GWh):** 12,090 (2000)
**System losses (%):**  13 (2000)
**Electricity consumption** *per capita* **(kWh):** 874 (2000)
**Number of customers in utility:** 499,117 (2000)
**Number of employees in utility:** 6,968 (2000)
**Number of customers/employee:** 72 (2000)
**Debt collection period (days):** 40 (2000)
**Electricity tariffs (US cents/kWh):** 4 (2000)
**Profit/loss (US$)** 65,200 (2000)
**No. of employees/installed capacity:** 3.55 (2000)
**No. of employees/generated capacity:** 0.58 (2000)
**Modern energy consumption levels (000 metric toe):** 4,722 (1994)
**Modern energy consumption** *per capita* **(kgoe):** 422 (1994)


Sources: *Business in Africa,* 2001; AFREPREN, 2001; World Bank, 2000; World Bank, 2001; Batidzirai 2002; IEA, 2001; Time Inc., 2002; ZESA, 2001; EIU, 2001; Mapako, 2001; Dube, 2001; Kayo, 2001; IEA, 2000; ZESA, 1992–9

# 11

Country Background

## Physical and socio-economic characteristics relevant to the energy sector

Zimbabwe's population currently stands at about 12 million (CSO, 1998), within an area of 391,000 square kilometres. The annual growth rate of the population is approximately 2.8 per cent. (World Bank, 1996c; see brief country profile opposite and additional time series data in Part V Appendix 1). The Limpopo River forms Zimbabwe's southern border with South Africa, while to the north is the Zambezi (the fourth largest of Africa's rivers after the Nile, Congo and Niger), which feeds the country's largest hydropower station. The land climbs from the hot lowlands of these two river valleys, up through small farming areas to a central plateau of Msasa and Mopane savannah woodland, which covers a quarter of the country. It is on this fertile, well-watered land that the country's main towns are situated.

Zimbabwe has no known oil reserves, and is a landlocked country. It has to depend on the seaport infrastructure in neighbouring countries to procure petroleum fuels. The importation of fuel accounts for a considerable chunk of the country's foreign currency expenditure. The long distances to be traversed, either by rail or road containers, contribute to the escalation of petroleum fuel prices at the point of sale. The country normally keeps large strategic reserves (worth several months of supply) of fuel, which translate into large outlays of tied-up capital.

Turning to the power sector, some of the noteworthy physical and socio-economic features include the course of the high-potential Zambezi River, which traverses the boundaries of a number of Southern African countries. Total exploitable hydroelectric potential is 19,281 MW (World Bank, 1996c) and in Zimbabwe installed capacity is 666 MW. Development of the hydroelectric potential of the Zambezi involves protracted consultations with the stakeholder countries. The case of the Batoka Gorge hydro scheme is an illustration of how protracted and frustrating these consultations can become. On a more positive note, the existence of large generating (and sometimes excess) capacity in such countries as Mozambique, the Democratic Republic of Congo and South Africa led to the concept of a regional power pool. The success of this concept is

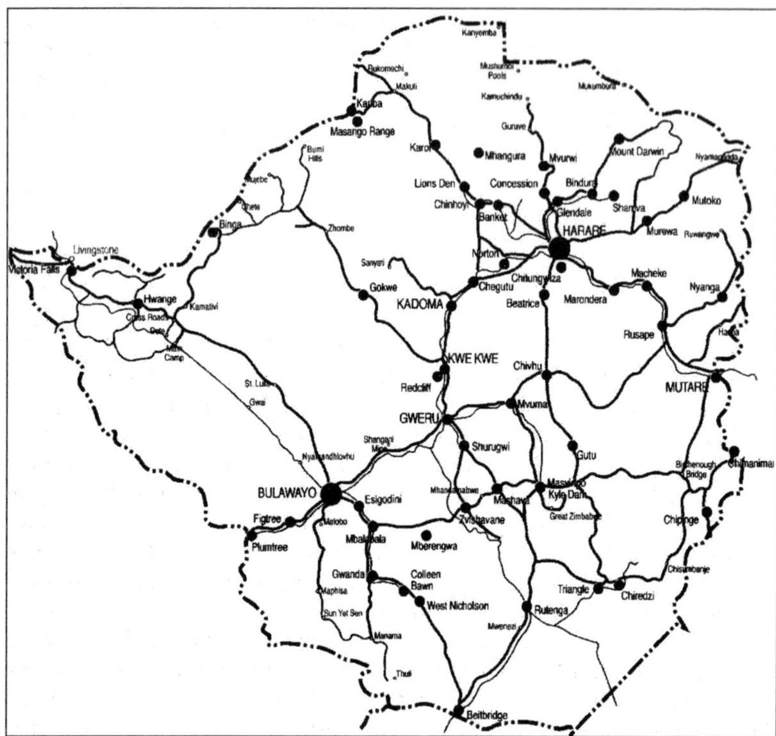


**Figure 11.1  Map of Zimbabwe**

Source: *Surveyor General, Zimbabwe*

enhanced by the prevalence of political stability and harmony among participating states, some of which were serious antagonists until a few years back.

Most urban households are connected to the electricity grid. An ethanol plant – the first in Africa – at Triangle in the lowveld produces 40 million litres of ethanol per annum from sugar cane, which for some time was blended with petrol but is now mainly exported due to the better prices fetched on the export market. The word 'blend' is still on every petrol station pump in the country, although such pumps now dispense leaded and unleaded petrol.

Zimbabwe was under white minority rule from the turn of the century until 1980, when independence was granted after a protracted armed struggle. The political system for most of the twentieth century favoured the ruling racial minority in terms of resource allocation and opportunities. The mass exodus of experienced and skilled (white) manpower at independence in 1980 dramatically changed the *status quo*. The new government therefore had to make far-reaching decisions to redress the imbalances existing at independence, including massive expansion in education and provision of social services. The establishment of the Ministry of Manpower Planning and Development at independence in 1980 demonstrated the government's immediate recognition of the key role of skilled manpower in the development process.

## The energy sector

The energy sector in Zimbabwe is, after South Africa, perhaps the most developed in sub-Saharan Africa in terms of its technological sophistication and integration into the rest of the economy. The 1992 World Bank/ ESMAP study estimated that the energy sector contributes between 8 and 9 per cent of GDP (mainly duties levied on liquid fuels). In the period 1980–9 it accounted for approximately 12 per cent of the country's gross domestic capital formation. About three quarters of this investment was carried out for the electricity subsector. The cost of importing liquid fuels accounted for about 27.1 per cent of the country's foreign exchange earnings in 2000 (Dube, 2001). Energy imports, together with servicing of the debts incurred by investment in the energy sector, required between 16 and 22 per cent of total export earnings throughout the 1980s.

The energy sector in Zimbabwe has a pronounced dual character: on one hand a well-established commercial sector, on the other a subsistence sector catering for the needs of the rural majority. Not surprisingly, biomass dominates the energy supply picture. For historical reasons – the heritage of colonialism – and more recently for economic ones, invesment (both public and private) is heavily skewed in favour of the commercial sector.

*Energy supply*
The Department of Energy maintains an energy information system and also publishes a yearly energy balance. In 1995 the total energy supply was 279,472 TJ, made up of biomass, coal, liquid fuel and electricity (Figure 11.2).

The final energy supply picture had changed little by 1997, with the total rising to 291,836 TJ. Biomass dominated all other sources of energy, its contribution being 52 per cent in 1995 and 49.6 per cent in 1997. Save for charcoal and ethanol, which are produced commercially, all other data for biomass are estimates. In the communal lands, biomass (mainly trees) is severely depleted owing to the clearing of forests for agriculture.

Figure 11.3 shows the 1999 electricity supply pattern, dominated by imports through regional interconnection and thermal generation (Hwange). The picture had changed considerably in response to growing internal demand and limited growth in local generation.

Zimbabwe imports power from South Africa, Mozambique and the Democratic Republic of Congo. ZESA has been responsible for all stages

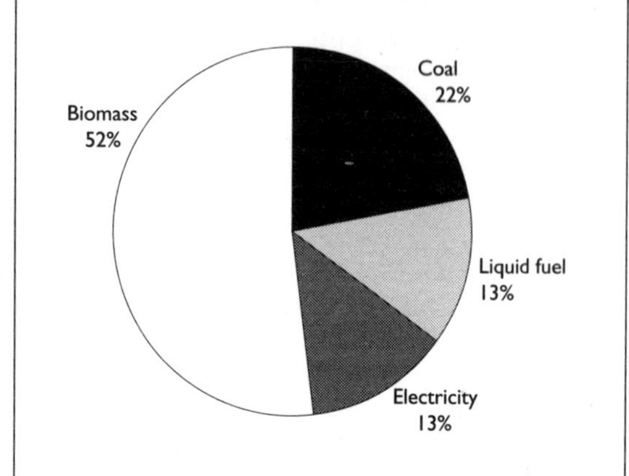


**Figure 11.2**
**Final energy supply by fuel, 1995**

Source: Ministry of Transport and Energy, 1997

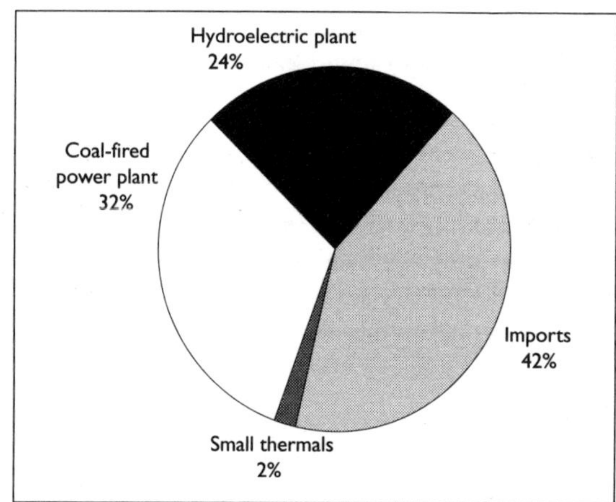


**Figure 11.3 Electricity supply by source, 1999**

Source: ZESA, 1999

of power supply: generation (except for minor contributions from small private generators), transmission and distribution. Preparations are at an advanced stage, however, to allow the participation of independent power producers in the power sector. To that end, new legislation is being formulated to create the office of a regulator of the power sector, who will deal with the licensing and monitoring of power producers. Enactment of this proposed legislation would be accompanied by the repeal of the current Electricity Act.

The Wankie Colliery Company (WCC) is the major supplier of coal followed by Rio Tinto, which started coal-mining operations on the Sengwa coal fields in Gokwe district. The selling price of coal at a given location changes in proportion to the distance it has been ferried from the point of supply. This non-uniform price structure, coupled with the absence of distribution outlets in many parts of the country, has

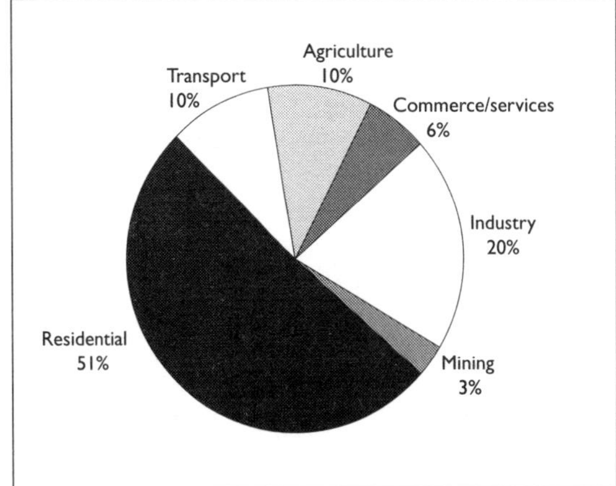



Figure 11.4
Sectoral energy
consumption, 1996

Source: Ministry of Transport and
Energy, 1999

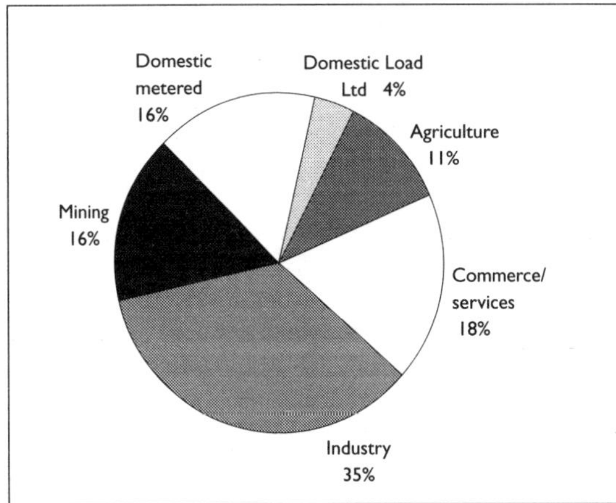



Figure 11.5
Sectoral electricity
consumption, 1998
(total 15,534 GWh)

Source: ZESA, 1998b

contributed to the minimal utilization of coal in many areas that seem to have consumption potential.

The bulk of liquid fuel supply is via a pipeline from Mutare to Harare where it is stored in strategic reserves. The National Oil Company of Zimbabwe (NOCZIM) is in charge of all bulk oil procurement on the international market. NOCZIM sells the petroleum products to oil companies (Shell BP, ExxonMobil, Total, Caltex and several other smaller local companies), which have fuel distribution networks.

*Energy demand*

According to the energy balances of the last several years, the residential (domestic) sector has the highest consumption of energy followed by industry, transport, agriculture, commerce and services, and mining. A comparison of consumption in the transport and agriculture sectors indicates that these two are more or less at par. The total energy consumption for 1996 was 272,753 TJ, with a sectoral consumption illustrated in Figure 11.4.

The sectoral electricity consumption for 1998 is illustrated in Figure 11.5, which shows the dominance of industry, domestic metered, mining, and commerce and services customers. A negligible amount of electricity is consumed by the electrified railway line between Harare and Gweru.

*Institutional structure of the energy sector*
It should be noted that the Department of Energy has been part of many different ministries over the years. It is currently under the Ministry of Mines and Energy. For most of the time covered by this study, it was under the Ministry of Transport and Energy.

The energy sector in Zimbabwe is overseen by the Department of Energy (DoE) within the Ministry of Mines and Energy. The manpower complement of the DoE stands at approximately 40 professionals. The Ministry of Mines oversees coal mining operations, while the National Economic Planning Commission has authority in the allocation of public funds or government loans for large investments in the energy sector.

Parastatals dominate the energy sector in the country. There are two main energy utilities: the National Oil Company of Zimbabwe (NOCZIM)

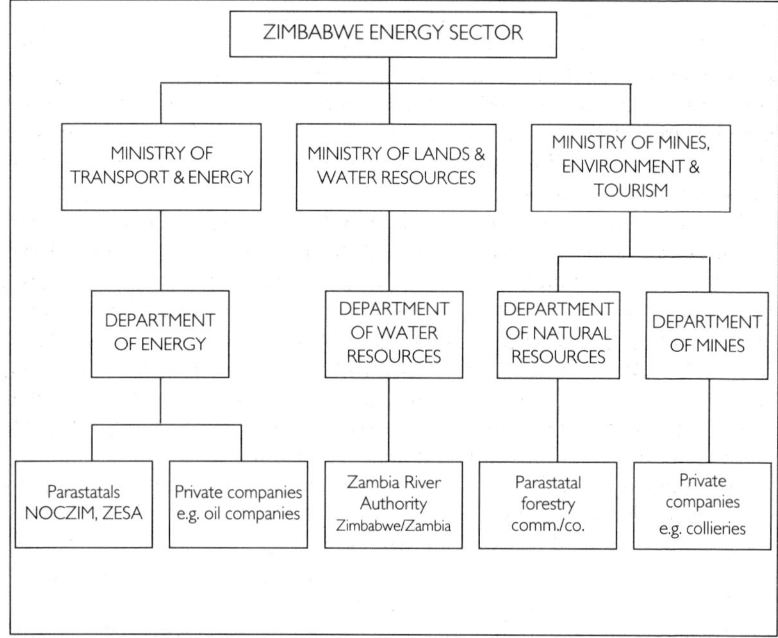


Figure 11.6 Institutional structure of the energy sector in Zimbabwe

and the Zimbabwe Electricity Supply Authority (ZESA). Both are answerable to the Department of Energy. ZESA has a staff complement of nearly 8,000 and NOCZIM about 150. The Department of Energy also sits on the Board of the Zambezi River Authority (ZRA), a body jointly administered by Zambia and Zimbabwe to control the shared Zambezi River resources. The ZRA has an environmental and hydrological focus, giving particularly close attention to the generation of hydroelectric power. Commercial sector players include the Hwange and Sengwa collieries, four multinational oil companies and Anglo-American's ethanol-producing sugar estates around Chiredzi in the southern lowveld.

*The national energy policy*
The objectives of the national energy policy focus on the provision of safe, adequate and environmentally acceptable forms of energy to all sectors of the economy in an economically sustainable manner. Pricing is one mechanism that government employs to achieve the policy objectives. For example, the pricing structure of the three most commonly used petroleum fuels (paraffin, diesel and petrol) incorporates a cross subsidy for the first two fuels, while petrol sells at a 'true' price that reflects all the costs.

Paraffin is subsidized to cater for the needs of the lower-income segments of society who use paraffin both for lighting and cooking. There is now differential pricing of paraffin, with commercial users paying more-or-less the full price while domestic consumers pay a subsidized price. This differential is difficult to enforce and is based on bulk versus small volume purchases. The small subsidy on diesel is meant to subsidize the production of both goods and services in the agricultural, commercial, industrial and other sectors. The price structure of electricity also incorporates differentiation in the power unit costs for various categories of consumers.

The woodfuel supply sector is largely informal and to a large extent uncommercialized, yet biomass constitutes more than 50 per cent of the national energy balance and is the main energy source for most low-income families (Ministry of Transport and Energy, 1997). The national energy policy supports the search for acceptable alternatives to fuelwood, including options for more efficient utilization of it. There is recognition that the biomass issue spans much more than the energy sector, and that the formulation of strategies for its sustainable production, supply and utilization demands the participation of other relevant sectors.

An important development is the proposed reform of the power sector, which is intended to remove ZESA's power sector monopoly and allow the operation of independent power producers (IPPs) in a conducive environment.

The next section will examine Zimbabwe's education and human resource development policy, which provides the framework for capacity building in the power sector – the focus of the next chapter.

## Review of education and human resource development policy relevant to the energy sector

Zimbabwe was colonized by the British at the end of the nineteenth century and was under British rule until 1965. Following the Unilateral Declaration of Independence (UDI) in 1965 by the local white minority, a new *Plan for African Education* was announced in 1966. Under the plan, only 12.5 per cent of primary school children could proceed to academic secondary education. This was part of a discriminatory policy aimed at keeping the indigenous population as a labour reserve for the settler-controlled economy (Zvobgo, 1994).

A new, more vocational stream, termed FII (Government of Southern Rhodesia, 1963) was introduced and attracted much resentment as it was clearly described officially as being for the less-gifted students. Most FII schools were in rural areas and the system was widely viewed as part of the racist approach to education. It is also true that when qualifications were being considered, FII students were regarded as inferior to those from the FI (more academic) stream.

**Table 11.1  Rate of growth of African secondary education between 1962 and 1971**

| Type of school | 1962 | 1963 | 1964 | 1965 | 1966 | 1967 | 1968 | 1969 | 1970 | 1971 |
| --- | --- | --- | --- | --- | --- | --- | --- | --- | --- | --- |
| Government | 8 | 10 | 12 | 14 | 16 | 16 | 15 | 15 | 17 | 17 |
| Mission | 33 | 39 | 47 | 61 | 71 | 75 | 75 | 82 | 83 | 83 |
| Total | 41 | 49 | 59 | 75 | 87 | 91 | 90 | 97 | 100 | 100 |

Source: Zvobgo, 1994

As shown in Table 11.1, growth in the number of government schools stagnated between 1966 and 1971. The number of missionary schools, which were also dependent on government funds, experienced only a slight rise. Government had adopted a policy of freezing growth of the so-called FI (academic stream) schools for African students. Table 11.2 brings out the impact of the racially biased education policies that severely curtailed African secondary education. It will become clear how this policy contributed to the future manpower situation in Zimbabwe, particularly as it encouraged the emergence of a predominantly white skilled manpower base. Table 11.2 also brings out clearly the impact of the racial policies of the government of the day. Figures 11.7 and 11.8 show the strong impact of independence policies on education.

Whereas the African (black) pupils were an overwhelming majority at primary schools level in keeping with the population composition, almost all 'European' (white) pupils progressed to secondary school compared to just over 3 per cent of the 'African' pupils! Austin (1975)

Table 11.2.  Colonial European and African enrolment 1970–4

|  |  | 1970 | 1971 | 1972 | 1973 | 1974 |
|---|---|---|---|---|---|---|
| Totals (primary) | European | 33014 | 33386 | 34396 | 34432 | 33620 |
|  | African | 671457 | 639043 | 695432 | 733562 | 776963 |
| Totals (secondary) | European | 22367 | 23115 | 24194 | 24896 | 35066 |
|  | African | 21040 | 22270 | 28602 | 24624 | 25532 |

Source: Zvobgo, 1994

further highlights the serious discrepancy between the races in the then Rhodesia: 10 African (black) apprentices out of 436 nationwide in 1962, and 7 out of 445 in 1965.

With the coming of independence in 1980, many changes were introduced, including the abandonment of racial segregation in schools, and the standardization of curricula. Massive expansion in the education system was undertaken as shown in Figures 11.7 and 11.8, and it remains one of the key successes of the new majority government. Figure 11.7 illustrates the dramatic increase in the number of both primary and secondary schools since 1980. The rise in secondary school enrolment was less dramatic, but nevertheless sustained after independence. The new government introduced free primary education. Figures 11.7 and 11.8 clearly show the results of this policy.

A *National Manpower Survey* was carried out in 1982. One of the results of this survey was the establishment of the Ministry of Higher Education in 1988 by the amalgamation of departments which were

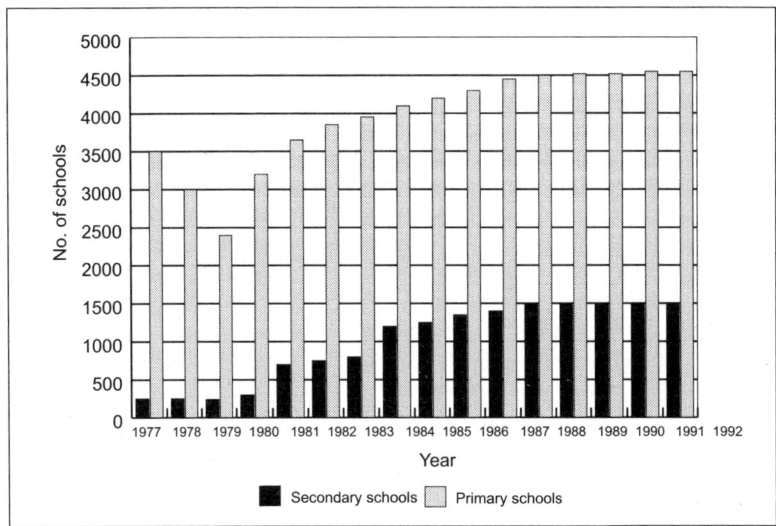


Figure 11.7  Number of primary and secondary schools 1977–92

Source: Plotted from CSO data

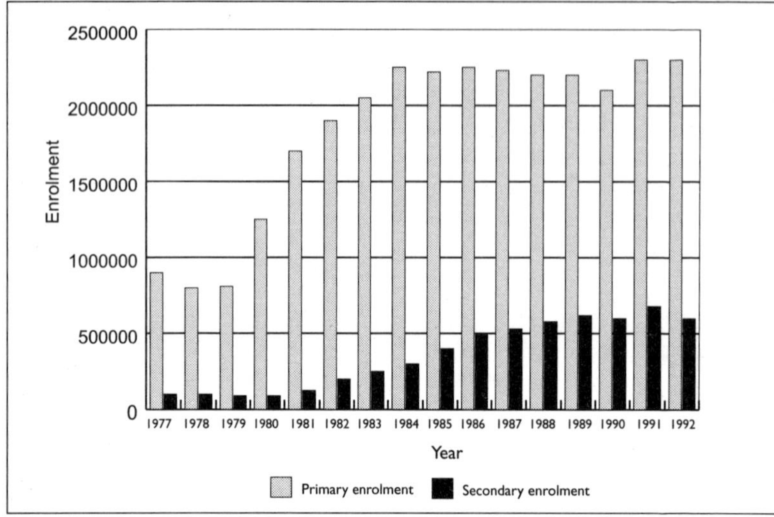


Figure 11.8 Primary and secondary school enrolment, 1977–92

Source: Plotted from CSO data

scattered in different ministries, particularly the Ministry of Labour, Manpower Planning and Social Welfare, and the then Ministry of Education. This effectively consolidated the bulk of tertiary education in one ministry, except that carried out by the Ministries of Health and of Agriculture.

The Education Act, administered by the Minister of Education, regulates school education in Zimbabwe. The head of the Ministry is the Secretary for Education, who supervises four deputy secretaries who head their divisions: schools; education development; administration, finance and policy planning; and adult and non-formal education.

The national education system has five levels: pre-school, primary, lower secondary, upper secondary and tertiary. Primary school lasts seven years, followed by four years of secondary school to reach GCE Ordinary Level. Fewer schools offer sixth form or GCE Advanced Level tuition, which is taken over two years. Successful completion of Advanced Level (upper sixth form) education is required for university entrance. Persons leaving school generally do so after completing their Ordinary Level at the age of about 16. The education system has gone through a number of changes since independence in 1980.

The Ministry of Higher Education runs a revolving fund to assist needy students who cannot afford to pay for their tertiary education. Such children can borrow money from this fund and pay back after completion of their education so that new needy students can also benefit. During the 1980s and early 1990s, the government used to pay 100 per cent of the total expenses. Of this amount, 50 per cent would be a grant and the other 50 per cent a loan. The latest policy is that government pays 50 per cent of the support rate, 30 per cent representing a loan while 20 per cent is a grant. The other 50 per cent is financed by students from their own resources. The above support is to students enrolled at local universities, technical colleges, polytechnics and agricultural colleges. Selected students can also be supported to study overseas in areas considered critical to the country. In practice this is difficult without external sponsorship due to the very high costs. Table 11.3 shows the current structure of the Zimbabwean education system.

University education is controlled by specific Acts. The University of Zimbabwe Act, 1982, regulates the operations of the University of Zimbabwe (UZ). The National University of Science and Technology Act, 1990, regulates the operations of the National University of Science and Technology (NUST). The National Council for Higher Education Act, 1990, regulates the operations of other institutions of higher learning.

**Table 11.3  Zimbabwe school system summary**

| Level | Age (years) | Academic | Vocational |
| --- | --- | --- | --- |
| Primary | 6 – 12 | Grade 1 – 7 | |
| Secondary | 13 | Form I | PVC |
| | 14 | Form II | |
| | 15 | Form III | NCF |
| | 16 | Form IV | |
| | 17 | Form V | NC |
| | 18 | Form VI | |
| Tertiary | 19 University | Year 1 | ND |
| | 20 | Year 2 | HND |
| | 21 | Year 3 | |
| | 22 | Year 4 (Bachelors) | B.Tech., B.Ed. |
| | 23+ | Higher degrees | |

There are five universities, namely UZ, NUST, Africa University, Solusi University and Bindura University College of Science Education (BUCSE). Solusi and Africa are church-affiliated universities and do not have a science bias. The other three are government institutions. In addition, numerous other universities have been proposed: Midlands, Masvingo, Catholic, Anglican, Open, New Life and an International University of Medicine and Dentistry. The country has ten technical colleges and polytechnics, with each major town having at least one and Harare having three. A Bachelor of Technology programme was started in

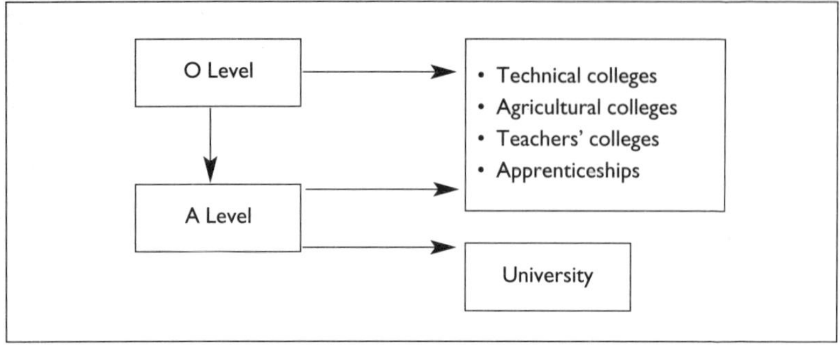


Figure 11.9  Options for Ordinary Level and Advanced Level students

1986 at Harare Polytechnic. The programme was affiliated to UZ, but was discontinued with the establishment of NUST.

The Minister of Higher Education is responsible for the administration of all the Acts specified above. The administrative provisions for UZ and NUST are very similar. This arrangement allows each university to prepare its own curricula, examinations and standards. The composition of the councils is the same and comprises a wide spectrum of the Zimbabwean society. Thus, apart from the wide array of those employed by the universities, there are representatives from industry, commerce, agriculture, engineering, teachers, trade unions, mines, youth, women and churches. Both universities have higher education and research as their objects. While UZ embraces both arts and science, however, NUST has a special bias towards the diffusion and extension of science and technology.

NUST is very young, with its first intake of students effected in April 1991, and is still experiencing staff and other resource problems. The NUST campus is still under construction on the outskirts of Bulawayo. UZ, on the other hand, was founded in 1953 and has accumulated more resources over the years, including better staff. Yet it is because UZ was no longer able to cope with the demand for university education and the pressure on its resources that NUST had to be established. UZ has other institutions affiliated to it, and both institutions have expansion plans.

Besides the two private universities already mentioned, there are numerous private training institutions, mainly in the two largest cities of Harare and Bulawayo. Courses offered are generally vocational and academic, up to Advanced Level, and in elementary technical disciplines. Where private training institutions have an academic orientation, they are required to register with the Ministry of Education. If they are technically oriented, they are required to register with the Ministry of Labour, Manpower Planning and Social Welfare. The movement of students after 'O' and 'A' Level is summarized in Figure 11.9.

More recently there has been growing official realization that the output of the current educational system was not geared to the needs of the Zimbabwean economy. This has partly been blamed on the confusion between levels of education and skills (Dube, 1997). The last time the education system was reviewed was in 1962 and standards are known to be falling. In view of this, the government of Zimbabwe in January 1998 swore-in a twelve-member Education Review Commission (*The Herald*, 3 January 1998). The Commission was multidisciplinary and included two foreign members, one being from the United Nations Educational, Social and Cultural Organization (UNESCO).

The next chapter opens its examination of capacity building in the power sector by presenting, in some detail, the status and structure of Zimbabwe's electricity industry.

# 12

## Capacity Building
## in the Energy Sector

## The power sector in Zimbabwe

The formation of ZESA through the Electricity Act of 1985 saw the amalgamation of four electricity utilities, the Electricity Supply Commission and part of the Central African Power Corporation. This change called for a structure that streamlined functions into one organization. Four deputy general manager positions were formed under the leadership of a general manager. Below them were assistant general managers.

The first restructuring occurred in 1993 and was necessitated by the need to respond to the demands of the economic structural adjustment programme as spearheaded by government. The Department of Generation and Transmission was split into two departments, each headed by a director, and the Corporate Planning Division was elevated into a department headed by a senior manager who was at the level of director. The structure was made flatter than before to facilitate effective coordination and delegation and shorter lines of communication. The spans of control were made wider. For instance, the level of assistant general manager was scrapped and replaced by at least two or more managerial posts reporting directly to the director.

It has been noted in a research study that the new organizational structure was insufficiently equipped to respond to the needs of the strategy and that there were no significant changes to the intended organizational structure (Kayo, 1995). There were still too many hierarchical reporting structures, which impinged on the quality and timeliness of information received by management. Some groupings of work units into departments resulted in conflicts between and within departments, and did not yield efficiency as intended.

As ZESA started implementing reform programmes and published its first-ever corporate business plan in July 1995, the shortcomings of the then structure became manifest. It should be noted that there is a close relationship between structure and the objectives of the organization (Kayo, 1995). The organogram of ZESA was revised once again, effectively from July 1997. This saw the Department of Technical Services being split into two departments, Technical Services and Transmission, both headed by directors. This was done to magnify the importance of transmission of electricity as a core business. The Generation Department

---

**Box 12.1 Summary: some features of the new Electricity Act (2001)**

On 30 January 2002 the Parliament of Zimbabwe ratified the Electricity Act of 2001. This new Act replaces the Zimbabwe Electricity Supply Authority Act of 1985 and provides for the appointment of a Zimbabwe Electricity Regulatory Commission (ZERC) which will oversee the operations of the power sector. The Minister of Mines and Energy will regulate the ZERC, and will appoint its commissioners. This implies that the Minister will still have the final say on key policy matters such as tariffs.

The new Act provides for the transformation of the current ZESA into a wholly government-owned company called ZESA Holdings Limited. The new company will be run on commercial lines. It is the responsibility of the present ZESA board to oversee the transformation and creation of ZESA Holdings Limited. The government-approved structure for ZESA Holdings Limited consists of four companies:

- The Zimbabwe Power Company, established in October 1996, will be in charge of generation.

- A national transmission company, the name of which is still to be decided, will be in charge of transmission and grid assets.

- A national distribution company – name still to be decided – will be in charge of distribution and supply.

- Other support departments such as public relations, treasury and corporate planning will comprise the non-core function of ZESA Holdings Limited.

The Parliament of Zimbabwe has already ratified the Rural Electrification Fund on 23 January 2002. A 13-member Rural Electrification board and a Rural Electrification Agency (REA) will be set up under this Act. Of the 13 board members, eight will be Provincial Administrators; the balance will be appointed by the Minister of Mines and Energy. The REA will embark on an expanded rural electrification programme.

---

was viewed as a manufacturer, the Transmission Department as a wholesaler and the Distribution Department (Consumer Services) as a retailer.

The number of managers reporting to the Consumer Services Director rose by three following the realization of the importance of focusing on the customer and of marketing electricity as a product. The importance of rural electrification was emphasized through the establishment of a managerial post in charge of the function. The Corporate Planning Department reverted to the Chief Executive's Office.

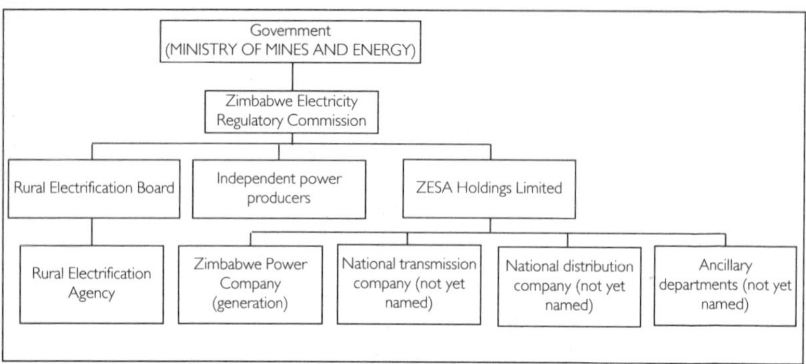



Figure 12.1  ZESA organogram, July 1997

In 2000 ZESA saw more change, with the appointment of an executive chairman. The incumbent chief executive contested this on the grounds that such an appointment had no legal basis, as it was not provided for in the existing Electricity Act. The matter was still unresolved by the end of 2001. Meanwhile the White Paper on electricity reform was circulated in 2001, and on 30 January 2002 the Parliament of Zimbabwe passed the Electricity Act of 2001. Box 12.1 presents some of the features of the new legislation.

The passing of the latest Electricity Act made far-reaching changes to the structure of the power sector, particularly to ZESA, as shown in Figure 12.1. The new arrangement is expected to result in the institutional structure depicted in Figure 12.2.

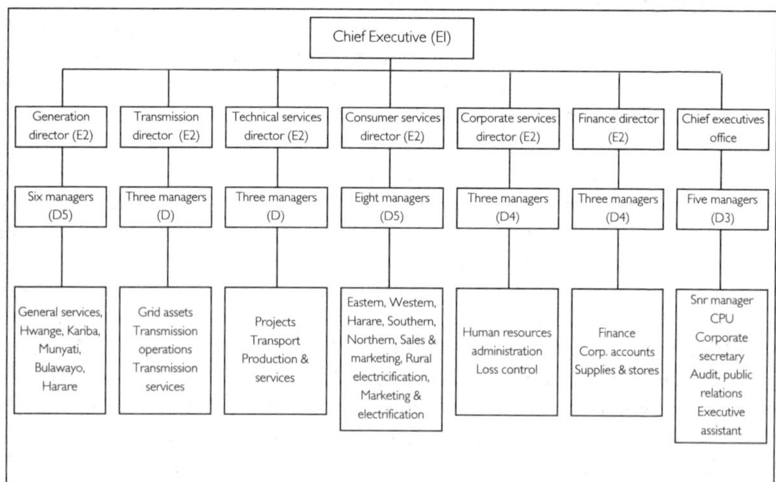



Figure 12.2  Expected structure of the power sector in Zimbabwe

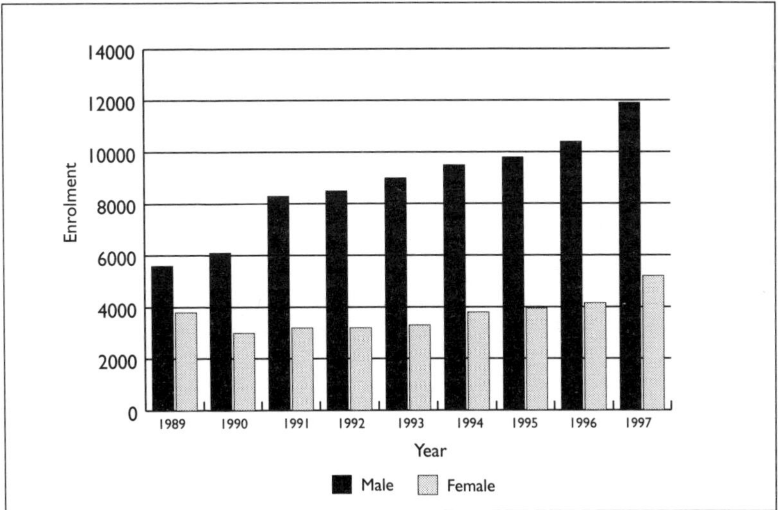


Figure 12.3  Technical college enrolment, 1989–97

Source: Plotted from CSO data

## Staffing issues

The power sector derives its manpower mainly from the output of the universities and the technical and vocational colleges. The enrolment at technical colleges has grown considerably as shown in Figure 12.3, and is characterized by strong male numerical dominance.

Similarly, the University of Zimbabwe enrolment has grown steadily and more recently a number of new universities have also been established, as shown in Figure 12.4.

The impact of the economic structural adjustment programme is seen clearly in the pronounced reduction in enrolment in the early 1990s. Table 12.1 shows the engineering student output from the University of Zimbabwe from the immediate post-independence era in 1982 to 1994. The trend shows the levelling off in the early 1990s and the 1994 total output of 148 is quite paltry when compared to the *annual* skilled manpower requirements estimated 11 years earlier at 130 to 150 for the electricity sector alone.

It will be shown that less than 2,270 of ZESA's workforce can be classed as professionals, of whom some 732 are degreed. The other organizations involved in power generation are Rusitu Power Corporation (700 kW), Triangle Limited (seasonal, up to 33 MW) (Kayo, 2000), Wankie Colliery Company and various mining and smelting companies, all totalling 110 MW. This private generating capacity is 6 per cent of the total capacity, and (proportionately) suggests that about 140 power-sector

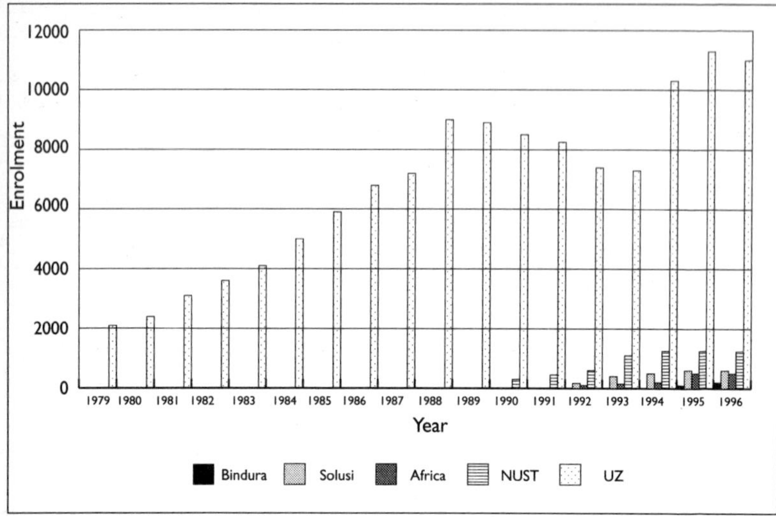



Figure 12.4 University enrolment, 1979–97

professionals are currently working in the private sector. The national total for ZESA, the private sector and about ten professionals in the Department of Energy adds up to about 2,420.

Since 1994, ZESA has used the Paterson Grading System together with its job evaluation methodology. The Paterson method of job evaluation

Table 12.1. Engineering student output from the University of Zimbabwe

| Year | Electrical | Civil | Mechanical | Metallurgy | Mining | Survey | Total |
|------|-----------|-------|-----------|-----------|--------|--------|-------|
| 1982 | 2 | 7 | 1 | | | | 10 |
| 1983 | 14 | 7 | 5 | | | | 26 |
| 1984 | 13 | 15 | 8 | | | | 36 |
| 1985 | 21 | 15 | 14 | | | | 50 |
| 1986 | 18 | 17 | 5 | | | | 40 |
| 1987 | 27 | 29 | 15 | | | | 71 |
| 1988 | 27 | 35 | 15 | 4 | 3 | 3 | 87 |
| 1989 | 27 | 29 | 19 | 8 | 10 | 4 | 97 |
| 1990 | 44 | 45 | 15 | 9 | 9 | 10 | 132 |
| 1991 | 34 | 54 | 24 | 6 | 11 | 10 | 139 |
| 1992 | 36 | 56 | 24 | 12 | 12 | 9 | 149 |
| 1993 | 35 | 46 | 23 | 17 | 9 | 9 | 139 |
| 1994 | 33 | 55 | 18 | 20 | 9 | 13 | 148 |
| Total | 331 | 410 | 186 | 76 | 63 | 58 | |

uses six bands of decision making common to all companies. The decision bands are related to the commonly used grading levels as shown in Table 12.2. The Paterson System emphasizes the decision-making levels of a job. The higher the level of decision making, the greater the value of the job to the organization, and the greater the compensation or reward. The different decision grades or levels determine wage rates. For instance, in ZESA, Bands F and E are in charge of the policy making which guides the organization. Decision making here is unlimited and only constrained by law. The compensation is therefore greater. The reasoning progresses that way downwards.

**Table 12.2 Detailed description of the decision bands: Paterson System used in ZESA**

| Band | Complexity of decisions | Grade |
|---|---|---|
| F | The vision, direction and key policy decisions of the company are made here. The major operational areas are guided by decisions made here. | Coordinating – 11<br>Non-coordinating – 10 |
| E | Executive policies in line with top management decisions made at this level. Broad programmes for each operational area are made here. Organizational structures are also mapped out at this level. | Coordinating – 9<br>Non-coordinating – 10 |
| D | Interpretative decisions are made which involves analysis of best options using discretion. The best use of resources available is done here. Decide on systems, procedures, rules and regulations. | Coordinating – 7<br>Non-coordinating – 6 |
| C | Routine decisions, which involve determining the best way, the work is to be done given the established processes, systems and procedures. | Coordinating – 5<br>Non-coordinating – 4 |
| B | Automatic decisions made by semi-skilled personnel. The choice is restricted to operations. | Coordinating – 3<br>Non-coordinating – 2 |
| A | Decisions are defined already and the unskilled work is implemented. | 1 |

The method enhances morale and lowers the incidence of industrial problems (Siegel and Myrtle, 1985). Use of the method in ZESA improves employee retention due to appropriate compensation strategies, but does not eliminate all the problems, as will be illustrated using staff turnover figures.

The significant vacancies rate within the professional and skilled sections of ZESA in part indicates a lack of suitable skilled manpower on the market. Certainly, the output of local institutions is not sufficient to ensure adequate manpower resources for both ZESA and the economy. In 1994/5, ZESA lost some 708 staff for numerous reasons, the greatest losses being in Generation and Technical Services. The second most important cause of staff loss is death, which showed an 18 per cent increase in 1995/6 compared to the 1994/5 period (ZESA, 1996). The cause of death is not always recorded but the trend is nevertheless worrying and has implications for the future manpower situation, not only in the power sector.

**Table 12.3 Overall staffing position within ZESA, 1999**

| Department | Overall establishment 1977 | Current strength | Variance |
|---|---|---|---|
| Chief Executive | 44 | 33 | –11 |
| Corporate Planning | 55 | 43 | –12 |
| Corporate Services | 609 | 515 | –94 |
| Finance | 139 | 150 | 11 |
| Generation | 1651 | 1733 | 82 |
| Technical Services | 374 | 319 | –55 |
| Consumer Services | 4674 | 4302 | –372 |
| Transmission | 409 | 367 | –42 |
| Total | 7955 | 7462 | –493 |

**Table 12.4  Breakdown of staff by department and type**

| Department | Executive/ Snr mgr | Mgr/Snr supervisory | Degreed professional | Non-degreed professional | Semi-skilled | Total |
|---|---|---|---|---|---|---|
| Chief Executive | 3 | 5 | 14 | 6 | 5 | 33 |
| Corporate Planning | 3 | 7 | 16 | 14 | 3 | 43 |
| Corporate Services | 3 | 11 | 15 | 46 | 440 | 515 |
| Finance | 4 | 27 | 4 | 58 | 57 | 150 |
| Generation | 9 | 176 | 65 | 411 | 1072 | 1733 |
| Technical Services | 6 | 12 | 18 | 95 | 188 | 319 |
| Consumer Services | 13 | 194 | 66 | 800 | 3229 | 4302 |
| Transmission | 2 | 35 | 24 | 107 | 199 | 367 |
| Total | 43 | 467 | 222 | 1537 | 5193 | 7462 |

Table 12.3 shows the approved establishment for ZESA to be 7,955 posts with 7,462 filled by 1997. A breakdown of the type of staff by department is given in Table 12.4. The ratios arrived at using these figures

should be interpreted with the classification system adopted here in mind. For example, the second-largest group pools together the non-degreed professional staff, skilled staff and junior supervisory staff. Also, the two most senior grades, the executive/senior manager group and the manager/senior supervisory group, are grouped together with the degreed professional staff as 'professionals'. In Table 12.4, the 'degreed professionals' category represents degreed staff outside top management (that is, those who are not senior managers and above). For our purposes, all top management are assumed to be degreed.

**Table 12.5  Staff movements 1994/5 and 1995/6**

| Type of movement | 1994/5 | 1995/6 | Variance | % change |
|---|---|---|---|---|
| Appointments | 548 | 178 | −370 | −67% |
| Transfers in | 197 | 168 | −29 | −15% |
| Resignations | 75 | 56 | −19 | −25% |
| Dismissals | 66 | 49 | −17 | −26% |
| Transfers out | 353 | 227 | −126 | −41% |
| Retirements | 110 | 139 | +29 | +26% |
| Deaths | 104 | 122 | +18 | +17% |
| Net gain/loss | +37 | −247 | −132 | |

The staff turnover ratio for 1994/5 works out at 11.4 per cent while that for 1995/6 works out at 9.6 per cent. However, recent staff turnover ratios indicate a reduction to the tune of 4.5 per cent in 1997/8 and 4 per cent in 1998/9.

*Performance indicators*
The Capacity Building Theme Group agreed to use a standardized 'ideal utility' to facilitate comparison, and proposed a set of ratios to be compared with utilities under consideration. These ratios are given in Table 12.6 in comparison with ratios derived from ZESA data.

**Table 12.6  Comparison between ZESA and ideal utility**

| Ratio | Ideal utility | ZESA |
|---|---|---|
| Manpower per GWh (produced) | 2 | 1.8 |
| Customers per employee | 125 | 51.6 |
| Technical to administrative manpower* | 3 : 1 | 9 : 1 |
| Semi-professional to professional manpower | 6 : 1 | 2.1 : 1 |
| Non-professional to professional manpower | 43 : 1 | 9.2 : 1 |
| Manpower per installed capacity (MW) | 5 | 3.87 |

* Based on the strength figures of technical departments (Generation, Transmission, Consumer Services and Technical Services) and non-technical departments (Finance, Planning, Corporate Services and Chief Executive's Office)
Sources: ZESA1995a; ZESA 1997a

The above comparison between ZESA and the ideal utility shows ZESA to be better in terms of manpower productivity at 1.8 staff per GWh of energy produced. The customers per employee figure is poorer than the ideal utility figure by a wide margin, which means that, by the standards of the ideal utility, ZESA could handle considerably more customers with its current staff.

One important factor that can explain this apparent inefficiency is the fact that much of the power sold is consumed by a small number of large consumers in industry. Of total sales of 10,088 GWh in 1996/7, 39 per cent was taken by the industrial sector, with 57 per cent of this figure (which is over 22 per cent of national sales) accounted for by just four large consumers. In the year 1996/7, ZESA had 410,782 customers, 6 per cent more than the previous year. Over the same period, an 8 per cent growth in units sold was realized.

The ratios for the technical, administrative, professional and non-professional staff vary considerably from the ideal utility. The reason for this is that the format of ZESA data does not always allow for direct comparison because the categorization is not identical.

The manpower per installed capacity is better in ZESA's case, with a figure below four compared to the ideal utility's figure of five. In 1996/7, ZESA managed to reduce the average debt collection period by more than a third, from 56 days in the previous year to 37 days, and realized a sales growth rate of 7.7 per cent, which is 1.3 per cent above the set target (ZESA, 1997a).

Maximum system demand grew by 4.8 per cent (to reach 1,828 MW) compared to the 1995/6 period. Total energy sent out was 11,310 GWh, which represents an increase of 7.8 per cent over the previous year, also exceeding the target of 10,976 GWh by 3.1 per cent. Of the total energy supplied, 7,279 GWh was internally generated while 4,012.9 GWh was imported from South Africa (65.1 per cent), Zambia (20.1 per cent) and the Democratic Republic of Congo (14.7 per cent). Imports accounted for 35.5 per cent of the total. This imported power has become increasingly costly for ZESA in view of the depreciating Zimbabwe dollar, which lost 50 per cent of its value against the US dollar in 1998. The power import bill presently stands at US$6 million per month. In Zimbabwe dollar terms, ZESA is paying Z$70 million per month. Before November 1997 (when the Zimbabwe dollar crashed), the average retail tariff stood at US$0.42, compared to the level in 1999, which was US$0.15, very much lower in US dollar terms.

Transmission faults numbered 437 in 1995/6 and, of these, 215 resulted in loss of supply (ZESA Annual Report 1996/7). In 1996/7 there were 418 faults, of which 143 caused loss of supply. The largest number of faults generally occurs between October and February each year (the rainy season). Causes cited are lightning, bush fire, primary and secondary equipment failure, human error and unknown. Twenty-two faults (about 5.3 per cent) were attributed to human error in 1996/7 and, of these, 15 (about 68 per cent) resulted in loss of supply. In terms of number of line faults per kilometre, the figures predominantly fall between one and a maximum of 2.5 faults per kilometre of transmission line per annum.

## Supply of manpower

*Manpower estimates*
Mordell and Coales (1983) provide an estimation methodology and apply this to a selection of Commonwealth countries, including Zimbabwe. The assumptions for Zimbabwe are based on a projected year 2000 population of about 17.4 million, with a GNP *per capita* figure of US$717. More recent data (World Bank, 1996c) point to a significantly lower population growth rate (2.8 per cent per annum in the past decade) and an annual average GNP *per capita* of about US$490 in the 1990s. This figure has been declining gradually from as high as US$710 in 1989. The revised forecasts are given in Table 12.7. It is important to appreciate that the accuracy of this method is of the order of plus or minus 30 per cent, so no undue emphasis should be given to the precision of the calculated estimates.

**Table 12.7  Manpower demand forecasts for 1998, 2003 and 2008**

| Year | Approx. population | | Professional/technical staff required | | |
|---|---|---|---|---|---|
| | | | Constant GNP (@ US$500 per cap.) | 2.5% GNP growth p.a. | 5% GNP growth p.a. |
| 1998 | 12.5m | Engineers | 4125 | 4125 | 4125 |
| | | Technicians | 16500 | 16500 | 16500 |
| 2003 | 14.4m | Engineers | 4719 | 5363 | 6435 |
| | | Technicians | 18876 | 21450 | 25740 |
| 2008 | 16.5m | Engineers | 5346 | 7290 | 8991 |
| | | Technicians | 21384 | 29160 | 35964 |

Technicians are those who hold a diploma (or ten years' experience instead) and have completed two years' experience. The figures given by the Zimbabwe Institute of Engineers (ZIE) in 1998 (verbal communication, 1998, Mrs Gatsi, ZIE) are as follows:

| | |
|---|---|
| Engineers (fully qualified) | 860 |
| Engineers (still under three years' experience) | 437 |
| Students (on degree/diploma course) | 689 |

The calculated figure of 4,125 engineers required in a population of 12.5 million represents a ratio of 0.33 engineers per thousand of population. This ratio becomes 0.54 per thousand in 2008 with an assumed 5 per cent per annum growth in GNP *per capita*. (The level of growth in the Zimbabwean economy has been near zero, which makes it somewhat academic to use the figures based on higher growth scenarios.)

Compared to even the modest actual figure of two engineers productively employed per thousand of population in Latin America, this ratio needs to be boosted 3.6 times (if we take the high figure of 0.54) or six times (taking the low figure of 0.33). The more realistic low ratio needs to go up 21 times to approach US figures of around seven employed engineers per thousand of population (Mordell and Coales, 1983).

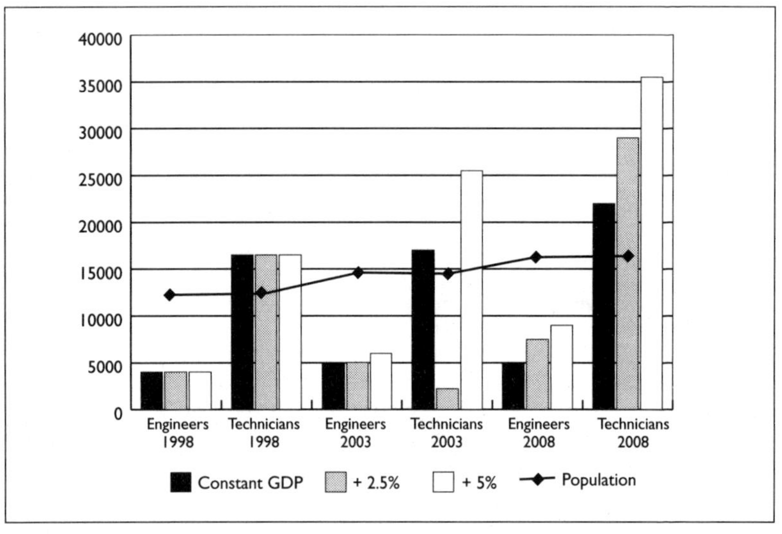


Figure 12.5  Total manpower demand forecast (population-driven)

The reality in Zimbabwe is rather more pessimistic. ZIE membership, required by many employers of engineering staff, is divided into two general categories: engineers and technicians. Registered engineers hold a degree and at least three years' experience. In Figure 12.5, each cluster of three bars represents estimates for engineers or technicians for the years 1998, 2003 and 2008. Each bar represents a specified annual GDP growth rate as shown in the legend. The estimated population is given in thousands. The ZIE membership figures do not represent the national total, since some large employers like the Posts and Telecommunications Corporation (PTC), a parastatal that employs many engineers and technicians, do not require ZIE membership of their employees. Nevertheless, it can be expected that most engineers, even those whose present employers do not require ZIE membership would seek such membership because it considerably improves their mobility within the engineering field, both in Zimbabwe and elsewhere. The implication of this is that the number of engineers in Zimbabwe is of the order of a few thousand, perhaps 2,000 based on the ZIE membership of nearly 1,300 member engineers. By 2001, increasing economic hardship, and growing political uncertainty have tended to encourage migration out of the country. This factor considerably increases uncertainty over the number of engineers and other skilled manpower in the country at present.

In conclusion, based on the above assumptions, the actual ratio of engineers to population for Zimbabwe would seem to be 2,000 in a population of around 14 million, or 0.14 per thousand. Compared to the ratios of two for Latin America, or seven for the USA, the numbers of employed engineers would need to be increased between 14 and 50 times. This suggests that there is a shortfall in engineering manpower at the national level. The seriousness of the shortfall cannot be judged on the basis of the examples quoted above, because of the differences in the structure of the economies. It cannot be refuted, however, that more developed economies have much better ratios of engineers to population than that estimated for Zimbabwe.


## Retention and capacity mobilization
## (including in-service training)

The government of Zimbabwe introduced the Zimbabwe Manpower Development Fund (ZIMDEF) in 1995 through the Manpower Planning and Development Act of 1994. The Fund seeks to finance the development of highly skilled and competent human resources for the nation. Under this Act, levies are collected from all employers in order to fund the programme.

Levies are calculated as 1 per cent of the total wage bill of employers. Every employer with a wage bill of Z$2,000 or more per annum is liable for payment of the levy. Employers undertaking 'approved training' are eligible for levy rebates. Approved training is that based on national interest and national standards and objectives as determined by the Minister of Higher Education. Grants are based on the number of instructors approved by the Ministry of Higher Education. Rebates are based on the number of trainees enrolled. The details of grant and rebate calculation are outlined in Appendix II.

Generally, government salary levels tend to be among the lowest while the most attractive salaries are offered in the private sector. Parastatal salaries generally bisect these. It is not surprising that many ZESA staff employed with work experience tend to be from government ministries, while skilled staff leaving ZESA generally go to the private sector or leave the country. The level of remuneration is only one of many factors influencing job satisfaction, however, and hence the ability to retain staff.

The departments most affected by staff losses are Generation and Technical Services, which show losses of 11.7 and 4.6 per cent respectively over the 1993–5 period. No other department showed a net loss of staff, giving rise to an overall 0.9 per cent rate, which tends to mask the more marked changes noted above.

On a broader level, there is also competition between countries for highly qualified manpower, leading to labour migration across boundaries. In particular, the newly independent countries such as Namibia and South Africa, experiencing immediate manpower shortages, prove very attractive. In time, however, the situation slowly changes as the need to satisfy demand for local employment grows. In South Africa there are already high-level moves to replace expatriate experts with local manpower. This will, to some extent, force expatriates home if they have no suitable alternatives.

Specific retention measures that can be singled out include:

- Periodic review of remuneration – ZESA carries out annual market surveys to ensure that its remuneration is market-based and competitive.

- Need to update competitiveness of conditions of service to adapt to changing times.

- Implementation of human resource management policies:

  - ZESA's performance management systems, based on rewards to recognize employees who beat set targets and to identify gaps and remedial measures for under-performing employees.

  - Succession planning – employees can chart out progression/career paths.

  - Dissemination of information to the grassroots on crucial organizational issues that affect the welfare of the employees and the goal of the organization.

  - Long-service awards.

- ZESA encourages employee-initiated staff development through financial assistance and study leave.

ZESA's plans show appreciation of the fact that the organization's success in the future will depend on having competent staff. The stated aim is therefore an environment 'where the best can bloom'. ZESA's Performance Improvement Centre (formerly the National Training Centre) is an in-house training facility that also services the region. Strategies adopted by ZESA to upgrade staff and improve morale include training, personal development of employees, education and effective induction, employee empowerment, good corporate governance, appropriate reward systems and employee productivity measurement.

A system of performance contracts has been instituted. The quarterly in-house magazine, the *Megawatt Bulletin*, regularly devotes several pages to staff-related issues, including training courses held, staff movements, promotion announcements and introduction of new staff.

*Key constraints to recruitment and retention of skilled manpower in ZESA, and suggested solutions*
Most of the constraints outlined below were identified through a study undertaken by Electricité de France (EDF) and KPMG Consultants as part of their assignment during reform programmes (Ministry of Transport and Energy, 1993). Clearly ZESA has taken steps to address many of the constraints, as will become apparent in this section.

1  Inadequate updating and implementation of human resource management policies and conditions of service that would enable ZESA to attract and retain suitably qualified and experienced staff. This problem could be solved through continuous updating of policies to ensure competitive conditions of service for all skills categories. ZESA should also improve manpower planning and succession planning.

2  The legal framework that empowers the Minister to regulate, among other things, staff conditions of service, is also a constraint. There are bound to be delays in implementation of conditions of service proposed by ZESA, even when approved. Such legislation should be changed. It was hoped that the incorporation of the new ZESA under the Companies Act would solve the problem, but it seems that the new ZESA Holdings Limited will still be subject to pronounced ministerial supervision.

3  Historically, there was insufficient employee motivation due to factors such as restrictive movement within grades and inappropriate grading, lack of responsibility and empowerment, and lack of performance incentives. This could be solved through increasing employees' responsibilities and empowerment and development of a performance-related incentive programme. Although a considerable effort has been made to implement these recommendations, future trends are not yet clear in view of ongoing changes.

4  Insecurity and anxiety caused by frequent restructuring exercises and the commercialization/privatization exercise. It is hoped that once these are complete, the environment in which the organization has to operate will stabilize. This problem persists, as the future shape of ZESA has remained unclear for several years.

The corporate business plan (1995) indicated that management has undertaken to promote teamwork, total customer satisfaction, performance-based reward systems, empowerment and accountability as part of creating an enabling organizational culture. A management committee has already been tasked with development of a code of ethics for the organization.

As an incentive to retain qualified and competent staff ZESA pays a 'critical allowance' to staff deemed critical to its operations. ZESA has also instituted a performance-related reward system with the twin objectives of raising productivity and rewarding staff competitively. ZESA carries out annual market surveys to ensure that its remuneration is market-based and competitive. This has reduced staff turnover rates significantly and also virtually stopped the brain drain to other utilities in the region.

ZESA also encourages staff personal development. Staff can initiate their own relevant training programmes and pay for them using their own resources. On successful completion, ZESA reimburses the full costs of the course or programme. There is also a successful effort at image building to make staff proud to be ZESA employees.

It is important to realize that present plans to encourage the entry of other major players will cause some upheaval. These new companies and utilities will initially offer packages specifically designed to attract the best from both Zimbabwe and the region. ZESA cannot escape the impact of such moves, but in a national perspective such a development may be beneficial if it entices expatriate Zimbabweans to return home to work for the new utilities and companies.


## Policy challenges: restructuring and after

Major policy changes at ZESA have been categorized as falling into five periods. Most of the changes were externally induced in response to government policy changes; some, however, were induced from within.

*Formation of ZESA*
ZESA was formed in 1985 through an Act of Parliament. The Act came into operation in January 1986, paving the way for the amalgamation of the electricity departments of the municipalities of Harare, Mutare and Gweru, the Electricity Supply Commission (ESC) and part of the Central African Power Corporation (CAPCO). ESC's mandate was to supply, transmit and distribute power from CAPCO's generation stations. The latter supplied power in bulk to the urban councils of Harare, Mutare, Bulawayo and Gweru, which had the mandate to supply and distribute power. Each of the utilities mentioned earlier acted independently on power matters.

There was no streamlined energy policy on electricity. Tariffs charged to the same group of consumers varied. It was therefore thought necessary to create a unified electricity supply service for Zimbabwe with the main functions of acquiring, generating, distributing and supplying electricity. The major benefits realized under the Act were the adoption of a uniform national structure and a streamlined management structure for the electricity sector (ZESA, 1995a). This arrangement enabled the maintenance of reasonable technical performance standards at prices that were lower, in real terms, than those prevailing at the passing of the Act. Amalgamation, however, also confronted ZESA with difficulties in mobilizing and motivating employees who had come from diverse cultures and were used to different conditions of service.

ZESA posted profits for the first two years. However, the three financial years beginning with 1989/90 ran deficits for various reasons. The first reason was the result of a legal framework that gave the Minister the power to regulate the price of electricity, investments in the utility, the disposal of its assets and its borrowing. The Minister would not agree to any real tariff increases, creating a situation that resulted in cash flow and profitability problems. This was compounded by the fact that, at the amalgamation, billing remained with the Harare City Council. Consequently ZESA could not control debt collection and billing cycles. Foreign currency, which was a problem during the period in question, affected the importation of spares and materials required for maintaining the system.

In 1991/2, only 9,248 GWh of total energy could be supplied against a demand of 10,256 GWh (ZESA, 1995a). ZESA was forced to introduce a combination of load shedding, and a tariff-based rationing system in order to curtail demand. Inadequate electricity supply continues to bedevil Zimbabwe to date, with load shedding intensified.

*Economic Structural Adjustment Programme (ESAP)*
In 1990 the government of Zimbabwe introduced economic reforms that sought to correct fundamental macro-economic problems such as the budget deficit and low economic growth. High levels of direct and indirect subsidies to public enterprises were a significant contributor to this fiscal problem. This meant that to comply with ESAP objectives ZESA had to change the way it operated and government had to make regulatory changes to create an enabling environment.

A major problem for ZESA was the need for a pro-reform management energetic enough to implement the drastic changes in, for example, management style, environmental impact analysis and the adoption of technological advances. Old management was retrenched: it was doubtful that they would be able to effect the turnaround policies. At the same time, there were grave conflicts between the board, management and the Minister of Transport and Energy that led to the ZESA board being fired before the appointment of another general manager. The new board appointed a new management team, which was placed under performance contracts.

There were some positive aspects to these developments. A young management team was appointed, the majority of whom (including the chief executive) were promoted from within. Most of them were in their late thirties. This brought about the chance to institute performance-based contracts and bonuses, and set targets. The management employed conventional methods of management and a culture of professionalism unfolded. For example:

1  For the first time, all projects were subjected to cost-benefit analysis.

2  Performance management for the whole organization was introduced.

3  Job evaluation was undertaken and the Paterson System, which as we have seen rewards decision-making responsibilities, was adopted.

4  Improvements in long-service awards.

5  Emphasis on focused training policy.

ZESA was restructured to streamline operations and reduce duplication (Ministry of Transport and Energy, 1993). In 1994 a new organizational structure was established that was supposed to be in tune with ESAP demands. The number of top management layers was reduced and spans of control widened. Separation of functions among divisions was defined to minimize overlap. A job evaluation exercise was undertaken.


*ZESA's Corporate Business Plan (CBP) and Performance Improvement Programme (PIP)*
ZESA contracted Electricité de France (EDF) and KPMG Consultants to provide assistance in implementing a reform programme within the parastatal. Assistance included the design of a performance improvement programme (PIP) and operations agreements for the financial years 1993/4–1994/5 geared towards improving the performance of ZESA to that of a well-managed power utility through immediate and longer-term measures (Ministry of Transport and Energy, 1993: 1). These reforms included:

• Operational improvements in the distribution system, which had a direct interface with customers that significantly influenced the image of the Authority. Employee training emphasized the linkage between the customer and survival of the organization.

• Human resource management planning, including a review of organizational structure. This meant the introduction of manpower planning and succession planning for high-level management posts.

CORPORATE BUSINESS PLAN (CBP)
The CBP was based on the general principles and vision of a new ZESA defined by the government, the board and the chief executive (ZESA, 1995a). Its aim was to address deficiencies identified by KPMG Consultants. The plan was a result of numerous strategic planning workshops held at operational level to develop strategies to achieve corporate objectives. ZESA applied 'management by objectives' skills,

which empower employees to be part of the critical decision-making processes to enhance successful implementation.

## Mission statement

To guide the planning process, the direction as defined by the board and government was captured through a mission statement: 'We are committed to the total electrification of Zimbabwe at world class standards and competitive prices' (ZESA, 1995a). The statement focused employees on how to perform their roles efficiently and effectively.

The fundamental cultural and ethical standards endorsed by ZESA and implicit in the statement include issues of capacity building: 'teamwork, commitment, national service, customer service, social responsibility, efficiency and excellence' (ZESA, 1995a).

## Vision

The plan also included the vision of ZESA as a utility, to be counted among the world's best electric utilities, thereby maintaining and enhancing the utility's leadership role in the electricity supply industry in Zimbabwe and the Southern African region (ZESA, 1995a). By this ZESA meant, for example, its ability to attract and retain the technical and management skills needed by the utility through providing a working environment conducive to productivity and innovation. Human resources were seen as a factor critical to the success of the utility's reform programme and privatization. The human resources management function was to tackle this challenge through the facilitation of organizational development and cultural change, change management, the development and standardization of skills and processes, and performance management.

A mission statement for the human resources function was also developed through brainstorming by practitioners within the organization under the direction of corporate planners. Critical success factors were isolated that included effective consultancy in recruitment/selection issues, skills retention, industrial relations, training and development, performance management, compensation and reward systems, succession planning and employee productivity. Performance indicators were given, including targets by the year 2000: professional staff turnover, for example, was set at 5 per cent, down from a previous 8 per cent.

## PERFORMANCE IMPROVEMENT PROGRAMME (PIP)

The programme identified major causes of poor performance and suggested actions that could be taken to improve performance. It was realized that no human resources strategic plan had been included in the overall corporate plan. The introduction of manpower planning and succession planning for high-level posts was suggested. The daily management of human resources had been emphasized by ZESA at the expense of long-term human resources planning. There was no comprehensive information on jobs and employees. Data were not analyzed.

Training was limited in scope; it focused mainly on technical skills. Training needs were not being identified comprehensively, nor was the impact of training on performance being monitored.

*PIP recommendations*

1  *Operational improvements in consumer services and management, and in the distribution plant system.* This area was regarded as being of critical importance to ZESA's image because of the direct interface with customers. It is also the area with the greatest number of employees because it is labour-intensive and the main source of revenue.

   In the past, ZESA considered its customers as consumers instead of clients. Press reports and internal assessments had indicated that ZESA's image to its customers was negative. Some of the reasons were long delays in connections after payment, and estimations of consumption of electricity instead of monthly readings. The PIP recommended the introduction of computerized billing in some areas and this has since been done. It also recommended the creation of a customer support unit, reducing intervention time on fault correction, and decreasing both customer debt and billing lag. Most of these recommendations have been effected.

2  *Improvement of generation plant and system.* It was recognized that it was necessary to minimize the severity of power shortages in Zimbabwe caused by droughts by increasing the performance and reliability of the Hwange coal-fired power station and reducing blackouts. This called for the implementation of a power system development plan. The plan included rehabilitation of old thermal power stations by 1993 and the addition of further capacity from the Cahora Bassa Interconnector (1995), Kariba South upgrading (1997), Hwange Stage III (1998/9), Batoka (2002/3) and Grassroots Thermal (2004). Implementation was on schedule at the end of the 1990s.

3  *A human resource management plan including organizational structure.* We have seen that such a plan was absent from the overall corporate plan and that both manpower planning and succession planning for high-level management positions were lacking. This resulted in delays in filling strategic posts and low morale among good management performers who had to fill in the gaps, usually without reward. Training in ZESA was also thought to be parochial as it focused on technical skills at a particular level and there were no management courses within the electrical and engineering courses in general.

   The PIP therefore recommended the introduction of management training for ZESA managers to assist them in implementing reform programmes and to equip them with skills to identify the training needs of their staff adequately. To date, almost all managers in the middle-to-senior levels have gone through the programmes. Another recommendation was the development of a results-oriented management style; shifting from norms and reports to objectives and results and appraising performance in fields delegated to line managers. A results-oriented performance appraisal system has since been installed.

4   *Reform of the financial management system.* Financial management in ZESA was poor at the time. Information was received too late and was so often inaccurate that it could not be relied upon. This made planning for the future difficult. There were also delays in the preparation and approval of financial information and reports. It was important, therefore, to improve access to timely and accurate information by introducing internal controls and management information systems.

It should be noted that implementation of the PIP recommendations was monitored by a project steering committee headed by the permanent secretary of the Ministry of Transport and Energy. The committee consisted of Ministry of Finance and ZESA representatives at the highest level. Progress meetings were held as often as once a month.

## Sale of the Hwange power station to YTL

As part of the reform programme, the government of Zimbabwe decided to privatize the Hwange power station and called for tenders. In a dramatic move, however, the government shelved the tender process and announced the sale of 51 per cent of shares in the station – the major supplier of electricity in the country – to a Malaysian company, YTL. ZESA was to retain the balance of the shares. The ZESA board opposed the deal; it was therefore fired and a new board was installed. The new board was not enthusiastic about the terms of the deal, either, and little progress was made.

## Second organizational restructuring

ZESA embarked on yet another organizational restructuring in 1996, about two years after the first one. The restructuring was to take into account the shortcomings of the current structure in view of the dynamic changes that were occurring both within and outside the organization. Marketing of electricity was emphasized in the new structure that became effective in July 1997 in recognition of the fact that in Zimbabwe, electricity constitutes only 12 per cent of the energy market (ZESA, 1995a). This is because households, which constitute the bulk of energy users, have easier access to fuelwood and petroleum products, energy sources that account for two thirds of the market.

One other feature of the restructuring was the splitting of the Technical Services Department into Technical Services and Transmission departments, both headed by directors. This was in recognition of the importance of transmission as a core business. The Department of Corporate Planning was moved back to the Chief Executive's Office.

## Summary of major issues

At this point it can be seen that a number of major issues have emerged regarding capacity building and retention in the power sector. The most important among these are:

- The need to reform the education system in Zimbabwe to better suit the requirements of the national economy. The present curriculum is highly academic.

- The need to maintain and improve training in the power sector in view of the clear national deficiency in skilled manpower. The ZESA staff turnover ratio of around 10 per cent per annum, and the impending changes due to the entry of IPPs into the sector, clearly point to a need to address the issue of skilled manpower supply.

- The need for ZESA to be granted greater autonomy to enable it to run with less disruption and to make business decisions that will ensure its continued viability.

  These issues will be examined in more detail in the next chapter.

# 13

## Policy Options and Assessment

The foregoing discussion has shown the existence of a number of issues that need attention if the power sector in Zimbabwe is to further improve on what up to now has been a comparatively good general performance. Remuneration and conditions in ZESA are competitive in Zimbabwe mainly because of the regular survey of prevailing market rates that enables ZESA to adjust pay levels in time. Of course the ability to pay competitively presupposes a sound financial performance and on the whole ZESA achieved this before the collapse of the Zimbabwe dollar at the end of 1997.

The major player in this sector in Zimbabwe, ZESA, has until 2002 been a parastatal or quasi-governmental institution, unlike its sister organization NOCZIM, which operates as a company although it is 100 per cent government-owned (Mashange, 2001). The latter has enjoyed greater autonomy from government control. There have been complications that seriously upset the smooth running of ZESA, such as disagreements between the parent ministry and the ZESA board. This has happened on several occasions, disrupting the smooth professional administration of ZESA, leading to disillusionment and increasing the risk of (particularly) senior staff loss.

The reform of the power sector is now fact in Zimbabwe, with the entry of new players and more power stations expected. There could be a further demand for skilled manpower due to these changes, which imply increased competition. Of direct relevance here is the education system, which has been found to be ill-adapted to local requirements, developed as it was during the colonial era and based on British curricula. There is also a need to improve gender representation as part of power sector reform: the present situation exemplifies virtually unrelieved male domination at the top.

The following policy options may be considered worth pursuing in view of the foregoing observations. The options are presented in order of perceived priority, and will require not only power sector attention but also national-level intervention in some cases. Each of the options in turn will be considered from several comparative perspectives: legal, financial, institutional, organizational and managerial. This will enable the feasibility of each option to be be assessed by weighing the factors for and against.

## Strengthening of in-house training

The expected expansion in the power sector will lead to greater demand for skilled manpower. Training in the power sector is therefore important to meet the demand. At present the ZESA Performance Improvement Centre (PIC) is the major specialist training centre serving Zimbabwe and the region. It is likely to be the nucleus of any future power sector manpower training even when the power sector includes other signficant players.

*Legal*
There are no legal implications to be dealt with as far as power sector internal training is concerned, and hence no legal obstacles are foreseen for this option.

*Financial*
The corporate business plan identified the management of human resources as a critical issue if ZESA is to achieve its developmental and growth goals. To achieve the various developmental programmes, all business plans have capacity development and staff retention strategies and action plans. The budgeting process thus makes available funds to implement these action plans. Autonomy in management of financial issues enables the centre to get the information it requires and to recover more costs. The finance section is headed by a qualified accountant. The fact that the centre is expected to sustain itself on revenue generated from its activities may be problematic if it does not perform well.

*Institutional*
The key step was to establish the autonomy of the training centre as a business unit and allow it to charge other business units within ZESA for its services. This has gone a long way towards improving the quality of the training courses being offered, as the customers now demand value for money, forcing improvements in the quality of the service. As a stand-alone unit, PIC is better able to look at corporate training needs and plan to meet them, as its role and mandate has now been clearly defined. The approach to training is now more focused and a lot of duplication and overlaps by individual business units have been eliminated.

Some functions – catering, for example – were removed from the centre, so that it now concentrates on its core business of training. The post of the head of training of the training centre has been elevated to managerial status, moving up from fourth level to third level, thereby enabling the head to command more respect and more authority. The fact that the centre is facing competition from other training centres in and outside the country for its traditional clientele will encourage it to strive for higher standards. Its survival will depend on its efforts, as it is no longer subsidized by ZESA.

The restructuring of the centre in 1997 has strengthened its position in the delivery of high-level and junior-level courses. The changes involved the redesign of lecturers' tasks and the centre's organizational structure to achieve specialization, enhance coordination and centralize decision making.

The reduction of the centre's establishment is viewed as a positive move in that the centre will be able to hire resource persons to run any courses deemed necessary in strengthening in-house skills. This could have been costlier if the previous complement of permanent training staff was still in place.

The fact that the centre has been removed from the ZESA system means that it must run cost-effectively in order to sustain itself. There is the possibility that the centre could fail and close down. If that was to happen ZESA would still be able to train its employees at other institutions in and out of the country, but conditions may be less favourable and ZESA may not be able to influence these new independent training facilities easily.

*Organization and management*
ZESA has planning processes that ensure a systematic approach to the organization and management of staff training, development and retention. Every year a general training needs analysis is carried out, looking at operational skills requirements including apprentice and postgraduate training. Specific management development needs are also established. Programmes are then designed to meet these needs through staff training and development and external recruitment. To monitor the realization of these objectives, performance standards are set and their achievement is monitored at regular intervals.

The following specific developments have taken place:

- Identification of training needs is now done professionally, with close liaison between management and the training centre.

- Realization of the need to market PIC activities to encourage production of quality courses.

- Commercialization of the centre is creating positive competition with similar institutions across the country.

- Training done at the centre is now being monitored to assess impact.

- Because the centre offers both technical and non-technical courses a broad range of performance-inhibiting deficiencies will be tackled.

- ZESA management itself has recognized the importance of training; hence the function is guaranteed to get the necessary support (ZESA, 1995a).

- ZESA has set targets for PIC to measure performance (ZESA, 1995).

Conflicting requirements and an atmosphere of competition are factors likely to hamper the smooth functioning of a common training facility. It is important that such a facility is not strongly associated with any one utility, particularly if relationships within the power sector are not cordial.

## Affirmative action

Affirmative action here means the enhancement or promotion of the advancement of disadvantaged groups of the population such as the disabled, women or minorities. The discussion will deal only with gender, specifically noted as an issue needing to be addressed. The issue of racial imbalance, by contrast, has received comprehensive attention in government institutions.

### Legal
Positive national policy, which has progressed in line with international trends towards improved gender sensitivity and in some cases affirmative action, is taken to accelerate the correction of glaring imbalances. There are, however, no legal barriers to the advancement of women in the power sector.

### Financial
There is the conflict of combining work with family responsibilities, and lack of provision of crèche/nursery facilities for working mothers, for example. The need for paid maternity leave may also worry employers when considering employing an increased proportion of women.

### Institutional
At the University of Zimbabwe, women with lower entrance qualifications (on a points score) are accepted into the system. In a recent development, women are also accepted as electrical apprentices (and in other trades), although relatively few women have taken up the challenge to date.

Occupational segregation still flourishes, however, and the discipline of engineering is male-dominated at present. When women are employed they are often not genuinely accepted by their male counterparts and may not get a fair chance to occupy responsible positions.

Social attitudes remain biased against women employed in high-level jobs. In such circumstances education for women tends to be geared to low-level jobs. By comparison, expectations of men as breadwinners are high, and therefore social action is geared towards education, training and support of men in employment. Consequently, the chances of women to gain management positions are poor. There is a general belief that males are better than women even in non-technical areas. High-level promotions of women are therefore less likely even if the women are well-qualified and perform impressively. This is a cultural problem the world over, including Zimbabwe. By the end of the 1990s there were no women in ZESA's executive group of 44 employees. This has been the case for many years.

*Organization and management*
There is a need for enhanced training opportunities for potential managers that would be open to all ZESA employees, male and female, and would create new challenges and experiences in management roles. There are, however, relatively few women who can be considered for posts. Women themselves are hesitant to take up engineering and other technical courses. In a way, this is a chicken and egg situation: realizing that opportunities in technical fields are often closed to them, young women opt for other fields of study – and this very choice helps to ensure that the *status quo* is maintained. The causes of this deadlock lie beyond the sectoral level: they are based on cultural beliefs and accepted norms regarding gender roles, and require solutions at national level.

The overall impression in the case of this option is that most factors affecting the subject of improved gender balance are outside the control of the power sector and have to do with institutionalized social attitudes that affect preferences, subjects and career choices according to what is perceived as proper for each gender. There are, nevertheless, growing numbers of women in the power sector and it is important that appropriate efforts should be made to take them fully on board.

## Educational system reform

The need for a more appropriate educational system in Zimbabwe has already been demonstrated, and the government, indeed, has appointed a commission of inquiry. This discussion will not attempt to pre-empt the commission but will touch on issues of importance to the power sector.

*Legal*
The legal framework is conducive, mainly owing to the ongoing changes necessitated by the economic reform programme. However, the speed of reform may be slow and could prove to be a constraint, since new or revised statutory instruments are likely to be required in the near term.

*Financial*
Private sector participation is pronounced and active, and this lessens the burden on the government at a time when it is forced to cut expenditure as part of ongoing economic reforms. The freedom to set fees for their services provides the private sector with the opportunity to ensure viable operations. The government of Zimbabwe is also still strongly committed

to education as evidenced by the budgetary allocations to the relevant ministries. Uncertainty due to prevailing economic problems of high inflation and a weakening Zimbabwe dollar could dampen investor confidence, however, and delay investment in the education sector.

*Institutional*
The government recognizes the need for change in the educational sector and is acting. In addition, relations between government and the private sector are good and allow for collaboration. No major difficulty is foreseen in view of the relatively stable institutional establishment in the education sector.

*Organization and management*
The government ministry in charge of the coordination of higher education and training is the Ministry of Higher Education. There are many private sector training institutions and this means a high degree of decentralization of organization and management within the sector. This situation is conducive to greater responsiveness because it makes it difficult for bureaucracy to delay decisions and the speed of change.

The outlook for this option is good as the government has acknowledged the need for reform of the education sector and is taking action. The recent rapid expansion in the number of tertiary institutions, mainly through private sector initiatives, is indicative of a viable sector.

## Increased autonomy from government

The problems stemming from ZESA's parastatal status have been highlighted, particularly the conflicts between the ministry responsible for energy, the ZESA board and ZESA top management. Tariffs are approved by government and may not necessarily be what ZESA needs to ensure its viability. Government decisions may often be influenced by political considerations, such as the need to avoid price rises near election time. ZESA management is, therefore, placed in a difficult position: on one hand, government expects profits to be made; on the other hand, extraneous decisions have to be accepted by management.

*Legal*
The legal framework is conducive, particularly the enactment of the Electricity Act of 2000 which opens up the power sector. This will necessitate the freeing up of ZESA to enable it to compete more effectively.

*Financial*
Private sector participation in the power sector will reduce the need for government to invest in and subsidize it. This should make it easier for decisions to be made without the fear of financial risks, which are borne

by other bodies. Uncertainty due to prevailing economic problems of high inflation and a weakening Zimbabwean dollar could dampen investor confidence and delay investment in the power sector.

*Institutional*
The presence of other large and powerful independent power producers will enable the power sector to negotiate from a stronger position with government. The possibility, recently announced by Shangani Energy Exploration of Zimbabwe, of coal-bed methane contributing to the generation of electricity, points to the likelihood of even more private sector players in the power sector, all contributing to an increasingly liberalized and competitive power sector.

*Organization and management*
The power sector is not directly in control of developments in the wider training of manpower, but the involvement of more power producers will make it necessary for the sector to reach an understanding on issues of common interest. This could become more difficult in an increasingly competitive environment.

The outlook for this option is very good as the government has already acknowledged the need for reform of the power sector and taken steps to facilitate that reform.

# 14

## Conclusions and Recommendations

The power sector in Zimbabwe is set to expand in the medium-to-long term, especially with the expected entry of independent power producers such as National Power. The extent of the expansion will partly depend on decisions that the government of the day makes between reliance on regional interconnection and local self-sufficiency in power. With the prevailing shortage in foreign currency, the government may wish to maximize local self-sufficiency to avoid costly power imports that must be paid for in foreign currency.

If increased dependence on expatriate skills is to be avoided, it is crucial that sufficient suitable local manpower is available. A case exists for measures to encourage the return of skilled African expatriates in view of the unfortunate situation whereby Africa is proving to be a rich hunting ground for expatriates from the developed world while a large number of highly skilled African experts are employed in the developed world. Karekezi (1995a) has highlighted this anomaly and estimates that the number of foreign experts in sub-Saharan Africa is comparable to the number of skilled Africans working abroad, roughly 100,000.

The analysis carried out in this study so far leads to the following conclusions:

- *In-house training* in the power sector is a reality, and a new approach, that of having an autonomous training centre, has been adopted. At this stage, with ZESA the only dominant player, the mechanism is relatively simple. However, with the possibility of significant players such as National Power running major power stations, the Zimbabwe power sector is set to change considerably.

  The issue of in-house training in the power sector could therefore be approached in several ways. One approach could be each player making its own arrangements, which would entail considerable duplication of facilities and equipment. It would be more logical for the various players to agree on minimum requirements for a training centre that could be jointly equipped, and that could then charge service fees based on service delivered.

- *Curriculum reform* has already been identified as an area in need of attention. This is largely an issue for the state. In Zimbabwe the subject is already under consideration but this does not guarantee that the existing problems will be satisfactorily resolved. The following conditions also need to be met:

- Political will must be there to take up the recommendations of the Review Commission and base policy on those found to be acceptable.

- The various sectors of the economy need to realize the importance of the presently ongoing review and put their views across vigorously. There is unlikely to be a similar review for many years to come.

- More could be done to excite nationwide debate on the subject of curriculum reform, for example by featuring it on radio and televised debates. The efforts undertaken to date have been formal and relatively low key.

One of the of the key constraints which government will face is how to finance any proposed curriculum reform in a situation where it is under pressure to reduce spending, and industry is also faced with greater competition due to globalization. Greater willingness to contribute will certainly result from a sense of identity with the process of defining the needed reforms in manpower development. This will to some extent reduce the need for government to bear the burden alone. Incentives could also be put in place to induce private sector participation, for example tax-linked credits tied to participation in important areas of manpower development.

The various laws governing education and training in Zimbabwe need to be integrated and harmonized. The history of education has tended to encourage a piecemeal approach whereby each university is subject to a specific Act of Parliament, mainly because for a long time the country had only one university with its own unique Act. A common Higher Education Act or similar instrument would bring together the provisions for training and education into one Act and provide some coherence of approach.

- *Affirmative action* in the correction of racial imbalances has been facilitated by a prevailing political climate that strongly supported its implementation. It can be argued that, at this stage, the area needing attention remains that of gender imbalance. To be fair, it may be that in great part the problem lies beyond the control of the power sector: it is a national issue. The solution can only be long term, in that the more young girls see women doing jobs traditionally seen as 'men's work', the more likely they are to opt for more technical subjects at school, and for engineering and similar disciplines at universities and colleges.

What the power sector can do is actively avoid gender bias in considering candidates for promotion. It can be difficult for a male-dominated management unit to look objectively at a small minority of female colleagues without applying culturally accepted gender stereotypes that prejudge the chances of such female colleagues.

One potential advantage with women employees is that the place of residence and work is often dictated by the husband's situation. Married women are therefore less likely to move to another country or town for a new job, a move that generally would force their husbands to relocate with them. The reverse, however, is commonplace and is generally readily accepted. The pool of manpower potentially available is likely to be much improved if efforts are made to tap into the full population rather than one (male) half of it.

- *Autonomy* from excessive government interference remains a difficult issue. Because of the strategic nature of electricity, total autonomy is unlikely. Certain non-core sections of ZESA will be sold off or privatized. Government should seriously consider the history of its control of ZESA, however, and make concerted efforts to minimize imposition of decisions on ZESA by national authorities that will not be held ultimately accountable for the results of such decisions.

# Part V Appendices

## Part V Appendix 1 Selected time series data Zimbabwe (table and figures)

Table VA.1.1  Selected time series data, Zimbabwe

| Zimbabwe | 1991 | 1992 | 1993 | 1994 | 1995 | 1996 | 1997 | 1998 | 1999 | 2000 |
|---|---|---|---|---|---|---|---|---|---|---|
| Population (millions) | | 10.4 | 10.8 | 11.2 | 11.5 | 11.5 | 11.5 | 11.7 | 11.9 | 12.1 |
| GDP (US$ million) | | 7156 | 7280 | 7690 | 7610 | 8260 | 8475 | 6500 | 6000 | 4500 |
| GDP growth rate (%) | | | 1.7 | 5.6 | −1.0 | 8.5 | 2.6 | 2.5 | −0.4 | −6.1 |
| GNP *per capita* (US$) | | 688 | 674 | 687 | 662 | 718 | 737 | 556 | 504 | 688 |
| Electrification levels (%) | | | | | | | | | | |
| National | | 28 | 29 | 31 | 32 | 34 | 35 | 36 | 39 | 40 |
| Urban | | 69 | 67 | 69 | 72 | 70 | 74 | 78 | 80 | 84 |
| Rural | | 11 | 14 | 15 | 14 | 17 | 16 | 15 | 18 | 18 |
| Installed capacity (MW) | | 1961 | 1961 | 1961 | 1961 | 1961 | 1961 | 1961 | 1961 | 1961 |
| Electricity generation (GWh) | | 10282 | 8760 | 9544 | 10123 | 10495 | 11311 | 11891 | 12363 | 12090 |
| System losses (%) | 11.0 | 8.6 | 11.0 | 12.1 | 11.0 | 11.0 | 10.8 | 10.7 | 13.2 | 13 |
| Electricity consumption *per capita* (kWh) | 931 | 931 | 948 | 924 | 927 | 839 | 791 | 774 | 672 | 874 |
| Number of customers | 308201 | 333390 | 333218 | 356395 | 368687 | 387593 | 410432 | 437523 | 473586 | 499117 |
| Number of employees | 7674 | 7603 | 7531 | 7975 | 7903 | 7655 | 7462 | 7273 | 6486 | 6968 |
| Number of customers/employee | 40 | 44 | 44 | 45 | 47 | 51 | 55 | 60 | 73 | 72 |
| Debt collection period (days) | 74 | 85 | 99 | 61 | 50 | 56 | 37 | 32 | 32 | 40 |
| Average electricity tariffs (US cents/kWh) | 3 | 2 | 3 | 3 | 3 | 3 | 3 | 1 | 2 | 4 |
| Profit/loss (US$ 000s) | −24.1 | −14.5 | 6.7 | 9.9 | 10.0 | 10.0 | 9.6 | −174.1 | 44.1 | 65.2 |
| No. of employees/installed capacity | | 3.88 | 3.84 | 4.07 | 4.03 | 3.90 | 3.81 | 3.71 | 3.31 | 3.55 |
| Electricity generated per employee (GWh) | | 1.35 | 1.16 | 1.19 | 1.28 | 1.37 | 1.51 | 1.63 | 1.90 | 1.73 |

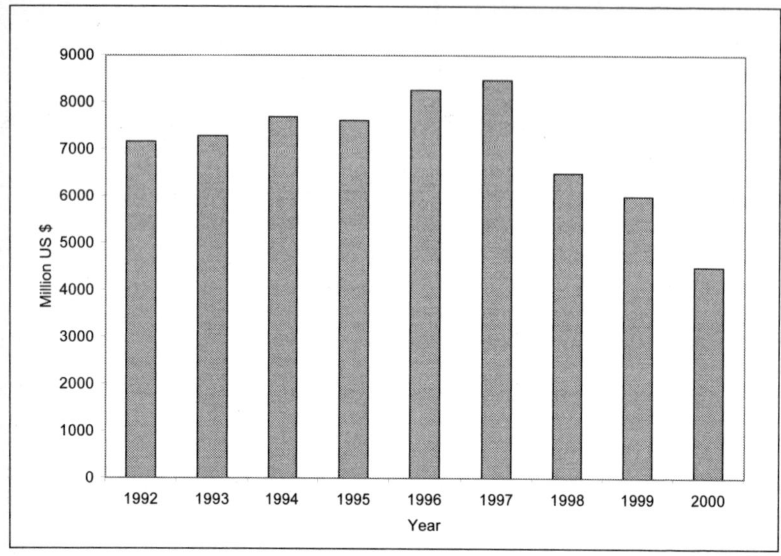

Figure VA.1.1  GDP, 1992–2000 (US$ million)

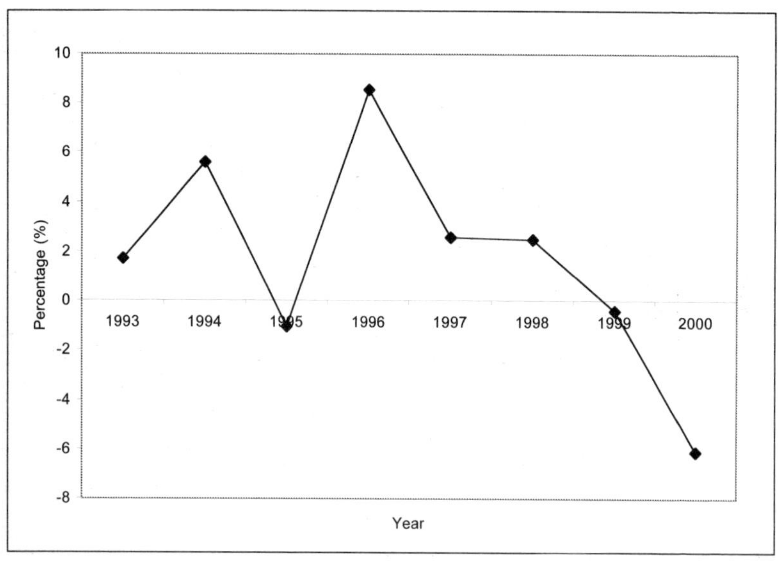

Figure VA.1.2  GDP growth rate, 1993–2000 (%)

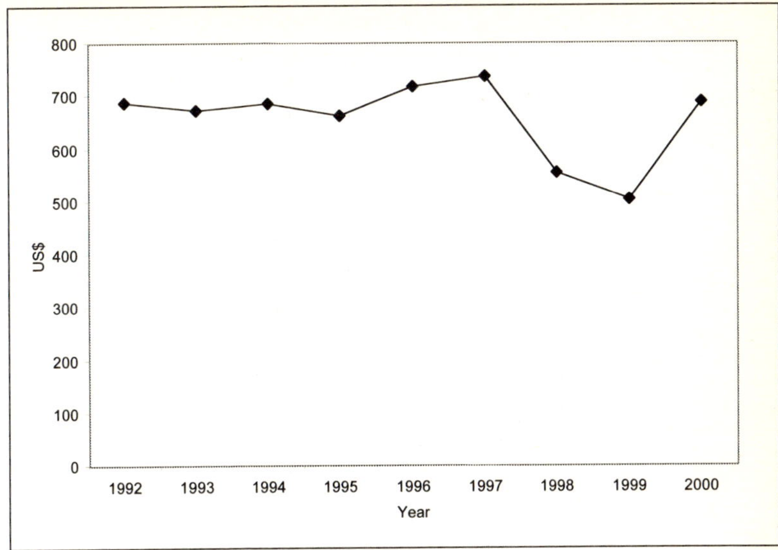

Figure VA.1.3  GNP *per capita*, 1992–2000 (US$)

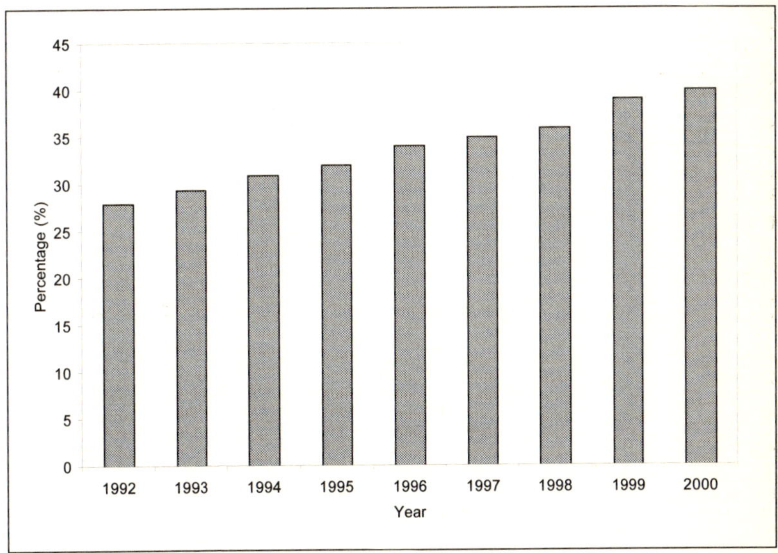

Figure VA.1.4  National electrification levels, 1992–2000 (%)

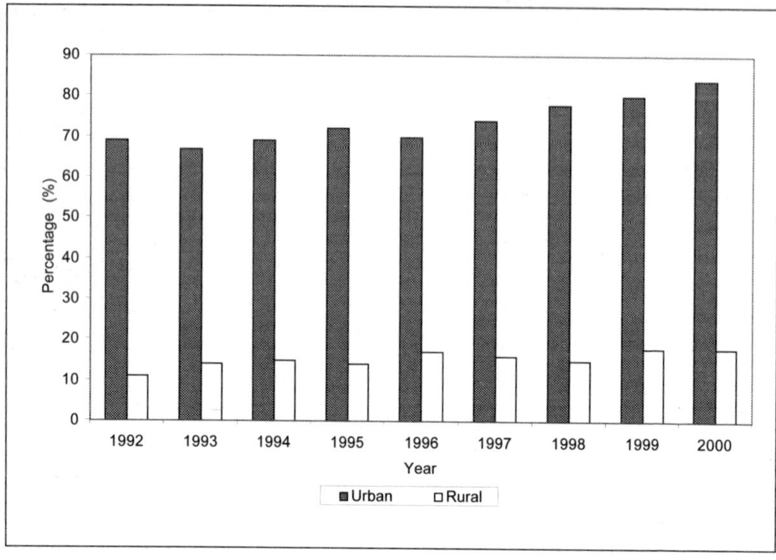


Figure VA.1.5  Urban and rural electrification levels, 1992–2000 (%)

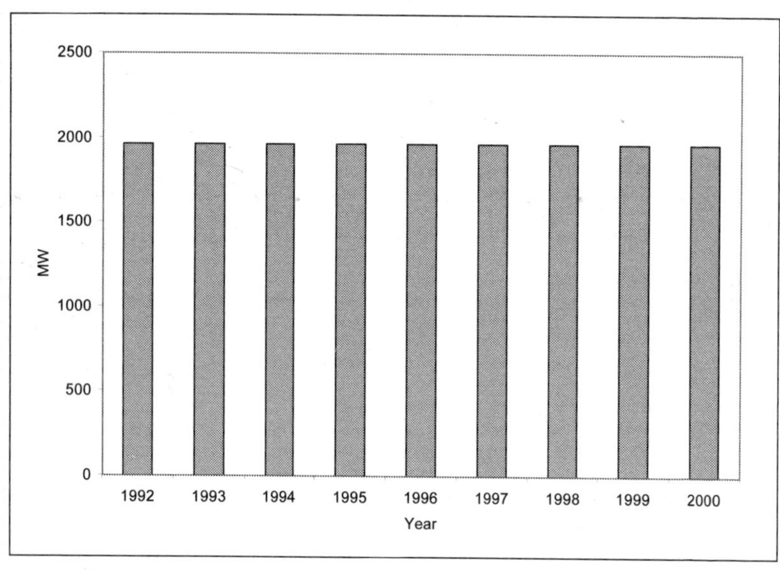


Figure VA.1.6  Installed capacity, 1992–2000 (MW)

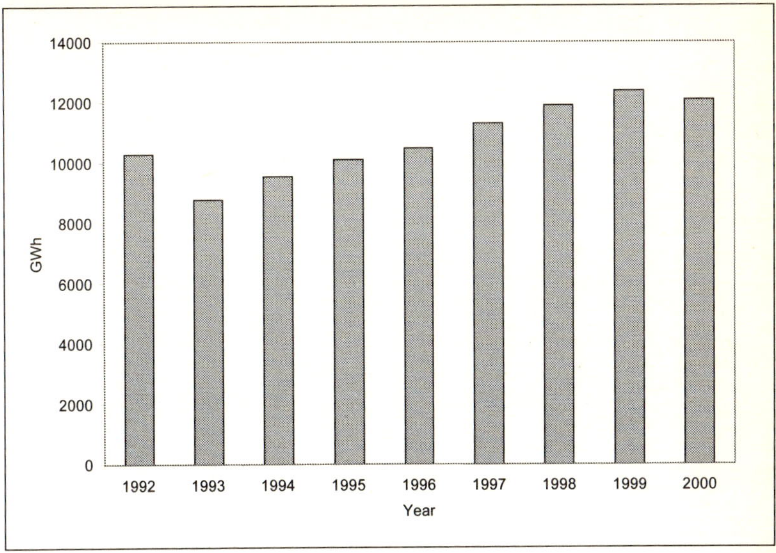

Figure VA.1.7  Electricity generation, 1992–2000 (GWh)

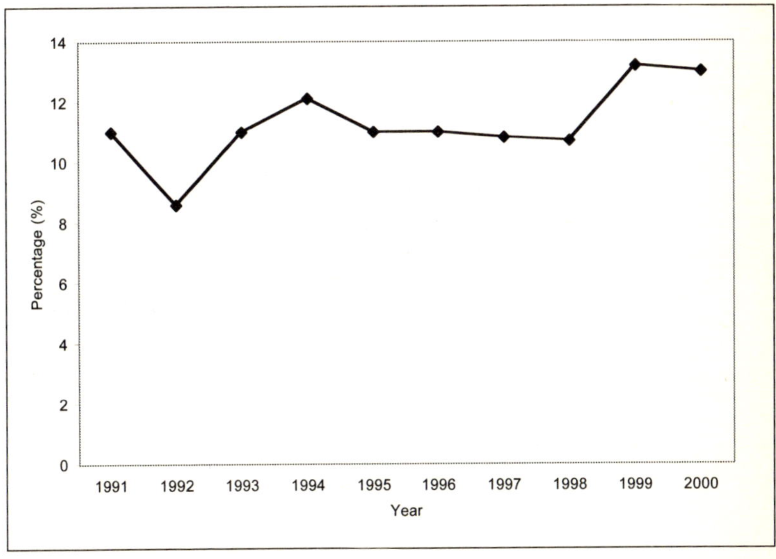

Figure VA.1.8  System losses, 1991–2000 (%)

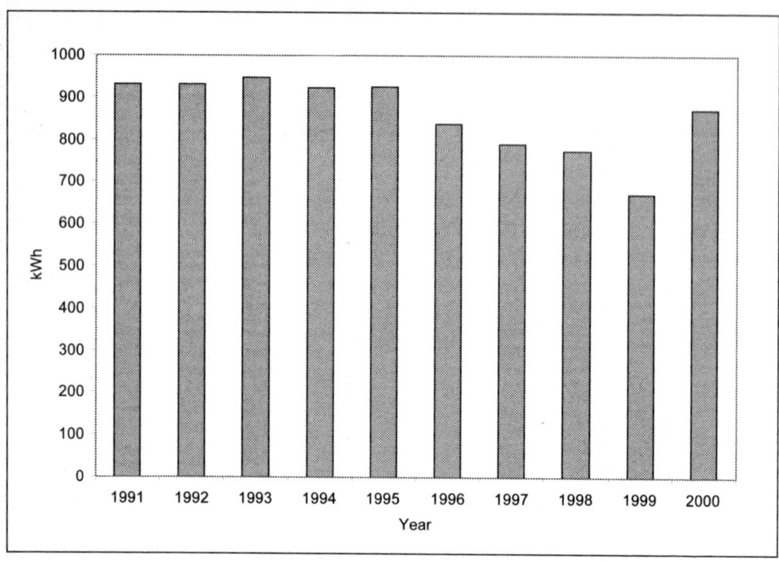

Figure VA.1.9  Electricity consumption *per capita*, 1991–2000 (kWh)

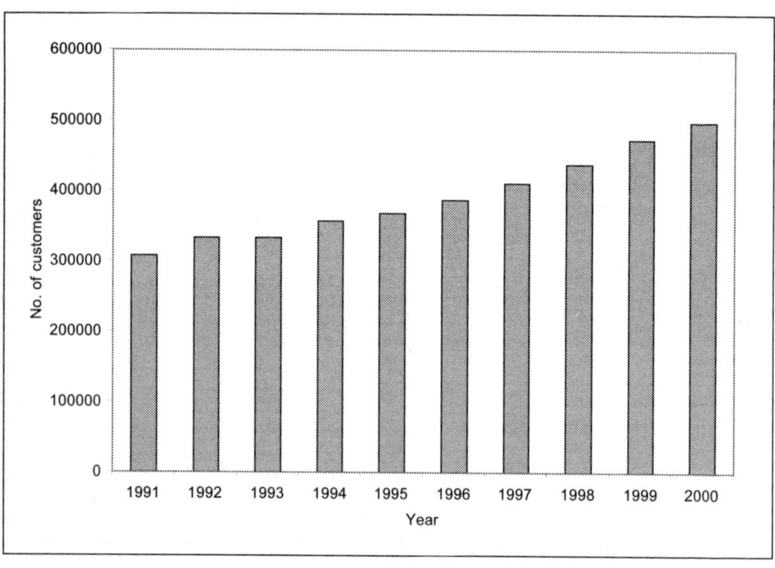

Figure VA.1.10  Number of customers, 1991–2000

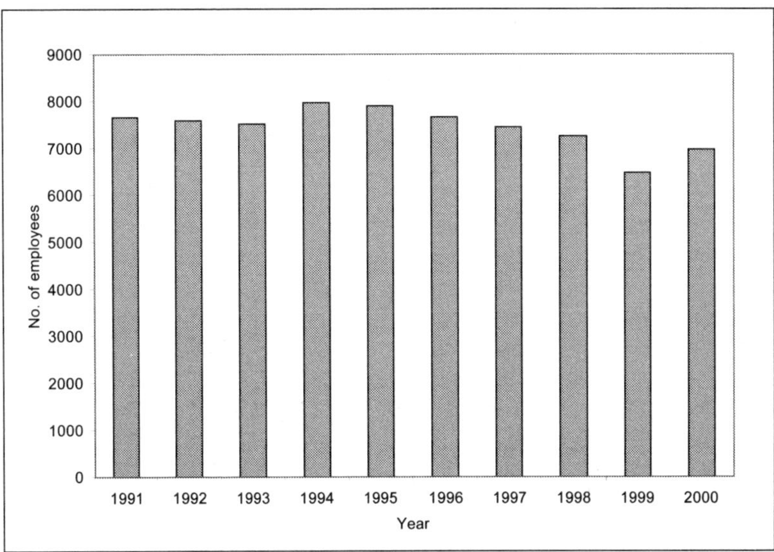

Figure VA.1.11  Number of employees, 1991–2000

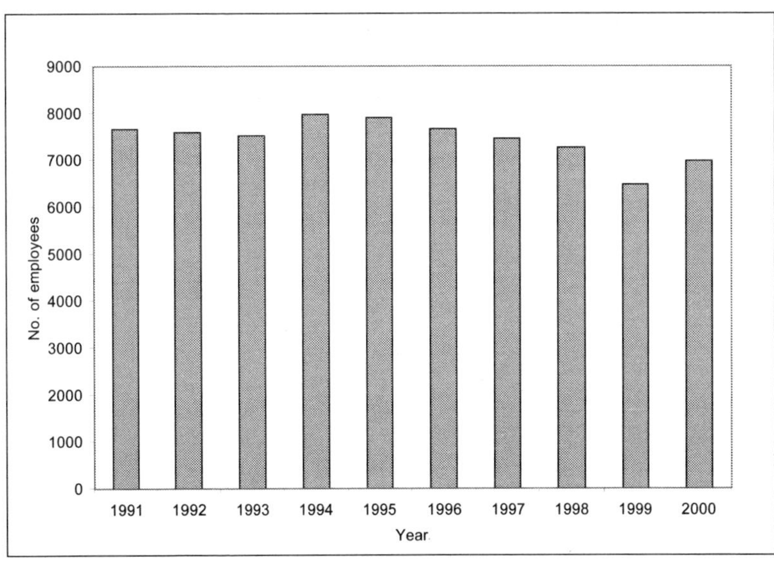

Figure VA.1.12  Number of customers per employee, 1991–2000

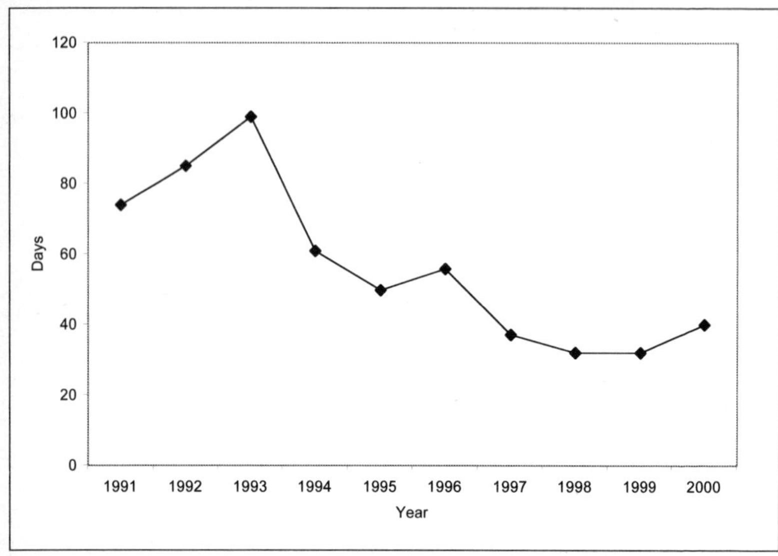

Figure VA.1.13  Debt collection period, 1991–2000 (days)

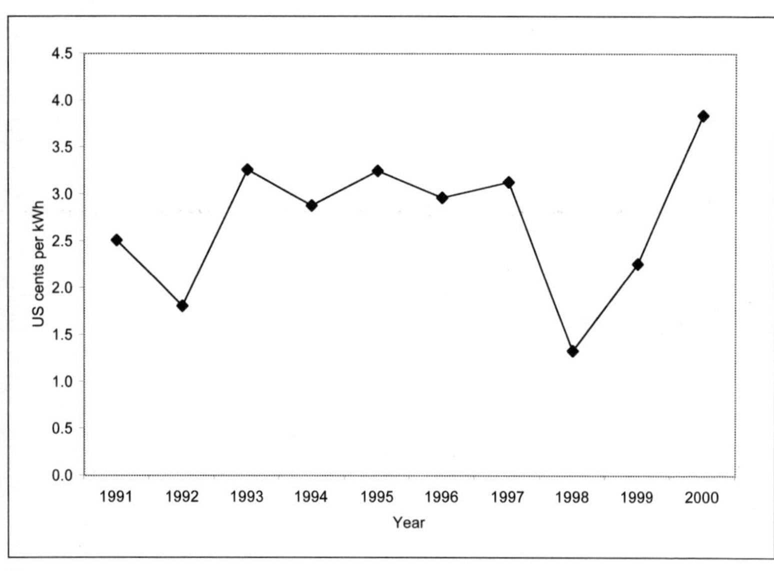

Figure VA.1.14  Average electricity tariffs, 1991–2000 (US cents per kWh)

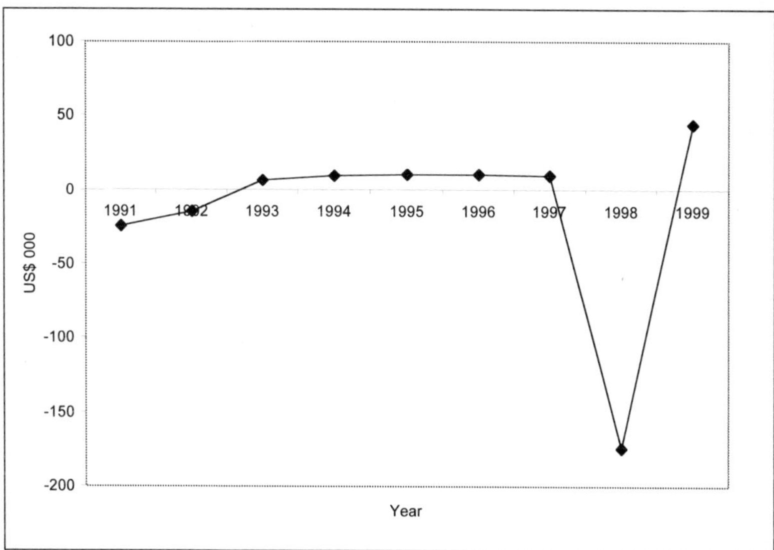

Figure VA.1.15  Profit/losses, 1991–9 (US$ 000)

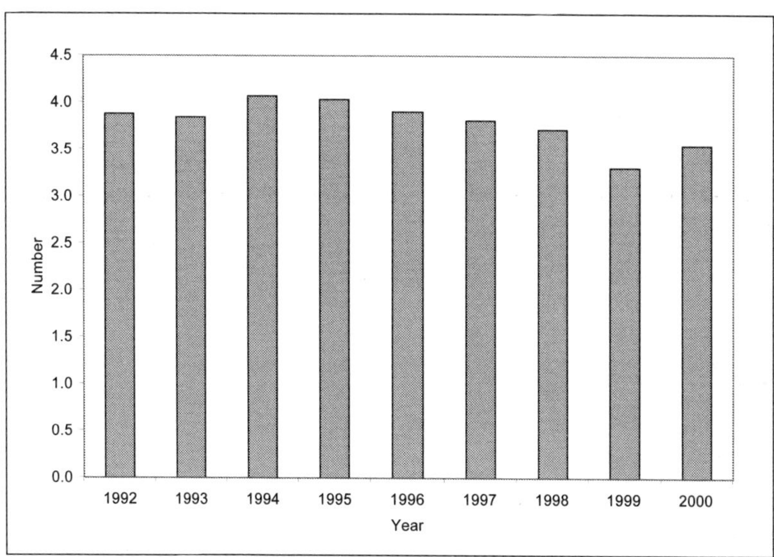

Figure VA.1.16  Number of employees per MW installed capacity, 1992–2000

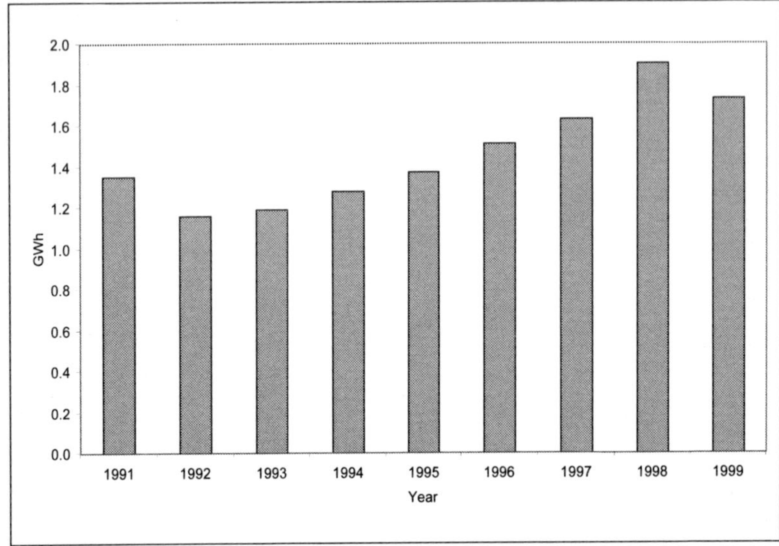

Figure VA.1.17  Electricity generated per employee, 1991–9 (GWh)

## Part V Appendix 2  ZESA staff breakdown 1999

| Department | Executive & senior management staff | | |
| --- | --- | --- | --- |
| | Establishment | Strength | Variance |
| Chief Executive's Office | 3 | 3 | 0 |
| Corporate Planning | 4 | 3 | −1 |
| Corporate Services | 3 | 3 | 0 |
| Finance | 4 | 4 | 0 |
| Generation | 9 | 9 | 0 |
| Technical Services | 7 | 6 | −1 |
| Consumer Services | 14 | 13 | −1 |
| Transmission | 7 | 2 | −5 |
| Total | 51 | 43 | −8 |

| Department | Managerial & senior supervisory staff | | |
| --- | --- | --- | --- |
| | Establishment | Strength | Variance |
| Chief Executive's Office | 7 | 5 | −2 |
| Corporate Planning | 10 | 7 | −3 |
| Corporate Services | 13 | 11 | −2 |
| Finance | 28 | 27 | −1 |
| Generation | 186 | 176 | −10 |
| Technical Services | 27 | 12 | −15 |
| Consumer Services | 236 | 194 | −42 |
| Transmission | 59 | 35 | −24 |
| Total | 566 | 467 | −99 |

| Department | Degreed professional staff | | |
| --- | --- | --- | --- |
| | Establishment | Strength | Variance |
| Chief Executive's Office | 21 | 14 | −7 |
| Corporate Planning | 23 | 16 | −7 |
| Corporate Services | 18 | 15 | −3 |
| Finance | 5 | 4 | −1 |
| Generation | 61 | 65 | 4 |
| Technical Services | 26 | 18 | −8 |
| Consumer Services | 94 | 66 | −28 |
| Transmission | 33 | 24 | −9 |
| Total | 281 | 222 | −59 |

| Department | Non degreed professional, skilled & junior supervisory staff | | |
| --- | --- | --- | --- |
| | Establishment | Strength | Variance |
| Chief Executive's Office | 8 | 6 | −2 |
| Corporate Planning | 15 | 14 | −1 |
| Corporate Services | 55 | 46 | −9 |
| Finance | 54 | 58 | 4 |
| Generation | 432 | 411 | −21 |
| Technical Services | 121 | 95 | −26 |
| Consumer Services | 1011 | 800 | −211 |
| Transmission | 175 | 107 | −68 |
| Total | 1871 | 1537 | −334 |

| Department | Semi-skilled & general staff | | |
| --- | --- | --- | --- |
| | Establishment | Strength | Variance |
| Chief Executive's Office | 5 | 5 | 0 |
| Corporate Planning | 3 | 3 | 0 |
| Corporate Services | 489 | 440 | −49 |
| Finance | 48 | 57 | 9 |
| Generation | 963 | 1072 | 109 |
| Technical Services | 193 | 188 | −5 |
| Consumer Services | 3319 | 3229 | −90 |
| Transmission | 135 | 199 | 64 |
| Total | 5155 | 5193 | 38 |

# Part V Appendix 3  Calculation of annual grant: Zimbabwe Manpower Development Fund

(a)   For technical practical subjects offered in workshops and laboratories
   Grant (G) = Total number of approved trainees (T) x Annual basic entry salary grade of lecturer II (S) at Ministry technical colleges based on a ratio of one trainer to 12 trainees (R)

   i.e.      $G = \dfrac{T \times S}{R}$

(b) For non-technical/ancillary subjects offered in classrooms
   Grant (g) = Total number of approved trainees (T) x Annual basic entry salary grade of lecturer III at Ministry technical colleges.

*Calculation of rebates*
Rebates are calculated according to category of approved training programmes as shown below.

A   Apprenticeship and upgrading training. Employers claim rebates in respect of expenses incurred.

B   Industrial attachments
   Rates:   $3 per hour per trainee in the first and second years of their training programmes.
            $2 per hour per trainee in the third and final years of their training programmes.

C   Formal courses offered by either the national training institutions or professional bodies recognized by the Ministry: employers facilitating the training of their employees at these institutions may claim rebates calculated as follows:
   (i)   Courses at government institutions: Rebate = 100 per cent of total expenses
   (ii)   Courses at other institutions
      (a)   For courses on which expenses are less than or equal to those in (i) above:
            Rebate = 10 per cent of total costs.
      (b)   For courses on which expenses are more than those in (i) above:
            Rebate = First amount equivalent to government rate + 25 per cent of excess expenses.

D   Practical on-the-job training leading to either membership of professional bodies recognized by the Ministry or registered by a body established by a local statute:
   Rate: $1.50 per hour per trainee.

E   Training in essential non-designated trades/occupations:
   Rate: $2 per hour per trainee.

F   Industrial training centres
   Employers with industrial training centres offering certain apprenticeship and upgrade training programmes, with the approval of the Ministry, may claim rebates as under Category C.

G   Provision of trade testing facilities: employers who provide such facilities may claim rebates at $100 per candidate.

H   Release of employees for part-time teaching at Ministry technical institutions:
   Rates:  Full rate per hour based on the employee's basic salary plus $60 per hour payable to such lecturers through the employer.

# Part VI

## SOUTH AFRICA

**Peter Ngobese and Mankone Ntsaba**

# South Africa

**South Africa: selected indicators**
**Area (km²):** 1, 221,038
**Population (millions):** 43.4 (2000)
**Capital city:** Pretoria
**GDP (US$ million):** 127,000 (2000)
**GDP growth rate (%):** 3.0 (2000)
**GNP *per capita* (US$):** 3,170 (2000)
**Literacy levels (%):** (1998)   **Total:** 85
                      **Male:** 85
                      **Female:** 84
**Official exchange rate (Rand: US$):** 7.7 : 1 (2000)
**Economic activities:** Agriculture, mining, tourism, commerce, financial services, textile manufacturing, construction
**Energy sources:** Coal, hydro, nuclear, oil, solar, biomass, bagasse
**Name of dominant electricity utility: ESKOM**
**Installed capacity (MW):** 39,186 (2000)
**Total modern energy consumption (000 toe):** 48,087.2 (1999)
**Modern energy consumption *per capita* (kgoe):** 1,108 (2001)
**Electricity consumption *per capita* (kWh):**  4,336 (2000)
**Electricity generation (GWh):)** 189,307 (2000)
**Electricity generation per employee ratio:** 5.77 (2000)
**System losses (%):**  5 (2000)
**Electrification level (%):** (2001)  **National:** 70.4
                       **Urban:** 83.5
                       **Rural:** 50.3
**Number of customers:** 3,110,405 (2000)
**Number of employees in dominant utility:** 32,882 (2000)
**Customers per employee ratio:** 95 (2000)
**Employees per installed capacity ratio:** 0.84 (2000)
**Employees per GWh of generation ratio:** 0.17 (2000)
**Profit/loss (US$ million):** 3,049 (2000)
**Transmission line length (km):** 358,370 (1999)

Source: AFREPREN/FWD, 2001

# 15

## Country Background

## Physical and socio-economic characteristics

With a population of over 40 million, South Africa has a total land area of 1,223,201 square kilometres, accounting for 4 per cent of the African continent (see brief country profile opposite, and additional time series data in Part VI Appendix 1). Average annual rainfall is 464 mm, about half the world average. Drought is a common feature in many parts, which limits the potential for hydropower and constrains the availability of water for cooling in coal-fired power stations. The average annual temperature of 17 Celsius reflects hot summers and temperate winters. The moderating influence of the sea and altitude results in moderate temperature variations across the country in the order of 6 Celsius. In contrast to most African countries, lower winter temperatures imply a high demand for space heating. As a result, the energy sector is characterized by peaky winter electricity consumption patterns and problems of indoor pollution in poor households that rely on coal for heating.

**Table 15.1  Key economic indicators, 1992–6**

| Economic indicator | 1992 | 1993 | 1994 | 1995 | 1996 | 1997 | 1998 | 1999 |
|---|---|---|---|---|---|---|---|---|
| GDP at current market | | | | | | | | |
| prices (Rand bn) | 341.0 | 383.1 | 432.8 | 484.6 | 542.7 | 594.9 | 737.0 | 795.6 |
| Real GDP growth (%) | −2.5 | 1.5 | 2.8 | 3.1 | 3.3 | 1.4 | −0.4 | 1.9 |
| Consumer price inflation (%) | 13.9 | 9.70 | 9.00 | 8.60 | 7.40 | 8.50 | 7.00 | 5.10 |
| Exports ($bn) | 23.60 | 24.10 | 24.90 | 28.00 | 30.23 | 31.17 | 29.26 | 28.62 |
| Imports ($bn) | 19.80 | 20.00 | 23.40 | 27.00 | 27.40 | 28.35 | 27.21 | 24.47 |
| Trade balance ($bn) | 5.80 | 5.80 | 3.40 | 1.60 | 2.10 | 3.75 | | |
| Total external debt ($bn) | 27.2 | 25.5 | 27.9 | 22.3 | 23.6 | 25.2 | 24.7 | 24.2 |
| Manufacturing production | | | | | | | | |
| (1990 = 100) | 92.4 | 92.3 | 94.7 | 103.0 | 100.5 | 103.6 | | |
| Mining production | | | | | | | | |
| (1990 = 100) | 85.2 | 79.6 | 77.9 | 99.3 | 98.8 | 100.9 | | |
| Exchange rate (R : $) | 2.90 | 3.30 | 3.60 | 3.60 | 4.30 | 4.60 | 5.50 | 6.10 |

Source: EIU, 1997b; AFREPREN/FWD, 2001

A striking feature of South Africa is a combination of indicators associated with middle-income countries, such as the GDP, and those displayed by very poor countries, such as low literacy, high population growth and very high unemployment (see country profile on page 220 and Table 15.1). With a GDP *per capita* income of R17,545 (US$3,579) South Africa is generally classified as an upper-middle-income country. South Africa has one of the highest income inequalities in the world, with a Gini coefficient of about 0.7 (Table 15.2). Income inequality is also reflected in the fact that the bottom 20 per cent of income earners receive only 15 per cent of national income, while the wealthiest 10 per cent of households receive 50 per cent (International Labour Organization, 1997).

The poverty line for a household with two adults and three children in 1994 has been drawn at approximately R10,080 and R8,880 for urban and rural households respectively (Whiteford *et al.*, 1995). On this measurement it has been estimated that close to half of all households in South Africa live in poverty, with slightly more than half (59 per cent) of all women living below the poverty line (Banda, 2002). As of 1995, just over a third of households had access to electricity (DMEA, 1995). It is now estimated that close to 70 per cent of the county's population have been connected to power supplies (NER, 2001b). Mass unemployment is one of the features of South African society. The unemployment rate is about 36 per cent (Central Statistical Services, 1996), and is further aggravated by the inaccessibility of land, which in many countries forms a basis for rural livelihoods.

GDP growth figures have shown an upward trend in the 1992–6 period, reaching a peak of 3.4 per cent in 1995 (Table 15.1). The government's Growth Employment and Redistribution (GEAR) strategy proposes a growth rate of 6 per cent for the country to meet its poverty reduction and employment creation obligations. The political changes that have occurred in South Africa in the last few years have led to many economic policy reform initiatives.

While South Africa has solved most of its political problems and created a democratic society, the country faces the challenge of redressing developmental backlogs created by the apartheid policies of the past. Major challenges include social and economic inequalities: a large number of people living in poverty; unemployment; and little or no access to education and training for the majority of the population. Part of the country's poverty reduction strategy is the expanded provision of key services such as health, education, water, sanitation and electricity. A further challenge will be the development of human and institutional capacity to manage development programmes and deliver services. In terms of human resources development performance, the World Competitive Report (1996) ranked South Africa last out of 46 developing countries. This poor performance can be attributed directly to poor access to education and training by a large majority of the population.

**Table 15.2  Comparative indicators for selected countries, 1999**

| | Middle-income countries | | | | | | | Sub-Saharan Africa | | |
|---|---|---|---|---|---|---|---|---|---|---|
| | Thailand | Poland | Chile | South Africa* | Brazil | Malaysia | Venezuela | Kenya | Nigeria | Tanzania |
| Life expectancy (years) (1998) | 72.5 | 73 | 75 | 65 | 67 | 72.5 | 73 | 52 | 54 | 48 |
| Infant mortality rate (1998)** | 29 | 10 | 10 | 48 | 33 | 8 | 21 | 74 | 77 | 85 |
| Adult illiteracy rate (%) (1998) | 5 | 0 | 4.5 | 16 | 16 | 13.5 | 8 | 21 | 40 | 28 |
| Total fertility rate (1998) | 1.9 | 1.4 | 2.2 | 2.8 | 2.3 | 3.1 | 2.8 | 4.7 | 5.3 | 5.5 |
| Access to safe water (%) (1998) | 89 | 82 | 85 | 59 | 72 | 89 | 79 | 45 | 50 | 49 |
| Gini coefficient | 0.42 | 0.33 | 0.57 | 0.69 | 0.6 | 0.49 | 0.49 | 0.51 | 0.45 | 0.365 |

* The South African data are an average of all races. There are large differences between the races in these social indicators

** Death of infants under 1 year old per 1000 live births

All Gini coefficients are based on income, except for those for sub-Saharan Africa, which are based on expenditure (a Gini of 0 signifies absolute equality and 1 absolute concentration)

Source: RDP, 1995; World Bank, 1999

## The energy sector

This section briefly discusses South Africa's energy sector with an emphasis on the power sector. It examines the interrelationships between various energy sources, the institutional structure of the sector and policies for human resources development.

*Energy supply*

The energy sector of South Africa combines a number of different fuel types, with various sources of supply and a host of governing institutions. The sector operates within a dynamic policy environment, closely linked to policies in other sectors such as the environment, forestry, finance, trade and education. Capacity building, which is the central theme of this study, is linked to educational and associated human resources development policies.

South Africa is a major coal producer and exporter, and has a sophisticated synthetic fuel industry that is led by the SASOL conglomerate. It is therefore not surprising that the country's energy economy is predominantly coal-based, with about 80 per cent of domestically produced coal utilized by ESKOM for power production and by SASOL for petroleum production. The country's energy balance sheet is given in Table 15.3. Coal, as the primary fuel produced, is also the second-largest foreign exchange earner. The total annual coal production of over 200 million tonnes is comprised of mainly bituminous coal with a relatively high ash content (DMEA, 1995). About a third of the total coal produced is exported, mainly to Europe and the Pacific ocean countries. Domestic consumption is about 163 million tonnes annually, used mainly in the production of electricity. Other domestic consumers of coal include the gold mining industry, steel manufacturing and the various industrial processes required in the production of synthetic fuel and petrochemicals. Some of the coal beds have been identified as having a potential for coal-bed methane development. This potential was investigated through a project supported by the US Department of Energy as an alternative energy source for domestic and industrial sectors.

South Africa generates over half the electricity produced on the whole African continent. The power utility ESKOM is ranked as the fifth-largest in the world in terms of installed capacity. ESKOM is responsible for most of the generation and transmission in the country and has been able to generate power at some of the world's lowest prices. Very low electricity generation costs have limited the development of independent energy producers (IPPs). Anderson (1994) notes that industries such as gas, coal mining and pulp and paper manufacture have the potential to produce a sizeable amount of power for themselves. This potential has not been realized because of the low-cost electricity that ESKOM can deliver. A larger component of distribution to the domestic market is the responsibility of municipalities.

Table 15.3  Energy balance (million tons of oil equivalent), 1999

|  | Oil | Gas | Coal | Electricity | Other | Total |
|---|---|---|---|---|---|---|
| *Primary supply* | | | | | | |
| Production | 1.5 | 1.6 | 118.5 | 4.4 | 11.5 | 137.5 |
| Imports | 19.0 | 0.0 | 0.0 | 0.6 | 0.0 | 19.6 |
| Exports | −4.0 | 0.0 | −30.5 | −1.2 | 0.0 | −35.7 |
| Stock change | 0.0 | 0.0 | 0.0 | 0.0 | 0.0 | 0.0 |
| Total | 16.5 | 1.6 | 88 | 3.8 | 11.5 | 121.4 |
| | | | | | | |
| *Processing and transformation* | | | | | | |
| Losses and transfers | −22.0 | −1.6 | −69.5 | −6.0 | −3.0 | −102.1 |
| Transformation output | 26.5 | 0.6 | 0.0 | 17.5 | 0.0 | 44.6 |
| Total | 4.5 | −1.0 | −69.5 | 11.5 | −3.0 | −57.5 |
| | | | | | | |
| *Final consumption* | | | | | | |
| Transport | 16.5 | 0.0 | 0.0 | 0.3 | 0.0 | 16.8 |
| Mining & industrial | 1.5 | 0.6 | 9.0 | 9.5 | 1.5 | 22.1 |
| Residential etc. | 2.3 | 0.0 | 4.0 | 5.5 | 7.0 | 18.8 |
| Non-energy uses | 0.7 | 0.0 | 5.5 | 0.0 | 0.0 | 6.2 |
| Total | 21.0 | 0.6 | 18.5 | 15.3 | 8.5 | 63.9 |

Source: EIU, 1997b; AFREPREN/FWD, 2001

The planned power sector reform will see ESKOM divided into several separate entities. The distribution will be transferred to a separate holding company named EDI (Electricity Distribution Industry) Holdings (NER, 2001a). In 2004 the firm will be divided into separate units that could merge with municipalities to form independent regional electricity distributors.

Since the country relies on coal for 83 per cent of its primary energy consumption it is one of the highest producers of greenhouse gas emissions in the world (Group for Environmental Monitoring, 1994).

GENERATION

South Africa currently has substantial excess generating capacity mainly from ESKOM's 24 power stations. ESKOM's generation group maintains a portfolio of 13 coal-powered plants; of the other 11, two use gas turbines, six are hydroelectric, two rely on pumped storage and one is nuclear-powered. ESKOM's 39,870 MW nominal capacity comprises of (NER, 1999):

- 35,627 MW coal-fired (89 per cent);

- 2,061 MW hydroelectric (5 per cent);

- 1,840 MW nuclear (5 per cent);

- 342 MW gas turbines (1 per cent).

TRANSMISSION

ESKOM's transmission group manages a network of about 280,000 km of power lines, of which about 26,000 km constitute the national grid. The Southern African Power Pool network is interconnected with the electricity grid of neighbouring countries. In 1996, exports of energy by ESKOM to South African neighbours was 2.7 per cent of South African consumption and amounted to US$75 million. The main interconnection with the north is the 420 km 400 kV Matimba–Bulawayo line which carries 300 MW to Zimbabwe (ESKOM, 1997a). It was hoped that by the middle of 1997 ESKOM would become a net importer of energy, through the rehabilitation of the 533 kV DC lines linking South Africa to Cahora Bassa in Mozambique. This major project, involving the reconstruction of about 2 x 800 km of line, will soon be finalized as negotiations between the two countries on electricity pricing have now been concluded.

Discussions between SADC countries and the Democratic Republic of Congo are well advanced with regard to the further development of the Southern African Power Pool (SAPP). According to the White Paper, ESKOM will be representing South Africa in these discussions, as the SAPP is largely a utility-driven initiative. However, the National Electricity Regulator (NER) may also be required to participate, in particular to ensure that the regulatory arrangements within the countries comprising the SAPP are consistent with those operating within South Africa (NER, 2000).

DISTRIBUTION

While generation and transmission are relatively well managed and coordinated, distribution is poor because of the fragmented nature of the industry. Distribution has generally been poor in the apartheid-era black municipalities, which were plagued with problems of poor infrastructure, lack of trained personnel and poor financing and cost-recovery mechanisms. This was a direct result of years of neglect caused by the policies of the apartheid governments. The new democratic local authorities are faced with the problem of integrating the former 'white' and 'black' municipal services. Many municipalities do not have the expertise and experience necessary to deal with the new areas they have to serve.

The planned restructuring of the electricity distribution industry will partially address this issue. The blueprint report was submitted to the Cabinet Committee for the Economic Sector in March 2001. It is expected that EDI restructuring will be completed in 2004, when the national holding company will be unbundled into separate entities. There is the possibility that the unbundled entities could merge with municipalities to form independent regional electricity distributors.

*Energy demand*

South Africa is a high-energy, semi-industrialized country and accounts for 45 per cent of total energy demand on the African continent. High energy intensity has been encouraged by low prices. Energy intensity is the energy used per unit of output. In this respect, the World Bank (1994) notes that only ten out of 111 surveyed countries have higher industrial primary energy intensity than South Africa. This high energy intensity points to the urgent need for a re-examination of energy efficiency management in the country.

At the same time the current electricity demand projections of ESKOM, which are based on the GDP growth of 3 per cent per annum, are lower than the potential electricity growth. The main consumers of electricity are mining and industry (Table 15.3). Although this pattern is not expected to change drastically, the growth rate of domestic consumers is likely to be considerably higher. Management of domestic demand will differ from that of industry as domestic demand has greater demand peaks. This poses a challenge for the service providers who will have to design management strategies appropriate for meeting the envisaged peaks.

The average electricity consumption of wealthy households is in the region of 600 to 800 kWh per month. With a target of 400,000 to 450,000 new household connections to electricity per year, it was envisaged that an accumulative total of approximately 65 per cent of all households would have been electrified by 1999. By the end of that year this target had been met in full through the commitment of ESKOM and local governments (NER, 2000: 13).

ESKOM maintains that it produces some of the cheapest electricity in the world. Its coal-fired power stations are backed by the country's total coal reserves of about 55 billion tonnes (DMEA, 1998), enough to last for up to 50 or 60 years. Thus, existing stations could meet new demands for electricity, assuming that demand grows by between 3 and 3.6 per cent. Industry, which accounts for 52 per cent of the energy consumption in the country, utilizes mainly coal and electricity. Coal and electricity account for 58 and 36 percent respectively of total energy consumption in the industrial sector (DMEA, 1995). Energy consumption in the industrial sector is mainly for mineral beneficiation and manufacturing, which make up 50 and 20 per cent respectively of energy requirements in the sector.

Given the growth in demand for electricity of 2.8 per cent per year, it was estimated that up to 1,000 MW more electricity would be required by the year 2000, and that by the year 2004/5 South Africa would begin experiencing a shortfall in electricity supply (Barraclough, 1997).

*Institutional structure of the energy sector*
Energy cuts across a number of sectors and, therefore, has a broad range of stakeholders. There are a number of government departments and institutions involved in energy management in South Africa. Their functions include planning and policy formulation, policy implementa-tion and advocacy, service provision and research. ESKOM employs about 39,000 people and electricity entities controlled by local authorities

**Table 15.4  Employment in the energy sector**

| Entities | Employment levels |
| --- | --- |
| ESKOM | 33000 |
| Local authorities | 36000 |
| Liquid fuel service stations | 45000 |
| SASOL and MOSSGAS | 27000 |
| Crude oil refineries | 6000 |
| Coal mining | 59000 |
| Coal vendors | no data |
| Woodfuel vendors | no data |
| Total employment | 206000 |

Source: ESKOM, 2001

about 33,000. The energy sector as a whole is estimated to employ as many as 250,000 people, as indicated in Table 15.4.

Investments in the electricity sector, particularly in ESKOM power stations, have made a major contribution to the country's gross domestic fixed investment (GDFI) (Van Horen, 1994). For example, ESKOM's capital expenditure of R5.25 billion in 1985 represented as much as 18 per cent of the country's GDFI. This has declined over the years, however, owing to excess capacity on ESKOM's part: its capital investment of R3.6 billion in 1992 represented only 7 per cent of GDFI for that year. In the petroleum sector, most of the institutions are in the private sector although the state has invested heavily in the synthetic fuel plants of SASOL and more recently in MOSSGAS (*ibid.*)

The process of formulating energy policy is therefore complicated by numerous stakeholders in the energy sector (DMEA, 1995). For example, within the power sector the NER licenses, regulates and sets standards for the electricity supply industry. The Department of Mineral and Energy Affairs (DMEA) formulates policy and administers all legislation relating to energy, such as the Electricity Amendment Act of 1994 that established the NER.

*National energy policy*

National energy policy is driven by international forces which impact on South Africa's reintegration into the global economy, and also by domestic forces determined by the country's national priorities and needs. During the apartheid era, South Africa was exposed to economic sanctions, which included an embargo on fuel oil. In response, South Africa formulated policies driven by the need for security and self-sufficiency.

Measures associated with these policies included:

1  Development of the synthetic fuel industry which entailed producing oil from coal at SASOL and the production of gas from coal at MOSSGAS.

2   The development of a nuclear industry that currently consumes two thirds of the DMEA budget.

3   Stockpiling of oil reserves through the Strategic Fuel Fund.

All these measures are being reviewed, and the DMEA plans to scrap the massive subsidies to the synthetic fuel industry. With the abolition of apartheid and the lifting of sanctions, South Africa's new international outlook includes the need to attract investment by creating an environment where energy sources are widely accessible and affordable. Global competition has forced the country to re-examine how energy impacts on industry's performance in world markets.

Within the SADC region, South Africa participates in the Energy Cooperation Policy Strategy, which seeks to promote energy trade within the SADC countries. Participation in the Southern African Power Pool also requires that South Africa develop policies that are in harmony with the region's electricity sector.

Since the inception of the Government of National Unity, South Africa has embarked on a policy reform process that endorses the principles of equity and efficiency as opposed to the past policies that were driven by the need for security and energy self-sufficiency. Equity, economic efficiency and sustainability have therefore become key requirements. The current developments in energy policy reform occur within a broader economic context defined by GEAR and the Reconstruction and Development Programme (RDP).

International treaties such as the United Nations Framework Convention on Climate Change will require South Africa to review how its energy operations affect the environment. The White Paper on Environmental Management identifies the energy sector as the largest single source of greenhouse gases in Africa, and proposes that South Africa should consider measures to control emissions. The Paper further identifies measures to deal with defaulters. This implies that key actors in the energy sector will have to devise means to deal with the emission problem. The White Paper also identifies indoor pollution as a major environmental problem affecting poor households. The main source of indoor pollution is the burning of fuels such as wood and coal as a result of poor access to 'cleaner' energy such as electricity. There are instances, however, where electricity is available but not affordable. Current energy reform processes should therefore consider mechanisms that will ensure that electricity and other cleaner energy sources are affordable to the poor.

## Education and human resource development policy

Key human resources development challenges are posed by the current levels of education and the need to respond to the mentioned imperative of economic development. The government has embarked on a process of policy reform that would increase the level and relevance of skills in the country. The Department of Labour has recently produced a Skills Development Bill proposing a new approach that complements the formal education system. It attempts to link skills development to the requirements of a growing economy and extends education and training to people both within and outside formal employment. It is primarily concerned with industry-based training to improve the intermediate-level skill base of the country's workplaces and labour market. It also targets groups that are considered to be underprivileged on the basis of financial status. The objectives of the proposed Skills Development Bill are as follows:

- to increase the skills profile of the population in south africa;

- establishment of national coordination among qualification authorities, industry and government so as to increase awareness of the skills that are in high demand;

- partnership between public and private sector;

- promoting investment in or funding of skills development in the workplace.

The White Paper on Public Service Training and Education, on the other hand, recognizes a number of problems that hinder the proper training, and therefore empowerment, of public servants. The problems can be described broadly as:

- the fragmented and uncoordinated approach to education and training across the public service;

- the lack of a strategic approach to public service training and education based on needs, outcomes and competence;

- the inappropriate nature of training and education provided by external service providers.

The resultant policy reforms have analyzed a variety of options. Ultimately the country's education and training of public servants will reflect the competence-based model proposed in the Skills Development Bill. This has major implications for capacity building in the power sector.

# 16

## Capacity Building in the Power Sector

Capacity building in the power sector is a sub-component of a broader demand for human resources development in South Africa. Factors that affect human resources development, especially in science, engineering and technology, will affect initiatives in the power sector. These factors include past and present policies on education/training and the availability, allocation and management of resources.

This chapter looks at the current capacity-building initiatives in the power sector. Sources of manpower for the sector are identified. An assessment is made on how this manpower is deployed and mobilized for the success of the sector. Also identified are the challenges facing the sector in relation to manpower needs and skill gaps within the overall energy sector.

Capacity building and human resources development in the power sector are being transformed in response to changes in the country's broader national priorities and the related energy needs. Notable initiatives include the establishment of energy policy institutes at various universities; the establishment of energy training and policy NGOs; and outreach programmes for energy users. Curriculum reform has been made through modest attempts to integrate energy studies into the broader educational system. These initiatives occur as isolated efforts by individual institutions in a policy vacuum, however, or in response to a number of sectoral policies. So far there has not been an attempt to integrate capacity building or training and education policies with sectoral policies such as those of energy or the environment.

Important priorities in ongoing capacity-building initiatives in the power sector include:

- Awareness of capacity-building needs in the power sector among government officials and other decision makers in state corporations. This can be encouraged through the various university energy and policy institutes, workshops, conferences, bi-national training programmes and in-house training.

- The need to increase the technical and management capacities of power sector personnel who are trained in tertiary institutions. This can be addressed mainly through the curriculum and research programmes of the relevant faculty.

- Enhancement of power sector research capacity in universities and other research institutions in collaboration with regional and international research networks.

- Enhancement of technical and management capacity within key institutions in the electricity supply industry such as ESKOM, municipalities, consultants and regulators.

- Initiatives to enhance capacity among urban and rural energy users on the basic technical, social and environmental dimensions of electricity use.

## The power sector

In this chapter, the power sector refers to all those institutions, companies or other entities and activities that are concerned with the planning, generation, transmission, distribution and broader management of power. It also includes regulators and policy makers in the power industry and in government.

*Department of Mineral and Energy Affairs*
The Department of Mineral and Energy Affairs (DMEA) has initiated programmes of capacity building and training throughout all staff levels in the Department. The DMEA has embarked on a training programme with components that range from basic literacy through technical training to policy training. One such course introduced cleaning and associated personnel to computers. The Department also uses some of its associated institutions such as the Atomic Energy Corporation and the Institute of Geoscience to provide training in science and mathematics to post-matriculation students.

Higher management and policy training is facilitated through university bursaries offered by the Department to qualifying students. The Department of Energy of the United States and the DMEA in South Africa have established a Sustainable Energy Committee co-chaired by the US Secretary of Energy and the South African Minister of Mineral and Energy Affairs. The Committee aims to create a market for renewable energy and standards for energy efficiency that will contribute to South Africa's electrification goals while benefiting the economy and environment.

The Committee has also initiated a programme with US government and industry funding to train public officials in the energy sector. The US Department of Energy has also funded the training of entrepreneurs to establish and run renewable energy businesses. The Committee is supporting the DMEA proposal for a programme to increase citizen's awareness of energy and environmental issues.

DMEA has further commissioned the Energy and Development Group, a private consultancy firm, to develop a capacity-building and awareness strategy for low-income rural and urban households. The project, known as Household Energy Action Training (HEAT), has a number of objectives which include:

1  Development of content and methodology for household energy capacity-building initiatives.

2  Development of materials for information dissemination.

3  Identification of target groups for the initiative.

*Private companies*
At the end of 1996 there were four licensed private power-generating plants in the country: a bagasse plant operated by the Tongaat Hullet Sugar Company, two coal-based chemical and fuel processing co-generation plants operated by SASOL and a mini-hydro plant.

The total capacity of these plants was 881 MW, of which 769 MW was provided by the SASOL plants (NER, 1999). Although these private plants were generating electricity primarily for their own requirements, there is potential for co-generated power to supply the national grid at some point in the future (Anderson, 1994). The manpower requirements and training for these co-generated plants are generally met through the companies' own policies on human resource development.

Although private companies and consultants offer in-service training, this has generally been low by international standards. South African private companies spend about 2 per cent of overheads on training as opposed to an international average of at least 10 per cent. The corporate sector as a whole, however, contributes significantly to trusts and foundations that provide support for education, health and other aspects of social development. Total corporate expenditure on these amounted to R56.7 million in 1995, with the bulk spent on education. It is estimated that between 1987 and 1990 the corporate sector spent as much as R167.4 million on education in South Africa in terms of either scholarships or vocational training. Umbrella business organizations such as the South African Chamber of Business (SACOB) and others have established the Private Sector Educational Council (PRISEC) to lobby for changes to the educational system.

*Municipalities*
Municipalities in South Africa have an electricity generating capacity of 2,436 MW, of which 45 per cent is generated by the Greater Johannesburg Metropolitan Municipal Council. The other significant generating capacity is shared amongst Pretoria (21 per cent), Cape Town (18 per cent), Port Elizabeth (11 per cent) and Bloemfontein (4 per cent). The municipalities are organized into four to five departments, which are defined as clusters: technical, finance, human resources, community services, and urban planning and development. Although they often have policies for the maintenance of appropriate workforce skills, this is not always the

case. Shortages of skills are most prevalent in the smaller municipalities with modest budgets.

In order to maintain efficiency, municipalities insist on employing personnel with recognized qualifications. Technical staff must have an approved apprenticeship certificate obtained from the Apprenticeship Board, which is in constant liaison with the education boards of the various universities and technikons. This practice allows the quality of training to be constantly improved in line with emerging sectoral trends.

Training of employees is encouraged and supported by an independent fund, which is obtained from electricity tariffs. Training courses vary between two weeks and three years, and vary according to the skills needs expressed by each municipality. The current electricity management reforms may have an impact on the sources of funding for training. One of the proposed policy actions is that electricity tariffs should no longer be used to finance or subsidize other activities of the municipality. It is currently unclear how training will be financed in the future.

### National Electricity Regulator (NER)

Because of tight financial resources, the National Electricity Regulator (NER) does not currently have any bursary or other financial support programmes for engineers and technicians. If resources become available, however, the NER will support bursary programmes for the study of electricity regulation. The NER believes that operators in the industry should build the basic level of technical expertise, while the NER should support the training of regulation specialists.

In order to achieve its goals, the NER ensures that its employees attend various training courses to enhance their knowledge and levels of skill. Employees are also granted financial assistance to enable them to further their academic qualifications in fields of study that will be beneficial to the NER. In addition, both management and junior cadre employees undergo management training in areas such as team building (NER, 2001b).

### ESKOM

ESKOM's human resources management recognizes the need to increase employee skills in order to improve productivity and enhance efficiency in all its operations. Until 1995, ESKOM had been spending about R200 million per annum on various educational and training programmes. This figure increased to R300 million in 1996. ESKOM has taken cognizance of the fact that the South African education system is deficient in science, engineering and technology, which limits the availability of graduates for recruitment. Furthermore, ESKOM has noted that it is no longer sufficient to have professionals with qualifications limited to engineering. Other areas of expertise such as business administration and leadership are also required. In response to these challenges, ESKOM has established a number of training programmes for various staff categories.

High-level technical training takes place in local universities in the

Faculties of Engineering and Science. This is supplemented with technical training overseas. Trainees are supported by ESKOM's bursary scheme, which is also extended to employees' children (ESKOM, 1997a).

At the artisan level, training in technical skills takes place at the ESKOM Training Centre in Midrand. The centre also trains employees from other companies, and from outside the country. In order to meet its affirmative action targets, ESKOM has committed itself to increasing the intake of black students at the centre.

Apprenticeship training takes place at the Wilge power station. The station provides training on the technical operation and management of a power station. Many of ESKOM's plant operators have been trained at Wilge. To increase its management capacity and to fast-track black and female employees in management positions, ESKOM has introduced a management development training programme. Over 800 staff members have completed the course. Of the total participants, 22 per cent were either black or female.

To increase literacy within its labour force, ESKOM has invested in adult basic education. In 1996, 1,356 employees completed the course at a cost of R32 million. To date, close to 10,000 employees have undergone literacy and numeracy training with an average pass rate of 57 per cent.

STAFFING ISSUES AT ESKOM

ESKOM has a current total staff complement of 32,832 and is the largest single employer in the power sector (Statistics SA, 2001). Although municipalities collectively employ more people, no single municipality employs as many individuals in the power sector. ESKOM's staffing profile is historically derived, and consequently has a skewed racial and gender profile. Since the 1980s, however, there has been an attempt to institute affirmative action and a proactive corrective recruitment policy. The policy is supported by strategies such as the 'pipeline' development of staff, whereby the organization provides scholarships at high school and tertiary level as a 'seedbed'. On the other hand, the organization has embarked on external recruitment from other power utilities from the region when the local pool was insufficient to meet 'affirmative action' appointments. This was supplemented by aggressive headhunting.

As far as affirmative action is concerned, Kobokoane (1995) argues that there are at least three South African companies that are considered as leaders in this field, namely ESKOM, the Development Bank of Southern Africa (DBSA) and African Life, an insurance company. These are the only companies where more that 10 per cent of the total number of middle to upper managers are black. At ESKOM, the target to which the organization committed itself was that at least 50 per cent of its junior to senior managers would be blacks by the year 2000. At present above 42 per cent of senior management positions are held by blacks, up from 5 per cent in 1992. ESKOM's employment by race over a ten-year period (1984–94) is indicated in Table 16.1.

**Table 16.1  ESKOM employment by race over a ten-year period (1984–94)**

| Year | Total | Asian | Coloured | Whites | Blacks |
|---|---|---|---|---|---|
| 1984 | 63600 | 100 | 4000 | 24600 | 34900 |
| 1985 | 66200 | 100 | 4100 | 25800 | 36200 |
| 1986 | 63760 | 60 | 4000 | 24700 | 35000 |
| 1987 | 56840 | 40 | 3400 | 22800 | 30600 |
| 1988 | 57170 | 70 | 3300 | 24100 | 29700 |
| 1989 | 52400 | 100 | 3100 | 23000 | 26200 |
| 1990 | 50920 | 120 | 3000 | 23200 | 24600 |
| 1991 | 47940 | 140 | 2600 | 22400 | 22800 |
| 1992 | 45890 | 190 | 2500 | 22000 | 21200 |
| 1993 | 42480 | 248 | 2319 | 20751 | 19162 |
| 1994 | 39972 | 336 | 2314 | 19147 | 18175 |

Source: Central Statistical Services, 1996

Over a ten-year period employment levels in ESKOM have decreased by 37 per cent. The employment of blacks has decreased by 48 per cent whereas for whites the decrease has been 22 per cent and for coloured people 42 per cent. The number of Asians employed, on the other hand, has increased three-fold, although they constitute less than 1 per cent of total employment. The decrease in total employment has not been uniform across racial categories and relative to occupational classes.

## Supply of manpower to the power sector

The preceding sections describe the status of skilled manpower in the power sector while this section looks at the supply of manpower to the sector. Supply in this context refers to the quality and quantity of personnel available to the sector. A description of supply should contain not only the numbers and sources of trained manpower, but also the type and content of training that is available in the country. The supply of qualified manpower is determined by the ability of the tertiary institutions to produce the required manpower. On the other hand, the universities are dependent on the number and quality of incoming students who are willing and able to start tertiary education.

The power sector in South Africa draws its skilled manpower from various sources. These include universities for high-level management and engineering personnel; technikons for technicians and engineering diplomas; and technical high schools for assistant technicians. The rest of the support staff, such as clerks and secretaries, is obtained from the general population of school leavers. The sector still employs a large number of semi-skilled and unskilled workers from the general population. The current study will only look at skills and staffing in those areas that are specific to the power sector, as opposed to general support staff, who are present in every sector.

*The education system*

The shortcomings of the education system in South Africa are different from those of many countries in sub-Saharan Africa. Reasons cited for educational shortcomings in the wider region include public spending cuts under structural adjustment, reduced foreign aid, falling personal incomes and high population growth (Noonan, 1994). South Africa, on the other hand, has a somehow different set of problems, mainly related to the negative consequences of the legacy of apartheid.

On the positive side, South Africa has achieved the most developed and well-resourced system of education and training in Africa (*ibid.*), known for the high quality of its diplomas, degrees and postgraduate research output (National Commission on Higher Education, 1996). South African education, however, also displays characteristics of the extreme racial segregation that dates back to 1948, when education was officially structured along racial and ethnic lines. This effectively excluded blacks from quality education and other forms of training. The net result has been a large pool of uneducated and unskilled labour. This in turn has had a negative impact on productivity and economic growth (Preece, 1990). The link between the lack of education and the incidence of poverty is well established in South Africa (Whiteford *et al.* 1995). Access to education has had a racial and gender dimension, with African females and white males being the least and the most advantaged social groups respectively, as indicated in Table 16.2.

**Table 16.2 Level of education by race and gender among those aged 20 years plus (percentage of group with particular level)**

| | African female | African male | Coloured female | Coloured male | Indian female | Indian male | White female | White male |
|---|---|---|---|---|---|---|---|---|
| Higher | 6 | 6 | 5 | 5 | 9 | 15 | 24 | 30 |
| Std 10 | 12 | 15 | 12 | 15 | 29 | 36 | 42 | 42 |
| Std 6–9 | 33 | 36 | 40 | 40 | 35 | 40 | 33 | 26 |
| Std 4–5 | 15 | 14 | 22 | 17 | 11 | 6 | 1 | 1 |
| Grade 1–Std 3 | 15 | 15 | 13 | 14 | 7 | 2 | 0 | 0 |
| None | 20 | 14 | 9 | 9 | 9 | 2 | 0 | 0 |

Source: Central Statistical Services, 1996

South Africa presents the anomaly of a high expenditure on education coupled with a high illiteracy rate (Preece, 1994). About 15 per cent of the population is illiterate (World Bank, 2000), yet the country spends 6 per cent of its GDP on education and training, which remains the largest single item on the government's budget, being 21.3 per cent of total government expenditure. However, the budget allocation to education as a proportion of GDP is expected to decline in real terms over time (Department of Education, 1997).

The government has recognized that the crisis in education is not solely financial but due to a lack of capacity in the management of the education system. Nevertheless, the country has an inverse skills profile whereby 76 per cent of the workforce is either semi- or unskilled. In the energy sector, 63 per cent of the workforce is in this category (DMEA, 1995). The low levels of education within the labour force impact negatively on productivity. The challenge here is for the country to work better and more efficiently with limited resources. This can only be achieved if there is a concerted effort to introduce training initiatives that will improve skills and, ultimately, performance.

The labour force skills distribution profile should also be understood within the context of the competing sector requirements for training in science, engineering and technology. The country's human resources performance in any particular sector is determined by the rate at which South African universities produce graduates and technologists trained in science. Currently, South African universities are producing appreciably higher numbers of social science graduates than those in science and technology. This has a bearing on ratios of scientists, engineers and technologists to the rest of the population. In 1994, for example, the country had a total of 392,688 degree holders, whose breakdown between engineering and science and by racial groupings is

**Table 16.3  Types of degrees held by South African population, 1994**

|  | Total | Asians | Coloureds | Whites | Blacks | Unspecified |
|---|---|---|---|---|---|---|
| Engineering | 26289 | 425 | 149 | 24378 | 234 | 1103 |
|  | (6.7%) | (1.6%) | (0.6%) | (93%) | (1%) | (4.2%) |
| Science | 34120 | 1796 | 1165 | 27429 | 2057 | 1673 |
|  | (8.7%) | (5%) | (3%) | (80%) | (6%) | (5%) |
| Total all graduates | 392688 | 19730 | 14537 | 298582 | 42345 | 17494 |
|  |  | (5%) | (4%) | (76%) | (11%) | (4%) |

Source: Human Science Research Council, 1996

indicated in Table 16.3.

Whites had 76 per cent of all degrees held in the country and 93 and 80 per cent respectively of those in engineering and science. Blacks, on the other hand, held 11 per cent of all degrees but 1 and 6 per cent respectively of those in engineering and science.

*Supply of matriculants to universities and technikons*
The aforementioned imbalances in the levels of education for the country as a whole originate from inequalities engendered at lower levels of education, particularly at secondary school matriculation level. Matric-

ulation results differ significantly amongst the races, with pass rates in the core science subjects and mathematics being in the region of 20 per cent for blacks and 80 per cent for whites. Current levels of unemployment and attendant poverty force many black children to drop out of school and seek employment in a bid to support themselves and their families. In the process, many black children never get an opportunity to finish their secondary education, let alone attain tertiary qualifications.

Furthermore, only a small proportion of black matriculants are enrolled in mathematics and physical science. In the 1980s, for example, only 30 per cent and 15 per cent of black matriculants were enrolled in mathematics and physical sciences, respectively (*ibid.*). This was also a reflection of the fact that teacher shortages in science, technology and mathematics in black schools were as high as 70 to 90 per cent.

Results from the Department of Education and Training, responsible for black education at that time, indicate that black matriculants who wrote examinations in mathematics and physical science in the 1980s had very high failure rates (see Figure 16.1). This has had a negative impact on the ability of the country to produce black scientists and technicians. Preece (1994) stresses the need for appropriate education of the highest quality in the future if the skills profile of the country is going to meet the demands of the economy and reflects the nation's racial profile.

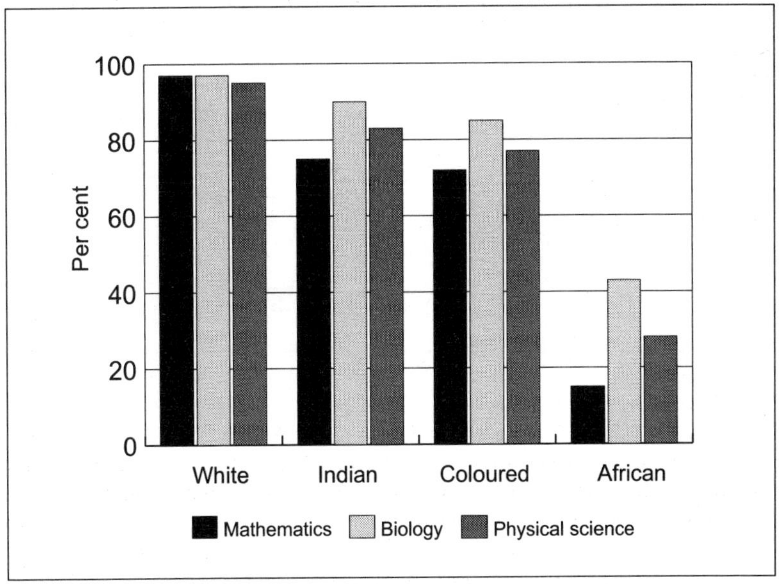


Figure 16.1 South African matriculation results: % pass in science and mathematics, 1980s

Source: FRD, 1995a

South Africa's language of business and education is mainly English, yet in many instances student performance in English at matriculation level is very poor. English is also an entry requirement in all English-speaking universities. While a lot of attention should be paid to mathematics and science, similar efforts are required to improve performance in English as the main language of instruction and broader communication.

### Universities and technikons

In South Africa there are various institutions offering degrees, diplomas and courses in a wide range of fields such as economics, engineering and management. Table 16.4 presents the names of tertiary institutions that offer Electrical Engineering studies. Most of these institutions are 'historically white universities' from which the power sector draws most of its high-level technical manpower. The introduction of engineering in South Africa was influenced by the country's mining history. Tertiary institutions developed curricula that reflected the mining industry's past dominance of the country's economy.

**Table 16.4  Listing of electrical engineering departments by province**

| Province | Tertiary institutions | Province | Tertiary institutions |
| --- | --- | --- | --- |
| Western Cape | University of Cape Town<br>University of Stellenbosch<br>Cape Technikon<br>Peninsular Technikon | Gauteng | Rand Afrikaans University<br>University of the<br>    Witwatersrand<br>University of Pretoria<br>Technikon Witwatersrand<br>Technikon Pretoria<br>Vaal Triangle Technikon<br>Technikon Northern<br>    Gauteng |
| Eastern Cape | Rhodes University<br>Port Elizabeth Technikon<br>Border Technikon | KwaZulu–Natal | University of Natal<br>University of Durban<br>    Westville<br>Natal Technikon<br>ML Sultan Technikon |
| Free State | Free State Technikon | North-West | Potchefstroom University |

Source: Modified from Braun, 1997

Later, the focus shifted from mining to industrial engineering. The tertiary institutions then began to focus on power, electronics and communications engineering. Most of the engineering degrees from the different universities are recognized by South African and foreign professional associations. The Engineering Council of South Africa (ECSA) accredits engineering graduates for electrical, electronic, mechanical and civil engineering.

As far as degree curricula are concerned, the universities believe that the students must have a wide range of knowledge and skills. The various types of engineering courses that are available include courses on management, report writing and presentation skills; important aspects of training if students are to be deployed successfully in the power sector.

Theoretical training in these institutions is not the only type of training offered. Practical training is emphasized from the first year. Engineering design programmes have been introduced throughout the curricula and a vital Design Project is presented during the third year of study. Vacation work is also important for students, in order to promote 'hands-on' experience and skills training.

The University of Cape Town (UCT) has perhaps the most comprehensive energy training programmes, some of which are specific to the power sector. The Faculty of Engineering has established a new inter-disciplinary programme in electro-mechanical engineering. The programme emphasizes integrated studies to produce graduates who are generalists rather than specialists, at home in a broad area of professional engineering practice.

Another aim that is driven by the needs of the power sector is to produce engineers with cross-disciplinary skills, particularly in the fields of electro-mechanical power systems and mechatronics. The programme also includes components from the fields of economics and management, to provide a broad range of skills required by the job market. The content of the programme has been influenced by a number of companies who also sponsor students for future recruitment.

UCT also houses the Energy for Development Research Centre (EDRC) whose main areas of activity are in energy research and consulting and in educating and training students for employment in the energy sector. EDRC has consolidated its research activities into a number of programmes, including 'Energy Markets and Governance'. The programme researches policy in the electricity and gas sectors, with a special emphasis on governance, regulation, restructuring, pricing and finance (EDRC, 1997). For example, EDRC has undertaken a project to develop policy options for widening access to basic energy services for the urban and the rural poor. The major aim of the project is to ensure the maximum amount of interaction between researchers and key decision makers in energy institutions and other relevant stakeholders. Another aim of the project is to produce a cadre of energy policy specialists who can influence policy to address the needs of the poor.

The Rand Afrikaans University (RAU) houses the Institute of Energy Studies. The Institute provides both education and research, concentrating mainly on energy policy support and on energy planning. The Institute is also involved in generating national statistics and modelling future energy supply and demand.

The Department of Engineering at the University of the Witwatersrand has a dedicated research programme in power engineering. Funded by

ESKOM's tertiary education support programme, it provides specialist training and research in the area of electricity and allied industries. The programme also runs the Power Engineering Winter School, which attracts students from the university and participants from the electricity industry.

*Supply of engineers, economists and scientists*
South Africa had over 200,000 'professional, semi-professional and technical workers', of whom 91 per cent were white and the rest black in 1990 (Commonwealth Expert Group, 1991). The racial breakdown in the fields of engineering, management and related fields in that year is indicated in Table 16.5.

**Table 16.5  Selected professionals by race (1990)**

| Occupational category | Total number | White | Blacks |
| --- | --- | --- | --- |
| Electrical and related | 1675 | 1648 (98%) | 27 (2%) |
| Electronic, civil and related | 4798 | 4735 (99%) | 63 (1%) |
| Computer science/computer programmes | 6580 | 5727 (87%) | 853 (13%) |
| Personnel and management service/ manpower planning | 310 | 280 (90%) | 30 (10%) |

Training in energy-related disciplines in South Africa has tended to focus on the purely technical aspects of professional qualifications and skills to be utilized, as opposed to their social context (*ibid.*, 1991). Such training has not taken sufficient cognizance of the developmental status of the country and has thus tended to create an élite professional class somewhat out of touch with the country's development needs. Thus the question of the relevance of the curriculum is now beginning to predominate. At the aforementioned University of Cape Town, the design of degree programmes is also being re-evaluated.

It is now recognized that there is a need to transform the academic programme for engineers at South African universities. Changes would include more training in the fields of management, the behavioural sciences and information systems. To achieve this paradigm shift, South African engineering students need better career counselling to show students how their skills could be optimally utilized. According to the Foundation for Research Development (1996), the balance between teaching and research at universities used to be tilted 80 per cent towards high-tech solutions and only 20 per cent towards developmental aspects.

In addition to the high-tech bias of the product of South African engineering education there is also a spatial concentration of this product. A comparison of the number of professionals, technicians and managers across South Africa's nine provinces indicates that at least a third are located in one province, Gauteng, as indicated in Table 16.6. Although

Table 16.6  Comparison of the number of professionals, technicians and managers across South Africa's nine provinces (1994 )

| Province | Number | Percentage of SA |
| --- | --- | --- |
| Western Cape | 278878 | 14.04 |
| Northern Cape | 24073 | 1.21 |
| Free State | 89509 | 4.51 |
| KwaZulu–Natal | 409815 | 20.63 |
| Eastern Cape | 213210 | 10.73 |
| Mpumalanga | 73508 | 3.70 |
| Northern Province | 149928 | 7.53 |
| North-West | 99857 | 5.0 |
| Gauteng | 647606 | 32.63 |
| Total | 1986384 | 100.0 |

Source: FRD, 1995b

this is a reflection of the dominance of this one province in the country's economy, greater numbers of scientists, engineers and technologists are surely needed in the other provinces (FRD, 1995b).

The power sector in South Africa is driven by engineering and technology, and, like many technology-based sectors in South Africa, it suffers from a lack of properly trained scientists and engineers able to incorporate important aspects of the social sciences into their operations. It was estimated that for the economy as a whole there would be a shortfall of 200,000 workers with a degree, diploma or comparable skills by the year 2000. The fact that there is very little in-depth and policy-oriented research around the question of the mobilization and utilization of human resources is a cause of concern. Part of the reason for this is that there appears to be a lack of consensus between academics and employers.

While employers and some academics are pushing for graduates with more general knowledge and life skills, some academics believe strongly in specialization. There is also disagreement on whether an interdisciplinary focus should be emphasized at undergraduate or postgraduate level. Debate on this question is compounded by the historical pattern of employment as reflected in the occupations filled by Africans and whites by gender (Table 16.7). Therefore, the supply of manpower to the power sector needs to focus on numbers, the racial and gender dimension, and the relevance of training. However, an exclusive focus on the least advantaged, although necessary, is not sufficient in itself.

One can determine shortages in manpower in any sector by examining the vacancy rate of particular professionals and relating it to the ability of the utility to recruit. Successful recruitment is determined, among other factors, by the ability of academic and other training institutions to supply the required number of professionals. There is an annual output of 100 graduates from South African university departments offering broadly

**Table 16.7 Occupation of employed Africans and whites by gender (percentage of persons in each occupation)**

|  | African female | African male | White female | White male |
|---|---|---|---|---|
| Managers | 2 | 4 | 8 | 19 |
| Professionals | 3 | 2 | 7 | 9 |
| Semi-professional/ technicians | 15 | 6 | 21 | 17 |
| Clerks | 10 | 7 | 47 | 7 |
| Sales/service | 11 | 11 | 11 | 10 |
| Artisan/crafts | 4 | 15 | 3 | 29 |
| Operators/assemblers | 4 | 20 | 1 | 6 |
| Elementary | 50 | 34 | 1 | 2 |
| Other and unspecific | 1 | 1 | 1 | 1 |
| TOTAL | 100 | 100 | 100 | 100 |

Source: Central Statistical Services, 1996

defined electric energy technology, but only some of them are available to the electrical industry (*ibid.*) For South Africa to reach the level of graduate output in this field of countries such as Canada or the United Kingdom, it would have to increase this output by between 900 and 1,000 over the next 25 years.

The vacancy rate measures vacancies as a percentage of total posts, and is therefore an indication of a shortage of manpower. Researchers in this field note that this index can be misleading, however, as it does not indicate the quality of labour. It may just indicate labour turnover. In some instances, posts may be frozen because the company has given up searching for the right skills. Wage rates may also be used as an index to show job categories where manpower is scarce. Vacancy rates are calculated using the following equation:

$$\text{Vacancy rates (\%)} = \frac{\text{Vacancies} \times 100}{\text{Employment} + \text{vacancies}}$$

At national level, South Africa's vacancy rates are highest in the fields of health, science and technology in the professional category (FRD, 1996). In the case of ESKOM, which has been in the process of reducing overall numbers of staff, the vacancy rate is somewhat misleading in that there has been a fair amount of internal rationalization and redeployment of staff.

One of the arguments advanced by ESKOM on why it has been able to maintain output in spite of shedding labour is that the nature of the industry itself is changing because of technological advancements. For example, at a typical ESKOM power plant that in the 1980s employed about

1,200 persons, 600 will do in the future. ESKOM reckons that the average technician is now able to do more, thereby contributing to increased productivity. Although ESKOM is more or less self-sufficient in its manpower requirements, it has had to increase the number of artisans it has under its artisan bursary scheme. On balance the utility produces slightly more than its requirements, given changes in the industry.

## Effectiveness and retention of skilled personnel

Using various measures and ratios, this section examines the effectiveness of existing skilled personnel in the electricity industry. It also reviews the extent to which the power sector has been able to retain and attract qualified and skilled manpower.

*Assessment of effectiveness of existing pool of energy professionals*
Areas where high-level manpower will be required in the electricity industry include generation, distribution and reticulation, utilization and manufacturing (Van Wyk and Reynders, 1990). This requirement will comprise not only technical competencies but also management, economic and financial skills. There is also a major gap in energy policy analysis.

As far as generation equipment is concerned, South Africa is not in a position to manufacture large generating equipment but will require the appropriate manpower to manufacture ancillary equipment. It is in distribution and reticulation that there is greater scope for developing appropriate technological solutions for the country. A correct proportion of electrical engineers at all degree levels (Bachelor, Master, Doctor) is required.

Another area of manpower requirement will be in environmental management. Apart from its corporate environmental programme, ESKOM has established an environmental management system throughout all its operations, and therefore requires qualified environmental scientists and managers.

There are certain internationally recognized indices for estimating the effectiveness of manpower, the efficiency of a power utility and the general capacity of a country to manage energy. (Some of these indices are presented in Table 16.8.) For example, an internationally accepted indicator of manpower efficiency power utilities is the ratio of employees per gigawatt hour (GWh). Thus the calculated generation efficiency of less than one person per GWh for ESKOM is extremely high when compared to other countries. This measurement is distorted, however, by the fact that ESKOM has a distribution subsystem that is smaller than that of comparable utilities. In many utilities, distribution employs a larger number of employees who are involved in a wide range of operational tasks such as billing, collection of cash, customer complaints, operations and maintenance and tariff setting. Furthermore, the ratio of employees

**Table 16.8  Power utility efficiency ratios**

| Efficiency ratio | ESKOM |
| --- | --- |
| Ratio of employees per GWh | 0.17 |
| Ratio of employees per customer/s | 95 |
| Wage bill per GWh | R23918 |
| Wage bill per customer/s | R2279 |
| Electricity revenue per employee | R717860 |

Source: Ntsaba, 2001; NER, 2001b; AFREPREN/FWD, 2001

per GWh may get distorted where there are large differences in the quality and seniority of the staff in question. In this respect, a more representative ratio would be the salary bill or the average salary to the amount of electricity produced. The wage bill per GWh for ESKOM is R23,918 (US$4,500).

Another internationally accepted indicator of manpower performance is the ratio of customers served per person employed. This ratio for ESKOM is distorted, too, since ESKOM sells power to a few large customers who further distribute what they purchase. More recent adjustment numbers for ESKOM indicate an employee ratio of about 230. A less distorted ratio could be the amount of electricity revenue per person employed. ESKOM has experienced a decline in staff numbers at an average rate of 3.1 per cent per year since 1985 (Table 16.1). On the other hand, customers have increased by an average of 46.5 per cent per year in the period 1992–6. This means that total electricity sold per employee has increased over the years.

*Retention and capacity mobilization (including in-service training)*
The retention of energy professionals, particularly in the public sector, is proving to be a challenge for South Africa. For instance, the Chief Directorate on Energy in the Department of Mineral and Energy Affairs had a vacancy rate of 17 per cent in 1994. The reasons advanced for the low retention of energy professionals in the Department include the relatively low pay scales of government and poor perceptions of the conditions of service in the public sector. The Department has been forced, in consequence, to recruit professionals with few if any specialized energy skills. The critical areas in which the Department has not been able to attract skilled personnel are multidisciplinary professionals with qualifications in engineering, business and economics (DMEA, 1995). The Department is particularly deficient in energy economists and energy system planners.

The Department has an affirmative action plan with set targets for the employment of blacks and women. These targets have still to be met. The apparent lack of affirmative action in the public service contrasts with internal staff development programmes in ESKOM. ESKOM has at entry level a 'graduates in training programme' which is compulsory and allows newly recruited graduates to cope with the organizational culture of ESKOM. In addition, ESKOM has an 'accelerated development programme' for blacks who have been with the organization for a long period. The programme is designed to equip them for senior positions. We have seen that its management development training programme is similarly designed to prepare staff for advancement and that its adult basic education programme aims at overcoming illiteracy within the organization.

The fact that ESKOM is the fifth-largest electricity utility in the world (Pickering, 1994) probably explains its attention to staff career development. Because of restructuring and commercialization, ESKOM has shed about 25,000 jobs, mostly in the unskilled and low-skilled categories (thus disproportionately affecting blacks) (Manga, 1996) This contrasts with gains in the higher skilled categories that have resulted in the somewhat changed racial profile of the organization, specifically at top management level (see Table 16.9).

**Table 16.9  Permanent staff strength by race, gender and skill level, 1994**

| Paterson grade | White | Black | Coloured | Asian | Total | Women |
|---|---|---|---|---|---|---|
| F | 17 | 5 | 0 | 0 | 22 | 1 |
| E 4-5 | | | | | | |
| E 1-3 | 190 | 9 | 1 | 2 | 202 | 4 |
| D 4-5 | 289 | 14 | 1 | 0 | 304 | 11 |
| D 1-3 | 1731 | 74 | 12 | 18 | 1835 | 161 |
| C 4-5 | 4380 | 176 | 36 | 49 | 4641 | 532 |
| C 1-3 | 4988 | 481 | 101 | 107 | 5677 | 748 |
| B | 7772 | 7033 | 1203 | 131 | 16139 | 3391 |
| A | 0 | 10359 | 932 | 1 | 11298 | 187 |
| Total | 19367 | 18151 | 2286 | 308 | 40118 | 5035 |

| | |
|---|---|
| Paterson F | Executive directors |
| Paterson E 4–5 | Senior–Executive management |
| Paterson E 1–3 | Senior management |
| Paterson D 4–5 | Middle–Senior management |
| Paterson D 1–3 | Junior–Middle management |
| Paterson C 4–5 | Assistant management–Senior supervisory & Junior professional graduate entry, Supervisory, Artisan & technician, Senior operative & Senior administrative/clerical/secretarial |
| Paterson B | Operative, administrative/clerical/secretarial |
| Paterson A | Entry-level operative & labourer |

South Africa as a whole has been experiencing significant shortages of skilled personnel and emigration has been increasing. In a recent survey of some 84 businesses it was found that two out of five respondents described the availability of top management as scarce and very scarce, suggesting that a skills shortage might constrain the economy sooner rather than later. Reasons given by scientists for emigrating include, among others, the diversion of resources from basic science; political and economic uncertainty; changes within their institutions; and general deficiencies in the way research is structured and funded in South Africa (FRD, 1995a).

ESKOM seems to have escaped this affliction in that it has managed to attract high-level skilled manpower from the rest of Africa (countries ranging from the Democratic Republic of Congo to Zimbabwe and Lesotho) and Eastern Europe. There has been less movement in the middle-management ranks.

## Policy challenges – power sector reform

This section reviews the prospects for manpower development in an electricity sector that is undergoing rapid restructuring and reform. As part of the socio-political changes that were initiated in 1991/2, a number of initiatives have been established to investigate and report on the problems of poor management in the electricity supply industry. In 1993, the National Electrification Forum (NELF) was established to design proposals and policy guidelines that would improve the management and efficiency of the electricity supply industry. The NELF proposed the establishment of the National Electricity Regulator (NER). NER's objective is the establishment and enforcement of order, structure and good decision making in the electricity supply industry while also ensuring that customers and stakeholders get an acceptable level of service from the various service providers.

NER has been granted power to issue licences for generation, transmission and distribution. This means that NER also has a regulatory control over ESKOM. Issuing licences to service providers is expected to improve performance. Municipalities, which in general have been understaffed and underperformed, will have to invest in human resource development in order to meet the performance standards set by the NER.

Many municipalities have been deriving much of their revenue from electricity sales and in some instances have used this income to subsidize other services. A review of this practice will require major changes. An issue currently threatening some of the service providers is that if a licence is awarded and the service provider is unable to meet the standards, the NER has the power to withdraw such a licence. Performance standards will obviously be determined by, among other things, availability of skilled manpower both in the technical and management fields, financial capability, technical innovation and appropriate infrastructure. This will pose a challenge to poorly financed and understaffed municipalities.

During 1997, however, the Electricity Restructuring Inter-Departmental Committee (ERIC) submitted its report, which recommended the establishment of a restructuring task team at ministerial level (Cowan, 1997) to give impetus to the restructuring of the sector. Government, mindful of the fragmented nature of the electricity distribution industry, has proposed in its ERIC report that ESKOM and the municipalities form regional electricity distributors (REDS).

The restructuring task team will determine the number, format and boundaries of the REDS (du Plessis, 1997). This will mean that ESKOM and the municipalities will now become involved in joint ventures in the operation and management of REDS, with generation being 'ring fenced' or incorporated into the REDS (Cowan, 1997). The NER meanwhile will undertake an economic and financial analysis of the electricity supply industry during 1998 and advise government accordingly on the options that are available for restructuring (NER, 1998). It is envisaged that the industry will be completely restructured by 2001/2. The human resources implications of such restructuring will also need to be taken into account, particularly as it relates to the demands for electricity.

A further challenge facing the electricity supply industry is respond-ing to the government's challenge to increase the level of electrification to 70 per cent of the population by the year 2000 (RDP, 1995). The rate of electrification has to be accelerated and extended to the rural areas where the backlog is greatest. This poses a further challenge to both trans-mission and distribution, as some of the rural areas are in remote parts of the country and are also dispersed.

The electrification of schools is one of the programmes contributing to the government policy of providing basic needs. The aim of the programme is to provide electricity to schools in all provinces. Partners in this venture are the Department of Mineral and Energy Affairs, ESKOM, and the provincial departments of education. The aim is to electrify 9,500 of the 25,000 schools that are without electricity. The remaining 15,500 will be provided with power by means of photovoltaic cells. It is believed that the schools electrification programme will present opportunities for labour-intensive construction and training.

All SADC countries except Mauritius are members of the Southern African Power Pool. The SAPP is guided by two principles of cooperation, which are:

- the obligation to wheel energy for others if technically feasible;

- the obligation to supply emergency energy to a neighbour in difficulty.

South Africa's participation in the SAPP includes plans to import low-cost hydropower from other countries in the region. This may require the development of new transmission capacity. For example, Mozambique has the potential to increase its hydropower generation five-fold from its current installed capacity of 2,200 MW to about 12,000 MW, a good proportion of which could be exported to South Africa (Barraclough, 1997). The combined effects of mass electrification, power importation and the current initiatives of the NER will impose ever increasing demands on the sector. These demands will be on the various components of the sector such as operations and maintenance, construction, management, information systems, cost recovery, environmental management, research, and education. The human resources base responding to these challenges has to grow both in sheer numbers and in technical expertise.

# 20

<hr>

## Policy Recommendations

The preceding chapters provide a basis for policy recommendations in capacity building for the power sector. The following policy recommendations are based on some of the proposals made within the current policy debate, and on policies implemented with varying degrees of success in other parts of the world.

## Dedicated power sector training fund

Development of a dedicated sector training fund for the power or any other sector is a common and tested option for funding capacity-building initiatives relevant to the sector. One advantage of having a dedicated sector training fund is that training budgets are separated from the day-to-day operating budgets of the utilities. In many instances, training and research-and-development budgets are the first to be cut in times of financial strain. Currently, companies' expenditure on training varies. Many take a short-term view of providing training in those skills which are of immediate need to the company, without due consideration of long-term needs or the needs of the broader sector. A dedicated sector training fund can be seen, therefore, as a means of injecting long-term strategic human resources planning in the sector.

To have legal standing, the fund would have to be established through an enforceable Bill. The government has proposed in its Skills Development Bill that dedicated sector training funds be established. This Bill calls for a levy equivalent to one per cent of the employers' payroll as the minimum level of investment required to finance skills development. However, 80 per cent of the funds would be retained by the Sectoral Education and Training Authorities (SETAs). The remaining 20 per cent would then finance a National Skills Fund (NSF). It is envisaged that the NSF would cover targeted training not covered by SETAs.

To be successful, the National Skills Fund should operate within an institutional structure that clearly defines roles and responsibilities. SETAs are in the process of being established. They will be responsible for (without being confined to) formal sector training. There are currently existing sector and professional training bodies. Many of these concentrate their training on individuals who are already in or are being prepared to enter a sector. This leaves out the majority of people who are unskilled and not associated with any particular sector. The NSF, on the other hand, will target people outside the formal sector, as well as the unemployed, women and the disabled.

## Affirmative action

Affirmative action is used in many parts of the world to redress inequities created by various forms of discrimination. In the South African context, affirmative action is used to create opportunities for groups historically subjected to discrimination such as blacks, women and the disabled. These groups are underrepresented at decision-making levels and in technical occupational classes. A number of policy documents and the Constitution support equal representation.

Implementation of affirmative action policies is not only meant to satisfy the Constitution or national policy, but should also be seen as a business imperative meant to improve the skills of the previously excluded. As mentioned earlier, the power sector is currently recruiting from a relatively narrow base when compared to the potential total workforce of the country. This is mainly because many people who could be providing the necessary skills base have been left out of the training and education programmes, which would make them eligible for employment.

By law, designated employers (those with 50 employees or more) are obliged to develop 'employment equity plans' aimed at achieving a workforce which mirrors national and/or regional demographics. In general, they must thus aim at a workforce, which is 75 per cent black at all levels, as well as 52 per cent female and some 5 per cent disabled. Some variation may be possible based on economic and financial factors, as well as the pool of 'suitably qualified' people available, but it remains uncertain how the size of this pool should be determined. Unfair discrimination is punishable by both compensatory and punitive penalties.

Programmes of staff support through training and the creation of career opportunities should accompany the implementation of affirmative action. All these initiatives have financial implications, which at present are the responsibility of the individual companies. Affirmative action, if made a component of the strategic human resources plan in the broader sector, should be financed like all other strategic initiatives within the sector. For instance, if the sector agrees to affirmative action targets, they should be allocated an appropriate proportion of the sector training fund.

The availability of funding for training and skills development programmes that would in turn feed into the affirmative action programmes in the power sector is one of the key factors. It is common knowledge that even though many students from disadvantaged communities desire to enrol in technikons and universities for engineering-related degrees and diplomas, they are incapable of paying the required fees.

## Curriculum reform and development

The White Paper on Transformation of Higher Education sets the scene for tertiary education reform in South Africa. It focuses on a number of issues such as equity, redress, autonomy, staff development and curriculum reform. Curriculum reform tends to be an expensive process, bearing in mind that its necessary conditions include the retraining of instructors, research for the development of materials and methodologies, and, in some cases, pilot programmes. Currently in South Africa, the individual institution or faculty finances curriculum reform in tertiary education. The degree of reform and the implementation may well be hampered by financial constraints within the institution.

A common option worldwide is to approach industry to finance reform initiatives that affect the sector in which the industry is operating. For instance, ESKOM contributed to the development of courses at the University of the Witwatersrand. The typical form of such arrangements is a private agreement between the two parties. This is a policy option that should be considered while disbursing funds for the dedicated sector training fund, so that the sector may have a say in the curriculum content of institutions that are training prospective employees.

## Regional capacity-building initiatives

A variety of capacity-building initiatives throughout sub-Saharan Africa have attempted to deal with the weaknesses in human and institutional capacity. There is general agreement on the need to invest in both technical advance and human resources development. Many of these efforts are externally funded; often they bring with them a large contingent of foreign expertise that pursues its own agenda, not necessarily in the national interest. This has been noted as a major reason for the failure of most African capacity-building initiatives.

Regionalization has been advanced as an approach through which African institutions can share knowledge and resources, creating fewer but more robust capacity-building initiatives. The major challenge in eliciting support for regional initiatives is to ensure that standards and accreditation are harmonized at the regional level.

There are various models for financing regional initiatives. Within Southern Africa, the existence of SADC sectoral structures and the SAPP present a platform from which broader regional financing initiatives can be created. A pool of funding generated from contributions by member countries or their institutions will be required, on a scale to be determined by a training assessment needs analysis. If, as we have seen, donor agencies fund most initiatives in sub-Saharan countries, part of this donor funding can also be pooled together to support regional capacity-building initiatives on a broader scale. In some instances, a single donor may be funding similar initiatives in more than one country. This creates an opportunity for recipient countries to pool these resources.

The existence of the SAPP will ensure that there is greater regional integration and scientific and technical progress in the power sector. This integration calls for communication and cooperation among member states and their institutions; it will require not only trained individuals, but also institutions with the capacity to run and maintain the various regional programmes. Multiple partnerships among countries, institutions and donors in the power sector should be identified to provide the basis for capacity-building initiatives in the sector.

An international institution that is operational in the region, and which can be used as a model, is the Carl Duisberg Gesellschaft (CDG), a German foundation for advanced international training in human resources development. CDG has established partnerships with various governments and organizations to offer people from all over the world training and practical experience to gain qualifications in diverse fields such as the environment and natural resources (including energy), infrastructure and communications, economics and social statistics, and poverty alleviation.

Another example is the African Capacity Building Initiative in policy analysis and development management. In its formative stages, the initiative formed a partnership between states, institutions, regional networks and donors. This was followed by a survey of existing regional capacity-building programmes and an investigation into the capacity of institutions in relation to national and regional needs. A similar but more localized sub-regional initiative is the Eastern and Southern Africa Management Institute (ESAMI), which conducts management capacity-building courses in the various sectors, including energy. (Selected energy-related management courses offered by ESAMI are shown in Table 17.1.). Finally, the African Energy Policy Research Network (AFREPREN) makes part of its contribution in this area by running a programme of short-term training courses on energy policy and a Masters degree programme in the same subject.

**Table 17.1  Energy-related management courses offered at ESAMI**

| | Course title | Target group |
|---|---|---|
| 1 | ESAMI/SADC Energy Ministers Seminar | Ministers from SADC member states |
| 2 | Rural Project Planning and Environment Management | Energy specialists from government utilities, NGOs and the private sector |
| 3 | Environmental Management | Staff working in all social and economic development sectors |
| 4 | Public Enterprise Restructuring and Privatization | Senior government officials in state-owned enterprises |

Source: ESAMI, 2001

# Part VI Appendices

## Part VI Appendix 1 Selected time series data, South Africa (table and figures)

Table VIA.1.1  Selected time series data, South Africa

| | 1992 | 1993 | 1994 | 1995 | 1996 | 1997 | 1998 | 1999 | 2000 |
|---|---|---|---|---|---|---|---|---|---|
| Population (millions) | 35 | 35.8 | 36.4 | 37 | 37.6 | 40.4 | 41.4 | 42.1 | 43.4 |
| GDP (US$ million) | 108390 | 105902 | 108486 | 133600 | 137008 | 136000 | 133000 | 130000 | 127000 |
| GDP growth rate (%) | −2.5 | 1.5 | 2.8 | 3.1 | 3.3 | 1.4 | −0.4 | 1.9 | 3 |
| GNP *per capita* (US$) | 2670 | 3320 | 3420 | 3550 | 3520 | 3409 | 3310 | 3316 | 3170 |
| Installed capacity (MW) | 36846 | 37637 | 35926 | 35951 | 36563 | 37175 | 37848 | 38517 | 39186 |
| Electricity consumption *per capita* (kWh) | 3942 | 3998 | 4216 | 4291 | 4306 | 4322 | 4302 | 4299 | 4336 |
| Electricity generation (GWh) | 149457 | 155812 | 167609 | 167552 | 179444 | 187811 | 183093 | 181818 | 189307 |
| System losses (%) | 7 | 7 | 6 | 6 | 5 | 5 | 5 | 5 | 5 |
| Exchange rate (SA Rand : US$) | 2.9 | 3.3 | 3.6 | 3.6 | 4.3 | 4.6 | 5.5 | 6.1 | 7.69 |
| National electrification (%) | 53 | 53 | 53 | 54 | 57.3 | 59 | 60 | 64 | 65 |
| Urban electrification (%) | 76.4 | 76.4 | 76.4 | 77 | 78.2 | 82 | 82 | 81 | 81 |
| Rural electrification (%) | 24 | 24 | 25 | 26.8 | 32.4 | 32 | 39 | 46 | 48 |
| No. of employees | 42223 | 40128 | 39760 | 39952 | 39857 | 39241 | 37311 | 34027 | 32832 |
| No. of customers (000s) | | | 1568 | 1568 | 1887 | 2224 | 2564 | 2856 | 3110 |
| No. of customers per employee | | | 39 | 39 | 47 | 57 | 68 | 83 | 95 |
| No. of employees per installed capacity | 1.15 | 1.07 | 1.11 | 1.11 | 1.09 | 1.06 | 0.99 | 0.88 | 0.82 |
| Electricity generation per employee (GWh) | 3.54 | 3.88 | 4.22 | 4.19 | 4.49 | 4.79 | 4.91 | 5.34 | 5.77 |
| Employee per GWh of generation ratio | 0.28 | 0.26 | 0.24 | 0.24 | 0.22 | 0.21 | 0.2 | 0.19 | 0.17 |

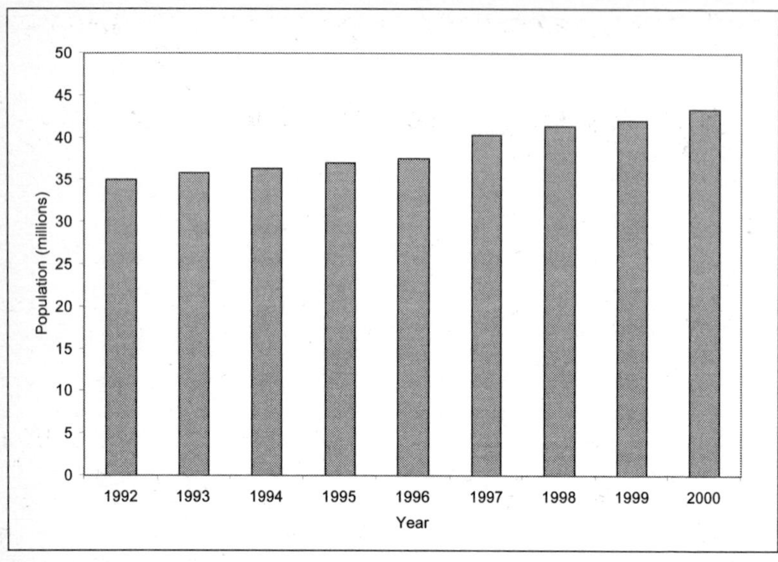

Figure VIA.1.1  Population, 1992–2000 (millions)

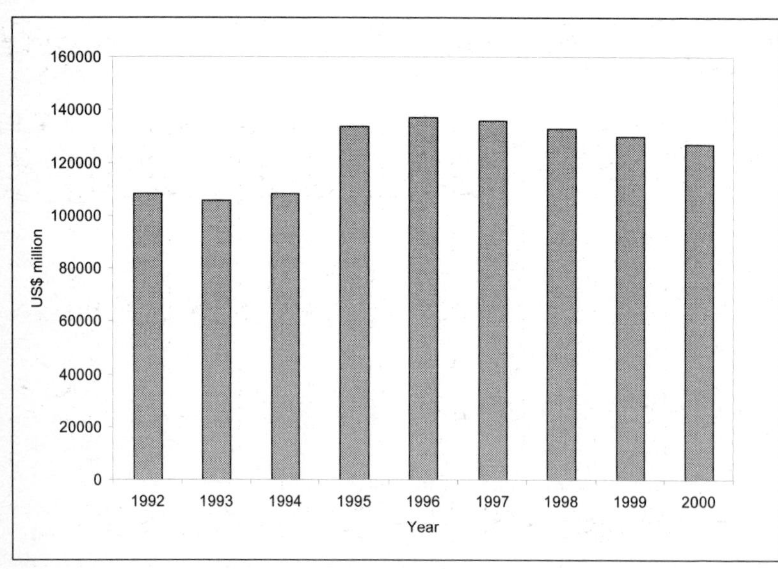

Figure VIA.1.2  GDP, 1992–2000 (US$ million)

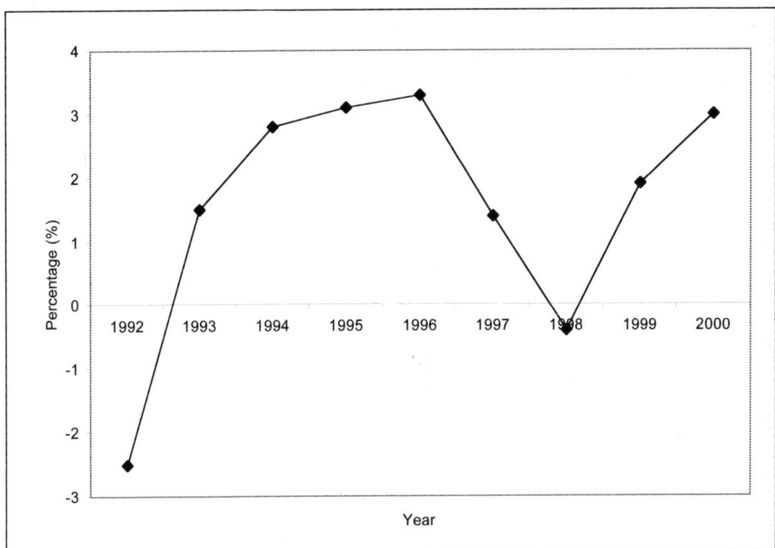

Figure VIA.1.3  GDP growth rate, 1992–2000 (%)

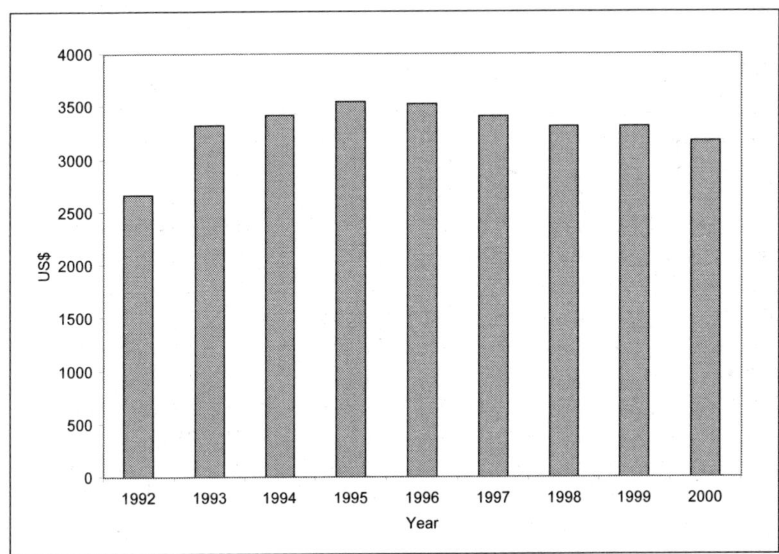

Figure VI.A1.4  GNP *per capita*, 1992–2000 (US$)

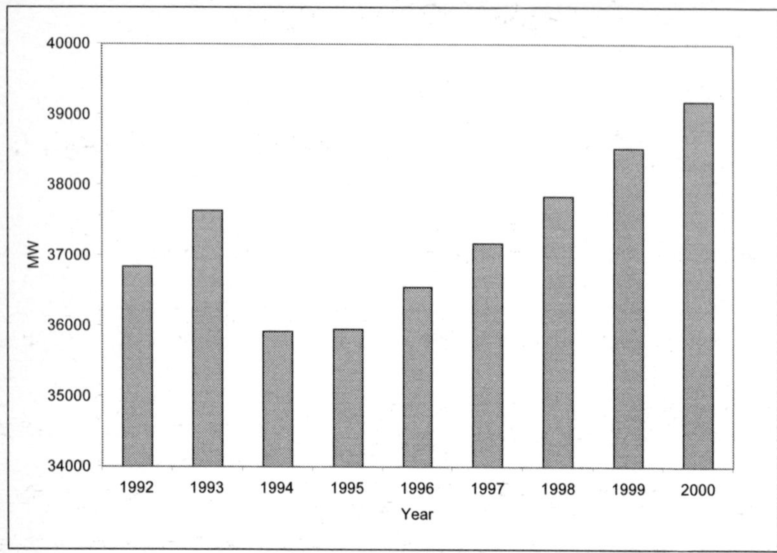

Figure VIA.1.5 Installed capacity, 1992–2000 (MW)

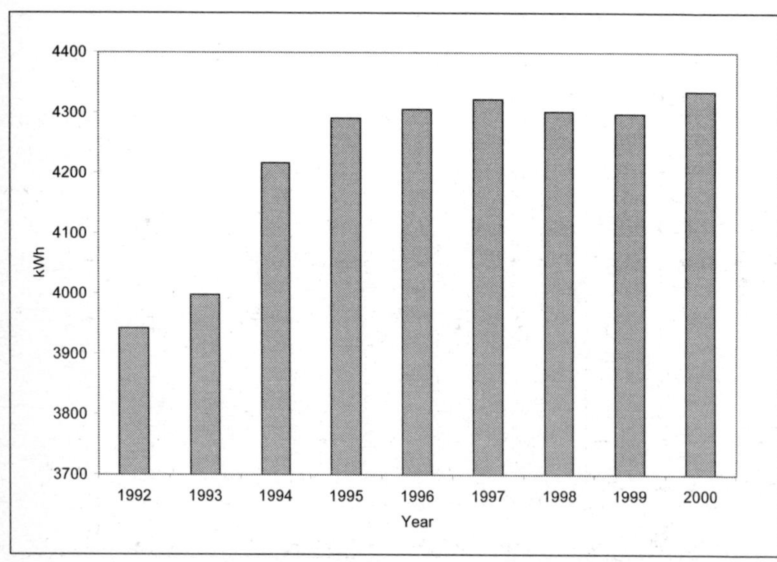

Figure VIA.1.6 Electricity consumption *per capita*, 1992–2000 (kWh)

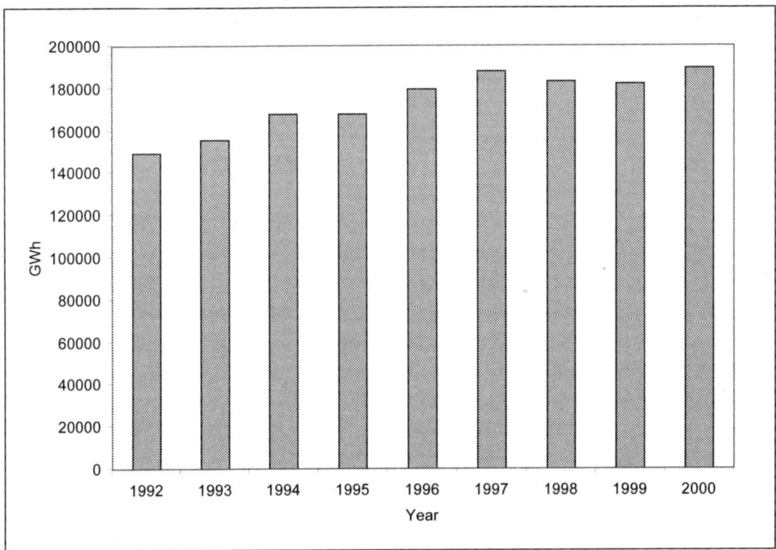

Figure VIA.1.7  Electricity generation, 1992–2000 (GWh)

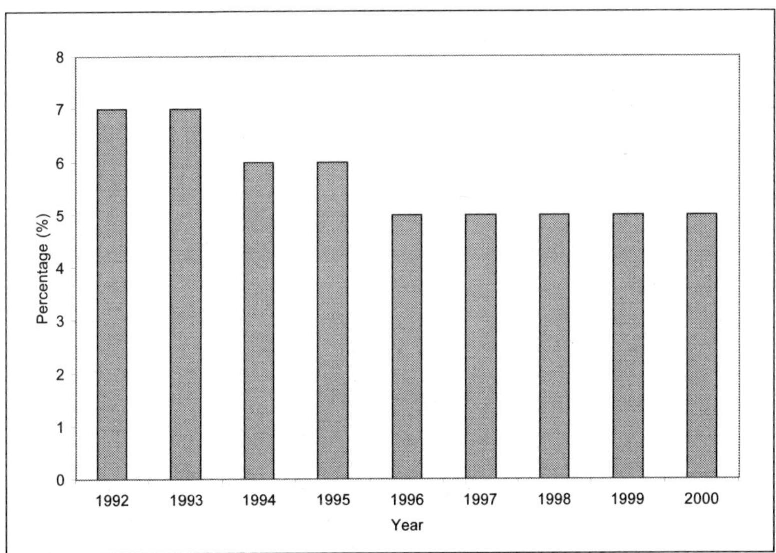

Figure VIA.1.8  System losses, 1992–2000 (%)

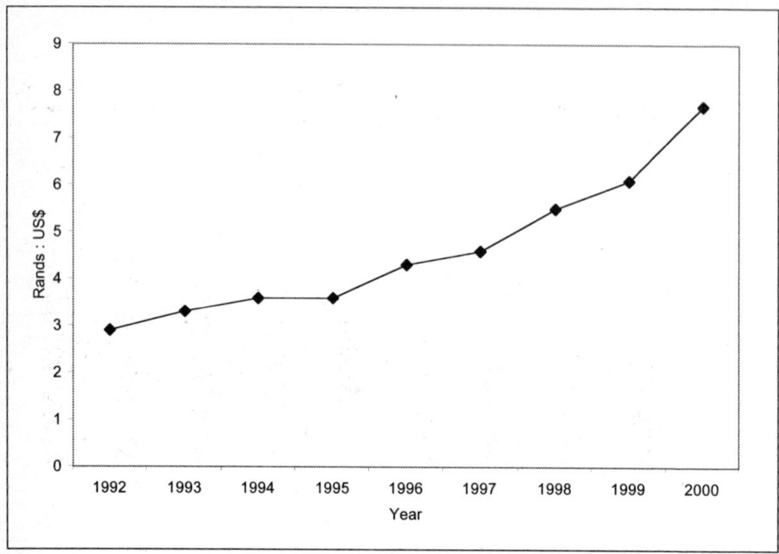

Figure VIA.1.9  Exchange rate, 1992–2000 (SA Rand : US$)

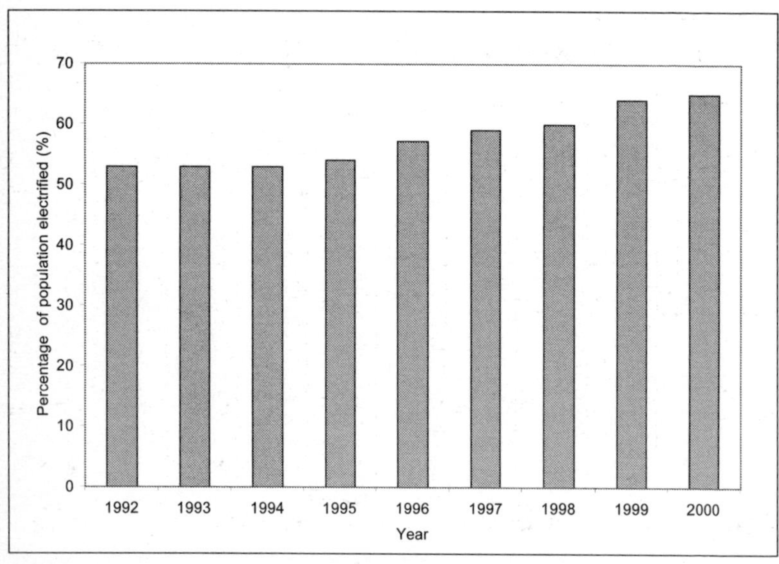

Figure VIA.1.10  National electrification levels, 1992–2000 (%)

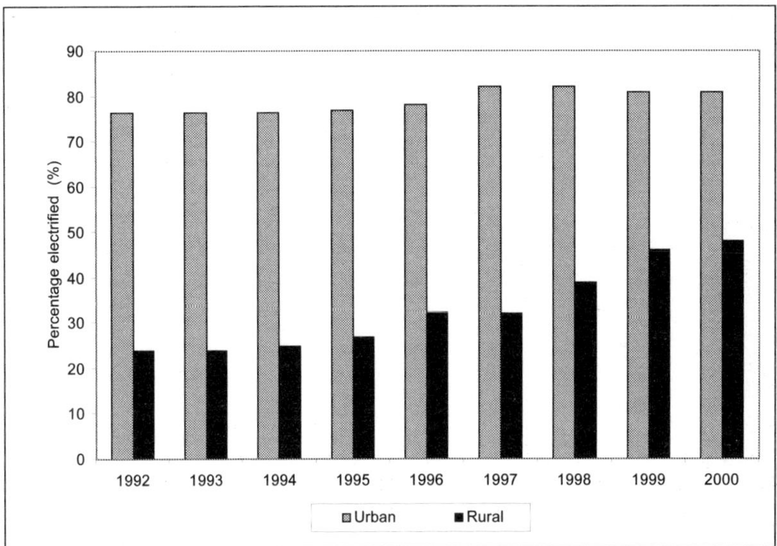

Figure VIA.1.11 Urban and rural electrification levels, 1992–2000 (%)

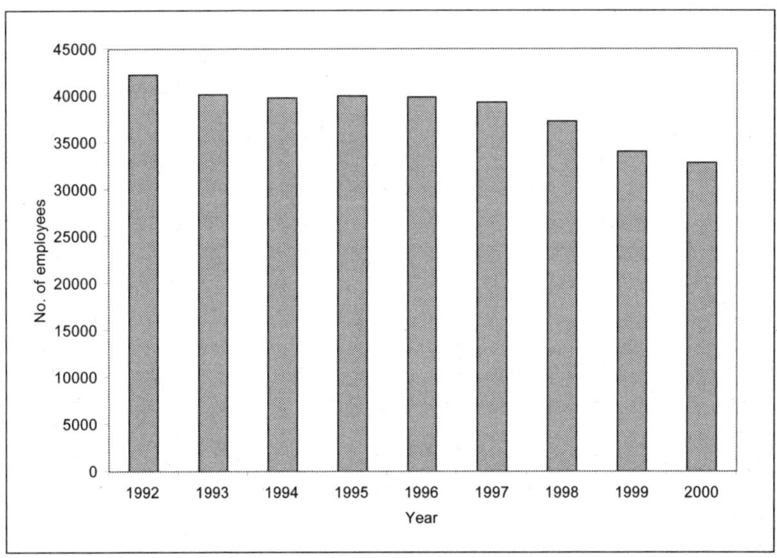

Figure VIA.1.12 Number of employees, 1992–2000

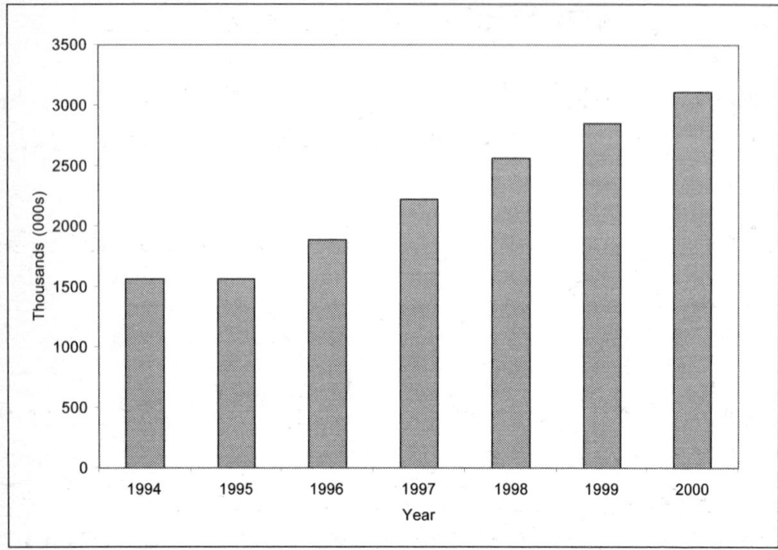

Figure VIA.1.13 Number of customers, 1994–2000 (thousands)

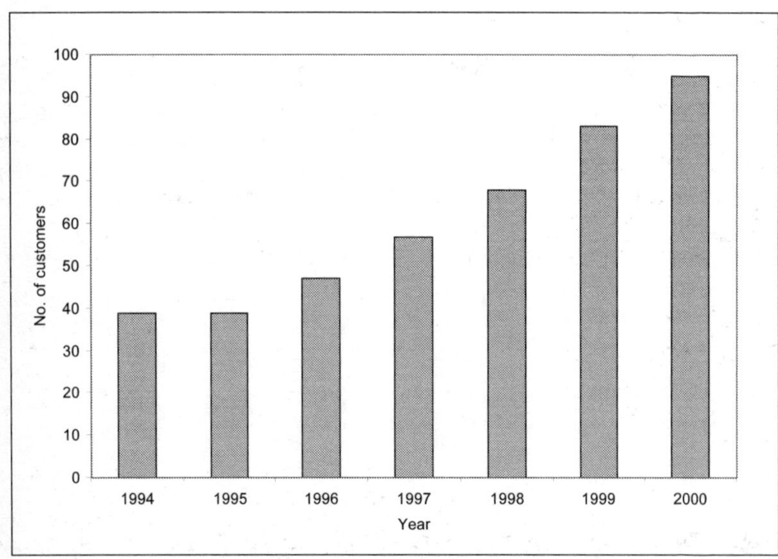

Figure VIA.1.14 Number of customers per employee, 1994–2000

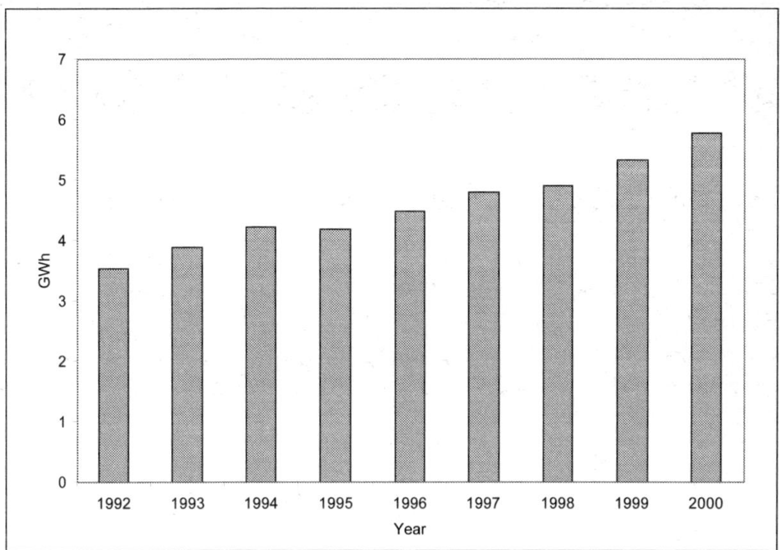

Figure VIA.1.15 Electricity generation per employee, 1992–2000 (GWh)

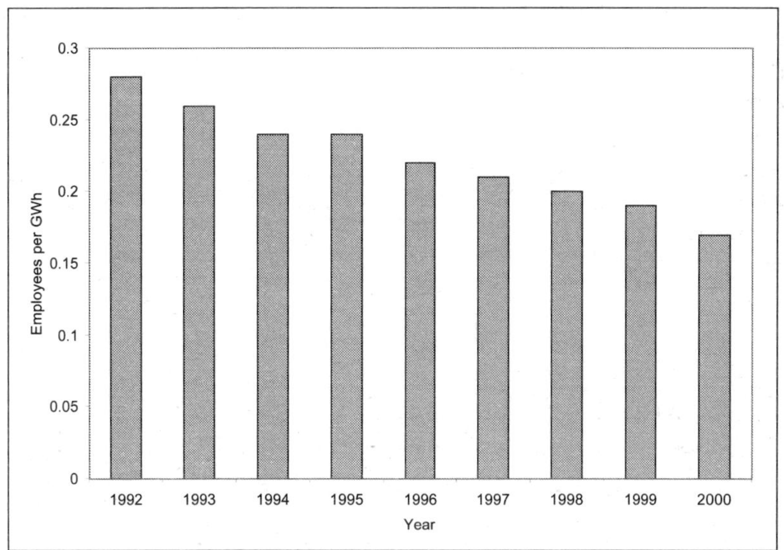

Figure VIA.1.16 Number of employees per GWh

# References

ACBF (African Capacity Building Foundation), 1992. 'Strategy and Indicative Work Programme, 1992–95', Harare: ACBF.

——, 1993. 'Building Capacity', *Quarterly Newsletter of the African Capacity Building Foundation*, Harare, Zimbabwe, Vol. 1, No. 1 (April).

ADB (African Development Bank), 1994. *Tariff, Fiscal and Financial Aspects of the Energy Sector in Africa*, African Development Bank, Abidjan, Côte d'Ivoire.

——, 1996. 'African Electricity Subsector is Facing Serious Shortages of Qualified Staff', *The Electricity Subsector in Africa*, African Development Bank, Abidjan, Côte d'Ivoire.

AEG (Applied Energy Group), 1997. 'Forecast of EELPA Electric Energy and Peak Demand for 1998–2016: Preliminary Report'. Addis Ababa: Ethiopia.

AFREPREN/FWD (African Energy Policy Research Network/Foundation for Woodstove Dissemination), 2001a. *African Energy Data Reference Handbook IV*, Nairobi: AFREPREN/FWD.

——, 2001b. *African Energy Data Reference Handbook 6*, Nairobi: AFREPREN/FWD.

AIT (Asian Institute of Technology), 1994. *Abstracts Prepared for the 4th International Symposium on Renewable Energy Education*, Bangkok: AIT.

Aldhous, P., 1995. 'Getting an Education in Cameroon: the Struggle Continues', *New Scientist* (October).

Ali, G. E. and A. R. Elgizouli, 1996. 'Sudan', in M. R. Bhagavan (ed.), *Energy Utilities and Institutions in Africa*, London and Nairobi: Zed Books in association with AFREPREN.

Anderson, 1994. *Potential for Electricity Co-generation*, Stellenbosch: University of Stellenbosch.

Austin, R., 1975. *Racism and Apartheid in South Africa: Rhodesia*, Paris: UNESCO, p. 49.

ATC (Appropriate Technology Centre), 1992. *Report on a Solar Energy Training Workshop*. Nairobi: Kenyatta University.

Bacon, R., 1995. *Appropriate Restructuring Strategies for the Power Generation Sector: the Case of Small Systems*, Washington DC: World Bank.

Baguant, J., 1990. 'Issues in Energy for the African Region: Higher Education Training with Particular Reference to Mauritius', University of Mauritius.

——, 1992. 'Energy Management in Africa: the Case of Mauritius', in M. R.

Bhagavan and S. Karekezi (eds), *Energy Management in Africa*, London: Zed Books.

——, 1996a. 'Human Resources Development and Training in the African Energy Sector', in *Science in Africa: Energy for Development Beyond 2000*, Washington, DC: American Association for the Advancement of Science.

——, 1996b. 'Capacity Building for the Energy Sector in Eastern and Southern Africa, with Special Reference to Mauritius', University of Mauritius, Interim Report No. 1.

——, 1996c. 'Transport Energy Management in Africa – Mauritius', in M. R. Bhagavan (ed.), *Transport Energy Management in Africa* , London: Zed Books.

Baguant, J. and R. P. Beeharry, 1998. 'Capacity Building in the Power Sector in Mauritius', report for the AFREPREN Capacity Building Theme Group, Nairobi: AFREPREN.

Baguant, J. and J. Manrakhan, 1994. 'Issues in Energy for the African Region: Higher Education Training with Particular Reference to Mauritius', University of Mauritius.

Baguant, J. *et al.*, 1997. 'Capacity Building Study  – Energy Sector with Special Reference to the Power Sector – Mauritius', report for the AFREPREN Capacity Building Theme Group, University of Mauritius.

Banda, G., 2002. 'Draft Short-Term Study Report', Nairobi: AFREPREN/FWD.

Bank of Mauritius, 1995. Annual Reports 1989–95, Port Louis, Mauritius.

Barraclough, C., 1997. 'High Hopes for Hydro in Mozambique', *African Review of Business and Technology* (November), p. 57.

Basson, J., 1995. 'The Demand for Energy in Southern Africa', *Journal of Energy in Southern Africa*, Vol. 6, No. 1.

Batidzirai, B. 2002. *Cogeneration in Zimbabwe: A Utility's Perspective*, Nairobi: AFREPREN/FWD.

Beeharry, R. P., R. Ramgulam and J. Baguant, 1994. 'Energy Data Book – Energy Supply And Consumption (1970–1993)', Reduit: Faculty of Engineering, University of Mauritius.

Bhagavan, M. R., 1992a. 'The SAREC Model: Institutional Cooperation and the Strengthening of National Research Capacity in Developing Countries', Stockholm: Swedish Agency for Research Cooperation with Developing Countries (SAREC).

——, 1992b. 'Technical Change and Restructuring in Asian Industries: Implications for Human Resource Development', paper presented at the ILO–ARTEP Regional Symposium on 'An Integrated Approach to Human Resources'.

—— (ed.), 1999. *Reforming the Power Sector in Africa*, London and Nairobi: Zed Books in association with AFREPREN.

Bossuyt, J., G. Laporte and F. van Hoek, 1991. 'New Avenues for Technical Cooperation in Africa – Improving the Record in Terms of Capacity Building', Maastricht: European Centre for Development Policy Management (ECDPM).

BP (British Petroleum), 1996. *BP Statistical Review of World Energy*, London: Group Media and Publications.

BPC (Botswana Power Corporation), 2000. Annual Report, BPC, Gaborone.

Braun M. R., 1997. 'Listing of Electrical Engineering Departments'. UCT web page, http://www.uct.co.za

Brew-Hammond, A., 1995. 'Electric Power Generation and Technological Accumulation in Sub-Saharan Africa: a Study of Kenya Power and Lighting Company with Reference to Volta River Authority, Ghana', paper prepared for the Energy Africa Conference, Accra, Ghana, November 1995.

——, 1997. 'Technological Capabilities in Electric Power Utilities in Sub-Saharan Africa: the Case of Ghana', PhD thesis submitted to the University of Sussex, Brighton.

*Business Herald, The*, 1996. 'Namaco Calls for Change in Training System', 26 September 1996, Harare.

Business in Africa, 2001. 'Exchange Rates', in *Business in Africa*, Vol. 9, No. 4, May 2001, Johannesburg: Goldcity Ventures, p. 77.


Cape Technikon, 1998. *Cape Town International Conference on Domestic Use of Electrical Energy – Proceedings* , Cape Town: Elektro Wise.

CEB (Central Electricity Board), 1994. *Annual Report 1994*, Curepipe, Mauritius: CEB.

——, 1995. *Annual Report 1995*, Curepipe, Mauritius: CEB.

——, 1996. *Annual Report 1996*, Curepipe, Mauritius: CEB.

——, 1999. *Annual Report 1999*, Curepipe, Mauritius: CEB.

——, 2000. *Mauritius Government Gazette, General Notice No. 1522 of 2000*, Curepipe, Mauritius: CEB,

Central Statistical Services, 1996. *Living in South Africa: Selected Findings of the 1995 October Household Survey*, Pretoria: Central Statistical Services.

CESEN–Ansaldo, 1986. *Cooperation Agreement in the Energy Sector*, Addis Ababa: Ministry of Mines and Energy, Ethiopian National Energy Committee.

Chandi, L. 2001. *Data and Statistics Compilation – Zambia*, Nairobi: AFREPREN/FWD.

Chiwaya, A., 1996. *Malawi Interconnected Power Systems Blackout.* Blantyre: Escom.

——, 2000: *Data and Statistics Compilation – Malawi,* Nairobi: AFREPREN/FWD.

—— and N. Mphasi, 1996. *Restructuring the Power Sector in Malawi*, Nairobi: AFREPREN/FWD.

Cole, G. A. 1997. *Personnel Management: Theory and Practice*, 4th edition, London: Letts Educational.

Commission on the Developing Countries and Global Change, 1992. *For Earth's Sake*, Ottawa: International Development Research Center (IDRC).

Commonwealth Expert Group, 1991. *Beyond Apartheid: Human Resources in a New South Africa*, London: Commonwealth Secretariat.

Council of Academics of Engineering and Technological Sciences, 1995. 'The Role of Technology in Environmental Sustainable Development', Kiruna, Sweden, 21 June.

Covarrubias, A., 1996. *Lending For Electricity in Sub-Saharan Africa: a*

*World Bank Operation Evaluation Study*, Washington, DC: World Bank.

Cowan, W.D., 1997 'Turbulence Ahead for Electricity Pricing in South Africa', *Elektron*, Vol. 9, No. 11 (November/December).

CSA (Central Statistical Authority), 1998. *The 1995/96 Household Income, Consumption and Expenditure Survey*, Addis Ababa: CSA.

CSO (Central Statistical Office), 1987. *Statistical Yearbook 1987*, Harare: Government Printer.

——, 1995. *CSO Stats Flash*, Harare: Government Printer.

——, 1998. Zimbabwe 1997 *Inter-censal Demographic Survey Report*, Harare: Government Printer.


Dag Hammarskjöld Foundation, 1990. *The State and the Crisis in Africa: in Search of a Second Liberation*, report of the Mweya Conference, Uganda, 12–17 May 1990, Uppsala: Dag Hammarskjöld Foundation.

DANIDA, 1990a. *Desk Evaluation of Electrification Projects in Sierra Leone*, Copenhagen: DANIDA/Department of International Development, Ministry of Foreign Affairs, pp. 11–12.

——, 1990b. *Desk Evaluation of Electrification Projects in Tanzania*, Copenhagen: DANIDA/Department of International Development, Ministry of Foreign Affairs, pp. 10–12.

——, 1990c. *Evaluation of Electrification Projects in Botswana*, Copenhagen: DANIDA/Department of International Development, Ministry of Foreign Affairs, p. 18.

——, 1990d. *Evaluation of The Four Towns Power Project in Sudan*, Copenhagen: DANIDA/Department of International Development, Ministry of Foreign Affairs, p. 19.

——, 1991. *Evaluation of Electrification Projects in Benin*, Copenhagen: DANIDA/Department of International Development, Ministry of Foreign Affairs.

Davidson, O. and S. Karekezi (eds), 1992. 'Environmentally Sound Energy Options for Africa – Final Statement of the African Energy Experts Meeting, Nairobi, Kenya (18–20 May, 1992)', Nairobi: AFREPREN, FWD and UNEP.

Deepchand, K., 2000. *Bagasse Energy Cogeneration in Mauritius and Its Potential in the Southern and Eastern African Countries*, Nairobi: AFREPREN/FWD.

——, 2001a. 'Bagasse Energy Cogeneration in Mauritius', in *AFREPREN Regional Policy Seminar on Renewables – Cogeneration Proceedings*, AFREPREN Occasional Paper No. 1, Nairobi: AFREPREN/FWD.

——, 2001b. *Bagasse-Based Cogeneration in Mauritius – a Model for Eastern and Southern Africa*, AFREPREN Occasional Paper No. 2, Nairobi:. AFREPREN/FWD.

Department of Arts, Culture, Science and Technology, 1998. DACST web page, http://www.dacst.gov.za/foresight/index.htm

Department of Education, 1997. Report of the Medium Term Expenditure Framework Education Sectoral Team, Pretoria.

Department of Labour, 1996. *Growth Employment and Redistribution; a Macro-economic Strategy*, Pretoria: Department of Labour.

Department of Water Affairs and Forestry (DWAF), 1995. Forestry Policy

Discussion Document, Pretoria: DWAF.

Development Bank of Southern Africa, 1994. *South Africa's Nine Provinces: a Human Development Profile.* Development Information Paper 28, Midrand: Development Bank of Southern Africa.

*Digest of Educational Statistics*, 1997. Volume 13 (1996), Port Louis: Central Statistics Office, Republic of Mauritius: Government Printer.

Diphaha, J. and R. Burton, 1993. 'Photovoltaics and Solar Water Heaters in Botswana', in S. Karekezi and G. A. Mackenzie (eds), *Energy Options for Africa: Environmentally Sustainable Alternatives*, London: Zed Books, pp. 139–53.

DMEA (Department of Mineral and Energy Affairs), 1995. 'South African Energy Policy: Discussion Document', Pretoria.

——, 1997. *Annual Report 1997*, Pretoria: Department of Mineral and Energy Affairs.

——, 1998. *Annual Report 1998*, Pretoria: Department of Mineral and Energy Affairs.

Doppegieter, J., J.J. du Toit and E. van Vuuren, 1993. *Energy Futures 1993*, Stellenbosch: Institute for Futures Research, University of Stellenbosch.

Drummond, R., 2001a. *Journal of Energy in Southern Africa*, Vol. 12, No. 1 (February), Cape Town: Energy Research Institute, University of Cape Town.

—— 2001b. *Journal of Energy in Southern Africa*, Vol. 12, No. 3 (August), Cape Town: Energy Research Institute, University of Cape Town.

Du Plessis, J., 1997. 'The NER Talks of the Challenges Facing Electricity Supply', *Urban Management* (November), pp. 42–3.

Dube, Danny, 1997. 'The Paradox of Education and Skills', *The Herald*, 10 July 1997.

Dube, I., 1996. *Restructuring the Power Sector in Zimbabwe: The Question of Privatization.* Nairobi: AFREPREN/FWD.

——, 1998a. *Power Sector Reform in Africa*, Nairobi: AFREPREN/ FWD.

——, 1998b. *ZESA System Load Forecast*, Harare: ZESA, p. 30.

——, 2001. *Data and Statistics Compilation – Zimbabwe.* Nairobi: AFREPREN/FWD.

Eberhard, A., 1992. 'Integrated Energy Planning for Widening Access to Basic Energy Services in South Africa: a Methodology for Policy Analysis and Research', Paper No. 2, Energy Policy Research and Training Project (EPRET), Energy for Development Research Centre, University of Cape Town.

ECA (Economic Commission for Africa), 1991. 'Africa's Human Resources Agenda for the 1990s and Beyond', paper presented at Fourth Meeting of ECA's Conference of Ministers Responsible for Human Resources Planning Development and Utilisation, Addis Ababa, 18–23 November 1991.

——, 1997. 'The Role of Private and Other Development Actors in Strengthening Subregional and Regional Cooperation in the Development and Utilization of Mineral and Energy Resources in Africa', paper presented at Regional Conference of African Ministers Responsible for the Development and Utilization of Mineral and Energy Resources, Durban,

21–22 November 1997.

*Economist, The,* 1997. 'World Education League: Who's Top?', 29 March, pp. 21–5.

*East African Standard, The,* 1995. 'Africa Loses 23,000 Academics', 8 June, Nairobi: Standard Ltd.

EDRC (Energy for Development Research Centre), 1997. UCT web page, http://www.uct.co.za

——, no date. *The Development Context for Energy Planning in South Africa,* Cape Town, EDRC, University of Cape Town.

EELPA, 1996. 'Restructuring Study for EELPA – Executive Summary for the Analysis Report', Addis Ababa: EELPA.

EELPA, 1997. 'Preliminary Power Demand Forecast', Addis Ababa: EELPA.

EEPCO, 1996. 'System Load Forecast and Supply–Demand Balance', Addis Ababa: EEPCO.

EGPC, 1996. *Egyptian General Petroleum Corporation,* Cairo: EGPC.

EIU (*The Economist* Intelligence Unit), 1995. EIU Country Report for Ethiopia, London: *The Economist.*

——, 1997a. Country Profile for Ethiopia, London: *The Economist.*

——, 1997b. Country Profile for South Africa, London: *The Economist.*

——, 1998a. Country Profile for Mauritius, Madagascar, Seychelles, London: *The Economist.*

——, 1998b. Country Profile for South Africa, London: *The Economist.*

——, 1998c. Country Profile for Ethiopia, London: *The Economist.*

——, 1999a. Country Profile for Ethiopia, London: *The Economist.*

——, 1999b. Country Profile for Mauritius, Madagascar and Seychelles, London: *The Economist.*

——, 2000a. Country Profile for South Africa, London: *The Economist.*

——, 2000b. Country Profile for Mauritius, Madagascar, Seychelles, London: *The Economist.*

——, 2000c. Country Profile for Ethiopia, London: *The Economist.*

——, 2000d. Country Profile for Kenya, London: *The Economist.*

——, 2000e. Country Profile for Zambia, London: *The Economist.*

——, 2001a. Country Profile for Ethiopia, London: *The Economist.*

——, 2001b. Country Profile for South Africa, London: *The Economist.*

——, 2001c. Country Profile for Zimbabwe, London: *The Economist.*

Electricité de France, 1993. *Zimbabwe: Training Development Scheme in the Electricity Power Sector. Book 1: The Harare Training System,* Harare: Electricité de France.

Eleri, O. E., 1996. 'The Energy Sector in Southern Africa: a Preliminary Survey of Post-Apartheid Challenges', *Energy Policy,* Vol. 24, No. 1, Oxford: Elsevier Science Limited, pp. 114, 117.

ENA (Ethiopian News Agency), 1998. 'New Universities to Be Opened', *Ethiopian Herald,* Addis Ababa, 17 April.

Engorait, S. P., 2002. *Data and Statistics Compilation – Uganda,* Nairobi: AFREPREN/FWD.

ERI (Energy Research Institute), 1994. Energy for Development Research Centre Brochure. University of Cape Town: South Africa.

ESAMI (Eastern and Southern Africa Management Institute), 2001. ESAMI web site.

——, no date. *SADC Training Programmes on Rural Energy Planning and Environmental Management*, ESAMI, in collaboration with University of Twente.

ESCOM (Electricity Supply Commission of Malawi), 1995. *Annual Report, 1994/5*, Blantyre: ESCOM

——, 1999. *Annual Report and Accounts 1999*, Lilongwe: ESCOM.

Eshetu, L. and W. Bogale, 1996. 'Power Sector Restructuring in Ethiopia', paper prepared for the AFREPREN Institutions Theme Group.

ESKOM, 1991. *Annual Report 1990*, Johannesburg: ESKOM.

——, 1992a. *ESKOM in Perspective*, Johannesburg: ESKOM.

——, 1992b. *Annual Report 1991*, Johannesburg: ESKOM.

——, 1993. *Statistical Year Book 1992*, Johannesburg: ESKOM.

——, 1994. *Statistical Year Book 1993,* Johannesburg: ESKOM.

——, 1996. *Annual Report 1995*, Johannesburg: ESKOM.

——, 1997a. *Annual Report, 1996*, Johannesburg: ESKOM.

——, 1997b. *Environmental Report*, Johannesburg: ESKOM.

——, 1997c. *Statistical Year Book, 1996*, Johannesburg: ESKOM.

——, 1998. *Annual Report, 1997 – Yesterday Is a Foreign Country*, Johannesburg: ESKOM Corporate Communications.

——, 2001. ESKOM web page, http://www.eskom.co.za

ESMAP (Energy Sector Management Assistance Programme), 1990. *The Interafrican Electrical Engineering College (IEEC) Proposal for Short and Long Term Development*, Report No. 112/90 (March), Washington DC: UNDP/World Bank.

——, 1999. *Global Energy Reform in Developing Countries*, Washington DC: UNDP/World Bank.

Europa, 1996. *The Europa World Year Book 1996*, Vols 1 and 2, 37th edition, London: Europa Publications Limited.

FAO, 1995. 'Future Energy Requirements for Africa's Agriculture', prepared for the African Energy Programme of the African Development Bank, Rome.

FDRE (Federal Democratic Republic of Ethiopia), 1996a. *A Five Year Programme on Development, Peace and Democracy*, Addis Ababa: FDRE.

——, 1996b. Proclamation No. 37/1996: Investment Proclamation of the Federal Democratic Republic of Ethiopia, Addis Ababa: FDRE.

——, 1997a. Council of Ministers Regulation No. 18/1997: Regulation to Provide for the Establishment of the Ethiopian Electric Power Corporation, Addis Ababa: FDRE.

——, 1997b. Proclamation No. 86/1997: A Proclamation Relating to Electricity, Addis Ababa: FDRE.

*Financial Gazette*, 2002. 'Power Sector Reforms Gets Green Light', Privatization Supplement to the *Financial Gazette*, 7–13 February.

*Financial Mail*, 1998. 'Top Companies: Special Survey', 26 June 1998.

*Financial Times*, 1996. *Electricity in Southern Africa*, London: *Financial Times* Energy Publishing.

——, 1999. *African Power Projects*. London: *Financial Times* Energy Publishing.

——, 2000a. *African Energy*, Issue 28, London: *Financial Times*.

——, 2000b: *African Energy*, Issue 30, London: *Financial Times*.

——, 2001a. *African Energy*, Issue 30, London: *Financial Times*.

——, 2001b. *African Energy*, Issue 42, London: *Financial Times*.

——, 2002. *African Energy*, Issue 45. London: *Financial Times*.

Fowler, A., 1993. *Institutional Development: a Focused View*. London: International Institute for Environment and Development (IIED).

FRD (Foundation for Research Development), 1995a. *Strategic Issues in Science, Engineering and Technology in South Africa*, Science and Technology Policy Series No. 4, Pretoria: FRD.

——, 1995b. *Research, Science and Technology in South Africa: Comparative Strengths of the Nine Provinces*, Science and Technology Policy Series No. 5, Pretoria: FRD.

——, 1996. *SA Science and Technology Indicators*, Pretoria: FRD.


GEF (Global Environmental Facility), 1993. Report by the Chairman to the May Participants Meeting, Washington DC: GEF.

Gielink, M. I. *et al.*, 1993. 'Energy Profile: South Africa', Report No. 158 (September), Plumstead, South Africa: Energy Research Institute (ERI).

Girod, J. (ed.), 1995. *L' Énergie en Afrique*. Daka: Enda.

Global Policy Network, 2000. *Highlights of Current Labour Market in South Africa (2000)*, Johannesburg: National Labour and Development Institute (NALEDI), www.GlobalPolicyNetwork.org

Government of Southern Rhodesia, 1963. *Reports of the Southern Rhodesia Education Commission, 1962*, Harare: Government Printer.

Government of Zimbabwe, 1979a. *Education Act, 1979*, Harare: Government Printer.

Government of Zimbabwe, 1979b. *Report of the Commission of Inquiry into the Establishment of a Second University or Campus*, Harare: Government Printer.

Government of Zimbabwe, 1991. *Second Five Year National Development Plan 1991–1995*, Harare, Government Printer.

Grey-Johnson, C. (ed.), 1990. *The Employment Crisis in Africa: Issues in Human Resources Development Policy*, Harare: SAPES Trust.

Group for Environmental Monitoring, 1994. *Climate and Africa: National Report, South Africa*, African Centre for Technology Studies (ACTS), Swedish Environment Institute (SEI).

Gutierrez, L., 1996. 'How Do Sub-Saharan African Utilities Compare?', paper presented at the Symposium on Power Sector Reform and Efficiency Improvement in Sub-Saharan Africa (5–8 December 1995, Johannesburg), Washington, DC: World Bank.


Habitat, 1996. *An Urbanizing World: Global Report on Human Settlements*, Oxford: Oxford University Press.

Habtetsion, S., 2002. *Data and Statistics Compilation – Eritrea*. Nairobi: AFREPREN/FWD.

Hebrard, G., 2001. 'Mauritius Power Sector Reform', paper prepared for the AFREPREN Uganda National Policy Seminar, Nairobi: AFREPREN/FWD.

*Herald, The*, 1996. 'ZESA Performance Improvement Centre (10th Anniversary Open Day Special)', 30 May 1996, Harare.

——, 1997. 'Private Hydro Power Station Comes on Stream', 9 July 1997, Harare.

——, 1998. 'Chinhoyi College to Be Upgraded', 25 June 1998, Harare.

——, 1998. 'Move to Revamp Education System', 3 January 1998, Harare.

——, 1999. 'Access to Tertiary Education Improved', 8 January 1999, Harare.

Holm, D. and R. Viljoen, 1996. *Primer for Energy Conscious Design*, Pretoria: Department of Mineral and Energy Affairs.

Human Sciences Research Council, 1996. 'The Job Market: Focus on Professions and Databases', in *HSRC/RGN in Focus*, Vol. 3, No. 4, Pretoria: Human Sciences Research Council.

IEA (International Energy Agency), 1994. *World Energy Outlook*, Paris: Organization for Economic Cooperation and Development (OECD) Publications.

——, 1999. *Energy Statistics and Balances of Non-OECD Countries*, Paris: OECD Publications.

——, 2000. *Energy Statistics and Balances of Non-OECD Countries*, Paris: OECD Publications.

——, 2001. *Energy Statistics and Balances of Non-OECD Countries*, Paris: OECD Publications.

International Labour Organization, 1997. *Report on the SA Labour Market*, report to the Department of Labour, Pretoria.

IVTB (Industrial and Vocational Training Board), 1998a. *Course Guide 1998 – a Handbook of Full-time and Part-time Courses at IVTB*, Port Louis, Mauritius: IVTB.

——, 1998b. *IVTB News, May 1998*, Port Louis, Mauritius: IVTB.

Jaycox, E. 1993. 'Capacity Building – the Mission Link in African Development', keynote address by Edward Jaycox, Assistant Director, World Bank, at the African-American Institute Conference on African Capacity Building: Effective and Enduring Partnerships held at Reston, Virginia on 20 May 1993, published in *Kenya Times* on 17 and 18 June 1993.

Jordanger, E., 1992. 'Power Cooperation in the Southern African Region', *SADCC Energy Quarterly*, Vol. 9, No. 24 (January–March), Luanda: SADCC Energy Sector Technical and Administrative Unit.

Kalumiana, O., 2002. *Data and Statistics Compilation – Zambia*. Nairobi: AFREPREN/FWD.

Karekezi, S., 1993. 'African Energy Research Networks: Impact on Policy Formulation and Implementation', in Anton Eberhard and Paul Theron (eds), *International Experience in Energy Policy Research and Planning*, Cape Town: Elan Press and Energy Research Institute, University of Cape Town, pp. 92–120.

Karekezi, S., 1995a. 'Capacity Building for Policy Analysis and Implementation in Developing Countries', in K. von Schlebrugge (ed.), *Research for Development – SAREC 20 Years*, Stockholm: Swedish Agency for Research Cooperation with Developing Countries (SAREC), pp. 65–78.

Karekezi, Stephen, 1995b. 'Capacity Building for Policy Analysis and

Implementation in Developing Countries', Working Paper No. 61 (March), Nairobi: AFREPREN/FWD, p. 10.

Karekezi, S., 1995c. 'Building a Policy Research Network: the Case of the African Energy Policy Research Network (AFREPREN)', Working Paper No. 74, p. 1.

Karekezi, S., P. Turyaaareeba, and E. Ewagata, 1994. *Renewable Energy Training in Kenya: The Case of Solar Photovoltaics*. Nairobi: AFREPREN.

Karekezi, S. and T. Ranja, 1996. 'Renewable Energy Technologies in Eastern and Southern Africa: Research for Dissemination and Implementation', Final Report, Nairobi: AFREPREN/FWD, pp. 164–71.

Karekezi S., J. Kimani and J. Wangeci (eds), 2001. *Power Sector Reform in Africa, Proceedings of a Regional Policy Seminar*, Occasional Paper No. 5, Nairobi: AFREPREN.

Kathambana, P. 1998. Personal communication.

Katyega, M., 2000. *Data and Statistics Compilation – Tanzania*, Nairobi: AFREPREN/FWD.

Kayo, D., 1995. 'An Analysis of the Fit between Organization Structure and Strategy: a Case Study of the Zimbabwe Electricity Supply Authority', MBA dissertation, University of Zimbabwe, February).

——., 2001. *Power Sector Reforms in Zimbabwe: Implications for Private Sector Participation*. Nairobi: AFREPREN, p. 13.

Kebede, B., 2001. *Data and Statistics Compilation*, Nairobi: AFREPREN/ FWD.

KPLC (Kenya Power and Lighting Company), 2001. *Annual Report and Accounts*, Nairobi: KPLC.

Khalema-Redeby, L. M. and K. E. Sefeane, 1996. 'Literature Review: Management and Maintenance in the Lesotho Power Sector', paper prepared for the AFREPREN Management and Efficiency Theme Group, Nairobi: AFREPREN/FWD.

Khalema-Redeby, L. M., H. Mariam, A. Mbewe and B. Ramasedi (eds), 1997. *Planning and Management in the African Power Sector*, London: Zed Books.

Khonza, R. M., 1997. General Report of the 12th Congress of UPDEA, 22–26 June 1996, Algiers, Algeria, UPDEA Homepage.

Kibwarata, D., 1995. 'Pay Hike for Power Staff', *The Standard*, Nairobi, 19 January.

Kimani, M.J. and E. Naumann. (eds), 1993. *Recent Experiences in Research Development and Dissemination of renewable Energy Technologies in Sub-Saharan Africa: Seminar Proceedings*. Nairobi: Kenya.

Kobokoane, T., 1995. 'South Africa's Big Employers Find Affirmative Action Works Best from within', *Business Times*, 15 October, p. 8.

Kyokutamba, J., 2001. *Country Data and Statistics*, Nairobi: AFREPREN/ FWD.

LEC (Lesotho Electricity Corporation), 1993. *Annual Report 1992/3*, Maseru: LEC.

Manga, A., 1996. 'Privatization: Unions Dig In', *New Nation*, South Africa, 19 January, pp. 12–13.

Mangwengwende, S. E., 2001. 'Experiences in Power Sector Reform in Zimbabwe', in Karakezi, S., Kimani, J. and Wangeci, J. (eds), *AFREPREN Occasional Paper No. 5: Power Sector Reform in Africa – Proceedings of a Regional Policy Seminar*, Nairobi: AFREPREN/FWD, pp. 63–4.

Manrakhan, J., 1992. *Varsity at Reduit: the Out-turn of a Calculated Risk, 1965–90*. Reduit: University of Mauritius.

Mapako, M. C., 1996. 'Draft Literature Review: Zimbabwe', paper prepared for the AFREPREN Capacity Building Theme Group, Nairobi: AFREPREN.

——, 1998. 'Capacity Building in the Power Sector in Zimbabwe', paper prepared for the AFREPREN Capacity Building Theme Group, Nairobi: AFREPREN/FWD.

——, 2001. *Data and Statistics Compilation – Zimbabwe*. Nairobi: AFREPREN/FWD.

Marandu, E., 2001. *Data and Statistics Compilation – Tanzania*, Nairobi: AFREPREN/FWD.

Mashange, Krispen, 2001. *Assessment of Liquid Fuel Policies in Zimbabwe*, Nairobi: AFREPREN/FWD.

Mauritius Chamber of Commerce and Industry, 1997. *Annual Report 1997*, Port Louis, Mauritius.

Mbendi, 1997. Mbendi Information Services, http://mbendi.co.za/htm

Mbewe, A., 1996. 'Management and Efficiency of the Power Sector: a Sub-Saharan Perspective', paper prepared for the AFREPREN Management and Efficiency Theme Group, Nairobi: AFREPREN.

McLennan, A., 1995. 'Exploring the Dynamics of Educational Change', in P. Fitzgerald, A. McLennan and B. Munslow (eds), *Managing Sustainable Development in South Africa*, Cape Town: Oxford University Press.

Ministry of Education, 1993. *Statistics on Higher Education*, Addis Ababa: Government of Ethiopia.

——, 1994. *Basic Education Statistics*, Addis Ababa: Government of Ethiopia.

——, 1995. *Education Statistics, Annual Abstract, 1993/4*, Addis Ababa: Government of Ethiopia.

——, 1997. *Education Statistics, Annual Abstract, 1995/96*, Addis Ababa: Government of Ethiopia.

Ministry of Education and Culture, 1980. *School List 1980*, Harare: Government Printer.

——, 1994. *Annual Report of the Secretary of Education and Culture for the Year Ended 31 December 1992*, Harare: Government Printer.

Ministry of Information, Posts and Telecommunications, 1995. *Zimbabwe in Brief 1995*, Harare: Government Printer.

Ministry of Public Utilities (Mauritius), 1999. *Mauritius Energy Indicators*, Port Louis: Ministry of Public Utilities.

Ministry of Transport and Energy, 1993. *ZESA: a Reform Programme*, Harare: Electricité de France International, KPMG and Management Consultants.

——, 1995. *Energy Information System*, Harare: Government of Zimbabwe.

——, 1996. *Energy Bulletin*, Vol. 6, No. 1, p. 2, Harare: Government of Zimbabwe.

——, 1997. *Energy Information System*, Harare: Government of Zimbabwe.

——, 1999. *Energy Bulletin*, Vol. 8, No. 1 (December),  pp. 3–4, Harare: Government of Zimbabwe.

Mkadawire, Thandika, 1992. '30 Years of African Independence: the Economic Experience', in Peter Anyang Nyongo (ed.), *30 Years of Independence in Africa: the Lost Decades?*, Nairobi: African Association of Political Science and Academy Science Publishers.

Mohahir, V. V., 1990. 'Capacity Building Initiative for Sub-Saharan Africa', paper presented at the seminar on 'Sub-Saharan Africa - Beyond Adjustment?', The Hague: Ministry of Foreign Affairs, Directorate-General for International Cooperation.

Mordell, D. L. and J. F. Coales, 1983. *A Proposal for the Developing Commonwealth: the Need for Engineers and Technicians and How to Meet It Effectively and Efficiently*, London: C. E. Hodgson and Sons.

Mugyenzi, J. E., 1996. 'Literature Review: Uganda', paper prepared for the AFREPREN Institutions Theme Group, Nairobi: AFREPREN/FWD.


National Commission on Higher Education, 1996. *A Framework for Transformation*, Pretoria: NCHE.

National Science Foundation, 1992. *Indicators of Science and Mathematics Education*, 1st edition, Port Louis: National Science Foundation.

Naumann, E., 1993. *Scientific Research, Education and Training in Renewable Energies*, Oldenburg: Renewable Energy Group.

NEC (National Electricity Corporation), 2001. NEC web site: www.necsudan.com

NER (National Electricity Regulator), 1997. Electricity Supply Statistics for South Africa, 1996, Sandton: NER.

——, 1998. *NER News*, No. 16, Pretoria: NER.

——, 1999. Electricity Supply Statistics for South Africa, 1999, Sandton: NER.

——, 2000. *Annual Report 1999/2000*, Pretoria: NER.

——, 2001a. *Electricity Regulatory Journal*, July 2001, Sandton: NER.

——, 2001b. *Annual Report 2000/2001*, Pretoria: NER.

Ngobese, P. and M. Ntsaba, 1998. *Capacity Building in the Power Sector of South Africa*, Nairobi: AFREPREN/FWD.

N'guessan, E., 1997. *Privatisation of the Power Sector in Côte d'Ivoire*, Nairobi: AFREPREN.

Noonan P., 1994. 'Continuing Crisis in African Education', *Africa Recovery*, No. 23.

Ntsaba, M., 2001. *Data and Statistics Compilation – South Africa*, Nairobi: AFREPREN/FWD.

Nyoike, P. and B. A. Okech, 1993. 'A Study of Appropriate and Performance of Energy Sector Institutions in Kenya', Interim Report, Nairobi: AFREPREN, pp. 40, 58.

——, 1996. 'Kenya', in M. R. Bhagavan (ed.), *Energy Utilities and Institutions in Africa*, London and Nairobi: Zed Books and AFREPREN.


Office National de L'électricité (ONE), 1995. Rapport D'Activité, Office National de L'électricité, Morocco.

Ogunlade, R. D., 1994. 'Energy and Power Development in Sub-Saharan

Africa: Challenges and Prospects for the Future', in American Association for the Advancement of Science, *Science in Africa: Energy for Development Beyond 2000*, Washington, DC: AAAS, p. 10.

Okech, N. and Nyoike, P., 2001. *Data and Statistics Compilation, Kenya.* Nairobi: AFREPREN/FWD.

Onyemelukwe, C., 1995. Personal communication.

Pachauri, R. K., 1993. *An Approach to Capacity Building in the Field of Environment and Development*, Geneva: International Academy of the Environment.

Percy, A., 1996. 'ESKOM: Southern Africa's Powerhouse', *African Review of Business and Technology* (July), London: Alain Charles Publishing.

Phuroe, T. and P. Mathaha, 1995. *Renewable Energy Technologies Dissemination in Lesotho*, Maseru: AFREPREN, pp. 8, 15–16, 19–20, 24.

Pickering, M., 1994. 'Electricity Pricing Policy', Energy Policy Research and Training Project (EPRET) Paper No. 19, Energy for Development Research Centre, University of Cape Town.

Preece, H., 1990. 'Poor Expectations: SA Will Have to Run Fast to Stand Still Over 1990–1995', *Finance Week*, No. 46, p. 22.

—— 1994. 'Education Revolution: SA Must Ensure That Its Schools, Universities and Other Areas of Training Produce Skills the Economy Vitally Needs', *Finance Week*, No. 60, pp. 9–10.

Provisional Military Government of Ethiopia (PMGE), 1984. *Ten-Year Perspective Plan: 1984/85–1993/94*, Addis Ababa: PMGE.

Ramsewak, D., 1991. *Mauritian Law – the Constitution, Its Legal Aspects and Political Philosophy*, Port Louis: Edition de L'Ocean Indien.

Rabor, J.A., 1992. *Biomass Energy Technologies for Small Industries and Institutions, Regional Training Course on Biomass Energy Development*, Nairobi: KENGO/RWEPA.

RDP (Reconstruction and Development Programme), 1995. *Key Indicators of Poverty in South Africa*, South African Communication Services, Pretoria: RDP.

Republic of Mauritius, 1992. *The Constitution, Republic of Mauritius*, Port Louis: Government Printer.

——, 1994. *Synopsis of Findings and Recommendations of the Training Needs Identification Survey of 12 Sectors of the Economy*, Port Louis: Government Printer.

——, 1995. *Biennial Report on Education (1993/1994)*, Port Louis: Government Printer.

Republic of South Africa, 1995. 'National Social Development Report', prepared for the World Summit on Social Development, Copenhagen, Denmark.

Ruiters, W., 1995. 'Affirmative Action in the Energy Sector', Paper No. 21, Energy Policy Research and Training Programme (EPRET), Energy for Development Research Centre, University of Cape Town.

SAD-ELEC, 1996. 'Electricity in Southern Africa – Investment Opportunities in an Emerging Regional Market', London: *Financial Times*.

SADC (Southern African Development Community), 1996. SADC Energy Cooperation Policy and Strategy Document, Luanda: SADC Energy Sector Technical Administrative Unit, p. 25.

——, no date. 'SADC Training Programme Brochure on Rural Energy Planning and Environmental Management', Luand: SADC.

SADCC (Southern African Development Coordinating Conference) *Energy Quarterly*, 1990. 'Kafue Gorge Regional Training Centre', *SADCC Energy Quarterly*, Vol. 8, No. 21, Luanda: SADCC Energy Sector Technical and Administrative Unit.

——, 1991. 'Training in the Power Sector', *SADCC Energy Quarterly*, Vol. 8, No. 23, Luanda: SADCC Energy Sector Technical and Administrative Unit.

Sampa, R. C., 1996. 'Literature Review: Management and Efficiency of the Power Sector in Zambia', paper prepared for the AFREPREN Management and Efficiency Theme Group, Nairobi: AFREPREN/FWD.

SAREC (Swedish Agency for Research Cooperation with Developing Counties), 1993. 'The Ownership and Cultivation of Knowledge – The Rationale for Swedish Support to Universities in Developing Countries', Draft Report, Stockholm: SAREC.

Sayce, K. (ed.), 1987. *Tabex Encyclopaedia Zimbabwe*, Harare: Quest Publishing.

Schramm, G., 1990. 'Electric Power in Developing Countries: Status, Problems, Prospects', *Annual Reviews of Energy*, Vol. 15, California: Annual Reviews, Incorporated, pp. 307–33.

——, 1991. 'Issues and Problems in the Power Sector of Developing Countries', paper prepared for the Stockholm Initiative on Energy, Environment and Sustainable Development (SEED), Stockholm, 13–15 November 1991.

Selvaratnam, V., 1994. *Innovations in Higher Education: Singapore at the Competitive Edge*, Washington, DC: World Bank.

Semere, H., 2002. *Country Validation Data – Eritrea*, Nairobi: AFREPREN.

Siegel, G.B and Myrtle, R.C., 1985. *Public Personnel Administration Concepts and Practices*, Boston: University Press of America Inc.

Sizoomu, G., 1994. *Diagnosis of Energy Education in African Energy Systems and Study of Skilled Manpower Requirements in the Field of Energy*, Abidjan: African Development Bank/African Energy Programme.

Sokona, Y., undated. *The Development of Requisite Energy Sector Management Capability und Skills – the ENDA Training Initiative*, Dakar: Environnement et Developpment du Tiers Monde.

South African Communication Services, 1994. *South African Yearbook 1994*, Cape Town: CTP Book Printers.

Southern African Development through Electricity and Minerals and Energy Policy Centre, 1996. *Electricity in South Africa; Investment Opportunities in an Emerging Regional Market*, London: *Financial Times* Energy Publishing.

Statistics South Africa, 1998. 'Labour Statistics: Employment and Salaries and Wages Summary' PO200 (May), Statistics South Africa at www.statssa.gov.za

——, 2001. 'Comparative Labour Statistics Survey of Employment and

Earnings in Selected Industries, September 2001', discussion paper, December, www.statssa.gov.za

Stavrou, S. E., 1992. 'Future Directions for the Electricity Supply Industry', Working Paper No. 4, Centre for Social and Development Studies, University of Natal, Durban.

Stoneman, C., 1978. *Skilled Labour and Future Needs* (From Rhodesia to Zimbabwe Series No. 4), Gweru: Mambo Press.

Suba, M. R., 1991. *Zambia – Rural Energy Institutions Study*, Zambia: ZERO.

*Sunday Mail, The*, 1997. 'Education System Reviewed', 15 June 1997, Harare.


Teferra, M., 1998. *Capacity Building in the Power Sector in Ethiopia*. Nairobi: AFREPREN/FWD.

——, 2001a. *Country Validation Data – Ethiopia*, Nairobi: AFREPREN/FWD.

Teferra, M. (ed.), 2001b. *Energy for Rural Development in Ethiopia – Proceedings of a National Policy Seminar*, AFREPREN Occasional Paper No. 11, Nairobi: AFREPREN.

Tibicke, H. L., 1997. *Research Environment in Zimbabwe*, Stockholm: SAREC.

Transitional Government of Ethiopia, 1991. 'Economic Policy During the Transitional Period', Addis Ababa: TGE.

——, 1992. Proclamation No. 25/1992: Public Enterprise Proclamation, Addis Ababa: TGE.

——, 1994. 'Education Sector Strategy', Addis Ababa: TGE.

Turkson, J., 1996. 'Meeting Institutional and Capacity Building Needs for Power Sector Restructuring and Environmental Regulation in Ghana – a Brief for Discussion', Roskilde, Denmark: UNEP Collaborating Centre on Energy and the Environment.

—— (ed.), 2000. *Power Sector Reform in Sub-Saharan Africa*, London: Macmillan Press Ltd.


UEB (Uganda Electricity Board), 1996. *Corporate Strategic Plan 1996–2000*, Uganda Electricity Board, Kampala.

United Nations (UN), 1988. *World Demographical Figure Estimates and Projection, 1950–2025*, New York.

——, 1997. *Energy Statistics Yearbook 1997*. United Nations Publications, New York.

UNCED (United Nations Conference on Environment and Development), 1992. *Agenda 21*, New York: United Nations Secretariat.

——, 2000. *Human Development Report 2000*. New York: Oxford University Press.

——, 2001. *Human Development Report 2001*. New York: Oxford University Press.

UNDP (United Nations Development Programme), 1993. 'Establishment of an Electrical and Electronics Institute: Report of the Evaluation Mission', Addis Ababa: UNDP.

——, 1994. *Human Development Report, 1994*, New York: Oxford University Press.

——, 1995. *Human Development Report, 1995*, New York: Oxford University Press, pp. 12–13.

——, 1996. *Human Development Report 1996*, New York: Oxford University Press.

——, 2000. *Human Development Report 2000*, New York: Oxford University Press.

——, 2001. *Human Development Report 2001*, New York: Oxford University Press.

UNDP/WB (United Nations Development Programme and World Bank), 1996. 'Ethiopia Energy Assessment Report No. 179/96', Washington, DC: UNDP/WB.

UNESCO (United Nations Educational, Scientific and Cultural Organization), 1982. 'Final Report of the Meeting of Ministers of Education and Those Responsible for Economic Planning in African States, Harare, 28 June–3 July 1982', Paris: UNESCO.

——, 1993. 'UNESCO Series of Learning Materials in Engineering Sciences', *UNESCO Bulletin*, Paris: UNESCO.

——, 1995. *World Education Report*, New York: Oxford University Press.

University of Cape Town, 1997. 'Energy Research Institute Web Page', http://www.eri.utc.ac.za/eri.html

University of Mauritius, various years. *Annual Report*, Reduit: University of Mauritius.

University of Stellenbosch, undated. *University of Stellenbosch Brochure*. Stellenbosch: Matieland.


Van Horen, C., 1994. 'Financing and Economic Implications of Household Energy Policies', Paper No. 18, Energy Policy Research and Training Project (EPRET), Energy for Development Research Centre, University of Cape Town.

Van Wyk, J. D. and J. P. Reynders, 1990. 'Supply and Education of Engineering Manpower in the RSA up to 2015', paper presented at the National Energy Council and ESKOM Workshop on 'Issues Affecting Future Electricity Strategies for South Africa', 25–26 April 1990.

Vermande, P., 1994. Paper presented at the Symposium on Science and Technology In Africa, Session II, 'Partnership Industry/University and Tertiary Research Institutions', 14–15 February 1994, Nairobi: UNESCO.

Viviers, C. D. and B. A. Statham, 1994. 'Integrated Resource Planning – the Opportunity for Africa', paper presented at the World Energy Council Regional Energy Forum for Southern African Countries: Mobility Energy for Growth, 13–14 October, 1994, Cape Town.


Walubengo, D., and J. M. Kimani, 1993. 'The Successful Dissemination of Renewable Energy Technologies in Sub-Sahara Africa', in J. K. Muiruri and E. Naumann (eds), *Renewable Energy Technologies in Sub-Sahara Africa*, Nairobi: KENGO, pp. 55, 59–60.

Welham, 1994. 'Non-OECD Energy Demand to 2010 – Its Growing Significance', Paris: International Energy Agency.

Werkman A., 1996. 'International Review of Government Energy Departments: Sample Answer – South Africa'.

Wheeler, J.C. 1990. Statement at the Africa Conference, Maastricht (the Netherlands), July 2–4, 1990, *Proceedings of the African Seminar: Sub-Saharan Africa: beyond Adjustment*, Copenhagen: Netherlands Directorate General for Development Cooperation (DGIS).

Whiteford, A., D. Posel and T. Kelatwang, 1995. *A Profile of Poverty, Inequality and Human Development*, Pretoria: Human Science Research Council.

Wield, D., 1991a. *Integrating Donor Reporting Systems to Support African Universities*, Research Surveys, Stockholm: SAREC.

——, 1991b. *Forging the Links: Evaluation of SAREC Support to Research Development in Engineering and Sciences in Mozambique*, Stockholm: SAREC Documentations.

Williams, P. R. C., 1989. *Report of the Commission of Inquiry into the Establishment of a Second University or Campus*, Harare: Commission of Inquiry.

Wils, Frits, 1995. *Building Up and Strengthening Research Capacity in Southern Countries*, Publication No. 5 (August ), The Hague: Advisory Council for Scientific Research in Development Problems (RAWOO).

Winter, B. H. A., 1995. 'Nuclear Power', *Journal of Energy in Southern Africa*, Vol. 6, No. 2, Plumstead, South Africa: Energy Research Institute.

Wolde-Ghiorgis, W., 2000. *Renewables and Energy for Rural Development in Ethiopia: Data and Statistics Compilation.* Nairobi: AFREPREN/FWD.

Wong, C. T., 1997. 'National Energy Data Profile: South Africa', Report No. 181 (September), Plumstead, South Africa: Energy Research Institute.

World Bank, 1987. *World Bank Technical Assistance Activities and Issues (FY82–86)*, Washington, DC: World Bank.

——, 1989. *Sub-Saharan Africa – From Crisis to Sustainable Growth: a Long-Term Perspective Study*, Washington, DC: World Bank.

——, 1991, The African Capacity Building Initiative – Towards Improved Policy Analysis and Development Management, Washington, DC: World Bank.

——, 1993a. *Staff Appraisal Report: Republic of Ghana National Electrification Project*, Washington, DC: World Bank.

——, 1993b. *Staff Appraisal Report: Zimbabwe*, Washington, DC: World Bank.

——, 1993c. *World Development Report 1993: Investing in Health*, Washington, DC: Oxford University Press.

——, 1994. *World Development Report 1994: Infrastructure for Development*, Washington, DC: Oxford University Press.

——, 1995a. *World Development Report 1995*, Washington, DC: Oxford University Press.

——, 1995b, *Labour and the Growth Crisis in Sub-Saharan Africa*, Washington, DC: World Bank, pp. 2, 20.

——, 1996a. *World Development Report 1996*, New York: Oxford University Press.

——, 1996b. *World Bank Atlas 1996*, Washington, DC: World Bank.

——, 1996c. *African Development Indicators 1996*, Washington, DC: World Bank.

——, 1997. *World Development Report 1997*, Washington, DC: World Bank.

——, 1999. *World Development Report 1998/9, Knowledge for Development*, Washington, DC: World Bank.

——, 2000. *African Development Indicators*, Washington, DC: World Bank.

——, 2001a. *African Development Indicators*, Washington, DC: World Bank,

——, 2001b. *World Development Report 2000/2001*. Washington DC: World Bank.

World Resources Institute, 1994. *World Resources: People and the Environment*, New York: World Resources Institute.

——, 1995. *World Resources Database,* Washington, DC: World Resource Institute.

ZESA (Zimbabwe Electricity Supply Authority), 1992. *Annual Report and Accounts, 1992*, Harare: ZESA.

——, 1993a. *Annual Report and Accounts 1993*, Harare:ZESA.

——, 1993b. *What is ZESA?* Brochure, Harare: ZESA.

——, 1994. *Annual Reports and Accounts, 1994*, Harare: ZESA.

——, 1995a. *Corporate Business Plan: July 1995–June 2000*, Harare: ZESA.

——, 1995b. *Annual Report and Accounts, 1995*, Harare: ZESA.

——, 1995c. *Megawatt Bulletin*, Harare: ZESA.

——, 1997. *Annual Report and Accounts, 1997*, Harare: ZESA.

——, 1998a. *Annual Report and Accounts, 1998*, Harare: ZESA, pp. 10, 15, 17.

——, 1998b. *Megawatt Bulletin*, Harare: ZESA.

——, 1999. *Annual Report and Accounts, 1999*, Harare: ZESA.

——, 2001. *2001 Load Forecast Report*, Harare: ZESA.

——, 2002a. *Corporate Business Plan, 2002*, pp. 26, 77.

——, 2002b. Expanded Rural Electrification Programme, Supplement to the *Financial Gazette*, 7–13 February 2002.

——, no date. Official opening of ZESA National Training Centre, Harare: ZESA.

ZESCO (Zambia Electricity Supply Corporation), 1999. *Annual Report and Accounts, 1998–1999*, Lusaka: ZESCO.

Zvobgo, R. J., 1994. *Colonialism and Education in Zimbabwe*, Harare: SAPES Books.

Zymelman, M., 1990, *Science, Education and Development in Sub-Saharan Africa*, Washington, DC: World Bank.

# Index